When Rituals Go Wrong: Mistakes, Failure, and the Dynamics of Ritual

Numen Book Series

Studies in the History of Religions

Edited by

Steven Engler (Calgary, Canada)
Kim Knott (Leeds, UK)
P. Pratap Kumar (Durban, South Africa)
Kocku von Stuckrad (Amsterdam, the Netherlands)

VOLUME 115

When Rituals Go Wrong: Mistakes, Failure, and the Dynamics of Ritual

By

Ute Hüsken

BRILL

LEIDEN • BOSTON
2007

Cover illustration courtesy C. Emmrich

This book is printed on acid-free paper.

ISSN 0169-8834
ISBN 978 90 04 15811 5

PRINTED IN THE NETHERLANDS

CONTENTS

PREFACE

> What happens, if a healing ritual fails to cure the patient?
>
> What if rituals, invented to create a communal identity, do not convince the audience?
>
> What if the ingredients of a Vedic sacrifice prove to be impure?
>
> What if two religious groups quarrel over the appropriate text to be recited in front of the god?

The present volume is entirely dedicated to investigating the implications and effects of breaking ritual rules, of failed performances and of the extinction of ritual systems.[1] While rituals are often seen as some kind of machines or infallible mechanisms which 'work' irrespective of the individual motivations of the performers,[2] it is clearly visible here that rituals can fail, and that improper performances do in fact matter. Without aiming at presenting a 'theory of ritual failure' the diverse contributions assembled here take a close look at failed or flawed rituals. This point of view opens up new perspectives on the ritual procedures, on the interaction which constitute these procedures and on the context in which these actions are embedded. The contributions to this volume approach these important issues from the angle of their respective disciplines.

This volume is the outcome of one and a half years joint endeavour of the working group 'ritual failure' within the Collaborative Research Centre on Dynamics of Ritual[3] and two other scholars closely related

---

[1] The intensive scholarly exchange on this topic, resulting in the present volume, was made possible by the generous funding by the Deutsche Forschungsgemeinschaft (DFG). Special thanks are due to Malcolm Green for revising the English.

[2] See, for example, Humphrey & Laidlaw (1994: 128): "Ritual is prescribed action, you have to get it right, and yet sometimes it seems that as long as you try, so long as you accept the ritual commitment, it is almost impossible to get it wrong."

[3] The Collaborative Research Centre's aim is to systematically analyse and develop theoretical models of the circumstances of change, as well as of the stable facets of ritual in historical and intercultural perspective. The Collaborative Research Centre is funded since 7/2002 by the German Research Council (DFG) and is planned to run for approximately twelve years. For details see http://www.ritualdynamik.uni-hd.de/;

to this project (Brigitta Hauser-Schäublin and Maren Hoffmeister). In late 2004 several members of this working group presented their ideas and concepts at the panel 'ritual failure' at the annual meeting of the American Academy of Religion (held in San Atonio, Texas), as part of the Ritual Studies Group's programme. At that occasion Ronald L. Grimes responded to the papers (see Grimes 2004). When the present collection reached its final stage, Edward L. Schieffelin, who had already taken interest in the project in its very beginning phase, kindly agreed to write the introduction to this volume.

This publication continues a sequence of monographs published in the context of the Collaborative Research Centre "Dynamics of Ritual", such as the volume *Ritualdynamik* (edited 2004 by Harth and Schenk), a collection of essays on *Dynamics of changing rituals* (edited 2004 by Kreinath, Hartung and Deschner), and the two recently published volumes *Theorizing rituals*, edited in 2006 by Kreinath, Snoek and Stausberg.[4] Like these monographs, the present volume is a collection of contributions from a great diversity of research areas and methods. The contributors are anthropologists with regional focus on South Asia, Taiwan, and the Pacific islands, Indian Studies scholars, scholars of Assyriology, of medical Psychology, of the history of Ancient Greece, a scholar of German language and literature and Religious Studies scholars.

The articles are arranged according to Schieffelin's suggestions in his "Introduction". The first section "Mistakes, Procedural Errors and Incorrect Performances" comprises six articles which unfold the potential diversity of mishaps in ritual traditions. The two articles in the second section "Preventive Measures and 'Quality Control'" refer to measures taken by ritual traditions themselves to prevent rituals from going awry, whereas the three contributions to the third section "Contingencies and Emergence" are mainly concerned with case studies in which a ritual's outcome does not answer all participants' expectations. The last section on "Competing Perspectives: the Discursive Production of Ritual"

for the history of this project see Schenk's introduction to the volume *Ritualdynamik* (Harth & Schenk [ed.] 2004).

[4] Whereas Kreinath's 2004 volume is mainly concerned with change in and of ritual ("modifications and transformations", see Kreinath 2004: 267f.) the present volume takes special interest in the evaluation of such changes. The first volume of "Theorizing ritual" was unfortunately not yet available when the articles were finalised. Therefore many contributors to this volume refer to the articles published therein without giving the page numbers.

concentrates on conflicting assessments of rituals, which is in all four cases strongly connected to politics. The volume concludes with the article "Ritual Dynamics and Ritual Failure" which takes up the theoretical issues raised by Schieffelin in his "Introduction" once more. All of the contributors had the opportunity to read the finished "Introduction" by Edward L. Schieffelin before making the final revisions to their essays. Especially the concluding article by Hüsken is decisively influenced by Schieffelin's contribution to this volume.

References

Grimes, Ronald L. 2004. Response to the contributions presented on the occasion of the panel 'Ritual Mistakes and Failure of Ritual' during the AAR conference, held in 11/2004 in San Antonio, Texas (unpublished).

Harth, Dietrich & Gerrit Schenk (ed.) 2004. *Ritualdynamik. Kulturübergreifende Studien zur Theorie und Geschichte rituellen Handelns*. Heidelberg: Synchron Publishers.

Humphrey, Caroline & James Laidlaw 1994. *The Archetypal Actions of Ritual. A Theory of Ritual illustrated by the Jain Rite of Worship.* Oxford: Oxford University Press.

Kreinath, Jens 2004. "Theoretical Afterthoughts". In: *The Dynamics of Changing Rituals. The Transformation of Religious Rituals within Their Social and Cultural Context*, Kreinath, Jens & Constance Hartung & Annette Deschner (ed.). New York: Peter Lang Publishing (Toronto Studies in Religion 29), 267–282.

INTRODUCTION

Edward L. Schieffelin

The idea that rituals can 'fail' is not new in anthropology or liturgical studies, but it is also a subject that has been very little explored in the literature. This collection is the first attempt by a group of scholars to address the issue of 'ritual failure' as a topic in its own right in the study of ritual. What is 'ritual failure', how may it be characterised? Why should it be a focus of study? These issues are very much alive in one way or another in all the papers in this collection—but they have been problematic for a very long time.

Clifford Geertz published what is probably the pioneering article concerning a failed ritual in 1957, entitled: "Ritual and Social Change, a Javanese Example". In it he described a funeral he had observed which, instead of producing the community harmony and inner quietude appropriate to the occasion, fell apart in active grief, recrimination and an acute social embarrassment that was excruciating to the Javanese sensibility. His analysis showed that the conflict which surfaced in the ritual had its origins in emerging social changes in the local community external to the ritual, which had outrun the villagers' traditional cultural capacity to absorb them. These changes in social relationship brought with them political differences which, when brought into the ritual, blew it apart. Geertz's interest, however, was not in exploring or explaining ritual failure *per se* but in launching a critique of functional analysis, the principle anthropological approach of the time. In it, Geertz was following an analytical strategy in anthropology dating at least back to Bateson (1936) where the investigator focuses on a single ritual (or other key practice or event) in order to pursue a broader theoretical agenda. In this case Geertz showed that a functionalist approach could not account for this ritual breakdown. But his novel approach of investigating a dysfunctional ritual as well as his masterful analysis of ritual failure in terms of the clash between traditional cultural understandings and new socio-political allegiances was highly original, leading eventually to a whole new approach in anthropology that remains influential to this day.

Concern with ritual failure *per se*, however, did not reawaken until 1990 with the publication of Ronald L. Grimes's book "Ritual Criticism". Grimes develops an approach for assessing rituals drawing on Austin's speech act theory. Applying Austin's idea of 'infelicitous performance' to the discussion of ritual evaluation, he works out a set of nine 'categories' or 'types of performative shortcomings' relevant to ritual failure. The strength of this approach is that it derives largely from a coherent body of pre-existing theory. The weakness is that it imports an approach to ritual studies derived from linguistics which may or may not be appropriate to ritual materials which involve considerably more than spoken language. To his credit, Grimes is aware of this and puts his categories forward experimentally, pointing out that they will need considerable testing and trying out to see whether they are useful. "Their worth", he says, "consists of their ability to point to troublesome dynamics [within rituals] and to provide a vocabulary for recognitions, debate and discussion. They are useless as some kind of performative canon" (Grimes 1990: 208).

Beyond questions about the usefulness of the categories themselves, Grimes recognized two further problems which remain as cautionary to anyone venturing upon the exploration of ritual failure. The first is the difficulty of sharply distinguishing between infelicities which are 'in the ritual' and those which are 'of the ritual': "In some [of the categories] the problem lies with the ritualists, in others with the rite itself, and in still others in the relation between the rite and the surrounding religiocultural processes" (1990: 209). To make things worse, these tend to change their relations in part depending on the nature of the rituals themselves. The second problem, Grimes points out, is that "the typology does not solve the problem of point of view: who, participant or observer, is to decide whether procedures fail, and if they do, what sort of infelicity has been committed" (1990: 207). This problem is probably the most productive one, pointing as it does to the exploration of a multi-perspectival approach to ritual which emerges in some of the papers in this collection.

A more recent paper by Schieffelin (1996) examines the failure of performance by a central figure within a ritual occasion (one medium in a spirit séance) in order to gain insight into the performative dynamics that make the ritual work. In this paper, the issues for exploration are, on the one hand, drawn from what seemed to be the most interesting and productive categories of performative dynamics at that stage on the theoretical development of the discipline. On the other hand, unlike Grimes, these categories of analysis are re-framed as 'issues' for exploration that denote interesting domains of investigation in the realm of ritual. In other words, these issues are meant to be open to critical discussion both by the investigator as to their usefulness and appropriateness to the material, and also by informants in the field whose realities they are meant to bridge or represent. In this way the attempt is made to ensure that categories of anthropological analysis cannot be uncritically imposed on their material, and that a variety of perspectives may be preserved and acknowledged even if, in the final analysis, the overarching analysis reflects western scholarly, rather than local social and political, interests. This kind of analysis might be taken to represent a theory of ritual, but what it really attempts to do is to constitute a broad approach to the understanding of ritual dynamics within which, local categories, multiple perspectives, and ritual failure may be accommodated. The approach is thus geared less to understanding ritual failure for itself than to understanding what such a failure may reveal about the dynamics of the ritual itself.

Taken together, these early examinations of ritual failure do not lay the groundwork for a theory of ritual failure so much as reveal some of the complexities and difficulties surrounding the subject. For one thing, there is no consensus as to what 'ritual failure' actually is. What counts as a failed ritual? For Geertz the ritual failed not just because it failed to produce the sentiments appropriate to the occasion, but the performance itself could not be completed, so that its ritual functions could not be accomplished. Moreover, the reasons for this had to do with changing social and political relations in secular life that had nothing to do with the ritual itself.

Grimes's typology of performative infelicities, on the other hand, suggests that 'ritual failure' is situated somehow in the poor design or improper performance of ritual procedures themselves. Here it is left unclear whether 'ritual failure' refers primarily to 'process' (proper performance of ritual) or 'outcome' (achieving the ends for which ritual is performed). This, in turn evokes questions about the degree to which, for a given tradition, ritual performance is about 'getting it right' vs. 'getting it done'. (We will return to this point.)

In Schieffelin's paper, the ritual (a séance) did not, in fact, fail. Rather, it was the performance by one of the spirit mediums that collapsed. But this failure did not break the performance; paradoxically, it ended up enhancing its intensity, credibility and success.

There is no final approach here. At best, some ground has been cleared, and, as we have seen, many of the principle issues and difficulties encountered in these early works are still very much alive for the contributors to this volume.

Like many attempts to explore new territory in the absence of an established framework, the authors of these papers draw on a wide range of ethnographic and theoretical sources, and a diversity of methods (ranging from interpretation of ancient texts to participant observation in active ritual settings) according to the nature of the material they deal with. In the midst of this variety of approaches there is also diversity of opinion on how to conceptualise the subject of inquiry itself. Although the various authors take different approaches to 'ritual failure', it is possible to tease apart several basic tendencies in the papers, according to how each investigator frames or focuses their discussion.

In the first, ritual failure is primarily conceptualised in terms of the failure of the ritual to produce expected results. Karin Polit's poignant story of a young Garhwali woman's search for a cure for her infertility is a case in point. Polit's investigation of the young woman's repeated failures to obtain (a ritual) cure shows that the conceived causes of ritual failure can quickly move outside the context of ritual form and performance (failures or inadequacies of the ritual specialists) and into the play of social issues within the larger society, and blame (as in this case) may fall on the victim herself. The social stakes here were high as her husband's family's honour (let alone continuity) was threatened. Indeed, her own status as a wife and woman was at risk as her husband began making moves to get a second wife. Fortunately, instead of this situation ending in domestic tragedy, a way out was found (by another ritual specialist) that, while it did not restore the woman's fertility, managed to restore her social respectability and her husband's family honour (and in the process, get the ritualists off the hook).

A further interesting use of this 'outcome oriented' view of ritual failure is provided by Maren Hoffmeister, whose paper analyses the acts of certain serial killers as ritual-like behaviour and explains the survival of some of their victims in terms of ritual failure. Hoffmeister argues that when the potential victim didn't respond to, or play along with, the killer in the manner he desired (i.e. when they 'misperformed' their part in his 'ritual') it spoiled his desire to kill so that he didn't go through with the murder. On the surface this is analogous to the stereotype of a ritual broken by failed procedure. However, in this case the question turns on the debate about the degree to which ritual can usefully be understood as analogous to psychopathology (specifically obsessive-compulsive behaviour). Taken as ritual theory, Hoffmeister's paper would represent an argument for a 'strong,' virtually causal relation between errors in ritual procedure and failure of outcome. However, as is clear from this collection, this relationship, while often theoretically postulated, is quite rare in actual ritual situations cross-culturally, even among the most demanding and punctilious kinds of ritual performance.

The latter point leads directly to the second way authors in this series tend to conceptualise 'ritual failure'. In this approach the failure of ritual *outcome* as the hallmark of 'ritual failure' fades into the background and the central focus of failure of ritual is seen mostly as a matter of mistakes, procedural errors, and incorrect performance.

It is perhaps not too surprising that this second or 'procedure oriented' view of ritual failure should be the perspective taken by nearly all the papers that deal with rituals from the Indian subcontinent. The high culture of India is renowned in the anthropological literature for the complicated and punctilious nature of its rituals which informants often insist must be performed without error. A number of these rituals are devotional in nature, without an observable worldly outcome. In these cases particularly, one gets the feeling that error-free performance—plus the fact that the ritual gets performed at the right time and place—is basically what is at stake in ritual. In other words, the correct procedure and timing of the ritual seem an end in themselves.

This perspective seems to lie in the background of Axel Michael's discussion of Vedic rituals. Vedic rituals are thought to be products of the Gods and hence they are perfect. Imperfections derive from their performance by men. Any mistakes, or failure to follow the prescribed procedures to the letter, are thought to 'break the ritual' bringing harmful consequences to the world and to the ritualist and his family. These are very high standards, extremely rigid and difficult to keep. Vedic priests were aware of this, and possessed a body of texts which outlined an array of remedies and atonements for ritual errors and provided alternative ways to perform ritual details and ritual segments—as well as admonitions not to take the prescribed rigidities too seriously. In this way, therefore, seemingly fixed and stereotyped Vedic rituals could be fairly easily adapted to the practical needs of the occasion or the capacities of the priest or sacrificers. Thus, even the integrity of the most formal, repetitive, and stereotyped rites could be actually full of adjustments and changes, and for all their fuss and detail even a messy performance did not necessarily invalidate or 'break' a ritual. This suggests that ritual punctiliousness existed more in the Vedic ideology (or imagination) of ritual than that it was realised in the real world, and that actual performances usually went to completion rather than being invalidated by mistakes or variations.

Punctilious ritual practice is also part of Hindu ritual ideology and there are likewise numerous rites for atoning for ritual errors in Hindu liturgy. In some cases these are so woven into the fabric of the ritual that it is tempting to believe the practitioners themselves lack confidence in what they are doing. Johanna Buss makes the point that the potential danger of misfortune from making ritual mistakes is particularly acute in rituals concerning life and death transitions. She describes the culminating rite of the Newar death rituals where a corrective offering is performed to ensure that nothing has been overlooked in that ritual or previous ones in the series that would prevent the soul of the dead from joining its ancestors. Buss argues that this corrective offering implies that the series of rituals which sustain the ghosts during their passage through the underworld is actually a failure. This seems to me a step too far—or at least one could plausibly make a case for a somewhat different view. In Buss's account, most of the perils encountered by the dead in their journey through the underworld are due to their encounters with other ghosts who are trapped there and who waylay them and steal their food. These 'other' ghosts are stuck in the underworld for various reasons including improper performance of their own death rituals—but not because of any failures of the present one. The 'corrective' offering is intended to provide them with the food they need so as to allow the recently deceased to make his or her way to the ancestors unmolested. Indeed, the offering intends to provide the 'other' ghosts with enough sustenance so that they can complete their own passages themselves. By this argument, Newar death ritual does not imply its own failure so much as to recognise the inevitable presence of human frailty and make an attempt to compensate for the shortcomings of the performers—present and past. But Buss also suggests that bigger issues are at stake. She concludes her essay by remarking that the hungry ghosts are not feared so much for themselves as because they represent elements of cosmic disorder. If so, the Newar death ritual would seem to pertain to more than just the wellbeing of the deceased, but also to act as a general rite against cosmic dissolution and decay—of which human frailty in ritual performance is acknowledged to be a part.

Jan Snoek in his study of European Masonic rituals shows that freemasons' attitudes towards ritual performance are very different from those held by the peoples of the Indian sub-continent. While freemasons make considerable efforts to perform their rites exactly, in the end it is the flow and progress of the overall performance that is important. Unless a slip is a very major one, it will be passed over as if nothing had happened. In fact, Snoek points out, a deviation from traditional procedure is occasionally seen as interesting or attractive enough to be incorporated without comment in later performances of the rite. For the freemasons, the slip-up must be bad enough to imply the ritual leader does not understand the procedure he is performing before it breaks the performance and requires the rite to be done over again. This is something that very rarely occurs.

It is interesting that the rituals discussed so far from this 'procedure oriented' view of ritual failure all get carried to their conclusion despite the errors and mishaps. Although such errors might be criticised or deplored, they could usually also be ignored—or corrected and atoned for—without invalidating the ritual as a whole. One wonders, at this point, what significance ritual errors really have if the rituals rarely fail in terms of their completion or outcome. Or, is it safe to assume that the 'corrective procedures' always work satisfactorily? Or that some ritual moves can safely be ignored? This seems to be a question that requires further exploration.

Between the 'outcome oriented' and 'procedure oriented' conceptions of ritual failure, a number of papers in this collection adopt a kind of middle-ground approach in which any unusual event or contingency that changes a particular ritual performance significantly from its usual appearance is deemed a potential instance of 'ritual failure'.

Clearly this category is a bit of a grab-bag and admits of a wide range of events with a wide range of possible effects on the performance of ritual and opens the door for considerable interpretive latitude. On the level of ritual performance, for example, Brigitte Merz describes a séance performed in Nepal in which a goddess manifesting through a female medium broke into an unusual bout of violent weeping for an extended period of time. Such a thing had never happened before and, although the séance went on to completion, the participants were unsettled and uncertain as to the portent and significance of what they had witnessed. An unusual event, yes, but, asks Merz, since the séance went on to its conclusion does it really count as a ritual failure? Would it not be more accurate to characterise this as a failure of the performance of one of the mediums within the larger context of a successful séance or is this a case of a variant but tolerable performance of a rite? This raises more questions than it answers and we will return to this case presently.

By contrast, a clear example is provided by Ambos' account of Assyrian King Esarhaddon's attempt in 669 BCE to return the statue of the deity Marduk to Babylon (from where it had been abducted by Sennacherib 20 years previously). This act of peacemaking and reconciliation was to be a crowning achievement for the ailing Esarhaddon's reign. However, just as the ritual procession bringing the statue reached the boundary of Babylonian territory, the god Marduk himself made an oracular pronouncement through the mouth of a servant that the journey had to be put off. The procession was halted, and the statue returned to Assyria. Because this ritual was broken off in the middle, Ambos denotes this disaster a ritual failure—it was certainly a failure of achievement for Esarhaddon, who died soon afterwards without completing the mission.

However, questions arise. Esarhaddon's ritual failed because it was brought to a halt by external circumstances (in the form of an unexpected pronouncement from the god). But is this to be counted as a failure of the *ritual*? Or an interruption or intervention by an external circumstance which prevented it from going to completion? Would it have been a *ritual* failure if the procession had been set upon by bandits and the statue despoiled of its lapis and gold?

We cannot answer this in part because we don't know whether the Assyrians thought about this incident in terms of 'failure'. But Christoph Emmrich, in studying a similar ritual mishap in modern Nepal, was able to discuss the issue with his informants. Once a year the statue of a Nepalese deity known as 'the red Matsyendranatha' is ceremonially transported in a huge chariot of primitive construction between the temples of the village of Bungamati and the town of Lalitpur. In the procession of 2004, the chariot broke down and dumped the god onto the ground. This disaster brought the ritual to a halt for a month. The god had to be lifted from the mud and the chariot completely rebuilt while appropriate rituals of atonement and exculpation were performed. Then the procession was resumed and the journey of the god completed.

Emmrich, seeking an explanation of what happened in terms of ritual failure, discovered that ritual experts and lay persons alike regarded the causes of the mishap to lie either in practical contingencies (like those pulling the chariot were drunk and going too fast), or as a kind of message from the god who was showing displeasure at the general period of ill-omen and political misfortune prevailing in the kingdom at the time. To Emmrich's surprise, the idea that ritual errors had been made or that the ritual had failed made no sense to them. Emmrich concluded that the language of failure and mistakes didn't address the perspective from which this event was understood by its participants. For them, the drama of the collapse of the chariot was a misadventure, which in due course was absorbed within the larger ritual process. It was a mishap, but not a failure.

This kind of complexity reveals there is a problem with applying the term 'failure' to any events or happenings that alter the course of a ritual or make it look particularly unusual or unconventional. While it is easy to assume that rituals (as social performances) must 'be successful' or 'fail' in some sense, Emmrich's example serves as a warning that these are not categories that an analyst can apply with impunity.

Moreover, if we think about this more closely, it throws doubt on our first two notions of ritual failure as well. Ritual performers and their constituencies usually have their own ideas corresponding to 'success' and 'failure' and the appropriate cultural domains to which they may be applied. Without an ethnographic exploration of these key terms of the analysis as they are conceived and used in the culture under investigation, we are unlikely to be good judges of what counts as 'failure' to those who perform a ritual or whether the discourse of 'success' and 'failure' is even relevant or appropriate to the event in question. If the investigator calls something a ritual failure, but his informants do not, there is something wrong.[1]

But more than this, by imposing a category inappropriately, something important may be overlooked. Asking ones informants what they think counts a ritual failure sometimes produces interesting surprises. Jan Weinhold approached his informants' notion of ritual failure obliquely through semi-structured interviews which aimed at determining how his informants thought about 'mistakes' and 'failure' in the performance of ritual in the Santo Daime Church. His interview protocol allowed the course of the discussion to outline implicitly the informants' understandings of these concepts. What emerged was a clear separation between their notions of mistakes or ritual disruptions, and ritual

[1] Of course the investigator needs to allow for the possibility that ritualists or others may deny failure in order to save face or avoid blame. But this cannot be assumed to be the case at the beginning without risking losing the real significance of the material.

failure. Moreover they held two notions of ritual failure depending on the perspective they took. On the collective level ritual was felt to have failed if the performance broke up prematurely before the last prayer was spoken. But from the individual perspective, the ritual failed when the participant left before the ritual was properly concluded. These two notions of ritual failure do not necessarily overlap, since a ritual could go on to its proper conclusion even if a participant left, yet this did not prevent informants from agreeing with both ideas. However, what Weinhold has tried to do here is more than determine local definitions of ritual failure. He has attempted to outline the larger conceptual field within which his informants think about ritual failure. Clearly interesting questions arise for analysis when informants conceptualise how key aspects of their social processes work differently from the analyist.

Without pursuing this point further, we may also point out that the 'ethnographic critique' of the terms of analysis that we have been discussing above has more than merely analytic or categorical implications. Analytic categories like 'failure' do not have neutral value in western usage. In English the term implies moral evaluation: connoting ethical fault or weakness, lack of normal capacity or incompetence, loss of authenticity or integrity. Whether these implications have any bearing on indigenous equivalents for the notion of 'failure' is an important question for assessing the significance of a ritual's not going properly. Does the local conceptual equivalent bear similar moral evaluations? Or does it perhaps simply imply misfortune or bad luck?

The issue here is not merely an analytical one of whether the values implicitly imported with our analytical categories distort the ethnographic situation. More importantly, as is clear from a number of the papers, the moral implications of 'ritual failure' frequently make it a subject of intense political contention and manoeuvre—which can be of considerable social consequence and hence critical for an analyst to understand. (We will return to this point in due course.) To reiterate my point before leaving it: whether the notion of 'ritual failure' is felt to be a well-defined analytical category, or whether, as in these exploratory papers, it is given a variety of meanings, it requires serious ethnographic interrogation and critique before it can be realistically applied to the material in a fully useful analytic way in any given case.

Before passing on to the discussion of rituals and politics which emerges in these papers, it is useful to make one more cautionary point that some of the papers touch upon. There is a further danger in being too keen to identify ritual mishaps or variant performances with 'failure' if that leads us to lose sight of other important perspectives on the processes that may also be going on in rituals. For example, some ritual 'failures' might also interestingly be interpreted as innovative moves within the ritual performance.

Merz's discussion of the weeping medium provides an interesting case of this. In the séance in question, there were three mediums, a woman and her two junior adepts. Normally the seniormost medium impersonated the highest of several middling gods (or goddesses) while junior adepts tended to manifest the lesser gods of the group. During one séance, the lesser god that came up on one of the junior mediums began to criticise the worshippers' offerings and object to shortcomings in their ritual preparations prior to the séance. This was a role more appropriately taken by the highest god who usually manifested herself in the oldest medium. Gently rebuked by the higher god for doing this, the lesser one began to weep violently through her medium, and wept for a long time. The junior god tearfully declared that she was no longer a child and should be allowed to comment upon the details of ritual just as the senior god (manifesting on the senior medium) did. After this unsettling performance, which caused a lot of local talk, the high god began manifesting himself more frequently in the junior medium.

Merz approaches this from the framework of failed performance (not failed ritual), but it also could be argued that this event was a highly visible performative move to shift the balance of entitlement and seniority amongst the performers within the performance—as it were between the gods rather than the mediums. It looks rather like stealing the show in hope of getting better notices. Viewed from the perspective of what happened afterwards, this performance looks very much like a move on the part of the junior medium to claim more space and authority in relation to the senior medium's role in these séances. While this performance was disconcerting, confused the congregation, and pressed the medium's behaviour to the edge of acceptability, *performatively*, it declared her intentions, and, more darkly, gave warning of what trouble she might cause in the group séance practice if she were not granted her desire. From this perspective, *performatively* the weeping god could be argued to be a success.

Michael Rudolph abandons the rhetoric of ritual failure altogether in his discussion of the restoration of a defunct Taiwanese Aboriginal ritual, which, after being performed for a few years, was again suppressed by the church (which had originally encouraged it) and the regional political elite. Far from being unsuccessful, this rite proved to be much more powerful and to have many more unforeseen consequences than its sponsors had intended. As a pagan ritual, it became too hot for the Christian church to handle and, politically, it began awakening sentiments in the Aboriginal people that undermined their political identification with the dominant Han state. So it had to be suppressed again.

Both of these examples can be seen as representing innovative moves, one in the structure of performative precedence within the ritual itself and the other in the ritual assertion of minority ethnic identity in relation to a dominant (and ethnically different) political society. Another case of ritual innovation that might, from one perspective, also be seen as a 'ritual failure' is discussed by Burckhard Dücker. He examines what happens for an award-winning ceremony when the designated award-winner refuses to accept the offered award. In this, the award winner's refusal is usually stated as a moral or political critique of the legitimacy or authority of the powers represented in the awarding institution. By refusing the Nobel Prize for literature, Jean-Paul Sartre, a communist, was rejecting both the implied legitimacy of the Swedish monarchy (the king customarily made the award) and the notion that any government institution had a right to be the arbiter of the quality of his work. Sartre's move caused a sensation and gained him enormous authority as an independent thinker. Here, by refusing to accept official honours on the grounds that the awarding person or institution is morally (or politically) unacceptable, the refusenik effectively garners the public prestige of having been offered the award while placing himself outside (and morally above) the awarding institution by refusing it. In effect, by refusing the perks of the awarding institution, he hijacks them instead. This clever ritual innovation can also be seen as representing one of our most profound examples of ritual failure (at least from the perspective of the awarding institution). According to those who refuse, part of what the awarding institution intends by the award is to gather socially recognized outstanding individuals to its virtual hall of fame, enhancing its own prestige and legitimacy as the arbiter of quality and honour. The refusenik's innovation upends this order, throwing the institution's claim to honour into question, while, for the moment, claiming the legitimacy of true honour for himself.

Looking at the collection of papers as a whole, it is notable how many of them describe moves—whether mishaps, mistakes, or innovations which can be seen to have fundamentally political value. They are (whether by intent, or in their consequences) transactions in power. Of course, rituals themselves are widely used as means for transacting empowerment: for negotiating transitions between statuses, group memberships, or life stages, conferring or exercising authority, making peace or war, ratifying judgements, aligning individual and society with earthly or spiritual forces etc. To this extent they are deeply implicated in the competition over, and exercise of, social status and political power. The stakes in ritual are often high and ritual outcomes consequential. So it is not surprising that ritual performances and ritual occasions become a focus for politically consequential contestation, manoeuvre and activity.

Claus Ambos' paper (already mentioned) gives a particularly vivid impression of ritual in a highly political context that can serve to point to its political significance in contexts of lesser political intensity. In his accounts of the Assyrian court during the reigns of Esarhaddon and Assurbanipal, he outlines a list of rites marred, contested or discredited by procedural mistakes, omissions, misdemeanors, and interruptions. But the main impression one comes away with from his paper is not so much that of types of ritual errors in the Assyrian court as the vast number of scribes, scholars, diviners, priests, and other ritual specialists (including different schools of ritual specialty, domestic and foreign) there were in attendance of the king. Most of the various kinds of mistakes, glitches, and unwanted outcomes of ritual situations that Ambos describes occurred as part of the exercise or support of kingly power in a court filled with intrigue and competition for influence.

This association between concern with ritual success/failure and political or social competition seems to have been widespread in the ancient world: Stravrianopoulou writes of laws being enacted in Greece to ensure proper precedence was observed among temple priests and officiants according to their ritual competence. But the close association between ritual criticism and political competition appears in papers drawn from contemporary ethnographic work as well.

Hüsken describes the contestation of rival sects of ritualists in a contemporary Indian Vishnu temple. Here officials and ritual servitors of the temple are divided between two sects with slightly differing ritual practices for accomplishing the same necessary acts of worship. Ritual services in the temple are linked with temple honours, perks and prestige that, in turn, affected group and individual status and identity in the larger society. Social competition and precedence in the community is fought out through fierce competition over ritual perks and precedence in the temple. The battle is typically joined around criticism of ritual procedures, each side claiming the other performs the rites incorrectly, while they alone practice them correctly. The resulting arguments sometimes have to be settled in court, thus becoming publicly legitimated. Here *accusations* of so-called 'ritual mistakes' have nothing to do with the efficacy of ritual (nor are they really mistakes). Rather, in the context of conflict over social status and honours which derive from roles served in rituals in the temple, spotting ritual mistakes provides an excuse for pushing ones own sectarian interests and discrediting rivals. (There is the strong suggestion from Ambos that this sort of thing was also going on in the court of Assurbanipal.)

A similar situation of status rivalry emerges in the Balinese temple rites described by Hauser-Schäublin. But here the conflict is itself ritualised, or rather incorporated within the ritual itself. High status Hindu gods appealed to by the local aristocracy are given central position in the temple building, while the statues of the lesser gods worshipped by the villagers are placed outside in the courtyard. During certain important rituals, some of the commoner (villager) participants fall into trance and become possessed by the lesser (courtyard) gods. These (low status) gods, speaking through their villager avatars, intimidate and humiliate members of the aristocratic bramanas community while also criticizing the way the lower status priests perform the ritual. Hauser-Schäublin shows that these ritual features articulate the lines of potential structural antagonism[2] in the community within the structure of the performance. Like Geertz's celebrated cock-fight (Geertz 1973), the ritual can be seen as a form of deep play or virtual status contestation that allows the expression of sentiments that inform social action but keeps them safely out of the arena of dangerous social consequences. Here, the ritual has incorporated the conflict within itself in a denatured form, as part of the ritual's function rather than to its discredit.

In each of the papers we have discussed so far we can ask the question: in what sense are we really talking about 'ritual failure' *vis-à-vis*, say, 'ritual mistakes', 'misadventures', 'deviations', 'variations', or something else? As Hüsken and Hauser-Schäublin suggest in their

[2] Hauser-Schäublin suggests factors that could potentially exacerbate tensions across aristocrat/commoner structural lines. Aristocrats in this area have always derived part of their prestige from their claim to greater religious and ritual knowledge than the common folk—a claim which the voices of the lesser gods (speaking through tranced commoner devotees) in the ritual vigorously contest.

conclusions, this is not necessarily a matter that can be determined objectively. When one tries to understand the issue of ritual failings in a competitive context, where accusations of ritual mistakes made by rivals appear as strategies for achieving advantage in a situation of power relations, the one who wins is the one who becomes right. Sorting out political differences as ritual mistakes in this manner is a clearly hegemonic move to assert one's own influence or faction in the situation. Identification of ritual error in this sort of situation becomes a matter of whose perspective is taken and is as much an artefact of political competition as of correctness. It is tempting to hypothesize here that ritual in India and ancient Mesopotamia may owe some of its punctilious concern with correct procedure to a history of vigorous political and sectarian rivalries which has driven rival ritualists to differentiate the details of their procedures from one another in detail, and to cement their claims to precedence by preserving their notions of correct performance in detailed texts.

Many of the problematic issues raised here are taken up and developed in Christiane Brosius's essay on "The Unwanted Offering". The complexity of Brosius's ethnographic material requires bringing the relations between politics and ritual dynamics to the forefront from the beginning. She describes a massive months-long pilgrimage-like procession across the whole of India organised by the radical right-wing VHP Hindu political party. The offering of the title was a stone pillar intended for the founding of a Hindu temple which this great procession was bringing to the intensely contested site of a famous ancient mosque. This 'ritual of confrontation' as Brosius calls it had several agendas: the highly provocative political aim of polarising Hindu/Muslim political factions, the enhancing of the VHP party's own political visibility and public attention, and the promoting of the Hindu ethnic cause.

Brosius identifies the success or failure of this inflammatory and highly media-genic event specifically with its ability to achieve its political aims, and associates the potential that it would not achieve these aims with a notion of 'ritual risk'. The argument turns on the idea that the management of this risk both by those involved in the rite, and by those opposed to it, is of central importance to the understanding of the ritual's success or failure.

However, this does not turn out to be a simple matter given that many different people and contending factions had important stakes in the outcome of this event. Moreover, this being the case, Brosius is compelled to adopt notions of 'failure' and 'success' that are graded and multi-faceted: a highly qualified matter of 'more or less', and 'from whose point of view', rather than a simple binary opposition of value. Brosius identified four different sets of relationships for which stakes in one outcome or another were significant. Success or failure of the ritual in relation to any of these would potentially affect the success or failure of the rite in achieving its aims as a whole. But the *attribution* of success or failure of the ritual depends on the agents' or factions' attitudes and interests as they seek to position themselves in the field of discourse about ritual. What is failure for some is successful performance for others. However, rather than taking these contesting viewpoints as problematic, Brosius incorporates them in her analysis theoretically by taking a multi-perspectival approach to assessing how the risks are played out and aims achieved in these different sets of relationships. The notion of ritual failure is not employed here as a final judgment on a ritual's efficacy or conduct, but as a way to enable the investigator to scrutinise how individual agents and factions play out their risks, and manoeuvre and position themselves to achieve political authority by means of (or in opposition to) the aims of the rite. In this way Brosius incorporates in one analysis both the processes within the rite that generate its movement and the forces in the external world which oppose it and with which it must contend.

The exploration and critique of the problem of 'ritual failure', as viewed across the whole breadth of the papers, has uncovered the complexities of the ethnographic material involved, the difficulty of clearly defining the subject of inquiry, and a broad range of analytical complications. The term 'ritual failure' has been used to characterise all manner of allegations, procedural errors, deviations, mishaps, internal contestations, and oppositional critiques in rituals that (with very few exceptions) seem, despite everything, to go to completion without losing their functionality, authority or credibility. Indeed, few of the essays discuss 'outright failure' itself. Rather their focus and concern might be usefully summarised under the heading 'ritual imperfection' with outright failure being reserved for that end of a continuum where ritual breaks down, loses its authority or becomes discredited. Changing the focus from 'failure' to 'imperfection' doesn't remove the difficulties we have discussed ('ritual imperfection' is still subject to ethnographic critique and the various perspectival views of those involved with it) but 'imperfection' is a term less loaded than 'failure', which allows discussion greater analytical space and nuance. It can accommodate a range of gradations of imperfection: infelicitous rites which do their job acceptably but don't do it well: e.g. not without conflict, or not without correction or not to everyone's satisfaction, or not in proper style—but don't actually "fail".

It may well be that a comprehensive theory of 'ritual failure' *per se* is not possible. But it may be possible, to attempt a broad *approach* to the phenomenon that incorporates many of the difficulties in a theorised manner. In order to do this, however, especially in the context of a wide range of analytical agendas represented in this collection of papers, we need to address the question: what are we approaching 'ritual imperfection' for? Is the notion of 'failed ritual' or 'ritual imperfection' ultimately something more than an anthropological curiosity? Does it have something useful and significant to contribute to our understanding of anything?

The study of ritual imperfections may be interesting for what it can contribute to the theory of ritual. In the first instance, this refers to ritual theory narrowly conceived, that is, a theory of ritual as a social fact or practice, an ordered process in its own right with the focus on its characteristic structure and performance: all those aspects of ritual which render it meaningful and make it 'work'. This is a domain investigated by a long tradition in cultural anthropology and more recently forms the special concern of Grimes's 'ritual criticism'. The investigation of marred or collapsed performances and ritual infelicities has considerable value for the understanding of the internal form and performative dynamics that make rituals work. This is especially useful in the field where flawed performances are often the topic of considerable discussion among participants and can provide a unique opportunity to learn how different players think or feel about the way their rituals work—as well as to track the effects particular errors or mishaps have on the ritual as a whole. Similarly, they provide an opportunity to investigate that little-studied phenomenon that forms an underlying issue in a number of the papers in this collection: the robustness of ritual—its capacity (and the limits of this capacity) to retain functionality, authority and credibility despite imperfect performance. This is a topic that has been virtually unexamined in the literature.

But the study of ritual imperfections has ramifications beyond the structure and process of the ritual performance itself narrowly conceived. It is clear from many papers in this collection, that many of the difficulties that afflict rituals have their origins outside the ritual itself or in the relation of the ritual enactment to its larger social, political and historical context. Rituals, of course, have been a central interest in anthropology for a long time, precisely because they are so frequently at the centre of activities of key cultural importance and social concern. Rituals bring core cultural values, ideology, knowledge and dramatic style to bear on real social relationships, problems and difficulties, often at key moments of transition or intensification. Rituals, in short, are often at the centre of the play of social and political forces operating in a society. For this reason anthropologists have often taken ritual events as a mirror in which the larger problems of particular interest in an ethnographic case may be reflected and become amenable to analysis.

Having said that, there is a weakness in this approach. Because rituals are relatively fixed and repetitive forms, fitted in a particular way to the events which they celebrate and facilitate, they present a particular version of the relationships and forces. It is relatively straight-forward to construct an analysis that shows how cultural sentiments, symbols, and dramatic processes frame a kind of canonical story 'that the culture tells itself about itself' in order to move forward the situation or circumstances to which the ritual pertains. These sorts of analyses tend to present typical or representative examples or at least to rely on exemplary ethnographic materials of properly performed rituals held in relatively stable social circumstances. But 'proper performances' are themselves constructions with agendas by and for the groups which perform them. Our analysis may be very good as far as it goes, but important aspects of the actual play of social forces between the ritual and wider social domain are likely to be hidden from, or deliberately and customarily mispresented in, the ritual performance itself. These hidden issues may be difficult to see in the smooth surfaces of well-done rituals performed in conventional circumstances. But rituals that are flawed or that fail can provide the opportunity to see them. Historically changing social values, shifts in social sentiments, or new implications for conventional symbols, all alter or affect the significance of what is being performed.

This collection has amply demonstrated that it is often out of this wider domain of social and political tension that allegations of ritual impropriety arise. Alternatively, circumstances may alter the conventional social relationships between ritual performers in such a way as to render their ritual roles awkward or impossible to perform (as in Geertz's example cited at the beginning of this paper). Shifting historical circumstances, changing social configurations, subtle (or not-so-subtle) political rivalries and manoeuvrings, important recent events, and all sorts of other contingencies affect the climate and context within which rituals are performed, the circumstances out of which they arise and to which they are addressed. And because of the central role rituals play in human affairs, it is sometimes by understanding what went wrong with the ritual that we come to realise that there is something amiss in the social/cultural world.

We are now in a position to sum up the lessons to be drawn from this collection. It is not obvious that a comprehensive theory of 'ritual failure' or more broadly of 'ritual imperfection' is called for (if it is indeed possible). This is partly because ritual imperfections have such a vast array of different kinds and levels of 'causes' and consequences as to challenge notions of straight-forward explanations. But more importantly, ritual flaws are much less interesting in themselves than they are for what they reveal about other things: the way the performative processes in rituals work, or, more broadly, what they reveal about a host of other issues relating to the complexities of wider social and political processes which rituals affect and which in turn have their impact on ritual. Because the study of ritual imperfection is likely to be grounded in an investigation about these wider issues of ritual and society, there are many possible starting points. However, it seems to me that any approach to the investigation of ritual imperfections must be established on the basis of answers to at least three questions.

First it is necessary to be clear about the agenda of the analysis—what is the investigator of ritual imperfection trying to find out? This concern is likely to differ from investigator to investigator as well as from the concerns the performers of the rituals investigated have about imperfections.

Second, the investigation must be sure to establish the various stakes and agendas of the participants, agents, or players in the ritual events, and to clarify how this positions them in relation to the allegations of flaws in the ritual. These positioned differences must be incorporated within whatever theoretical framework is being used. When this is done, allegations of ritual imperfections often emerge as a matter of political contestation deriving from tensions and struggles outside the ritual that are expressed in one way or another within it.

Finally (or perhaps firstly), the research must be done in the presence of an investigation of what local ritual experts and participants believe ritual is, what it does, how it works and how to perform it, in the context of the moral, aesthetic, emotional and socio/political values that inform their practice. That is, the investigation must determine ethnographically what might be called the local 'ideology of ritual', or the local 'ethno-understanding' of the theory and practice of ritual.

If properly pursued, this investigation should lead directly to useful questions concerning local cultural epistemology and sociology of knowledge. But more than this: if properly pursued, the investigation should emerge in the practice of what I have called the 'ethnographic critique of the terms of analysis', in other words, the problematisation of the way we approach our subjects of investigation in relation to how our ethnographic subjects think about the same (or related) things. This entails a problematisation of our own (western, academic) categories of analysis *vis-à-vis* the practices and conceptualizations of our ethnographic subjects. In this way our analytic categories become issues of conceptualization which may be pursued in dialogue with comparable local or 'native' notions to more finely align our understanding with their experience and way of being.

The payoff of this kind of disciplined approach to investigating flawed ritual is not thus just a greater understanding of ritual itself and the social and political processes in which it is embedded and participates. It also inspires broader investigation of the general problem of the creative role played by mishaps and failures in other key aspects of culture.

References

Bateson, G. [2]1958. *Naven*. Stanford, California: Stanford University Press (repr. of 1936).

Geertz, Clifford 1957. "Ritual and Social Change: a Javanese Example". *American Anthropologist* 59.1: 32–54.

—— 1973. "Deep Play: Notes on the Balinese Cockfight". In: *The Interpretation of Cultures*. New York: Basic Books, 412–453.

Grimes, Ronald L. 1990. *Ritual Criticism: Case Studies in its Practice, Essays in its Theory.* Columbia: University of South Carolina Press.

Schieffelin, Edward L. 1996. "On Failure and Performance. Throwing the Medium out of the Séance". In: *The Performance of Healing*, Laderman, Carol & Marina Roseman (ed.). New York & London: Routledge, 59–89.

MISTAKES, PROCEDURAL ERRORS AND INCORRECT PERFORMANCES

It seems that in ritual something always can go wrong, but this does not mean that a slip necessarily matters. The six contributions to this section give evidence of a wide range of possible deviations, errors, flaws, slips and mistakes, but also of the diversity of perspectives and modes of evaluation. The articles clearly document that rituals are always evaluated, assessed and interpreted, although the investigated traditions and the perspectives of the five authors could hardly be more different.

Claus Ambos in "Types of Ritual Failure and Mistakes in Ritual in Cuneiform Sources" demonstrates how much textual material cuneiform studies offers for the study of a ritual's risks and the attempts of the tradition to cope with it: ritual texts, oracular queries, wisdom literature, lamentations, and hundreds of letters from Assyrian and Babylonian scholars and ritual experts to the Assyrian Kings Esarhaddon (680–669 BCE) and Assurbanipal (668–627 BCE). Ambos presents several examples of ritual performances on the verge of failure. He analyses the textual representations of the risks of ritual and some instances of failed rituals in a long-gone civilization and studies the texts' rhetorics from the perspective of a textual scholar. Taking into account that texts sometimes tell us much about actual performances, but sometimes tell us little, he also presents cases in which he is confronted with two conflicting views of one and the same incident, namely two differing textual assessments of one single ritual. Moreover, Ambos vividly demonstrates that we always have to ask who articulates the reasons and consequences of ritual failure.

Jan Weinhold opens up individual perspectives of the participants on the issue in his "Failure and Mistakes in Rituals of the European Santo Daime Church: Experiences and Subjective Theories of the Participants". Weinhold's article is determined by participant observation, enriched by the analysis of interviews conducted with members of the Santo Daime church. He therefore mainly concentrates on the performance aspects of the rituals and on their subjective evaluations. The observed flexibility of ritual performance and its norms in emic views is often explained in that Daime itself is postulated as a superhuman agent, responsible for any practice, including deviations from the ritual norms. Moreover, it becomes clear that the 'flow' of a ritual performance can be perceived as more important than avoiding deviations.

Burckhard Dücker in his contribution "Failure Impossible? Handling of Rules, Mistakes and Failure in Public Rituals of Modern Western Societies" mainly concentrates on the participant institutions' evaluation of deviations. He gives a short historical survey of coronation ceremonies of poets in early modern times and other cultural honours from the mid-18th century where making ritual mistakes was possible but did not result in any spectacular actions: in many cases these deviations were incorporated as 'subversive elements' into the ritual systems. Dücker moreover highlights the reflexivity of tradition and ritual which he sees as essential for the relation between ritual criticism (as subversive element) and ritual performance. He argues that failure is an integral part of order. In and beyond the ritual, a mistake refers to systemic relations: on the one hand it refers to the synchronic and diachronic historical context of other rituals, on the other, to its contemporary socio-cultural context, where the deviation initiates a discourse about rules. "Deviation is the most latent element of the existing order, offering a new interpretation of the existing normality as and when it is activated" (Dücker, p. 79).

Jan A.M. Snoek in his article "Dealing with Deviations in the Performance of Masonic Rituals" explicitly takes on an extraordinary perspective: being a mason himself, he consciously chose a scholarly position, rather than an insider one. However, being a mason, he is in the position to report about the perspectives on ritual failures, mistakes or errors from within the tradition. Since masonic Grand Lodges are autonomous and independent, and since roughly speaking each country has its own Grand Lodge, some of which are several hundred years old, each developed in the course of time its own style, also in respect to dealing with deviations from the ritual norms. The examples given by Snoek give the reader a deep insight into the textual as well as the performance aspects of masonic Rituals.

Axel Michaels in his article "Perfection and Mishaps in Vedic Rituals" refers to several ways in which the rituals can be spoilt or endangered. The list of possible mistakes is long: unexpected incidents or obstacles, misbehaviour of the participants, pollution of the material, and so on. However, apart from the 'standard' methods employed to prevent a mistake's evil consequences (substitution, alteration, omission, fusion, reduction, repetition and invention), he argues, in Vedic ritual systems there is a very fundamental way of dealing with the risks emerging from procedural errors or slips, namely the internalisation of the entire ritual process. Michaels claims that a certain notion of internalisation and autonomy of the ritual is necessary for any kind of ritual thinking: rituals are dynamic events in their own right that cannot really fail on the doctrinal level. Internalisation here is the expression of the rituals' intrinsic "capacity of self-healing", he says (p. 131).

The tendency of some ritual systems to 'incorporate' deviations in ritual by attributing them to superhuman agency and thus considering them as part of the ritual process can also be interpreted as a means to cope with the riskiness of rituals. Christoph Emmrich in his contribution "'All the King's Horses and All the King's Men': the 2004 Red Matsyendranātha Incident in Lalitpur" describes and analyses how the ceremonial chariot carrying the god 'Red Matsyendranātha' on the sixth day of its procession through Lalitpur (Nepal) fell on its side. The procession was interrupted for one entire month due to necessary rituals of atonement and exculpation as well as the complete rebuilding of the vehicle. Now, as in earlier cases when the god 'fell', the incident is interpreted by many as the most recent one in a long line marking the country's troubled fate. Emmrich analyses how the damage was assessed in 'popular belief' and by the ritual specialists, which measures were recommended and how and for what purpose they were applied. Both interpretations—offence against the godhead or portentous omen—make Emmrich raise the question whether in this context there is any appropriate place for or a notion such as 'mistake' or 'failure'. He suggests rather that the event can be interpreted as pre-enacted and thus calculated catastrophe inherent in this particular ritual, which enables the performance of breakdown and recovery, mirroring on a small scale the fate of the world.

These six contributions reveal that deviations are constitutive features of ritual, and that dealing with such deviations is therefore an integral part of most ritual traditions: these methods can be interpreted as 'incorporation of risks', serving as means to avert the dangers arising from improper ritual performances.

TYPES OF RITUAL FAILURE AND MISTAKES IN RITUAL IN CUNEIFORM SOURCES[1]

Claus Ambos

The field of cuneiform studies can offer various and fascinating textual sources for the topic of ritual failure and mistakes in ritual.[2] Particularly interesting are hundreds of the letters from Assyrian and Babylonian scholars and ritual experts to the Assyrian Kings Esarhaddon (680–669 BCE) and Assurbanipal (668–627 BCE) unearthed at Nineveh, the last Assyrian royal residence. Through these letters we can obtain an amazingly vivid picture of ritual practice in the Ancient Near East in the 1st millennium BCE. These letters, stemming from real life, offer invaluable information which cannot be obtained from literary or propaganda texts. The following topics will be dealt with in this article:

- ritual failure brought about by the gods refusing to accept a ritual;
- ritual failure brought about by the gods interrupting a ritual by their own intervention;
- mistakes made by human participants and how to cope with them.

The discussion of these points will finally lead to the question of whether ritual failure or mistakes led to scepticism about the efficacy of divination and ritual. Up to now, the topic of ritual failure has never been treated coherently in Assyriological literature, so I have deliberately chosen a descriptive approach, collecting a representative sample of relevant primary sources rather than treating an isolated case study. By this, the reader will obtain an overview about the characteristics and expressiveness of both literary and everyday texts.

---

[1] Note the following conventions concerning the translations: uncertain translations and Akkadian words are in italics. Square brackets indicate damage to or a break in the cuneiform tablet, words in round brackets are supplied to aid comprehension. Dates mentioned in the texts presented here have been kept in the Mesopotamian calendrical system with the number of the month transcribed into Roman numerals; the date in our calendar is given in round brackets. e.g. 18.II. (16th May). Years are always BCE. I am grateful to Dr. Jon Taylor (London) for correcting my English.

[2] This article deals with material from Assyria and Babylonia. An informative and comprehensive introduction to Hittite rituals is found in Haas (2003).

Even to the present day, a considerable amount of cuneiform tablets already kept in museums and collections still remains to be published and analyzed. In contrast to the fields of classical philology or Old Testament studies, the already vast corpus of texts and archaeological artefacts is still increasing exponentially by scientific excavations, and, to a much larger degree, by illicit digging and looting. Any fruitful approach to Ancient Mesopotamian culture will always be based upon the study of primary sources, using philological methods as a starting point. The fundamental difficulties of how to approach the textual and archaeological remains of a long dead civilization have been discussed by Oppenheim (1977). A historico-cultural approach in dealing with Mesopotamian rituals has been chosen by Maul (1994) and Ambos (2004). An attempt to make use of theories and methods from other fields for dealing with Mesopotamian 'magic' in a broad sense of the word is offered by Binsbergen & Wiggermann (1999).

1. *Introduction: the divine origin of rituals, temples and cult statues*

The techniques of ritual and divination were transmitted to man by the gods themselves (see e.g. Lambert 1998). This idea, which can be found in exorcistic and healing rituals, also lies behind regular cultic rites performed daily in the gods' sanctuaries. When the gods created the universe, they themselves built their temples as their divine domiciles of eternal pleasure. Likewise the cultic images were created and the appropriate rites and cultic regulations introduced by the gods in these primeval times. The world with its raw materials, plants and animals was shaped to meet the needs of the gods and to serve as a source for the regular offerings and for furnishing the sanctuaries. This artfully shaped cosmic order could, however, be seriously disturbed.

As time went by, the old ground-plans of the temples would be forgotten, and the appropriate rites, cultic offices and divine images or symbols replaced with new ones. This was a serious threat to the good relationship between god and man and could lead to the deity abandoning his or her temple in anger, leaving the people without divine protection. This was obviously a very dangerous situation, only to be remedied by re-installing the temple, the rites and the divine image in their former, appropriate state (Ambos 2004: 45–61).

The following example is from a royal inscription of the Babylonian King Nabonidus (555–539 BCE). The text contains a report about improper changes made to the old rites, the statue and the temple of the goddess Ištar in the city of Uruk about 200 years earlier during the reign of King Erība-Marduk (8th century BCE). It was only under Nebuchadnezzar II. (604–562 BCE) that the sanctuary was restored to its proper state:[3]

> Ištar of Uruk, the lofty princess who dwells in a golden shrine, to whom are harnessed seven lions (and) whose hand-washing rites the Urukaeans changed during the reign of King Erība-Marduk, removing her shrine and unharnessing her team, left Eanna (her temple) in anger to dwell in a place not her dwelling. They made dwell in her cella a protective goddess not belonging to Eanna. He (Nebuchadnezzar II.) appeased Ištar, re-established her shrine for her (and) harnessed for her seven lions befitting her godhead. The inappropriate Ištar he removed from Eanna and returned Innin (= Ištar) to Eanna, her sanctuary.

The rediscovery of forgotten, neglected or maliciously altered rites is a regular topos in a lot of the texts. According to the colophon of a tablet from Uruk which describes the daily rites of the main temples of the city, the tablets containing these very rites were stolen by King Nabopolassar (625–605 BCE), taken away to the land of Elam in south-west Iran, and only rediscovered there in Seleucid times:[4]

> By the hand of Šamaš-ēṭir, son of Ina-qibīt-Anu, grandson of Šibqāt-Anu. Writing board of the rites of the cult of Anu, of the holy rituals (and) the ritual regulations of kingship, together with the divine rituals of the *reš*-temple, the Irigal, the Eanna[5] and the temples of Uruk, the ritual activities of the exorcists, lamentation-singers, the singers, and all the experts who follow the ... apart from everything that pertains to the apprentice diviners, according to the tablets which Nabopolassar, the king of the Sealand, took away from Uruk, and then Kidin-Anu, (...) the descendent of Ekur-zakir, the high-priest of the *reš*-temple, saw those tablets in the land of Elam, and copied them and brought them back to Uruk during the reign of Kings Seleucus (I.) and Antiochus (I.).

The topic of new as opposed to ancient rituals will be further dealt with below (section 4.2.). Real or alleged alterations did not necessarily take place hundreds of years ago in a distant past, as described in the

[3] Edition of Nabonidus' inscription by Schaudig (2001: 514–529); the English translation of the cited passage follows Beaulieu (1993: 45).

[4] Edition of the tablet by Thureau-Dangin (1921: 74–86); this English translation follows Beaulieu (1993: 47).

[5] These are the names of the main temples of Uruk.

texts presented above. A lengthy letter of complaint informs an Assyrian king of the activities of a lamentation-priest called Pūlu, who was turning the temple of the god Nabû upside down and affecting the sanctuary's building substance, furnishings, and cultic offices and rites (Cole & Machinist 1998: no. 134).

2. *Ritual failure caused by the gods*

2.1. *The gods refusing communication*

The plans of the gods were unfathomable to man, confusing even the ritual experts and diviners. This topic is often dealt with in the so-called 'wisdom literature'. As an example, some passages of the 'Poem of the righteous sufferer' will be cited and treated here.[6] The poem's protagonist is a man called Šubši-mešrê-Šakkan. An individual bearing this name is attested as a high-ranking official during the reign of the Babylonian King Nazimaruttaš (ca. 1307–1282 BCE) and may well have been the person mentioned in the poem. The extant manuscripts of the work are from the 1st millennium BCE.

Šubši-mešrê-Šakkan can best be described as the cuneiform equivalent of Biblical Job: albeit pious and devout, he is reduced by the god Marduk to a miserable state, stricken with illness and outcast by society. Since Šubši-mešrê-Šakkan always did his duty by god and man, he is utterly dismayed to find himself in a state which should rather be occupied by someone failing to honour the gods properly (Tablet II ll. 12ff.):

> Like one who had not made libations to his god,
> nor invoked his goddess with a food offering,
> who was not wont to prostrate, nor seen to bow down;
> from whose mouth supplication and prayer were lacking,
> who skipped holy days and despised monthly festivals,
> who was neglectful, omitted the gods' rites,
> had not taught his people reverence and worship,
> who did not invoke his god, but ate his food offering,
> who snubbed his goddess by not bringing a flour offering,
> like one *possessed*(?), who forgot his lord,

[6] The basic edition of this text was given by Lambert (1960 [repr. 1996]: 21–62). In his new (German) translation von Soden (1990: 110–135) offers a lot of important improvements. The translation of the passages given here follows Foster (1993: 308–325).

had frivolously sworn a solemn oath by his god—
(like such an one) did I appear!

Even if certain behaviour was conceived by man to be pious and pleasing to the gods, no one could know with certainty if the gods themselves would accept this behaviour as a proper way of acting. This does not mean that pious deeds, sacrifice and ritual were not effective, but that man had no insight into the real intentions of the gods. Šubši-mešrê-Šakkan was about to experience this himself. With the help of diviners and ritual experts, he tried again and again to determine the plans of the gods and, if possible, to soothe their anger by means of appropriate rituals. The gods, however, constantly refused all communication with him, both by divination and by ritual (Tablet I ll. 51f.; Tablet II ll. 6–9 and 108–111):

The omen organs concerning me were confused and *abnormal* every day,
(even) with (the help of) haruspex and dream interpreter my (bad) condition was not cut off.[7]
(...)
The haruspex with his extispicy could not get to the bottom of it,
the dream interpreter with his fumigation could not make manifest my case.
I implored the dream-god—he did not enlighten me!
The exorcist with his ritual could not appease the anger (of the gods).
(...)
The exorcist recoiled from my *sakkikû*(-illness),
while my portents have perplexed the haruspex.
The exorcist did not clarify the nature of my illness,
the haruspex could give no time limit for my illness.

Only after Marduk's anger at him had ceased, was the sufferer restored to his former health and position. Marduk himself announces Šubši-mešrê-Šakkan's recovery in several consecutive dreams. In each of these dreams a messenger appears, sent by Marduk in order to hand over the appropriate remedies to the sufferer. An example is cited here (Tablet III ll. 39–60):

In the dream [came] Ur-Nin-tin-ugga [...],
a bearded man with a tiara on his head,
he was an exorcist, carrying a tablet:
"Marduk has sent me:
To Šubši-mešrê-Šakkan I have brought a sw[athe].

[7] This line is cited in a royal inscription of King Nabonidus (Schaudig 2001: 493).

From his pure hands I have brought a swathe."
He entrusted it into the hands of my servant.
In waking hours he sent a message
and showed his favourable sign to my people
I was awake in my sickness, a (healing) serpent slithered by.[8]
My illness was quickly over, [my fetters] were broken.
After the mind of my lord had quietened,
and the heart of merciful Marduk was appeased
[after he had] received my prayers [. . .],
his sweet [relen]ting [. . .]
(. . .)
He made the wind bear away my offences.

The following lines describe how Marduk himself drives away every evil by which the sufferer had been oppressed. The sufferer's immediate recovery brought about by a merciful and appeased god contrasts sharply with the repeated but vain efforts of the diviners and ritual experts described above. Ritual could never work against the will of the gods or even force the gods to an action desired by the ritual's human participants. As long as Šubši-mešrê-Šakkan was exposed to Marduk's wrath and abandoned by his own protective deities, all the said efforts were doomed to failure.

The word of the gods, which is beyond human understanding, is a frequent topos in Sumerian lamentations: "His word has no diviner, no dream interpreter" (Cohen 1988: 123 l. 14; 277 l. b+100). Lamentations formed an important text genre in Sumerian literature and occupied a vital place in rituals and the regular cult to soothe the anger of the gods. One passage reads as follows (Cohen 1988: 124 ll. 35f.):

(Sumerian version)
Let me bring his (the god's) word to the diviner, and this diviner will lie, let me bring his word to a dream interpreter, and this dream interpreter will lie.

(Akkadian version)
His word is brought to the haruspex, and the haruspex will search for excuses, his word is brought to a dream interpreter and the dream interpreter will search for excuses.

[8] The serpent is the animal of Gula, the healing goddess.

2.2. *The gods' interruption of a ritual as exemplified by Marduk's failed return to Babylon*

As we have seen in the previous section, the gods could decide according to their unfathomable will whether to accept or to refuse a ritual. If the gods did not want to accept a ritual, they could interrupt the performance, while the ritual was still in progress, by their direct intervention. A good example is the failure of attempt by the Assyrian King Esarhaddon (680–669 BCE) to return the cult statues of the gods of Babylon.

In 689 BCE Babylon was destroyed by the Assyrians under their King Sennacherib (704–681 BCE), Esarhaddon's father and predecessor. Even the sanctuaries of the city were destroyed, and the images of their gods smashed or deported to the Assyrian capital Assur. After assuming power, Esarhaddon abandoned his father's rude politics towards Babylon and began to rebuild and resettle the city. Meanwhile, the statues of Marduk or Bēl, the city god of Babylon, and his consort Zarpanītu stayed in Assyria (it remains unclear whether they had been smashed by Sennacherib and fashioned anew under Esarhaddon, or simply deported to Assur). The return of the gods to Babylon would be the pinnacle of Esarhaddon's reconciliatory politics towards the city so cruelly destroyed by his father. The circumstances of Marduk's return had been object of several oracular queries. On 7.II. (5th May) 669, one day before his departure, Marduk's statue was consecrated by mouth-washing. On 8.II. (6th May) Marduk and his wife Zarpanītu left Assur on their way to Babylon. In eager anticipation, royal inscriptions were composed recording the solemn arrival of the deities in their city, an arrival which no one could doubt would shortly prove true. The inscriptions vividly describe the joyful entry of the statues into Babylon and their consecration by means of mouth-washing and mouth-opening, and suggest that the king himself took part in the ceremonies and rituals. The passage reads as follows (Walker & Dick 2001: 26f.):

> (The gods) travelled the road to Babylon, a festive way. From Assur to the quay at Babylon, every third of a double-mile piles of brushwood were lit, at every double-mile fat bulls were slaughtered. And I, Esarhaddon, led the great god in procession; I processed with joy before him. I brought them joyfully into the heart of Babylon, the city of their honour. Into the orchards, among the canals and parterres of the temple Ekarzaginna ('House-quay of Lapis Lazuli'), the pure place, they entered by means of

> the office of the *apkallu*,[9] mouth-washing, mouth-opening, washing and purification, before the stars of heaven, before (the gods) Ea, Šamaš, Asalluḫi,[10] Bēlet-ilī,[11] Kusu, Ningirim,[12] Ninkurra, Ninagal, Kusibanda, Ninduluma and Ninzadim. . . .[13]

In fact, only ten days after their departure, on 18.II. (16th May), Marduk and Zarpanītu arrived at Labbanat, a town at the border between Assyria and Babylonia, about 350 km south of Assur.

Then something totally unexpected happened which was to belie the already composed royal inscriptions with their anticipated arrival of the gods in Babylonia: Marduk made an oracular utterance through the mouth of a servant, according to which his and Zarpanītu's return had to be put off. Esarhaddon was informed about this serious event by his highest-ranking advisors, the chief scribe Ištar-šuma-ēreš, the king's exorcist Adad-šuma-uṣur, and the chief exorcist Marduk-šākin-šumi (Parpola 1983: no. 29; 1993: no. 24):

> To the king, our lord, your servants Ištar-šuma-ēreš, Adad-šuma-uṣur and Marduk-šākin-šumi. Good health to the king, our lord! May Nabû and Marduk bless the king, our lord!
>
> On the 18th day the god Bēl, together with his divine escort, was in the city of Labbanat. Everything was just fine.
>
> Bēl-erība and Nergal-šallim, servants of the household of the crown prince, under the jurisdiction of the governor of the city of Šamaš-nāṣir, were attending, in Labbanat, to a strong horse harnessed in trappings of the land of Kuš for the entrance into the city (Babylon). Nergal-šallim took hold of the feet of Bēl-erība and helped him to mount the horse. They saw (this), seized and questioned him. He said: "The gods Bēl and Zar[panītu] have sent word to me: 'Babylon—*straight*—the loot of Kurigalzu.'" [NN], the 'third man' [of . . .] claims as follows: "I know!—Those [robb]ers are waiting [in Dū]r-Kurigalzu."—What is it that the king, our lord, orders?

The servants' odd behaviour and the utterance were understood by the witnesses of this event as a message from Marduk (= Bēl) and Zarpanītu. The horse in question was harnessed in order to serve as a draught horse for the chariot of Marduk, not as a mount for the servant. The utterance was explained by a military official, the 'third man', as a warning

---

[9] Apkallu is the designation for a class of priests and a group of mythical sages.

[10] Ea, Šamaš and Asalluḫi are the gods who supervise the ritual.

[11] Bēlet-ilī is the mother goddess.

[12] Kusu is the high-priest of the gods, Ningirim is the goddess of exorcism.

[13] The aforementioned gods are the divine craftsmen who created the statue of Marduk.

about robbers lying in ambush in or near the city of Dūr-Kurigalzu.

The 'third man' reached his conclusion by deducing a meaning of each of these apparently incoherent words and connecting this meaning with the present situation: Kurigalzu was the name of two Babylonian kings of the second half of the second millennium BCE; individuals bearing this name are also attested during the 7th century BCE. The city of Dūr-Kurigalzu ('Kurigalzu-Castle') in northern Babylonia was founded by King Kurigalzu I and named after him. The gods and their escort had to pass this city on their way to Babylon. So the name Kurigalzu was linked to Marduk's return. The term 'loot' implied the presence of robbers, and 'Babylon' denoted both the goal of the procession and Marduk himself, the city god, whose procession was endangered by the activities of the just mentioned marauders. Of course, the presence of a 'third man', i.e. the third man in a battle chariot, implies that Marduk travelled under military protection, but the constant performance of the sacrifices outlined in the royal inscription cited above may well have been endangered by the presence of robbers, not to mention the fact that occasional fighting might have done some harm to the solemn character of the procession.

The concept of an oracular utterance is well attested in cuneiform literature and can best be compared with the Greek idea of *kledon*. If the 'third man' was right in his interpretation, it was something like a warning sent by the gods. We do not know what conclusion was reached by the scholars Ištar-šuma-ēreš, Adad-šuma-uṣur and Marduk-šākin-šumi in their own interpretation of the event, but the return of Marduk and Zarpanītu was put off.

The completion of his politics of reconciliation towards Babylon had been within Esarhaddon's grasp—but now this sudden and unexpected set-back! After all, a band of robbers (if the utterance was understood correctly) might have been a rather insignificant reason to stop this important enterprise.

Having been chosen to rebuild a temple and lead the deity back into his or her sanctuary in solemn procession was a proof of divine favour towards the ruler, and the joy expressed in Esarhaddon's royal inscription cited above was surely sincere and genuine. We can easily imagine the consternation that befell the king when he received the news of the gods' utterance at Labbanat. The disquieting fact that Marduk and Zarpanītu were apparently disinclined to continue their journey to Babylon meant that Esarhaddon was denied the accomplishment of his pious deed and enjoying its fruits.

And much worse, time was now running out fast for the Assyrian king and he did not live to see the return of the gods to Babylon. About half a year later, on 10.VIII. (= 1st November) 669 BCE he succumbed to the grave illness he had been suffering from for so many years. It was only in the first regnal year of his son and heir, Assurbanipal, that Marduk and Zarpanītu finally returned to their city, Babylon.

3. *Mistakes made by human participants and how to cope with them: general introduction*

Despite of all the efforts of the human participants, a mistake in performing a ritual could never be excluded. A mistake during the performance of a ritual or the recitation of a prayer led to the ritual missing its aim and arousing the anger of the gods. Another element of uncertainty was constituted by the mistakes that remained unnoticed to the participants.

Fortunately there was always a way to cope with this uncertainty, even while the ritual was still in progress. This is the case in the extispicy ritual of the haruspex, which includes in the so-called 'disregard-formula' a comprehensive list of possible mistakes that might happen during the performance of extispicy, and which Šamaš, the patron of divination, was asked to disregard (Starr 1990: xx–xxvii):

> Disregard the (formulation) of (the prayer for) today's case, be it correct, be it faulty,
> (and that) the day is overcast, and it is raining.
> Disregard that a clean or an unclean person has touched the sacrificial sheep, or blocked the way of the sacrificial sheep.
> Disregard that an unclean man or woman has come near the place of extispicy and made it unclean.
> Disregard that I have performed the extispicy in this unclean place.
> Disregard that the ram (offered) to your great divinity for the performance of extispicy is deficient or faulty.
> Disregard that I, the haruspex your servant, am dressed in my ordinary soiled garments,
> haven eaten, drunk, anointed myself with, touched, or stepped upon anything unclean,
> have seen fear and terror at night, have touched the libation beer, the flour, the water, the container and the fire,
> have changed or altered the proceedings,
> or that the oracular query became jumbled in my mouth.
> Let these (undesirable) things be excluded and left out of consideration!

This stereotyped formula gives a list of possible mistakes while performing the *agenda* or *dicenda* of the ritual. If a mistake had actually happened, it could be neutralised by a ritual against ritual failure (Maul 1994: 421–431). The title of this ritual was 'Apotropaic ritual to prevent the evil of cultic offices and the affliction (lit.: touch) of rites and hand-washing rites from approaching a man and his house'. These strategies to undo mistakes, be it by a prayer while the ritual performance was still in progress, be it by a special ritual performed after the incorrect performance, can best be compared with analogous strategies used in Indian rituals (see the introduction by Schieffelin to the present volume, and the article by Michaels).

4. *Mistakes and errors made by participants: case studies from Nineveh*

Let us now have a look at actual mistakes documented in cuneiform sources. The state archives of Assyria unearthed at Nineveh, the royal residence, offer plentiful and unique information for every aspect of the administrative, political or religious life of a long dead civilization.

The kings exchanged hundreds and hundreds of letters with scribes and scholars of every discipline. Legal documents of any kind, grants and decrees were issued by a bureaucratic administration and the governed people were thoroughly documented person by person in census lists. The government was kept up to date on anti-Assyrian activities inside and outside the frontiers by the reports of a well-organized intelligence service.

Most relevant for our topic is the correspondence of Esarhaddon and Assurbanipal with their scholarly advisors and ritual experts—exorcists, diviners, physicians, lamentations-priests etc. Best documented in these letters is the period from about 673 to 666 BCE, that is, the final years of Esarhaddon, overshadowed by his severe illness, and the first regnal years of Assurbanipal.

The senders did not provide their letters with a date, but this can often be reconstructed by astronomical facts mentioned in the texts. This chronological framework can further be supplemented by dates given in the letters when referring to certain events having already taken place or still to happen in the future ("on 8.V.", "tomorrow" etc.) (Parpola 1983).

The letters offer a rich insight into the working conditions of the ritual experts. In fact, working at the royal court at Nineveh was a balancing act. The scholars and ritual experts were dependent on the benevolence of the king. When they sent reports to the king about good omens which had been observed by them, they would include requests for a salary increase in their letters, but they always had to be careful never to fall out of royal favour, for the king's disgrace brought about dire consequences for the unhappy member of the court.[14]

4.1. *Omitting necessary rituals*

To keep the king in a happy state of mind, it is no surprise that from time to time the scholars made an agreement not to inform him about evil portents which had affected or could affect the ruler, and to play down these omens as obscure, but not inauspicious. This happened during the reign of Esarhaddon's father, Sennacherib, as the scholar Bēl-ušēzib reminds the king in one of his letters (Parpola 1993: no. 109 rev. 1–10):

> In the reign of the king, your father, Kalbu, the son of Nabû-ēṭir, without (the knowledge) of the king, your father, made a pact [with] the scribes and haruspices, saying: "If an untoward sign occurs, we shall [tell] the king that an obscure sign has occurred!"—For a period of time he censored all [. . .s], if a sign untoward to him [occurred], and that was anything but good. Finally, when the *alû*(-demon) had come, [he said: "If a sign] that is untoward to me occurs and you do not report it to me, [. . .]!"
>
> When the scribes and haruspices took heed of these words, [the gods of the king] surely know (it), [did they not report] when any portent whatsoever occurred during the reign of your royal father, and did your royal father not stay alive and exercise kingship?

Because of this pact among the scribes and scholars, the rituals necessary after an evil portent were not performed—to the disadvantage of the king, who suddenly became unexpectedly ill, without being warned by his scholars. Interestingly, even in this situation Sennacherib never cast the slightest doubt upon the efficacy of divination or ritual, but quickly recognised that he had fallen victim to treacherous advisors.

A similar case happened during the reign of Esarhaddon. Šamaš-šuma-ukīn, the king's son, informed his father that he had received a letter from some Babylonians about the misdeeds of several scholars (Luukko & van Buylaere 2002: no. 21):

[14] See e.g. Parpola 1993: no. 294 and no. 160.

> Now, Bēl-ēṭir and Šamaš-zēra-iqīša have neglected the order the king gave them (and) are acting on their own. Aplāja, whom the king sent (with the command): "Go (and) set up sanctuaries in Babylon!", has made common cause with them. They are observing the stars (and) dissecting lambs, but he does not report anything concerning the king, our lord, or the crown prince of Babylon.

4.2. *'New' or 'foreign' ritual techniques*

Even if Anatolian, Syrian and Egyptian experts were employed at the royal court at Nineveh and their techniques used in the interest of the king, the Mesopotamian arts of the exorcist, lamentation-priest, chanter, diviner and physician—with their tradition in cuneiform script stemming from the gods themselves—enjoyed highest authority (Parpola 1993: XIV). This is expressed in a letter to King Esarhaddon, in which rituals transmitted in cuneiform are mentioned as 'our rites', as opposed to other rituals without a tradition in cuneiform (Reynolds 2003: no. 204 rev. 3–10):

> [NN], a scholar from the Inner Cit[y] (and) [of . . . is in the presence] of the king, my lord. The king should question him.
>
> (Only) [rites that] are written down in the art of the cuneiform scribe are our rit[e]s. They have been performed by our forefathers, and they meet the needs of the ki[ng]. (There are) a hundred, (nay,) a thousand (rites) which, as far as I am concerned, would be suitable for the purification of the kings, my lords. But, because they are not our rites, they are not recorded in the art of the cuneiform scribe.

In another letter, the chief exorcist of Esarhaddon expresses his uneasiness about the king using foreign (Egyptian?) amulet stones (Parpola 1983: no. 181; 1993 no. 241):

> And concerning the string of (amulet) stones, what the king, my lord, said is quite correct. Did I not tell the king, my lord, (already) in the enemy country (= Egypt?) that they are unsuited to Assyria? Now we shall stick to the methods transmitted to the king, my lord, by the gods (themselves).

Likewise, new rituals not standing in the long tradition were conceived as ineffective by the Mesopotamian scholars, even if these rituals were introduced by the ruler himself, as the following letter to the Assyrian king demonstrates (Cole & Machinist 1998: no. 135 obv. 3–rev. 6):

> I will go to [. . .]. There is [a ritual]. In [the month of . . .], on the 16th day, in the even[ing, Ištar] will g[o] through the great gate [and] descend

into the cana[l . . .]. There is a ritual [*he* will perform]. She will then come up from the canal, go under the gate of the temple of Nabû, and take a seat in the shrine's gate. [Th]ere is a [ritual], *he* will perfo[rm]. She will then go d[own] from the shrine's gate in[to the . . .] of the palace which faces the [. . .] of the drinking place. He will fin[ish] 3 libation jars. This is not a ritual, this is nothing. It is not ancient—your father introduced [it].

4.3. *Incapacity or gross misdemeanour of ritual experts*

Working under difficult conditions in competition with each other, the scholars at court were not infrequently inclined to stress their own capability and the (real or alleged) incompetence or inability of their colleagues. The following example is from a letter from the exorcist Urad-Gula to Esarhaddon (Parpola 1983: no. 223; 1993: no. 290):

> Concerning what the king, my lord, said: "Which exorcists are with you?"—Nabû-lēʾûtī, his son and I. Now Adad-šuma-uṣur comes to us, checks our work and instructs us. We are collaborating closely. Because of this I am writing to the king, my lord. (When) Nabû-lēʾûtī and his son are alone, who can vouch for them, whether (the ritual) succeeds or not? I have seen that this son of his is still in the unsteadiness of his youth. (When) I stay with them, we are performing the ritual successfully—(but) can I leave them alone?

A remarkable fact is the 'hostile takeover' of a ritual mentioned in a letter from the exorcist Nabû-nādin-šumi to Esarhaddon. Nabû-nādin-šumi was employed by the king to perform the ritual 'to block the entry of evil into someone's house' for his sister, Šaddītu. When he had to interrupt the performance in order to participate in a treaty ceremony, his colleague Šumāja was suddenly on the spot to finish the ritual, as the very annoyed Nabû-nādin-šumi wrote to the king (Parpola 1983: no. 211; 1993: no. 273):

> To the king, my lord: Your servant Nabû-nādin-šumi. Good health to the king, my [lo]rd! May Nabû and Marduk [gr]eatly bless the king, my lord! [The king], my [lord], had sent me: "Go and perform the ritual for Šaddītu!"—So I did, (but) I could not perform the rest of the ritual, (because) I had to go for the treaty. Why then did Šumāja hurry from Kalḫu and said to Šaddītu: "This ritual [. . .] I will take over and perform for you!"—He should have asked me! (several fragmentarily preserved lines)
>
> He [is unable] to perform (the ritual) 'To block the entry of evil into someone's house', (but instead) [he has ex]posed her! The king sent me; why did he hasten to per[fo]rm (the ritual)! He is not able (at all)! I will perf[or]m it—or should I have learned from his example (lit.: looked on his hands)?

4.4. *On the verge of failure?—Performing anti-witchcraft rituals for Esarhaddon*

The difficulties and possible failures which could occur during the performance of a ritual can be illustrated by a group of several letters from Marduk-šākin-šumi, an eminent scholar and exorcist at the royal court of Nineveh, to the Assyrian King Esarhaddon. These letters, covering a time span from 22.IX. (24th December) 670 until 7.X. (7th January) 669, allow us to follow the preparation and performance of a ritual called *uš̌burruda*, directed against witchcraft. A performance of this ritual on behalf of the king and his family was scheduled for the end of the month Kislīmu; the preparation of the paraphernalia, however, proved to be so complicated and lengthy that it had to be postponed until the beginning of the following month, Ṭebētu. The letter of Marduk-šākin-šumi, in which he proposes the new schedule of the ritual performance, reads as follows (dated to the 22.IX.) (Parpola 1983: no. 173; 1993: no. 255):

> To the king, my lord: Your servant Marduk-šākin-šumi. Good health to the king, my lord! May Nabû and Marduk bless the king, my lord!
>
> Concerning the ritual about which the king said yesterday: "Perform it by the 24th day!"—We cannot make it, the tablets are too many, when shall they write (them)? Even the preparation of the figurines which the king saw (yesterday) took us five to six days!—Now, if the king, my lord, consents, the month Ṭebētu would be suitable for performing the counter-spells against witchcraft. Let the crown prince [perform] (his part) during that (month), and let the people of the king too perform (their parts) [during it. What harm (would it do)?]
>
> And concerning the Sumerian texts of the counter-spells about which the king said: "Send (word)! They should bring (them) from Nineveh!"—I shall send Iddin-aḫḫē; he will go and bring them. He will also bring with him the other tablets of the 'refrain series'.
>
> Let the king perform (his part) on the 2nd of Ṭebētu, the crown prince on the 4th and the people on the 6th. Alternatively, we may perform (the ritual) on [o]ther days, if (the proposed schedule) is troublesome or not executable.

The king had apparently no objections against the plan outlined in this letter and the ritual could start as proposed. During the performance, Marduk-šākin-šumi had to deal with questions and exhortations of the king and was confronted with ever new problems, as he informed Esarhaddon in another letter (dated to the 3.X.) (Parpola 1983: no. 174; 1993: no. 257):

> [To the ki]ng, my lord: [Your servant] Marduk-šākin-šumi. Good health to the king, my lord! May Nabû and Marduk bless the king, my lord!

> Concerning what the king, my lord, wrote me, I am heeding it and am currently making the preparations. As a matter of fact, the place (of the ritual) is very small to array (the participants). If it is acceptable to the king, my lord, those others should perform (their part only) after these have done with their performance. Or [should we choose anot]her place? (Break)
>
> [Nabû-g]ā[mil has come] to Nineveh and said that Rēmūtu, the [exorcist] who is in the service of the crown prince, is ill. Nabû-tartība-uṣur, Šumāja, the son of Nabû-zēra-[lēšir], Urad-Gula, Nabû-lēʾûtī, [Bē]l-nāṣir: Anyone of [the]se bearded courtiers [whom] the king, my lord, might choose can serve the crown prince!

In performing the ritual, Marduk-šākin-šumi collaborated closely with another high-ranking scholar and exorcist, Adad-šuma-uṣur. A letter, written by both of them to Esarhaddon, shows that the king and his experts sometimes lost the overview as to which of the participants already had performed their part of the ritual and who had not (dated to 5.X.) (Parpola 1983: no. 163; 1993: no. 259):

> To the king, our lord: Your servants Adad-šuma-uṣur and Marduk-šākin-šumi. Good health to the king, our lord. May Nabû and Marduk bless the king, our lord!
>
> Concerning the people about whom the king, our lord, wrote to us: "Can you not specify which (of them) are to come out?"—Those who have not performed (the ritual) should come out tomorrow and perform it. The king, our lord, knows who has performed it and who has not. Whence should we know?—May Bēl and Nabû indicate (the right persons) in the shadow of the king, and let them go out and perform (the ritual).

In this letter both scholars point out to Esarhaddon that the people of the king should go out the next day, i.e. the 6th of Ṭebētu, to perform the ritual. This was already proposed by Marduk-šākin-šumi in his letter dated 22.IX. Apparently not long after the above letter was written, it suddenly occurred to Marduk-šākin-šumi that the said day was not auspicious for performing a ritual. And so hastily this part of *uššurruda* for the people of the king had to be postponed until the day after next, the 7th, as Marduk-šākin-šumi informed Esarhaddon in a letter (dated to 5.X.) (Parpola 1983: no. 176; 1993: no. 260):

> To the king, my lord: Your servant Marduk-šākin-šumi. Good health to the king, my lord! May Nabû and Marduk bless the king, my lord! Concerning the ritual about which I just wrote to the king, my lord: "They should go out and perform it tomorrow!"—it had slipped from my mind that tomorrow is the day of the city god! I was too hasty there, it is not good to g[o out] and perform it. We shall get together and perform it only on the 7th day.

Even on the last day of the performance, Marduk-šākin-šumi had to deal with new problems. Apparently the heat led to yet another interruption of the ritual, as we can see in a letter written by the exorcist to the king (dated to 7.X.) (Parpola 1983: no. 177; 1993: no. 261):

> To the king, my lord: Your servant Marduk-šākin-šumi. Good health to the king, my lord! May Nabû and Marduk b[less] the king, my lord! Concerning the counter-spells which we earlier [had to interrupt] and did not finish performing, we could now, with the king, my lord's, permission, con[tinue with them]. Because of the *temperature*, [the ritual] was not comp[leted . . .] upon the [clothes] of the l[ater] people who [. . .]. At the same time we could also perform th[ose] rites of the series Šur[pu] about which I said to the king, [my] lord: "We should perform them for [. . .]." We will perform them in addition.

From these letters we can deduce that performing a ritual was a very stressful task and that Marduk-šākin-šumi surely was an eminent expert and scholar, who in spite of all the problems and obstructions led the performance of *ušburruda* to a successful conclusion. The problems in this specific performance of the ritual can be summed up as follows:

- complicated and lengthy preparation,
- too little space to perform the ritual,
- sudden illness of a ritual expert,
- lost overview of the participants,
- nearly overlooking an inauspicious day and
- interruption because of the *temperature* (?).

5. *Conclusion and outlook: ritual failure triggering critique or disapproval of ritual?*

Ritual failure could be coped with—at least up to a certain degree regarding mistakes made by human participants. But did perhaps failed or unsuccessful rituals sometimes trigger a general critique of the efficacy of ritual and divination, or bring about the development of different 'ritual schools' or the like?

Let us begin with the latter question. Ritual and divination were developed into a fairly homogeneous system, consisting of various disciplines like that of the exorcist, diviner, lamentation priest and singer. If we take a look at the letters from Nineveh, the scholars argue about technical and organisational details or how best to apply a certain treatment to a patient, but there were no fundamental differences in opinion pointing to different systems of thought.

Looking at Hittite ritual literature, we can discern kinds of schools or guilds formed by members of the various disciplines with their respective techniques, based on characteristic regional and local traditions (Haas 2003: 11ff. and 28ff.). These regional and local ritual specialities were not regarded as mutually exclusive; on the contrary, they all were collected at the Hittite court to be useful to the great King.

Let us now take a look at scepticism or critique regarding the efficacy of ritual and divination. Esarhaddon, royal patient over so many years, never cast the slightest doubt upon the efficacy of the traditional scholarly disciplines, although in spite of all the efforts of his scholars and physicians he was never to recover. His suffering can be deduced from his genuinely moving "agonized outcry" (Parpola 1983: 230) to the physician Urad-Nanaja "Why do you not diagnose the nature of my illness and cure it?" (Parpola 1993: no. 315 ll. 9f.). Recoveries from acute bouts of his illness (or other diseases which had befallen him) were attributed to the gods themselves.[15]

On the other hand there are quite a few (real or alleged) attestations of scepticism and indifference from the 3rd millennium onwards. At least according to the later tradition of the 2nd and 1st millennium BCE, King Narām-Sîn of Akkade (ca. 2254–2218) notoriously despised the will of the gods revealed to him by divination. When his empire was threatened by hordes of wild enemies, he performed an extispicy in order to obtain the agreement of the gods for a campaign (Westenholz 1997: 316f. ll. 72–83):

> I summoned the diviners and instructed (them),
> Seven before seven lambs I butchered.[16]
> I set up pure reed altars.
> I queried the great gods:
> Ištar, Ilaba, Zababa, Annunītum,
> Šullat, Ḫaniš, and Šamaš, the hero:
> The latch-hook of the great gods did not give me permission for my going and my demonical onrush.[17]
> Thus I said to my heart, these were my words:
> "What lion ever performed extispicy?
> What wolf ever consulted a dream-interpreter?

[15] Compare the statement of the king's exorcist Adad-šuma-uṣur: "[when] Bēl took away the illness of the king [...]" (Parpola 1993: no. 200 l. 10).

[16] That is perhaps: seven lambs for the seven gods mentioned below.

[17] 'Latch-hook' is an epithet of Šamaš, the sungod and god of extispicy.

I will go like a brigand according to my own inclination,
and I will cast aside that (oracle) of the god(s); I will be in control of myself!"

The performed extispicy was successful, but Narām-Sîn had hoped for another answer and simply did not accept the will of the gods. In spite of the negative decision, he set his army in motion and suffered a crushing defeat. It remains to point out that there is no proof for Narām-Sîn's scepticism from contemporary sources or his royal inscriptions.

The religious attitude of the ancient Mesopotamians was characterized by the premise of *do ut des*. Man venerated the gods by prayers, ritual and sacrifice, and in return expected a long and successful life. The pious man, however, often had to suffer the experience that less god-fearing people had much more success in life and found themselves in a much better position without bothering to behave properly towards the gods. This topic is treated in great detail in the so-called 'wisdom literature'. We already met the 'Poem of the Righteous Sufferer' in section 2.1 above. The protagonist describes the attitude of people with a rather impious life-style, who are indifferent towards the gods.

Another work relevant to our theme is the 'Babylonian Theodicy', a dialogue between a sceptic and his pious friend.[18] The sceptic points out that animals live without knowing the veneration of gods, a topic we have already heard allegedly from the mouth of Narām-Sîn (ll. 48–55):

The on[ager], the wild ass, that had its fill of [wild grass],
did it carefully ca[rry out] a god's intentions?
The savage lion that devoured the choicest meat,
did it bring its offerings to appease a goddess' anger?
The parvenu who multiplies his wealth,
did he weigh out precious gold to the mother goddess for a family?
[Have I] withheld my offerings? I prayed to my god,
[I] said the blessing over the regular sacrifice to my goddess, my speech [. . .].

The pious friend argues that wild animals or irreligious and primitive nouveau-riches will never consume the fruits of their improper behaviour, because sooner or later they will certainly fall victim to the wrath of the gods or their earthly representative, the king (ll. 56–66):

[18] Basic edition by Lambert (1960 [1996]: 63–91); new (German) translation with improvements by von Soden (1990: 143–157); this English translation after Foster (1993: 806–814).

O date palm, wealth giving-tree, my precious brother,
perfect in all wisdom, o gem of wis[dom].
You are a mere child, the purpose of the gods is as remote as the netherworld!
Consider that magnificent wild ass on the [plain],
an arrow will gash that headstrong trampler of the leas!
Come, look at that lion you called to mind, the enemy of livestock,
for the atrocity that lion committed, a pit yawns for him.
The well-heeled parvenu who treasured up possessions,
the king will burn him like Girra (the fire god) before his (appointed) time.
Would you wish to go the way these have gone?
Seek after the lasting reward of (your) god.

The sceptic, however, is not convinced by this point made by his friend, since he had already tried to succeed by means of religiousness and devoutness but never received anything in return from the gods (ll. 67–77):

Your reasoning is a cool breeze, a breath of fresh air for mankind,
most particular friend, your advice is e[xcellent].
Let me [put] but one matter before you:
Those who seek not after a god can go the road of favour,
those who pray to a goddess have grown poor and destitute.
Indeed, in my youth I tried to find out the will of (my) god,
with prayer and supplication I besought my goddess.
I bore a yoke of profitless servitude.
(My) god decreed (for me) poverty instead of wealth.
A cripple rises above me, a fool is ahead of me,
rogues are in the ascendant, I am demoted.

His investment in prayer and sacrifice, so to say, had not paid off—it remained 'a yoke of profitless servitude', as expressed in the text. A classical case of ritual failure! The sceptic expresses his desire to withdraw from society. This way of life without duly revering the gods is compared to the behaviour of a beggar or brigand, a comparison we have already found in connection with Narām-Sîn (see above) (ll. 133–143):

I will forsake home [. . .]
I will crave no property [. . .]
I will ignore (my) god's regulations, [I will] trample on his rites.
I will slaughter a calf, I will [. . .] food,
I will go the road, I will learn my way around distant places.
I will open a well, I will leave the ca[nal].[19]

[19] This translation follows von Soden (1990: 143–157). The sceptic wants to leave the area of civilization, cultivated by means of artificial irrigation, and go into the steppe, where water is only supplied by wells.

> I will roam about the far outdoors like a bandit.
> I will stave off hunger by forcing entry into one house after another,
> I will prowl the streets, casting about, ravenous.
> Like a beggar I will [...] inside [...],
> good fortune lies far off [...].

The wisdom literature criticizes indifference and tries to disprove scepticism. This scepticism was never developed into a coherent system and is only known through its opposite position. Both indifference and scepticism were expressed in the form of a general laxness towards the fulfilment of cultic duties.

The bare existence of these wisdom texts with their recurring topics points to the existence of critique, but it is difficult to assess how wide-spread this behaviour really was. Let us take a look at an example from everyday life. As hemerological texts show, every month had its auspicious and inauspicious days. A survey of the dates of several hundred legal documents from Assyrian cities has shown that there was a tendency to conclude financial transactions on auspicious days (Livingstone 1997: 175ff.). This avoidance of inauspicious dates by people doing business does not point to indifference or scepticism.

Sometimes we find a rather satirical scepticism, as in the so-called 'Dialogue of Pessimism', a dialogue between a master and his servant.[20] The master takes several decisions, including to fall in love with a woman, to marry, or to commit a crime, and the servant agrees pointing out various arguments in favour of this—and immediately afterwards the master decides to do the very opposite, and really his servant finds suitable reasons for his lord to do as he pleases. Performing rituals is also a topic of their dialogue (ll. 53–61):

> "Servant, listen to me!"—"Yes, master, yes!"—"Quickly bring me water (to wash) my hands; give it to me so I can sacrifice to my god!"—"Sacrifice, master, sacrifice! The man who sacrifices to his god makes a satisfying transaction, he makes loan upon loan."—"No, servant, I will certainly not sacrifice to my god!"—"Do not sacrifice, master, do not sacrifice! You will train your god to follow you around like a dog. He will require of you rites or a (magic) Latarak-figurine or whatever you have."

Performing sacrifice and ritual is characterised here as a rather annoying task, putting silly ideas into the capricious minds of the gods—ideas of

[20] Basic edition by Lambert (1960 [1996]: 139–149); new (German) translation with improvements by von Soden (1990: 158–163); this English translation after Foster (1993: 815–818).

always demanding more efforts from man than he is inclined to make.

It is instructive to read one more passage from the same composition. Here the sense of good deeds in general is dealt with (ll. 70–78):

> "Servant, listen to me!"—"Yes, master, yes!"—"I will do a good deed for my country!"—"So do it, master, do it! The man who does a good deed for his country, his good deed rests in Marduk's basket."[21]—"No, servant, I will certainly not do a good deed for my country!"—"Do not do it, master, do not do it! Go up on the ancient ruin hills and walk around, look at the skulls of the lowly and great.[22] Which was the doer of evil, and which was the doer of good deeds?"

References

Ambos, Claus 2004. *Mesopotamische Baurituale aus dem 1. Jahrtausend v. Chr.* Dresden: ISLET.

Beaulieu, Paul-Alain 1993. "The Historical Background of the Uruk Prophecy". In: *The Tablet and the Scroll. Near Eastern Studies in Honor of William W. Hallo*, Cohen, Mark E. & Daniel C. Snell & David B. Weisberg (ed.). Bethesda, Maryland: CDL Press, 41–52.

Binsbergen, Wim van & Frans Wiggermann 1999. "Magic in History. A Theoretical Perspective, and its Application to Ancient Mesopotamia." In: *Mesopotamian Magic. Textual, Historical, and Interpretative Perspectives*, Tzvi Abusch & Karel van der Toorn (ed.). Groningen: Styx Publications (Ancient Magic and Divination 1), 1–34.

Cohen, Mark E. 1988. *The Canonical Lamentations of Ancient Mesopotamia*. 2 vols. Potomac, Maryland: Capital Decisions Limited.

Cole, Steven W. & Peter Machinist 1998. *Letters from Priests to the Kings Esarhaddon and Assurbanipal.* Helsinki: Helsinki University Press (State Archives of Assyria 13).

Foster, Benjamin 1993. *Before the Muses. An Anthology of Akkadian Literature*. 2 vols. Bethesda, Maryland: CDL Press.

Haas, Volkert 2003. (With the collaboration of Daliah Bawanypeck.) *Materia Magica et Medica Hethitica. Ein Beitrag zur Heilkunde im Alten Orient*. 2 vols. Berlin & New York: Walter de Gruyter.

Lambert, Wilfred G. 1960. *Babylonian Wisdom Literature*. Oxford: Oxford University Press (repr. 1996 Winona Lake, Indiana: Eisenbrauns).

—— 1998. "The Qualifications of Babylonian Diviners". In: *Festschrift für Rykle Borger zu seinem 65. Geburtstag am 24. Mai 1994. tikip santakki mala bašmu . . .*, Maul, Stefan M. (ed.). Groningen: Styx Publications (Cuneiform Monographs 10), 141–158.

Livingstone, Alasdair 1997. "New Dimensions in the Study of Assyrian Religion". In: *Assyria 1995. Proceedings of the 10th Anniversary Symposium of the Neo-Assyrian Text Corpus Project, Helsinki, September 7–11, 1995*, Parpola, S. & R.M. Whiting (ed.). Helsinki: Neo-Assyrian Text Corpus Project, 165–177.

Luukko, Mikko & Greta van Buylaere 2002. *The Political Correspondence of Esarhaddon.* Helsinki: Helsinki University Press (State Archives of Assyria 16).

[21] That is, all good deeds are assembled and taken notice of by Marduk and rewarded.

[22] Or, according to von Soden (1990: 162): "look at the skulls of those having died recently and in the past".

Maul, Stefan M. 1994. *Zukunftsbewältigung. Eine Untersuchung altorientalischen Denkens anhand der babylonisch-assyrischen Löserituale (Namburbi)*. Mainz am Rhein: Philipp von Zabern (Baghdader Forschungen 18).

Oppenheim, A. Leo 1977. *Ancient Mesopotamia. Portrait of a Dead Civilization*. Revised Edition. Completed by Erica Reiner. Chicago and London: The University of Chicago Press.

Parpola, Simo 1983. *Letters from Assyrian Scholars to the Kings Esarhaddon and Assurbanipal. Part II: Commentary and Appendices*. Kevelaer: Verlag Butzon und Bercker; Neukirchen-Vluyn: Neukirchener Verlag (Alter Orient und Altes Testament 5.2).

—— 1993. *Letters from Assyrian and Babylonian Scholars*. Helsinki: Helsinki University Press (State Archives of Assyria 10).

Reynolds, Frances 2003. *The Babylonian Correspondence of Esarhaddon*. Helsinki: Helsinki University Press (State Archives of Assyria 18).

Schaudig, Hanspeter 2001. *Die Inschriften Nabonids von Babylon und Kyros' des Großen samt den in ihrem Umfeld entstandenen Tendenzschriften. Textausgabe und Grammatik*. Münster: Ugarit-Verlag (Alter Orient und Altes Testament 256).

Soden, Wolfram von 1990. "Weisheitstexte in akkadischer Sprache". In: *Texte aus der Umwelt des Alten Testaments III: Weisheitstexte, Mythen und Epen, Lieferung I: Weisheitstexte I*, Kaiser, Otto et al. (ed.). Gütersloh: Gütersloher Verlagshaus Gerd Mohn, 110–188.

Starr, Ivan 1990. *Queries to the Sungod. Divination and Politics in Sargonid Assyria*. Helsinki: Helsinki University Press (State Archives of Assyria 4).

Thureau-Dangin, Francois 1921. *Rituels Accadiens*. Paris: Éditions Ernest Leroux.

Walker, Christopher B.F. & Michael Dick 2001. *The Induction of the Cult Image in Ancient Mesopotamia. The Mesopotamian Mīs Pî Ritual*. Helsinki (State Archives of Assyria Literary Texts 1).

Westenholz, Joan G. 1997. *Legends of the Kings of Akkade: The Texts*. Winona Lake, Indiana: Eisenbrauns (Mesopotamian Civilizations 7).

FAILURE AND MISTAKES IN RITUALS OF THE EUROPEAN SANTO DAIME CHURCH: EXPERIENCES AND SUBJECTIVE THEORIES OF THE PARTICIPANTS[1]

Jan Weinhold

> So what can you do, when you fall down? Because, you know, then the rules fall as well, they are only [...] well, not 'only', but they are not absolute. Finally, the ultimate rule is the Daime itself, the Juramidam—the spirit, the soul of the ritual. That's the ultimate authority, is God, if you want (quoted from an interview with a member of the European Santo Daime church).

Research into ritual rules, mistakes and failure, and consequently the analysis of ritual dynamics can be fruitfully undertaken within different paradigms, for example through ethnographic research of ritual performances (Schieffelin 1996), the application of speech-act theory (Grimes 1988) or textual analysis (e.g. Ambos and Stavrianopoulou in this volume).

Most theories of ritual are based on ethnographic descriptions of ritual actions around the globe. While many of these theories deal with performative aspects of rituals (the most famous being Tambiah [1981]) and even more with the occurrence of possession within these rituals (see Boddy 1994), there are fewer accounts of rituals in which the central aspect is the participants' experience under the influence of psychoactive substances.

This paper focuses on the representations of experiences during rituals and on the subjective theories about these rituals by participants of the European Santo Daime church. My research is concerned with substance-induced altered states of consciousness and this paper attempts to link the insights of psychological knowledge about these substances with social theories on ritual. This approach presupposes that

[1] I would like to thank Howard Potter, Dan McIntyre, Fletcher DuBois, Ute Hüsken, Karin Polit, Eftychia Stavrianopoulou, Claus Ambos, and Kristin Benzinger for their help and comments on earlier drafts of this paper.

an understanding of ritual, ritual action or ritual failure is only possible through the consideration of the participants' own understanding of it, especially as it is impossible to observe what is happening for the different participants during such a ritual as it all happens "in another world", namely in the consciousness of the participants.

According to Humphrey & Laidlaw (1994) a ritual does not inevitably require a set of fixed rules or of speech-acts and even the meaning and the individual interpretation of a ritual action can vary. To them, it is "ritual commitment", the voluntary loss of one's own intention and one's subordination to the higher intentions of the ritual without, however, having to give up one's agency, which defines a ritual action as such. It is therefore the inner state of a person, his or her "meaning it to mean", that makes a ritual action effective and its absence can lead to failure. In a similar, yet different vein will this paper explore the intentionality of the human agents involved. The individual intentions and the understandings of human and divine agency become particularly important when it comes to explain mistakes within the rituals or even the failure of a ritual event. Since the participant's ideas about failure and mistakes include attributions of reasons why something or someone is regarded as wrong or not, the interface between human and non-human or divine agency in relation to ritual deviation will also be discussed here.

1. *Ayahuasca and Santo Daime—historical background*

Santo Daime is a religious institution that emerged in the 20th century in Brazil. A central aspect of the rituals of this religion is the ingestion of a psychoactive substance known as Ayahuasca,[2] a concoction of plants that grow indigenously in the Amazon basin of South America. The two most common primary plant materials used in Ayahuasca are the bark of the large forest liana *banisteriopsis caapi* and the leaves of a bush, *psychotria viridis* (McKenna 1999: 187).[3] Ayahuasca is prepared by

[2] The term Ayahuasca is a Quechua word which can be translated as 'vine of the soul' or 'vine of the dead'. Ayahuasca is known under a variety of names, depending on the context and region of its particular use, e.g. *caapi*, *yagè*, *hoasca* or *daime*. In this article the term Ayahuasca is used when the psychoactive substance is addressed generally, within the framework of the Santo Daime church, the emic term *daime* is used for the substance.

[3] The active biochemical substances are separate in each of the two plants: *Psychotria viridis* contains dimethyltryptamine (DMT), which has structural similarities with the human neurotransmitter serotonin. *Banisteriopsis caapi* contains the MAO-inhibitor

boiling the bark of the liana and adding the leaves of *psychotria viridis*, and depending on the particular context, other plant ingredients may be added (McKenna 1999: 187). Ayahuasca, a thick, dark-coloured, bitter-tasting brew is mostly consumed as a beverage. However, long before this psychoactive substance became an essential part of Santo Daime, Ayahuasca had been used in traditional and indigenous Amazonian cultures for healing, divination and as a means to contact the realm of the supernatural (Reichel-Dolmatoff 1972: 86).

Santo Daime was founded by Raimundo Irineu Serra, a rubber-tapper of African-Brazilian descent who came to the Brazilian Amazon state Acre to participate in the flourishing rubber industry in the 1920s (Shanon 2002: 21). Under the influence of the psychoactive drink he experienced a vision in which a female figure appeared. The visionary entity instructed Serra to prepare for a vision quest in the rain forest and to drink Ayahuasca alone and consecutively for eight days. The mission he received was to call the substance Daime[4] and to create a new church, in which the brew would be administered and play a dominant role as the sacrament—Santo Daime. In the 1930s Irineu Serra started his mission in Rio Branco in the Brazilian state of Acre and assembled his first congregation. Besides drinking the psychoactive brew another pivotal part of Santo Daime rituals, called *trabalhos* (works), became the singing of *hinos* (hymns), which were not composed but 'received' under the influence of the psychoactive drink. Since Irineu Serra was illiterate his followers wrote down the *hinos*. After Serra's death in 1971, Sebastião Mota de Melo led the Daime movement (Rohde 2001: 55). Santo Daime was initially established in the outskirts of Rio Branco and registered as CEFLURIS (Centro Ecléctico da Fluente Luz Universal Raimundo Ireneu Serra) in 1975. Later the small church moved further into the Amazonian jungle to establish the settlement Céu do Mapiá, a village which is the main seat of CEFLURIS to the present day. While Santo Daime initially was a rural phenomenon consisting mainly of farmers from poor socio-economic backgrounds as followers, it expanded in the last two decades of the 20th century. Nowadays

harmin, which enhances the effects of DMT. For significant psychoactive effects it is necessary to combine both plants (for details see Callaway 1999).

[4] The word *daime*—a colloquial phrase from the Portugese word *dai me* ('give me')—became the name of the movement as well as the name of the psychoactive drink. In some hymns the words often occur as a prayer—*dai-me forca, dai-me amor, dai-me luz*—"Give me strength, give me love, give me light".

there exist several communities of Santo Daime in major Brazilian cities as well as in smaller settlements. Since the 1990s congregations of Santo Daime were also established in several European countries (Rohde 2001: 64). While the psychoactive chemical DMT has an illegal status under international drug laws, the religious use of Ayahuasca is presently permitted in Brazil, the Netherlands and Spain.

Before introducing the rituals of Santo Daime, the spectrum of the psychoactive effects of Ayahuasca will be outlined. This is essential because Ayahuasca is not merely one of many symbolic elements within the Santo Daime system—comparable to wine in the Eucharist but the central core concept around which the doctrine and practise of the rituals revolve. Thus, mistakes and failure of Santo Daime rituals cannot be analysed without addressing psychoactive effects and socio-cultural meanings that are attributed to the substance and its effects within Santo Daime.

2. *Psychoactive characteristics of Ayahuasca*

Ayahuasca is often classified as hallucinogenic drug, since the effects partly resemble those of classic hallucinogens such as LSD. However, I follow Shanon (2002: 28) who uses the neutral term 'psychoactive substance'. He demonstrates that the spectrum of Ayahuasca experiences is significantly richer and more complex than merely non-ordinary perceptual effects. Moreover, the term 'hallucinogenic' may evoke negative connotations which mirror dominant frames of pathology and criminality in which hallucinogenic substances are currently discussed in public and in the medical sciences.

The effects of Ayahuasca—as with all psychoactive substances—are profoundly influenced by extrapharmacological factors. Elaborated as the theory of 'drug, set, and setting' (Zinberg 1984), this approach holds the central assumption that experiences with psychoactive substances are influenced by individual variables, which are denoted as the 'set' (e.g. expectations, prior experiences with psychoactive substances, emotional states, and belief systems), and context variables, the 'setting'. According to this model the setting not only denotes the actual physical surroundings of the experience but also the wider socio-cultural context, e.g. particular assumptions about reality, abnormality and epistemology. It should also be noted that no average or typical Ayahuasca experience can be delineated, particular qualities can vary inter- and intra-individually. Shanon (2002: 56) concludes: "No two Ayahuasca sessions are alike. Even very experienced drinkers fail to predict what might happen to them in a session, and the experience may surprise or stupefy even them". Although the effects of the substance depend on the specificity of individual and contextual factors, the variety, and to some degree the commonalities, of Ayahuasca experiences have been classified systematically by Shanon (2002).

Ayahuasca may change the perception of the general atmosphere and give participants the impression of being in another reality, whose primary characteristics can be beauty, enchantment, deep meaningfulness and sanctity. Shanon (2002: 59) introduces the term 'otherworldliness', a state in which "things are not as they used to be and one has the sense of entering into another, heretofore unknown, reality." Within this 'other world' sensations of a powerful energy are reported, which is often referred to as a divine force that sustains and permeates all creation. Affective states can range from love, elation and awe on the positive side to immense horror, anxiety and fear. Of the five perceptual modalities, in the Ayahuasca experience the visual is the most prominent: complex visualisations with open or closed eyes are common, and may include jungle motifs such as snakes, jaguars, birds, rain forests, or celestial scenes, ancient civilizations, cities, palaces, human and nonhuman beings such as deities, angels and demons. Ideational effects under the influence of Ayahuasca can vary from personal reflections and biographical insights to existential religious, philosophical and epistemological issues. Particularly important are changes in one's subjective sense of identity. Under the influence of the substance, occurrences of involuntary transformations are reported regularly. Effects range from a dissolution between internal and external reality, impressions that sensations, cognitions and actions are not self-controlled (e.g. in the phenomenon of receiving hymns) up to complete transformations of identity, e.g. dissociative episodes or transfiguring into animals. Although this article focuses on psychoactive effects, one major physiological reaction that should be mentioned is vomiting. Under the influence of the substance people regularly report nausea and a proneness to throw up that Shanon (2002: 57) characterizes as "a vomit like no other—drinkers often feel that they are pouring out the depth of their body and their soul". He points out further that these moments are said to be a transition from struggling with the effects to coming to terms with the experience. Within Daime rituals this procedure is also regarded as a physical and psychological cleansing process.

Despite the profound effects of Ayahuasca on the human psyche, people are able to participate in social activities. Complementary to periods when participants are completely absorbed by their experiences or even have to sit or lay down, the focus of attention can also be shifted away from the visions to the actual ritual scenery. Participants who are more experienced are better able to navigate and control the non-ordinary state of consciousness.

In summary, Ayahuasca can cause non-ordinary states of consciousness with significant changes in perception, emotion, cognition and modes of being in the world, states that are interpreted as religious experiences within Santo Daime.

3. *Cosmological elements of Santo Daime*

Santo Daime can be denoted as a religion integrating traditions from the Catholic Church, with indigenous Amazonian concepts and Afro-Brazilian elements (Larsen 1999: xii). Already in Serra's initial Ayahuasca vision a female figure appeared as a double-identity. The woman revealed herself as a plant being, Rainha de Floresta (Queen of the Forest), as well as Nossa Senhora da Conceição (Holy Virgin of Conception).

Ayahuasca is seen as a sacred drink, which both represents and embodies the divine aspect. Daime or Juramidam, as Ayahuasca is called within the church, refers to an animated force, residing in the substance, and beyond this, as a divine being and the source of life and knowledge. In several hymns Daime is understood as the 'teacher of all teachers'. Larsen (1999: xvi) points out that Sebastião Mota de Melo regarded Daime as well as nature in general as a body of knowledge and lessons for followers of the church. The visions induced by the substance, called *miração*, as well as other individual experiences are thus conceptualized as divine revelations. The substance is seen simultaneously as an intelligible being and a gateway for direct experience with the divine.

The concepts of illness and healing are closely related to the above. Illness is seen as an imbalanced state between the individual and the environment, while healing occurs when the individual corrects this imbalance (Rohde 2001: 58). Daime is seen as universal medicine and a pivotal key which offers insight into causes of the particular disease (physical or spiritual) as well as possible solutions. Larsen (1999: xv) characterizes this rather broad and dynamic concept:

> Enterprises that fail to inquire into divine intentions are doomed to failure—not through divine displeasure but through estrangement from the flowing source of all life, and failure to acknowledge the interconnectedness of all things.

Another influence upon Santo Daime is the cult of Umbanda, itself a system containing elements from various African and Brazilian religious traditions. One major feature of Umbanda and subsequently of Santo Daime is spirit possession, a concept that is applied in the Daime doctrine to dissociative episodes that occur especially during healing rituals. Animated individual entities or spirits are considered to enter humans under the influence of Daime. Healing of the spirit as well as the participant can occur when these entities are brought together with the positive and curative powers of the divine drink. Alverga (1999: 160) points out:

> These 'negative' spirit beings, if we can call them that, enter into contact with the 'positive' forces that are mobilized by the true self to help fight the fear, doubts, and seduction into sin, the favorite tricks of these demons. And this ends up making possible the healing inside the person, the dialogue between the positive and negative forces thus coming into the light. These are also the spirit beings or entities that 'having not prepared the ground, the spirit remains wandering,' as Mestre Irineu's hymn says. All of them are attracted by the quality of our vibrations and by our own inherent weaknesses that open our flanks to them.

The Santo Daime cosmology is mainly presented through *hinos*, hymns, which are sung during rituals. Hymns are relatively simple texts. They consist of several repetitive stanzas covering themes such as prayer, reports of visionary scenes, ethical and health related narratives, or references to Christian mythology. The hymns are the only teaching documents of the religion; apart from them the doctrine of Santo Daime is orally transmitted (Rohde 2001: 59).

Taking into consideration the model of 'drug, set and setting' (Zinberg 1984), the substance induced experiences and the cosmology of Santo Daime can be regarded as closely interrelated and recursively having influenced each other. Dobkin de Rios & Grob (1994) point out that through the use of Ayahuasca a hypersuggestible state is induced in which religious beliefs systems and culturally constructed narratives are reinforced, collective cohesion is strengthened and revelation, healing and ontological security are provided.

4. *Rituals of Santo Daime*

Trabalhos, the rituals of Santo Daime are conducted indoors, usually in bright illuminated rooms and churches. On average Daime is ingested every two hours. There exist different types of ritual. *Concentraçãos*, meditative rituals, are held on the 15th and 30th of each month. Central to these sessions are periods of concentration, lasting between 30 minutes and an hour. In the concentration periods all Daimistas, as the members are called, sit silently in chairs, focussing on the substance-induced inner experience. Legs and arms should not be crossed to avoid any interference of the energy flow, a rule which stands for the other Daime rituals as well. *Trabalhos de estrela* (works of the star) are explicit healing rituals, sessions with a small number of participants that are held on special occasions decided by the Padrinho, the leader of the ritual. In healing rituals the participants sit on chairs and there is singing but no dancing. Festive Daime sessions, called *hinário*, analogous to the name of the hymnals, are held on fixed dates such as Catholic holidays, Christmas, or special days in the biographies of the founders of the church. These rituals start in the evening and last between 6–12 hours. During a *hinário* the participants stand aligned in ordered formations according to height. This alignment means that everybody is able to see the table in the middle of the room. Set on the table are a wooden cross and three candles, symbolising sun, moon and stars. Around the table sit the Padrinho and musicians. In general, guitars are used but other instruments may be played as well, for example flutes. Several participants play the *maraca*, a small rattle instrument. During festive rituals the *bailado*, a synchronized dance is performed by participants. This highly formalized dance has the purpose of establishing harmony within the congregation and enhancing the flow of energy between participants.

During *trabalhos* women and men are separated and it is a strict rule not to move to the other's side. In the rituals participants are dressed in uniforms: novices in white, *fardados*, registered members of the church, according to the particular ritual type and gender in blue-white or green-white. Members of Santo Daime who have greater experience work periodically as *fiscal*. The task of a *fiscal* is to keep ritual order as well as to protect and assist participants (e.g. showing which hymn is presently being sung). *Fiscals* are not supposed to intervene with the participants' experience or address visions and unpleasant episodes directly. Their responsibility is just to secure the basic needs and the safety of the participants, for example to hand participants water or blankets if necessary, or direct them to the bathrooms. Usually there is one female and one male *fiscal* on the men's and women's side of the central table. At larger rituals a door *fiscal* makes sure that nobody leaves the *salão*, the building in which the ritual takes place.

5. *Methods: participant observation, interviewing, qualitative content analysis*

Within the research project 'Dynamics of ritual, Salutogenesis and the Use and Abuse of Psychoactive Substances', under the auspices of the collaborative research centre (*Sonderforschungsbereich*) 'Dynamics of Ritual', 22 people taking Ayahuasca are participants in the study, the majority of whom being members of Santo Daime. In this integrative longitudinal study, focussing on medical and psychological questions as well as ritual related research; interviews with participants have been held twice a year since 2003. As a subset of the sample twelve members of Santo Daime were explicitly interviewed about their experiences of failures and mistakes during their lifetime attendance of Santo Daime rituals. While questions concerning mistakes and failure were only a part of the second interview in a longitudinal sequence, a large quantity of interview data giving contextual information about biographical aspects of the interviewees has been amassed within the narrower context of specific Santo-Daime rituals as well as the wider socio-cultural context of the European Santo Daime Church.

The 'issue-related interview' ('Problemzentriertes Interview', Witzel 1982: 67) can be classified as a semi-structured interview that allows information to be obtained when certain topics of social reality are focussed on. An integral part of the interview is a set of questions, the 'Interviewleitfaden' (topic guide), which covers these topics of interest. This differs however from a standardized interview and the questions can be used flexibly to fit the interviewee's narration. The following questions were asked as part of the interview:

- What mistakes have the interviewees experienced in Santo Daime rituals?
- What are the experiences of the interviewees concerning failure?
- What reasons led to the mistakes and/or failure?
- Who was responsible for them?
- How were mistakes and failure coped with?
- How could they have been prevented?

To avoid suggestive questions, it was not specified or defined by the interviewers what the term 'mistake' (*Fehler*) and 'failure' (*Scheitern*) denotes, but left to the interviewees' perspectives and interpretations.[5]

During field research the interviewers were also able to visit three rituals (two festive and one healing ritual) that took place in middle-sized churches with more than 100 participants. They also attended another ritual of healing with only 25 participants that was held in a large room at a private house. Some of the interviews were conducted shortly after the rituals, which gave the interviewees the opportunity to directly refer to the prior events. The combination of interviews and participant observation can also be regarded as a way to improve the validity of the interviewee's reports in the sense of a multi-method triangulation (Flick 2004).

All interviews were transcribed word-by-word and interpreted with a qualitative content analysis system (Mayring 2002). This instrument allows the structuring of the interview texts according to topics of interest whilst simultaneously approaching the text through theoretical concepts. Matching text parts of the interviews were assigned to categories that mirror theoretical models regarding mistakes and failure. Hence, the category system is not only an ordering principle to structure extensive interview data in a comprehensive order, but can furthermore be seen as a set of hypothesises, considering which aspects of ritual failure and mistakes may be of interest for further research.

6. *Results*

The following categories were established:

1. preparatory neglect;
2. cognitive mistakes during a ritual;
3. mistakes in ritual performance (subcategorized into minor disturbances, interpersonal conflicts, and critical mistakes);
4. evaluation of mistakes and subjective theories about agency;
5. ritual failure (subcategorized into personal and collective failure);
6. coping with mistakes and prevention of deviation.

---

[5] Since the interviewees come from a German background all interviews were held in German with one exception, an Israeli participant, with whom the interview was conducted in English.

The descriptive categories '2. cognitive mistakes during a ritual', '3. mistakes in ritual performance' and '5. ritual failure' mainly contain information from reports referring to the inner frame of particular rituals.[6] The category '4. evaluation of mistakes and subjective theories about agency' refers to the interviewees' opinions and attitudes regarding the issues of mistakes and failure and is rather analytical. Results of the content analysis will be described and discussed according to the extracted categories. Original quotations from the interview texts will serve to illustrate examples. Quotations from interviews which were conducted in German are translated into English by the author.

6.1. *Preparatory neglect*

An example of preparatory neglect is given by a woman who remembers a ritual that was held early on in her personal involvement with Santo Daime:

> Once I took part in a work [= ritual; J.W.] with a shirt which wasn't ironed. One cannot imagine, it's ridiculous to even think about, but it really bothered me during the whole work. I had the feeling that it's not supportive... because I was concentrating the whole time its not having any pleats and I was distressed the whole time.... There are many small details that you notice, the more your attention is sensitized, the more you notice the little details that are not 100% right, when something could have been done before, which would have been much better. The room wasn't really tidy; people just put their belongings on one side and things like that.

What appears to be a small inattention in the preparations turns out to have a different quality when it is considered that Daime induces a highly suggestible state of consciousness. In accordance with the 'drug, set and setting' model it can be pointed out that any detail of a physical setting can assume subjective significance within the non-ordinary state of consciousness. This may apply to religious symbols or music, as features intended to evoke spiritual experiences but it may also be the case with flawed details that have been overlooked. In this example negative consequences arose only for the woman. However, future research may focus on how minor discontinuities in the preparation of rituals can add up to performance mistakes with collective consequences.

---

[6] Daime rituals are framed (Bateson 1972: 186) in an obvious way, so the separation between the actual ritual and the context is rather clear-cut and not as fuzzy as may be the case for other types of ritual.

6.2. *Cognitive mistakes during a ritual*

Since the efficacy of Daime rituals for the participants strongly depends on the experiential qualities of the intoxication, individual mistakes may occur that interfere with the 'right' experience. A woman describes her perceptual activities during one ritual:

> There was a conflict for me yesterday, so I temporarily broke the rules as well, if you view them really strictly. In these processes you are obliged to follow and to hold the energy. But I was curious about how Paulo Roberto is working, you know? That was on the other side, and because I've never seen him I watched him now and again, even if this is not according to the rules.

Her conflict resulted in an altered focus of attention—between her own experience on one hand and the performance of the ritual leader on the other hand—which can be seen as an example of what may be called a cognitive mistake within the 'cognitive rules'. However, this term may not only address cognitive information processing according to a computer model, but any of the psychological dimensions that summarize and influence the ritual experience, e.g. perceptual processes, the focus of attention, mental attitudes, the degree of participation or reflection, and the level of control over non-ordinary states of consciousness. Since these rules can be to a very large extent implicit or even unconscious, depending on the ritual involved, they may be hard to detect when not resulting in concrete action. From a methodological point of view this type of mistake can be seen as important example for the necessity of investigating psychological variables of ritual participants. Cognitive characteristics, individual framing processes, and the relationship between ritual mistakes and the degree of the 'ritual commitment' (Humphrey & Laidlaw 1994: 88) could be examined in further research.

6.3. *Mistakes during ritual performance*

This category addresses the most evident and most frequently reported form of rule-breaking. Included here are mistakes which are either made by the interviewees themselves or perceived by them as disturbances. Both perspectives are not strictly separable. Since the quality of performative mistakes can vary concerning their impact on the ritual as a whole, reports were subcategorized according the degree of endangerment to the flow and the phenomenological identity of the ritual.

A variety of minor and mostly unintentional mistakes and disturbances were reported, ranging from forgetting single hymns or passages of a prayer, mistakes in the *bailado* dancing steps and bumping into each other, singing too loud or out of tune, to being noisy while quietness is demanded. It seems that mistakes of this type have had no significant influence on a collective level and were consequently ignored. However, it should be noted that the reported slip-ups might have seriously disturbed individuals in their Daime experience, similar to the details mentioned under the category of preparatory neglect.

Another type of mistake during Santo Daime performances relates to interpersonal conflicts, mirroring power relations within Santo Daime.[7] In contrast to the above-mentioned category, these mistakes can be understood as deliberate transgressions, since the rules are essential and known by virtually every participant. Mistakes that were reported frequently refer to the spatial position during a ritual:

> There are rules that you know and there are rules that you are not sure of, and there are always things or so that happen in the work, like somebody wants to take your place and they think this is their place. You think that actually you are shorter than them standing on the other side and then you have these people because it goes by height... But it also goes by prestige of the person... you can be (laughs) very tall and still be on the first line because you are a very important person. There are all these politics there, it's just an observation.

A woman remembers a particular scene where spatial rules were broken:

> When I sat at the table playing [an instrument; J.W.] I had difficulties with another person. There was an American sitting there, I don't know if you noticed him. Normally the table is the place for musicians and for the people who sing and carry the work, who care for the right frame and for the other people, that they are supported. It is the central place, and when somebody sits there... who doesn't know that and just more or less hangs around... and he was somebody like that, it was really draining. You notice that you have to work for him as well to hold the energy. And I went to the *fiscal* afterwards and said: "He has to leave!" Because I noticed that other people had the same feelings, and when he was removed it was better.

---

[7] Mistakes of this category are reported as explicitly mirroring interpersonal conflicts. However, since the concept of power can be applied for any social reality it may also be the case for mistakes that are summarized under 'minor disturbances', as for instance when a small slip leads to an argument between participants.

Other reports describe broken rules and the subsequent negotiation of conflicts within the Santo Daime hierarchy, e.g. an argument between a *fiscal* and a novice who was not willing to step back into formation, or differences of opinion between the ritual leader and a musician about which songs to play.

Whereas the above mistakes during the performance can be evaluated as not interfering with the ritual's identity the following subcategory can be denoted as 'critical mistakes' concerning the integrity and stipulated form of the ritual. An example is reported by a woman who remembers a ritual she took part in, where one participant broke several rules which threatened to destroy the ritual:

> This guy on the men's side got possessed by . . . I don't know, himself. It started with some kind of . . . doing very gross sexual movements. Like, I don't know, touching himself and lifting his leg, all kinds of things. In his place, sitting down. Because when we were sitting down everyone had a little space to move. Then he started getting up and he was really, really strong and really aggressive, really pushing the boundaries and other people were trying to hold him and couldn't really hold him and he was trying all the time to get to the women's side. . . . And you know, everybody is high, so somebody is trying to hold him and then you put him down and then he gets up again. And he was always trying to get to the women's side. I was terrified . . . for ourselves, because it felt like nobody was really holding him together, and he could really get out of his place and move, and come to the women's side and somebody would pull him back, and this happened a few times back and forth. . . . We were on the fourth floor of the building and there was a balcony . . . and it was in the last moment that Ronaldo went out to the balcony and got him back in the room, because the guy could have jumped down. And they got him back to the room and the whole ritual continued, he locked the door, Ronaldo. So he couldn't go the way back, and the whole ritual continued with this guy trying to get to the women's side or doing kind of things on the other side and I was really scared, I think all the women felt like this . . . I think it was very wrong. He afterwards said that he had an amazing time [laughs]. He was so happy, he was mumbling all these kinds of words and screaming and we were trying to sing, and he was really screaming. And he said he was really, really happy. Never ever felt so happy in his life. . . . Afterwards people kind of forgave him, you know, there was this kind of compassionate attitude towards him, even if he screwed up everybody's ritual.

Nevertheless, the ritual was not interrupted but continued even under the adverse circumstances described.

6.4. *Participants' evaluation of mistakes and subjective theories on agency*

A comparison of the last two examples shows that the American participant, who sat at the table during the ritual, is replaced due to his 'unenergetic' behaviour, while the continuous breaking of basic rules in the second case, like moving to the women's side, is evaluated with an attitude of compassion. The examples show that 'mistakes' don't equal `mistakes' in every case. In the second example the transgression was perceived as helpful for the participant. The interviewee reflects on the event: "Maybe it's good that this situation happened. This guy had a release, he was doing really well with himself." It can be assumed that the evaluation of mistakes by the interviewees did not reflect the degree of threat to the course of the ritual, but mirrored rather the theories about why and for what purpose mistakes are made.

One suitable explanatory model for these different evaluations may be the attribution of agency in the subjective theories of ritual participants. In social psychology the attribution processes are assumed to be a cognitive need to find causal relations of perceived phenomena and therefore give meaning to subjective realities (Hewstone 1990). According to this theory the reasons and the control for certain behaviour or perceived phenomena can be attributed to either internal causes (the phenomenon is self-caused) or external causes (e.g. caused by other persons, circumstances, fate, chance or higher forces such as deities). The empirical analysis of attributions may be a useful way to reconstruct how agency is represented in the participants' view. Who or what is responsible for mistakes according to the participants' theories?

If mistakes are attributed to an internal cause and to the control of ritual participants, then human intentions are seen as reasons for the false action. These actions are evaluated as intentionally disturbing the flow of a ritual. The question how a ritual can go wrong is answered by an interviewee:

> Ego ... if there's too much ego, too much ... too little sense for the community, that will show up immediately. We have to stay within the energy together, and as soon as you go too far, that's a disturbance, in that moment everything goes wrong.

On the other hand, if actions are attributed to the external control of non-human agents, they are still reported as mistakes but the evaluation is quite different:

> Yes, and there are people who go so deeply into the process that they dissolve the ritual to a certain degree.... I once took part in a ritual, there was a woman yelling "Alfredo"... for three quarters of an hour or an hour. Again and again. And she was furious. It needed ten or twelve women to hold her, because she was so powerful.... But the ritual did not stop.

Asked, if participants in a dissociated state have more rights to act out she answers:

> When you are out of yourself, you are out of yourself, there's no question of being right or wrong.... You can't be different!

The subjective theory mirrors the view that human agency can be seen as bound to the individual's free will, presence of the self, or intentional control (Ahearn 2001: 114). If action is not controlled by the participant but by the non-human agency of the spirit, the participant cannot be blamed for the transgression. As shown earlier, Ayahuasca has the psychoactive power to dissolve the characteristics that would be demanded to purport individual human agency (Shanon 2002: 198). According to the doctrine of the church, the sacred substance Daime is the embodiment of the divine and the source of divine revelations. If these revelations manifest themselves in action, but are also mistakes, theories about agency could be stretched further by stating that anything happening during a Daime ritual is controlled by the divine, hence right. However, the interviewees' reports show a clear differentiation in the evaluations of mistakes. When questioned whether participants who break the rules cannot be held responsible for their transgressions due to a loss of personal agency, one interviewee replied: "Exactly, just in justified cases, but the difference is clear to see." Nevertheless, even this clarity can be flexible and inconsistent, therefore subjective theories may oscillate between human agency and the agency of the Daime. Thus, if subjective theories about the causes of deviation are changed, the rules of rituals may change as well, and the rituals therefore remain dynamic.

In general, the interviewed participants understand Daime rituals as processes of personal, social and spiritual development. This includes individual non-ordinary states of consciousness and inner realities, interpersonal behaviour and group processes, and ritual performances—as well as mistakes and deviations. An interviewee explains:

> It is my attitude to try to stay calm and stay with me, even when I notice something that worries me and which is not good for the ritual... Let's say someone is playing really loud and you can't hear anything, then I

> would try again and again not to take it as too important and simply think: okay, that's a detail, but what we want is something else, we want the connection with God, we want to call the powers and we want to care about healing. And then the detail is not so important anymore. . . . Mostly it is not perfect because it is conducted by humans, and therefore, the more I can forgive others making a mistake, the more I can forgive myself and admit that I sometimes make mistakes as well. . . . Sometimes the ego of the people appears, and you have to deal with it, with your ego and the egos of other people, and that can sometimes be confronting! And, yes, it is exactly what we can learn, because that happens to me in real life as well, and then I have to cope with it as well. And then I think to myself: I learn it in the church, then it will be easier in my life.

6.5. *Ritual failure*

Despite a high flexibility of Santo Daime rituals due to the assumption of a non-human agency, few cases of complete failure were reported by interviewees. The term failure is understood by participants as the precocious ending of a ritual against the rules, according to which a clear cut-off point is made to close the ritual, usually with three Lord's Prayers and three Ave Marias.

Before analyzing the interview data it should be noted that interviewees were hesitant to give information about ritual failure:

> Well, I believe after all these years of experience that the ritual cares for itself, that it can't go wrong. I still trust in it, even when difficult situations arise . . . It never failed, never.

The view that Daime rituals can't fail was expressed several times as a starting point in the interviewees' narratives. It couldn't be validated completely whether this is wishful thinking rather than actual experience. Even if most interviewees also hold a critical perspective towards Santo Daime, an overtly unfavourable opinion about their own religious practice (as it is the case in a recorded interview) may result in discomfort. However, this subjective theory can also be seen as mirroring the general assumption that ritual performances are invariably conducted according to fixed rules and that failure of rituals are hardly an issue within emic discourses.

The failure of a ritual is reported in two subcategories, the individual and the collective. While on a collective level a precocious ending is regarded as the collapse of the ritual, from an individual point of view a ritual fails when a participant breaks the rules by leaving before the last prayer is said. A woman describes:

> I left a ritual in the middle . . . went in the car and drove off. . . . I was really not well. I did not want to stay there. I fell down there, I injured my head. So, I left. And that's like the number one 'don't do'.

When questioned if other participants or *fiscals* argued or tried to stop her, she said:

> Nobody noticed me. I was so smooth. I stood up, I caught my boyfriend and we just left. We even managed to take our jackets from upstairs.

She accounts for her decision after questioned if she was aware of the rule not to leave the ritual:

> Oh, I knew that but there was no way that I was staying. I didn't care. I wanted to get out. I was really not well. I thought I was going to die. I kind of lost sensation in my hands and my feet and I was really not well so I did not trust anyone in this room anymore and I didn't want to be there. I just wanted to go and sort myself out.

The following day she went to the ritual leader, apologized and explained the situation. However, the ritual leader wasn't so much annoyed about the participant, but rather about the situation occurring at all and about the *fiscals* in charge.

The perspective of another participant who sometimes works as *fiscal* during Daime rituals is of interest here with respect to how these situations are coped with:

> There is the problem that people want to leave the work and go home. And then you start talking with them: "It'd be better if you'd stay." "But I don't want to, this is too much for me." You somehow try to influence, not only by talking, I often pray as well: "Give him the ease and power to go through, because this is just a period". And then they ask: "How long will it be? How long is the (Daime's) effect? I can't do it anymore. When does it stop? It's so strong in my head." . . . Well, then you try to talk with them, to encourage them, try to bring them back. But there were cases, when people left and went home. . . . You've said to them that staying until the end is the rule, but participants have their own will . . . they are not our property, finally they act according to what they want.

The question is addressed regarding the specific circumstances in which the major rule 'Nobody leaves the ritual before it is officially finished' is enforced, or the participants' wish to quit is accepted. According to interview data, no methods of pressure are applied to keep participants in the ritual and the criterion of respecting participant's individual needs is followed when it comes to the serious question of leaving a ritual. It should be noted that participation in Santo Daime rituals is fully voluntarily, the rules of the ritual are well-established and known, and the atmosphere is serious but friendly and supportive rather than forceful or strict. Further research may address the issue as to what extent rules (as collective ritual norms) are enforced and negotiated in relation or even contrary to individual needs and motives.

While in the case of a single 'personal failure' the ritual is not threatened, the summary of many individual mistakes may result in the collapse of the ritual, losing its phenomenological identity and integrating characteristics. A Santo Daime ritual may break down as soon as there is not a majority of participants who are able to continue performing. This was possibly the case in a reported ritual with seven, at that point rather inexperienced partakers. A woman who by now is a qualified and experienced member of the church remembers:

> Yes, I once experienced that a work had to be ceased.... The energy level in the room was so high that the leader couldn't hold it anymore at that moment. And because of this energy... well, he decided to interrupt the work, to stop it. That's something he wouldn't do nowadays, for sure, but back then in this work he did. He felt he couldn't hold it anymore.

Since it wasn't specified during the interview what exactly caused the premature end of the ritual it can be assumed that all participants were overwhelmed by the psychoactive effect of the brew and unable to perform any further in accordance with the existing rules. One has also to take into consideration that seven participants is a rather small number for Santo Daime rituals, which are usually larger. Nevertheless, one could ask whether the size of a certain group performing a ritual (and the ratio between experienced and inexperienced participants) predicts disturbances or even the failure of a ritual. Since it is stated by interviewees that Santo Daime rituals are the most suitable form for the intake of the psychoactive substance, it is not the question whether the participants want to continue the prescribed performance of singing and dancing but rather whether they are able to do so. This hypothesis also concurs with an interviewee's explanation:

> It also depends on the group. In large works... there are other possibilities than in a small one where you sit around a table with six people. Then everybody has to do more... because the energy is completely different and it is more demanding. If there's few people, everybody has to take a lot more care. If it's a large group and someone drops out, fine. But in a small work it is highly important if someone is absent.

It can be concluded that the size of a ritual group (and the accumulated experience of its participants) is one important factor for the correct conduction of a Daime ritual, even if a mere numerical perspective would oversimplify the social reality of the Santo Daime church.

6.6. *Coping with mistakes and prevention of deviation*

The issue of deviation is closely linked to attempts to regain or ensure/prevent the 'right' ritual order. Interviewees' reports in this category deal with either correctional attempts during rituals or preventive and evaluating activities outside ritual performances.

Mistakes detected during rituals were reported to be performatively corrected by other participants, *fiscals*, and in some cases the ritual leader. There exists a well established hierarchy of corrective instances. When asked who would be responsible for the avoidance of mistakes a woman said:

> The *fiscal* is responsible for the order, order or safety. He must know the rules particularly well and he has to decide what to do. Of course there are borderline cases, and there the commander (ritual leader) has to decide. But the *fiscal* asks him: "Okay, there's this and that . . ."—in exceptional cases! . . . Of course you can't disturb him permanently because the ritual leader has other things to do than to take care of the participants' positioning.

This quote also shows that the hierarchy of correction relates to the degree of seriousness of the mistake. While small slip-ups may be negotiated among the participants, more deviant actions demand intervention from the *fiscals* and leaders. A particular way to clarify an ambivalent situation is to interrupt the flow of the ritual and pause for a moment, mainly with the aim of quietening the audience and regaining the right 'energy', but also to give space to separate ritual groups and conflicting participants. Conversely, a correctional attempt is reported for the periods of concentration:

> Occasionally songs are reintroduced when somebody is too noisy during silence, then the singing is the carrying element and no longer his yelling.

Outside the ritual frame several activities ensuring the correct conduct of the religious practise are reported:

> There are regular *fiscal* meetings where such things can be talked about, problems that occurred, situations which were handled in the wrong

> way, any inattention... or how to deal with special people who act in a certain way again and again, how to cope with their behaviour, how to integrate them in such a way that the ritual remains harmonious for everybody... also how to improve the rituals.

The discourse about rituals (including any deviant occurrences) in more informal settings outside the ritual frame was reported by participants as well as observed by members of the research team. After a ritual is done, participants usually stay inside the church for a certain time to eat together, exchange experiences, socialize and review the ritual. Since the number of participants in the European Santo Daime Church is comparatively small, and some participants have a shared history not only as ritual participants but also as friends or partners, it can be assumed that this discourse permeates into private and informal spheres.

7. *Conclusion*

Contrary to the assumption that rituals are hardly ever conducted wrongly or cannot fail (see Merz and Polit in this volume), participants' accounts of European Santo Daime rituals deal with a broad range of errors. These vary from small slip-ups to the serious and complete failure of a single ritual performance and occur on an individual level as well as collectively. The ubiquity of potential mistakes and failure is reflected in the participants' discourses on the rituals. The interview data indicate that the study of mistakes and failure as well as the study of evaluative and correctional processes cannot be limited to the actual ritual performance, but that different contextual factors should be taken into consideration as well, such as how the fluid concepts of mistakes and failure are evaluated and negotiated outside the actual ritual.

Why are some performances evaluated as 'wrong', whereas others, which imply a serious breach of the rules, are not? The assessment of ritual actions by participants, *fiscals* or the *commander* as mistakes is highly dependent on information exceeding the actual ritual performance. Whereas some ritual actions are considered to be consciously motivated, and controlled by a human agency, others are regarded as controlled externally by the animated spirit of the psychoactive brew Daime, the superior ritual agent so to speak. This discourse clearly mirrors two different criteria for the evaluation process: human vs. nonhuman or divine agency. Since these criteria are closely related to the participants' states of consciousness it can be concluded that the analytical term 'altered states of consciousness' resembles 'altered mode of action control' and hence includes a more differentiated perspective on ritual mistake than just performative rule-breaking. If the question is raised whether the right to deviate from ritual norms represents different degrees of power, the analysis of the interviews shows that this is clearly the case. The negotiation of mistakes mirrors power-relations, e.g. between more and less experienced participants, the *fiscals* in charge or the *commander*. The motivation behind some mistakes may even be subversive, that is, to challenge these power relations. However, it is clear that at the top of the hierarchy of participants, *fiscals* and the ritual leader is the postulated being and power of the Ayahuasca: "Finally, the ultimate rule is the Daime itself, the Juramidam—the spirit, the soul of the ritual. That's the ultimate authority, is God, if you want."

Closely connected with the notion of different ritual agents are the criteria for judging the ritual's efficacy. One main criterion for assessing a ritual as successful is the 'right atmosphere', something that is empirically difficult to ascertain. This atmosphere or flow of energy between participants as well as between the congregation and the spiritual realm is effected by conducting the ritual according to the prescribed rules, e.g. the formalized dance. According to Moore & Myerhoff (1977: 12) this doctrinal efficacy is postulated by the cosmological understanding of the ritual.[8] However, performative mistakes, which seriously endanger this postulated efficacy by threatening the ritual order, are tolerated when interpreted as action that is controlled by the superhuman and divine agency of the animated being Daime. In these cases the emergent qualities of a ritual performance come into focus. Schieffelin (1996: 81) describes the emergent as "what performance as performance brings about". Here emergent efficacy is defined as its results in social reality. Schieffelin adds: "This is true even when what emerges in a given performance is not necessary predictable or is even the opposite of the performer's intentions." Implicit theories about the ritual's efficacy are related to the participants' differentiated evaluation of mistakes. While carrying out actions according to the rules is connected to human agency, the emerging results of the ritual are connected to the power of the Ayahuasca, the non-human agency. Thus, rituals are protected against failure to a certain degree, since in the case of grave mistakes the

[8] "The religion postulates by what causal means a ritual, if properly performed, should bring about the desired results. A religious ritual refers to the unseen cosmic order, works through it and operates on it directly through the performance. The gods, the ancestors, the spirits are moved."

focus of ritual participants may shift from human to nonhuman agency and from doctrinal to emergent efficacy. However, if the emergent results of a ritual performance—in this case study highly modulated by the effects of the psychoactive substance—reach a certain limit, then the ritual may fail in the sense that it is broken off before the official closing. As shown above, in this case the emergent qualities of the ritual became too predominant. In the described example the ritual leader "couldn't hold it anymore", and the ritual was abandoned.

It therefore seems that the issues of mistakes and failure highly depend on the participants' explanations of why and how some action is perceived as mistaken whereas other, and sometimes more serious rule-breaking, is not. As important as the analysis of ritual performances may be, for an understanding of why a particular action is considered to be wrong, additional information is useful. Intra- and extra-ritual critique are both closely related to questions of motivation, intentionality, the attributed agency of ritual actors and the substance-induced state of consciousness of the participants.

Lastly it is necessary to deal with methodological shortcomings. The use of in-depth interviews appears to be particularly useful when investigating apparently unimportant phenomena or idiosyncratic events, or cognitive or experiental processes and structures. However, as important as these individual perspectives may be, when focussing on the issue of deviation the tendency to give socially acceptable answers has to be taken into account, in particular when the interviewees are emotionally committed to a religious group, as is the case with Santo Daime. A related question is the heterogeneity of the participants, an issue that lies outside the scope of the present paper. What role does the socio-cultural background of the ritual participants play? Is there a different acceptance of mistakes when rituals are conducted in Europe instead of Brazil? To what degree are definitions of 'right' and 'wrong' exchanged and understood between the European and Brazilian participants of the churches of Santo Daime? These questions raise issues about intercultural differences and need to be addressed in further cross-cultural research.

References

Ahearn, Laura M. 2001. "Language and Agency". *Annual Review of Anthropology* 30: 109–137.

Alverga, Alex Polari de 1999. *Forest of Visions: Ayahuasca, Amazonian Spirituality, and the Santo Daime Tradition*. Rochester: Park Street Press.

Bateson, Gregory 1972. "A Theory of Play and Fantasy". In: *Steps to an Ecology of Mind*, Bateson, Gregory (ed.). San Francisco: Chandler Publishing, 177–193 (repr. of 1954).

Boddy, Janice 1994. "Spirit Possession Revisited: Beyond Instrumentality." *Annual Review of Anthropology* 23: 407–434.

Callaway, Jace C. 1999. "Phytochemistry and Neuropharmacology of Ayahuasca". In: *Ayahuasca—Hallucinogens, Consciousness, and the Spirit of Nature*, Metzner, Ralph (ed.). New York: Thunder's Mouth Press, 250–275.

Dobkin de Rios, Marlene & Charles S. Grob 1994. "Hallucinogens, suggestibility and adolescence in cross-cultural perspective". In: *Yearbook of Ethnomedicine and the Study of Consciousness* 3: 123–132.

Flick, Uwe 2004. *Triangulation. Eine Einführung*. Bohnsack, Ralf & Christian Lüders & Jo Reichertz (ed.). Reihe Qualitative Sozialforschung 12. Wiesbaden: Verlag für Sozialwissenschaften.

Grimes, Ronald L. 1988. "Infelicitous Performances and Ritual Criticism". *Semeia* 43: 103–122.

Hewstone, Miles 1990. *Causal Attribution. From Cognitive Processes to Collective Beliefs*. Oxford: Blackwell.

Humphrey, Caroline & James Laidlaw 1994. *The Archetypal Actions of Ritual. A Theory of Ritual illustrated by the Jain Rite of Worship*. Oxford: Clarendon Press.

Larsen, Stephen 1999. "Foreword". In: *Forrest of Visions: Ayahuasca, Amazonian Spirituality, and the Santo Daime Tradition*, Alverga, Alex Polari de (ed.). Rochester: Park Street Press, ix–xix.

Mayring, Philipp 2002. *Qualitative Inhaltsanalyse: Grundlagen und Techniken*. Weinheim: Beltz.

McKenna, Dennis J. 1999. "Ayahuasca: An Ethnopharmacologic History". In: *Ayahuasca—Hallucinogens, Consciousness, and the Spirit of Nature*, Metzner, Ralph (ed.). New York: Thunder's Mouth Press, 187–214.

Moore, Sally F. & Barbara G. Myerhoff 1977. "Introduction". In: *Secular Ritual*, Moore, Sally F. & Barbara G. Myerhoff (ed.). Assen, Netherlands: Van Gorcum, 3–24.

Reichel-Dolmatoff, Gerardo 1972. "The Cultural Context of an Aboriginal Hallucinogen: Banisteriopsis Caapi". In: *Flesh of the Gods: The Ritual Use of Hallucinogens*, Furst, Peter T. (ed.). New York: Praeger, 84–113.

Rohde, Silvio 2001. *Formen des religiösen Gebrauches des entheogenen Sakraments Ayahuasca unter besonderer Berücksichtigung des Aspekts ihrer Kriminalisierung*. University of Bremen: unpublished thesis.

Schieffelin, Edward L. 1996. "On Failure and Performance. Throwing the Medium Out of the Séance". In: *The Performance of Healing*, Laderman, Carol & Marina Roseman (ed.). New York & London: Routledge, 59–89.

Shanon, Benny 2002. *The antipodes of the mind: charting the phenomenology of the Ayahuasca experience*. Oxford: University Press.

Tambiah, Stanley 1981. *A Performative Approach to Ritual*. London: Oxford University Press for the British Academy.

Wilber, Ken 1996. *Eros, Kosmos, Logos: Eine Vision an der Schwelle zum nächsten Jahrtausend*. Frankfurt: W. Krüger (German translation of: *Sex, Ecology and Spirituality: The Spirit of Evolution*. Boston: Shambhala, 1995).

Witzel, Andreas 1982. *Verfahren der Qualitativen Sozialforschung: Überblick und Alternativen*. Frankfurt: Campus.

Zinberg, Norman 1984. *Drug, Set and Setting: The Basis for Controlled Intoxicant Use*. New Haven: Yale University Press.

FAILURE IMPOSSIBLE? HANDLING OF RULES, MISTAKES AND FAILURE IN PUBLIC RITUALS OF MODERN WESTERN SOCIETIES

Burckhard Dücker

Introduction

Public rituals in modern western societies will be the subject of this article. These rituals are part of the political or cultural field of society. They are performed by institutions which are exposed to the public eye. As a result, thanks to the media the general public has the possibility of essentially unlimited participation, which therefore can be considered constitutive. The performance ritual marks the social interface between the individual and the collective or the institution, which may change their mutual assessment. In the main a distinction can be made between three different types of ritual: those of consecration, initiation and conversion.

The rituals of consecration comprise according honours, tributes, awarding distinctions, awarding decorations in the military and political field, and prize award ceremonies in the literary-cultural field. For all these presentation ceremonies the religious connotation of the notion of consecration plays a part. The ritual of initiation or appointment means that someone is incorporated into an existing group or institution. In the third case—conversion—it is a question of changing from one group to another; this likewise religious notion is often executed by actions of separation, isolation and dismissal on the one hand, and by forms of purification and admission on the other hand. That is why parallels with the ritual of initiation are possible.

Such ritual performances, affecting a socio-cultural group or institution on the one hand, and the individual on the other hand, are about processes of legitimisation which affect the individual's feeling of identity in relation to a public institution, or his public prestige and perception by the institutional consecration. Since the individual is perceived differently after having passed through the ritual, the dimension of

'Statusmodifikation' (status modification)[1] has to be taken into account for the ritual performances to be analysed in this article.

In the following I will deal with the general criteria of the ritual action, then I will present the cases treated in this article. In a third section I will discuss the question of what happens if one of the two sides—the institution or the individual/prizewinner—cannot accept the result of the ritual process.

1. The basic interest in safeguarding continuity can be considered a universal phenomenon of cultural formation. This aim is made visible to society by the fact that the social and cultural knowledge of content, methods and the habitual course of events, as well as the visualisation of culture-specific norms and the values of one's own and of others, is passed on from one generation to the next by various forms of social learning. The temporarily restricted phase of socialisation, ending when the aspirant is entrusted with the rights and duties which he or she requires to participate in public life, is structured as is the individual's biography by privileged and habitualised events of legitimisation. These will inform both the individual and the society on the individual's position within the latter. This information can be given as a result of the extent and usage of the respective social and cultural knowledge. Usually the interfaces between individual and collective, between the story of life and its social background, between event and structure seem to appear as events or situations with ritual character.

The interfaces are focussed on a period of probation, verification or decision which legitimises the aspirant's transition from one level of social status to another, which usually goes hand in hand with a more extended range of social rights and duties. The dynamics of social change only take place in a specific segment of social reality. For a ritual process to be valid and officially accepted in social everyday life, its correct performance is indispensable. All participating protagonists officially have to be authorised according to the rules and regulations in effect.

The course of the ritual has to include all of the constituent sequences.

---

[1] In a case study Vogt (1998) demonstrates how the bestowal of the Order of Merit of the Federal Republic of Germany (*Bundesverdienstkreuz*) negatively influences the status of the honoured person according to his or her own perception: due to this recognition many former friends feel inferior and withdraw from him or her.

Regulations regarding for instance place, lapse of time, precise details (introduction, creating publicity, preparation of utensils) and the realisation of the event (order and correctness of particular sequences, use of correct terms) have to correspond to the structural guidelines. The respective ritual experts (priests, shamans, officials, chairmen, medicine men, wise women etc.) are responsible for their correct execution.

2. Every ritual considered in this article presumes the individuality and the self-determination of each person, as well as the authenticity of his action in the way it is interpreted by the institution. Of course, the aspirant follows the continuity of tradition, but through his personal performance he is able to give it a specific turn, a singular meaning. Through the process of ritual he is in return supposed to receive a form of gratification from the institution. The prize award ceremony is based on the elementary type of social activity which is known as the exchange of presents. The institution legitimizes a person's publications—gives recognition to his authorship—as an important present for his socio-cultural and aesthetic-literary continuity, and honours him in return by awarding the prize. In this way the honouring constitutes a social relationship between the institution and the individual who accepts not only the prize but also the value system of the institution.

The individual who is honoured with a prize has been able to prevail over other applicants through competition legitimised by a jury. As a result of his individuality, the aspirant has gained the benefit of distinction. On the one hand, the authenticity achieved through performance ritual distinguishes him from others but it has to be shared with all the other prizewinners. From this point of view, the aspirant might perceive his honour as a form of de-individualisation. Just as the institution, on the basis of its set of values, accepts his individuality as a representation of this same set, that is, just as the institution recognizes its orientation within this set and therefore cancels his individuality by giving its approval, the so honoured also accepts the institutional set of values if he accepts being confirmed in his individuality in regarding it as an honour to represent the values of the institution.

This ambivalence, which is created by the acceptance of individuality and the possibility of its political instrumentalisation, may be misinterpreted by the aspirant. As a result he may reject his prize or bring out a subversive dimension in his public expression of thanks. The institution on the other hand may withdraw the prize if afterwards it learns of details which would have made the honouring impossible.

3. In case of incorrect execution which calls the validity of the ritual into question, its validity and its roots will become the issue of reflexive and discursive work. Wrong moves may be perceived in advance of or during the performance, or in retrospect. They may concern the protagonist's actions, his behaviour, the preparation and check of the needed utensils such as a sacrificial animal, as well as the authorisation or worthiness of individuals in rituals of consecration, appointment or distinction. Furthermore they may concern place, time, set, sequence, publicity, the ritual's efficacy—in general all the elements that constitute the ritual process. Considering the number of possible sources of error one must assume that ritual performance, just like a theatre performance, is always characterized by a more or less visible deviation. "Rituals do not go smoothly; they often seem to be more trouble than they are worth" (Grimes 1988: 104).

Regarding public ritual or ritualised performances in socio-cultural areas of modern societies, it can be assumed that during the phase of performative execution mistakes will not lead to failure. Journalists or writers of a letter's page may criticise the poor design or the bad articulation of the speaker. Their observations presume a standard of success; the criticism does not however lead to the failure of ritual. Mistakes or rather deviations from the script during the performance of modern rituals are usually ignored or adjusted. When talking about failure of ritual in modernity it is either the before or the impact after the performance that is being discussed. In case a scholar of ritual or an observer finds out about details which would call into question the protagonist's ritual legitimacy, the planned performance will not take place or its reliability will be disputed afterwards.

The mediality of ritual in modernity has led to a new category of mistakes: the deficient technical recording of a ritual sequence which requires its repetition. Andreas Maier, aspekte-prizewinner in 2000, remembers:

> Prize-awarding ceremony took place at the book fair in 2000 with audience at stand of the Suhrkamp publishing house. "Aspekte" made a short film of this event, i.e. the whole ceremony was prepared for the film. Because the editing was not acceptable, the film was made twice, we have made the whole ceremony twice, once more with audience. The preparations were: Wolfgang Herles and me, we arranged the shooting, one shot to him, one pan with him to me, handing-over of the diploma, three questions for me, brief responses etc. In this way we have done it twice, the questions and responses, too. Because people were passing at the stand they didn't notice that I got the prize twice. Some left after the first, the others came only later (Ohmer 2004: XLI).

It is in the nature of such mistakes or interruptions that they will not be shown to the public since only the correct recording will be broadcasted. One has to assume that the broadcast of consecration-rituals can choose from various versions since it is common in the media scene to re-record particular sequences.

Another interference in the sequence of a performance is the prolongation of important gestures such as a handshake, a final photograph of all the participants, a demonstration of something new (for instance altered status) by touching a symbol (treaty or document) all together—in order to enable the media representatives to record the scene as perfectly as possible. This interference is not communicated as a mistake but it is mentioned by the media itself as a concession to the media. The same counts in other ritual contexts such as the first cut of a spade, the cutting of a ribbon at the inauguration of a public building etc.

Mistakes during ritual performance concern the understandable critique of institutions and their image management in ritual performance. At the beginning of his speech on the occasion of the Nobel Prize banquet in 1999 Günter Grass welcomed the Swedish Monarch with "Sehr geehrter Herr König" ('Dear Mr. King'). This was certainly perceived as an infringement of the rules (Hartwig 2002) but had no consequences. On the contrary, this mistake was perceived as a positive confirmation of the writer's unconventional and emancipated attitude and accepted as an expression of his poetic licence that allows, at least to a limited extent, a critical, subversive attitude towards power, institutions and control. Ritual criticism and ritual performance depend on each other. It is this interdependence that makes it possible for the individual to keep his independence by simultaneously being embedded in collectivism.

As the ritual performance approaches, delicate decisions regarding verification, purification, authorisation or selection of the prizewinner are principally taken during the non-public phase of selection. During the phase after the bestowing of the honours, especially if it is a public event in combination with a financial award, the prizewinner constantly has to demonstrate his worth. However, it is possible in principle to deprive or withdraw a prize for two reasons: first on the strength of detailed knowledge about the prizewinner's biography, which should have prevented the prize being awarded, second because the prizewinner withdraws because he does not want to be associated with the awarding institution or with preceding prizewinners. The first reason concerns the institution, the second the individual.

Wherever mistakes are made and perceived, in school or in another field of social life, they have deictic function for they draw attention to the rules that were broken, whereupon an explanation or justification is given to the public. Furthermore, the mistake draws (public) attention to the person held responsible for it. This mistake shall not be made again, the mistake is supposed to cause a learning effect. The possibility of making mistakes is the converse side of the possibility of exerting an influence on determining the correct form. In this case 'mistake' does not mean a wilful and intentional offence against or violation of a rule in order to gain profit (gain of symbolic, social or material capital) or to have a detrimental effect on another individual or institution which could be interpreted as an act of sabotage or criminal intent. The controlling instance, being authorised to impose sanctions, takes the view that the one responsible for the mistake unconsciously did not apply the rules correctly.

Looking at it from the responsible party's angle, the mistake could by all means have been made in order to express an innovative idea or to create something new. If that is the case the mistake is usually meant to have an imperative function. The public is to be motivated to accept and imitate it. Thus, its objective is to provoke structural, social and historical dynamics as a result of dynamics developed by means of personal experiences. This case polarizes the supporters of the existing and of the new order and thus leads to the expectation that negative and positive sanctions will be imposed on the protagonist within a public discussion. Even though this could prompt the possibility of "Statusverlust" (loss of prestige) and "Statusgewinn" (gain of prestige), of "Zeichnung" (stigmatisation) and "Auszeichnung" (Stagl 2001: 177) (honour, charisma), such a discussion usually means a gain of symbolic or social capital in favour of the actor—for he has been in touch with power, which in this case means the public opinion and the media.

Since the term 'mistake' is a notion which expresses a certain value (Luhmann 1971: 21) it draws attention to the actual purpose of the broken rule and the values it is based on. The term prompts the construction of deviation by the institution and causes interactions between the responsible individual, the observer, the involved institution and the interested public. Regarding the logical relationship between normality and deviation, the idea might be developed that variously deviation, opposition, or dynamics are tools of the order being criticized (see Dücker 2003: 142), or that the responsible party should be reintegrated or expelled by means of excuse, penance, or the restitution of the former situation. As a result, deviation is the most latent element of the existing order, offering a new interpretation of the existing normality as and when it is activated. Since normality or rather order obtains information about its own situation from the deviations, the deviation itself is the power that defines order. The latter has become reflexive, for a new potentiality of order has become apparent by means of deviation. This way deviation becomes a symbol of an institutional process—its deictic function is supposed to provoke situations which differ from reality but which, at the same time, refer to a normative, neglected and estranged element of reality. This is the situation where the old and ancient order becomes something new on account of an interpretation on the basis of deviation. The non-active norm is supposed to be reinvented (see Dücker 2003: 23f.). Thus, the genetic and historical relationship between an order and its deviation receives confirmation.

Generally speaking, the perception of mistakes has the catalytic effect to provoke a 'Regeldiskurs' (discourse about rules and regulations) in order to confirm or to transform the existing order. From this perspective the expression 'to learn from mistakes' reveals a second dimension. The learning effect results from the decisions and agreements underlying the rules, which concern norms and values of the socio-cultural setting that is organised by the rules that have actually been broken. Thus, the binary system of showing and hiding applies equally to the social phenomenon 'mistake'. If, on account of a certain constellation of interests, a 'Regeldiskurs' is desired, the range of tolerance and the scope of action concerning mistakes as a symptom of deviant behaviour can be defined as narrowly as possible.

Another observation concerns the universal significance of mistake as a term of social perception and interpretation. A mistake is made and then perceived, that is, it is part of a social acting-process with at least two protagonists. It is possible that both sides are represented in one person. The latter begins to construct deviation and to implement a 'Regeldiskurs'. Chronologically the mistake is being before it is perceived, but given the logic of deviation, a mistake is only perceived as such by applying normative rules. (Making mistakes only makes sense when a system of rules exists; making rules only makes sense when the possibility to make mistakes is given.)[2] Thus, the fact of mistake in the

[2] Within the discussion in ritual sciences, the study by Peter Winch (1958) apparently has been rarely noticed. In arguing against the pragmatic dimension of Ludwig

run-up and in the actual field of efficacy (retrospective) is the result of a process of interpretation and negotiation. Therefore, the agency for this interpretation is up to the representative of the system of rules which is effected by him. On the basis of the system's experiences as a controlling organ, its identity is defined and confirmed by the construction of deviation (see Foucault 1961). If a mistake is not perceived because it does not result in action—it does not exist.

Thus, one would be too shortsighted to take the mistake just as a deviation from material, arrangement and sequence of events within the rule. Mistake rather defines a socio-cultural generative complex of social meaning and its different forms of action. Its efficacy displays itself in dynamic processes. The actual extent (individuals concerned, institutions, interpretations of rules, period of time, intensity) cannot be precisely defined in advance. Since 'mistake' refers to the rule first and then to the values underlying the rules, the empiricism of the actual ritual process is already exceeded. Transcending rituals, a mistake refers to systemic relations: on the one hand it refers to the horizontally and vertically historical context of other rituals for which I have coined the term "Rituallandschaft" (see Dücker forthc.); on the other hand it refers to the socio-cultural context of the present where, caused by deviation, a discourse about rules is taking place. If the latter tends to be omnipresent in the media it is often talked about as a scandal. Considering the fact that mistakes can only be made in relation to a certain system of rules, we may conclude that every order with its system of rules and regulations contains its own definition of mistake. A mistake that is considered an offence against a rule in one order may be considered normal in another. From this point of view mistakes or deviation from rules can be of metonymic function for the respective system of norms.

Regarding the social and cultural field, it becomes obvious that the diagnosis of a mistake may refer to an inadmissible border crossing from one socially defined level to a higher one. Here we have a case of assumption of authority. Thus, in 1508 the honouring of Eobanus Hessus (see Schirrmeister 2003: 230ff.) failed because he sought to be honoured in an over-direct and intensive way—as if trying to avoid the

Wittgenstein's linguistic theory he states that mistakes and rules are mutually determined, that a mistake must be apparent, that private directives (according to Wittgenstein's notion of 'Privatsprachspiel') are possible but that they are socially not relevant because they lack intersubjective acceptance.

stages of appeal. By means of various applications and complaints he tried to put pressure on the bureau of the prince who was entrusted with bestowing honours. After having shown his interest in receiving an honour to a reliable person, Hessus would normally have had to wait until the office set up the required contacts in non-public negotiations in order to finally recommend him in public. Hessus was not able to correct this slip—he was not honoured. Another inadmissible case of personal arrangement regarding official symbolic performances between the literary field and the 'field of power' ("Feld der Macht", Schirrmeister 2003: 151) is the case of Johannes Fabri who, in 1531, published his work *De fide et bonis operis* with a dedication to the king without having required permission to do so through the official channels. On account of his assumption of authority, Fabri had to justify himself in public—which shows the existence of different standards and their respective interpretation of the offence 'mistake' in different social areas.

These examples of mistakes having been made in advance of and after the ritual process (failure of ritual performance) show that they attract great attention because, by means of suspension, they show up the habitual, traditionally legitimised sequence of symbolic events as a manifestation of power. Since Hessus and Fabri had to undergo sanctions for offending the social norm, they did not set a precedent for the de-legitimisation of symbolic forms and therefore the unchallenged validity of normative order was confirmed. Neither of them had been aware of their offence against the norm, say the documents. Fabri defended himself by pointing out other cases where the person honoured, who has not given explicit permission for the dedication, had even taken over the printing costs of the book (as a countermove). Hessus simply believes he is doing his protectors a favour. Both cases are about a conflict of values between innovation and tradition, between order and the principle of possible changes. Within the symbolic system the latter's dynamic potentiality indicates a change that continues, however, to remain latent.

Even though Hessus and Fabri were not successful with their offers of innovation, it caused a structurally analogous result—similar to that of success—concerning their prestige as writer and the related social capital. What counts is the contact with the institution that gives away this capital. This way, Hessus and Fabri, just like Sartre, Rich and Handke later on, have become individualised by their conflict with the institution. They have become 'visible' and 'recognisable' on account of negative qualifications and by these means they have entered literary history. Regarding the recollection of mistakes, one has to consider the further development of archives and historiography, on the tracks of which the production of deviation might almost be privileged.

Case studies

a) *Jean-Paul Sartre and his rejection of the Nobel Prize in 1964*

During the period of National Socialism, German citizens were not allowed to accept the Nobel Prize. By means of a media campaign, the Soviet government forced Boris Pasternak to refuse the Nobel Prize for Literature in 1958[3] ("for his important achievement both in contemporary lyrical poetry and in the field of the great Russian epic tradition", http://www.nobel.se/literature/laureates/1958; date of last access: 30/08/2006). In 1964 Jean Paul Sartre became the first to voluntarily decline the Nobel Prize.

Sartre heard about his potential honour by reading an article in *Le Figaro Littéraire* (12.10.1964, see Cohen-Solal 1988: 673), shortly before the Nobel Prize committee was to make its decision public. On October 14th 1964, Sartre wrote a letter to the Permanent Secretary of the Swedish Academy. He announced in advance that he would refuse the prize if it were really to be given to him, as was suggested in the article.

> Dear Sir,
> According to certain information which I have got today, I have some chances to get the Nobel-Prize. Although it may be strange to discuss a decision before it has taken place, I take the liberty of writing to you to prevent a misunderstanding. First, I assure you of my deep esteem for the Swedish Academy and the Prize with which the Academy has honoured so many writers. For personal and as well as for more objective reasons I don't want to figure on the list of the candidates for the Prize. I neither can nor want in 1964 or later accept this respectable award. (http://membre.lycos.fr/julbulus/sartrevie.htm; date of last access 1/6/2004).

It seems that the warning letter never reached its addressee for, on October 22nd, Anders Österling officially announced that the Nobel

[3] See Espmark 1988, Filser 2001, Pasternak/Freudenberg 1986.

Prize for Literature was to be awarded to Sartre. Thus, on the occasion of a press release on October 24th, Sartre repeated that he declined the prize and explained his decision in detail.

He distinguished between personal and objective reasons. The latter concern his understanding of authorship according to which "les distinctions officielles" have always to be refused: "The writer has to refuse to be transformed into an institution even if this occurs in a very respectable form" (http://membre.lycos.fr/julbulus/sartrevie.htm; date of last access 1/6/2004). Sartre wanted to avoid his institutionally legitimised exploitation, maybe even his exploitation as an author. Being a Nobel Prize winner, the authenticity of his works would receive the meaning of 'speaking in the name of', whereas Sartre defines 'author' or 'authorship' as 'speaking in one's own name', which includes the independence of political engagement with no regard to the institution which is entrusted with according the honouring. By refusing the "distinction" he gains distinction.

One of the objective arguments is his commitment "for the peaceful coexistence of the two cultures, the eastern and the western one". He says that he supports socialism but would not accept an honour from any side. According to Sartre, the Nobel Prize is reserved for authors of the West and oppositionals of the East (http://membre.lycos.fr/julbulus/sartrevie.htm; date of last access 1/6/2004).

Sartre's refusal to accept the Nobel Prize implied a non-acceptance of the consecration ritual and its monarchic-academic tradition. This tradition obliges the winner to accept the prize from the monarch's hands, which is interpreted by Sartre as accepting the monarchic system and its tradition as well as the way the image of monarch and his family is cultivated in public. For Sartre, the visible presence of the monarch and of the prize winner, who is often already world-famous, is the most important reason for the acceptance of the performative act. The participants as well as the world-wide public participating via the media know that this performance goes down in history—at least in national, institutional and professional history. The ritual gives the opportunity to be a part of history or to being stored. The experience of being a contemporary witness of historical events is completed by the spatial experience that arises from witnessing the transformation of the secular buildings *Konzerthus* (music hall, presentation of prizes) and *Stadthus* (city hall, banquet) into almost consecrated sites. Sartre saw neither a mistake that had to be corrected in advance, nor a flaw that, considering the aspect of the subversive dimension, had to be integrated into the ritual performance. Sartre criticised rather the ritual *per se*, taking a point of view that precludes not only the respective ritual performance but the institution of literary awards as such. According to Sartre, the failure of ritual consists in the choice of the prizewinner and in the choice of the type of ritual, that is, the Swedish Academy is to be held responsible for the crisis and the discussion about values afterwards.[4]

Thus, neither the institution's image management nor the author's self-presentation will be staged. Sartre did not obtain any physical presence as a prizewinner. The system of values the Nobel Prize of Literature is based upon ("the most outstanding work of an idealistic tendency", http://www.nobel.se/nobel/alfred-nobel/biographical/will/index.html; date of last access: 30/08/2006) could not be staged—it cannot become visible. In the course of the public discussion, which can be interpreted as a form of anti-ritualisation, the author's textual presence becomes more dominant than his physical presence. The evaluation of other cases shows that the refusal of a prize goes hand in hand with the publication of autobiographical and programmatic confessions which explain the refusal and constitute an individual poetry. The author presents himself as someone who speaks without a mask.[5] Being the negative of habitual expressions of thanks, confessional literature as a substitute for 'showing one's face' ('Ritual des Gesichtzeigens') can almost be assigned to the 'poetics of presentation'. The author presents his outlooks and attitudes, which deviate from the institutional ones, as well as his values and their genesis, whereupon the institution—with Foucault—may perceive and redefine its identity. Considering the fact that structures and contents of identity may be perceived as such by

[4] In May 2004 "the President of the Czech senate Petr Pithart refused the acceptance of the Bavarian Europe-Medal because of the dispute about the Sudeten Germans. The medal has been given [since 1990] for special merits of Bavaria in the united Europe" (Brössler in: *Süddeutsche Zeitung* 06/May/2004). Pithart had criticised the expulsion of Sudeten Germans. His refusal of the honour was a reaction to the fact that CSU-delegates disapproved of the entry of the Czech Republic into the EU on the occasion of the European Parliament in April 2003. Pithart refused in advance in order not to exceed the range of tolerance by extending the subversive dimension during the award of the honour. Thus, Pithart did not principally disapprove of presentation ceremonies. In this specific case he accords the failure of ritual to the ambivalence of the CSU-policy. (CSU: Conservative party in Bavaria)

[5] Cohen-Solal (1988: 674) resumes the details of Sartre's self-presentation. Even the refusal of a performative action has its performative frame: it is possible to present the refusal as an expression of authenticity.

means of deviation only, the term mistake or flaw is inappropriate because of its negative connotation, and should be substituted by deviation. It now has the constructive function of catalysing the processes of self-reflection and 'autopoiesis' (self-creation). Thus, Sartre deconstructs in his article the institution of the Nobel Prize by constructing the institution of independent authorship. The article is structured as a plea for public approval of his own awarding institution.

In his confession he elaborates on his decision to carry on looking at the community of Nobel Prize winners from the point of view of an outside observer. He refuses to be instrumentalised by propagating it from an emic perspective. Sartre explicitly disapproves of the bond which had been offered to him and confirms the dissociation. In his negative word of thanks he turns the contact function, being the central function of an expression of thanks, into a dissociating function.[6] Sartre explains his decisions by the fact that the anticipated effectiveness of the Nobel Prize, together with the new social status he would gain, would change the authentic image which he had gained so far on account of his works and his political actions, both in the cultural as well as in the political field. Sartre considers the Nobel Prize to be an indirect element of Western politics, so he is afraid of entering a moral conflict. Sartre's unexpected decision impressively confirms rules and agencies of the Nobel Prize ritual as a serious social institution. This information could hardly have been conveyed by a peaceful, conventional ceremony.

In order to judge the Nobel Prize's political function, Sartre may have remembered other unspectacular cases, besides the examples mentioned above (National Socialist Germany, Soviet Union), where a prizewinner would or could not accept the prize but did not want to refuse it either. For instance Carl Spitteler (1919; see Hjärne) and Hermann Hesse (1946; see Österling) sent the Swiss Ambassador as political representative of their home country to Stockholm rather than a relative or the publisher.

Institutional rituals dealing with consecration, honours or appointments legitimise a selected candidate and make him a member. They

---

[6] This function is performed in expressions like "Je regrette vivement, un prix est distribué et quelqu'un le refuse, mon refus n'est pas un acte improvisé, j'ai toujours déclinés les distinctions officielles, l'écrivain doit donc refuser . . ., c'est pourquoi je ne peux accepter aucune distinction, je serais donc incapable [. . .] d'accepter . . ." (http://membres.lycos.fr/julbulus/sartrevie.htm?; date of last access 1/6/2004).

make it perceptible that he turns from an outside observer into an inside observer. They expect him to actively prove his acceptance of his new status. For all these reasons there is always the risk that the candidate may want to keep his non-membership status. The ritual is always about the ritual integration of a candidate into the ritual community. Having been defined as a passive character before his integration, the candidate is supposed to turn into an active one once he has been accepted as a new member.[7]

A mistake makes perceptible non-membership and distinction, which can be annulled within the scope of cancellation of differences and which can be turned into membership. They can, however, also be perceived as a mark of distinction, in order to define one's own identity. However, Sartre's refusal to accept the Nobel Prize does not seem to have caused any increased dynamics within the performance of the Nobel Prize ritual, for the official reaction of the Academy was restricted to the following announcement:

> It will be recalled that the laureate has made it known that he did not wish to accept the prize. The fact that he has declined this distinction does not in the least modify the validity of the award. Under the circumstances, however, the Academy can only state that the presentation of the prize cannot take place (http://www.nobel.se/literature/laureates/1964/press.html; date of last access 1/6/2004).[8]

---

[7] In connection with the sacrificial ritual illustrated by Lawson/McCauley, Gladigow (2004: 68) refers to passive-active dynamics when "particularly in complex rituals the transformation from a passive participation of the gods to an active one is intended".

[8] S. Friberg, principal of the *Carolina Institute* tries to mediate in his banquet speech: "Mr. Sartre found himself unable to accept this year's Prize in Literature. There is always discussion about this prize, which every one considers himself capable of judging, or which he does not understand and consequently criticizes. But I believe that Nobel would have had a great understanding of this year's choice. The betterment of the world is the dream of every generation, and this applies particularly to the true poet and scientist. This was Nobel's dream. This is one measure of the scientist's significance. And this is the source and strength of Sartre's inspiration. As an author and philosopher, Sartre has been a central figure in postwar literary and intellectual discussion—admired, debated, criticized. His explosive production, in its entirety, has the impression of a message; it has been sustained by a profoundly serious endeavour to improve the reader, the world at large. The philosophy, which his writings have served, has been hailed by youth as liberation. Sartre's existentialism may be understood in the sense that the degree of happiness which an individual can hope to attain is governed by his willingness to take his stand in accordance with his ethos and to accept the consequences thereof; this is a more austere interpretation of a philosophy admirably expressed by Nobel's contemporary, Ralph Waldo Emerson: "Nothing is at last sacred but the integrity of your own mind" (http://www.nobel.se/literature/laureates/1964/press.html; date of last access: 23/08/2006).

What applies to Hessus and Fabri applies to Sartre as well: he certainly succeeds in acting out his non-membership (distinction), but he cannot avoid being qualified as the author who was the first to refuse the Nobel Prize for Literature. By changing the possible etic point of view into a seemingly emic one, simply another form of identity was created. Since Sartre is part of the unsuccessful ritual, he is—seen from an analytic and methodical point of view—a representative of one emic perspective.

The "conflict of values" (see Hondrich 2002) between the institution 'Nobel Prize' and the institution 'Sartre' confirms both of them. Cohan-Solal (1988: 677) states "daß diese erstmalige Ablehnung des Nobelpreises eine hervorragende Werbung [für Sartre] bedeute". The same applies to the Nobel Prize since Sartre has confirmed its global cultural and political publicity and definitional power in a very impressive way. The fact that the media pay so much attention to Sartre's refusal of the Nobel Prize gives him the chance to gain a considerable amount of symbolic capital. The elements that are said by Luhmann to constitute "Aufmerksamkeitsregeln" (rules guiding attentiveness) and which deal with the genesis of public events, such as scandals, might explain this phenomenon. These rules underline the risks entailed by refusal by less well-known people and the lack of media attention in cases when the honoured person and the institution involved are less famous. Luhmann's theory allows us to calculate—at least to a certain extent—the effect that will be caused by the perception of a mistake and by the respective action that is performed afterwards. To put it in slightly exaggerated terms: during the public process of competition, ritual mistakes can be employed as a strategic instrument to gain positionings ("positionnements", Bourdieu) in the socio-cultural and political field of society. To what extent this functional element of ritual mistakes applies to other cultures has to be decided on the basis of the respective research work.

First, Luhmann distinguishes "the outstanding priority of certain values" that appear uncertain. On the one hand, the validity of distinction and order, both factors within the institution Nobel Prize, is at stake. These factors safeguard to a great extent "the need for structures for the regulation of human experiences and behaviour" (Luhmann 1971: 13) within a segment of society. On the other hand, it is about the importance of individual self-determination. It has always been certain that it is a conflict of values. The maintenance of one value forbids the execution of another, for this would mean a modification of individuality. Second Luhmann distinguishes "the crisis and the symptoms of crisis" which concern not only a single value but "the existence of the system adequate to ones usual standard". That is, not only the architecture of values and traditions but also "the efficiency of the integration and innovations caused by a crisis" (Luhmann 1971: 16). Third he distinguishes "the status of the sender of a communication": since Sartre had already been world-famous, he got the appropriate attention. Luhmann further distinguishes "the symptoms of political success": the print-run of Sartre's books increased, especially his autobiography *Les mots* which appeared in 1964 and became much in demand. This shows that Sartre's cultural and political outlooks were accepted by the general public. The fifth distinction Luhmann makes is "the innovative character of events": the first spontaneous refusal of a Nobel Prize opens up a new dimension in its history. "The new has a value in itself". The Nobel Prize can no longer be considered unchallenged. The sixth distinction is: "pains or substitutes provoked by civilisation" (Luhmann 1971: 17). This aspect does not apply to the institution Nobel Prize. It might apply to Sartre, who cannot meet the demand of oppositional groups for financial aid.

Luhmann likewise sketches out a dramaturgy of scandal. In a first "latent phase" the scandal only "appears possible for those who are particularly informed and interested". As for Sartre, this phase is covered by the hint in *Le Figaro Littéraire* and his private letter to the Secretary of the Swedish Academy. Thus, Sartre's closer friends were prepared for the scandal. The "break through" (Luhmann 1971: 19) is marked by the official announcement that the Nobel Prize winner in 1964 will be Sartre. This phase is aggravated by Sartre's public refusal which is the "culmination point" of the scandal. During this phase it is possible to judge this 'case' in any possible way. Soon, there will occur "signs of tiredness" (Luhmann 1971: 19) and the public's attention will diminish, for neither Sartre nor the Academy will feed the scandal with further announcements. The scandal's potential to cause change will be unable to develop. There is no dynamising effect. However, the Nobel Prize's history has gained one more facet.

b) *Adrienne Rich: why I refused the National Medal for Arts*

In 1997, the American lyric poet Adrienne Rich refused the American National Medal for Arts in advance. Just like Sartre, she published autobiographical and programmatic articles in order to announce and to explain her refusal. She diagnosed an attitude towards the arts that was totally different from her own as mistaken. This attitude was supported by the Administration of the White House as well as by President Clinton, by whom she was to be awarded the prize. Unlike Sartre, Rich did not completely disapprove of the acceptance of the prize or of participation in the awards ritual. Her criticism only applied to Clinton's policy. She denied that Clinton had the ritual competencies that were required. There can be no mediation between her attitude towards art "as breaker of official silences, as voice for those whose voices are disregarded, and as a human birthright" and Clinton's policy of art "[to] honour certain token artists while the people at large are so dishonoured." There existed not even the possibility of mediation by activating the subversive function within the course of the ritual. "My concern for my country is inextricable from my concerns as an artist. I could not participate in a ritual which would feel so hypocritical to me" (Rich). Rich appointed herself representative of social underdogs to whom she lends her voice. Thus, she speaks 'in the name of' someone but not in the name of an institution. She speaks in the name of those who are supposed to form a community on account of her lyrics. Thanks to her own articles, Rich's refusal of the ritual had the catalytic effect of prompting a discourse about values by recalling the original vision of the American Constitution.[9]

Sartre and Rich replace the symbolic or social capital that is related to institutionally legitimised consecration with the capital they gain through their autobiographical and programmatic articles. The latter's generative 'coefficient' is higher than that of a conventional expression of thanks in response to a conventional eulogy during a conventional consecration ritual. Therefore such articles enrich the respective ritual history by highlighting its singular performances. The refusal of the ritual is explained from a systemic point of view which integrates the respective ritual into the socio-cultural context. Seen in this way, the ritual appears as an affirmative element of a general order that is judged critically.

[9] "My 'no' came directly out of my work as a poet and essayist and citizen drawn to the interfold of personal and public experience. I had recently been thinking and writing about the growing fragmentation of the social compact, of whatever it was this country had ever meant when it called itself a democracy: the shredding of the vision of government of the people, by the people, for the people" (Rich 1997).

c) *Ritual and anti-ritual: the Büchner Prize award ceremony in 1969*

This applies equally to rituals whose performance stands out from 'normal' performances on account of mistakes or flaws. The presentation of the Büchner Prize to Helmut Heissenbüttel[10] by the *Darmstädter Akademie für Sprache und Dichtung* in 1969 took place within the context of a local conflict situation (according to parents and authorities: suspension of a teacher on account of over-liberal sex education, or rather, according to pupils, on account of guidance to emancipation and self-realisation). With the help of collages made of texts from Georg Büchner and his milieu, as well as with present-day comments, students and pupils tried to prove that the structure of this situation (persecution of emancipatory action) as regards its revolutionary potential was comparable to the situation in 1830. Their aim was to prove Büchner's relevance, as a guide for social conflicts, to the present. During the ritualised presentation of the Büchner Prize, a group of students, ringing bells and screaming, passed down the aisle of the auditorium in the form of an antique 'pompa' (procession) and walked up to the lectern on the stage. There they read out a resolution via the microphone. After that, scuffling broke out. The police arrived and removed the demonstrators. In spite of the disturbance and the short outburst of zaniness, the presentation, as a correct performance with claims to validity, was brought to an end. After the award, a party political discussion on the responsibility for this interruption took place, or rather a discussion on the fact that inadequate measures were taken to prevent disturbances. Here it turned out that the interruption had apparently been announced several days in advance. There had even been the idea to integrate it into the performance by considering it a programme point (reading of a resolution) and harmonising it that way. The suggestion to change the structure, that is, to perform the presentation in the form of a private party, was not accepted. Finally, the structure remained the same even though the Academy was criticised on account of its inflexible attitude. Since the demonstrators' performance assumed the catalytic function of prompting a debate on the validity of presentations and their meaning in modern society, it occupied a larger part of the discussion in the media than the eulogy and the expression of thanks.

---

[10] I thank Judith Ulmer for allowing me to look at the documents about the presentation of the Büchner Prize to Heissenbüttel which she compiled as part of her thesis.

The revolutionary students confirmed the importance of the conventional consecration ritual by trying to convert it into a platform with which they could announce their interpretation of the given situation and the demands ensuing from it. At the same time they took the revolutionary poet Büchner seriously. They saw him as a figure of orientation. In the official speeches Büchner's political outlooks were regarded appreciatively as democratic and progressive. The students derived concrete practice from the officially represented values. They tried to visualise this value by performing it. Once again, deviation made it possible for the order to re-adjust itself. In his eulogy for Uwe Johnson (1971), Reinhard Baumgart confirmed that the students' performance opened up a new dimension in the history of the Büchner Prize: the establishment of reflexivity as a line of thought.

> We are celebrating a ceremony which was disturbed two years ago and that was the expression of the fact that people had taken it seriously. Today nobody is willing to do something alike, I can't either. I would wonder for some minutes how usual these kinds of prize-awardings has become. Until now I never witnessed such (Büchner-Preis 1971: 39).

He cites the exception of the disturbed ritual in order to define the awarding in the light of this event. He takes the basis of it as thinking model to make sure of himself.

d) *The case of Schneider/Schwerte*

Another constellation develops when an institution deprives an honoured person of the prize. It demands back the symbols of the honour, or rather, it forbids the person to hold the title. The institution repeals the whole consecration ritual on the strength of its authoritative function because the honoured person has proved unworthy of the honour by withholding facts beforehand that would not have allowed the ritual.[11]

[11] Another situation arose in the case of the 86-year-old Margarete Dierks. In 2000, she was supposed to appear in Darmstadt on the occasion of the "public event in the German Academy for Language and Literature in honour of the writer Dorothea Hollatz deceased in 1987" which was organized by the city of Darmstadt and the Elisabeth-Langgässer-Gesellschaft. Dierks was supposed to hold the eulogy. Beforehand, Dierks had to defend herself against the reproach that she had been a Nazi-writer. She justified herself by saying that she had spoken up "even for personalities who were condemned after 1945, as for example Hans Grimm or Hans Baumann." Grimm is the author of the novel *Volk ohne Raum*, Baumann wrote the lyrics "for the song roared by the Hitler youth 'Heute gehört uns Deutschland und morgen die ganze Welt' ('Today Germany is our, tomorrow the whole world')" (Feuck 2000). The town and the literary

By doing so, the institution withdraws symbolic and economic capital from the honoured person.

The case of Schneider/Schwerte (Sprache und Literatur 1996) throws light on a ritual of conversion and of re-conversion. It concerns a ritually legitimised falsification of a biography. In April 1995, the Professor emeritus of modern German literary studies unmasked himself—in order to avoid exposure by others—as a former member of the SS. He admitted as well that he has been an academic collaborator of the SS-organisation 'ancestors heritage' ('Ahnenerbe') in the 'Section of the Deployment for the Sciences based on the Germanic Tradition' ("Abteilung 'germanischer Wissenschaftseinsatz'", König 1998: 6). Further, he announced that he has changed his name and his identity: Hans Ernst Schneider turned into Hans Schwerte.[12] There were uncertainties about the doctorate he did in Erlangen in 1948, but they did not lead to his title being rescinded. Further, a doctorate (see Jäger 1998: 60–90) that he claimed to have passed in Königsberg in 1935 and the respective thesis could not be verified.[13]

The following instructions given by the administration are important for the history of rituals: his appointment as professor was re-voiced, the Order of Merit of the Federal Republic of Germany was withdrawn, and he was deprived of his status as civil servant, his pension, and his title as an honorary senator. The legal authorities checked whether Schwerte's activities during the period of National Socialism were sufficient to warrant legal proceedings on the basis of complicity to murder. ("His appointment as professor was cancelled, the Order of Merit of the Federal Republic of Germany[14] was taken away, the status

society realised the lack of suitability was a mistake. They cancelled the event in order not to institutionally legitimise Dierk's statements. They wanted to avoid her statements being honoured with public attention and symbolic capital.

[12] Schwerte "based his second life on five papers that were faked or obtained by devious means: 1. The marching orders from the camp of prisoners of war. 2. the identity card, 3. the official declaration of death, 4. the forged birth certificate (substitute), 5. the certificate of the university of Göttingen concerning the academic exams at the university of Königsberg" (Rusineck 1998: 32).

[13] As far as academic, administrative, biographical, psychological, moral, and general details of the case Schneider/Schwerte are concerned see Jäger 1998, König (ed.) 1998, *Sprache und Literatur* 77 (1996).

[14] This honour was given to Schneider/Schwerte by the Federal President Karl Carstens in 1982. "The order of Merit of the Federal Republic of Germany was founded in 1951 by the German Federal President Theodor Heuss. That is the unique and general Order of Merit, i.e. the most important recognition in the Federal Republic of Germany of merits for the public welfare." (http://www.bundespraesident.de/frameset/ixnavitext.jsp?node

as official, the pension and the title of an honorary senator were denied. The legal authority examined whether Schwerte's activities in the Nazi era were sufficient for a preferment of a charge for complicity in murder", König 1998: 7.). In various inquiries that reviews about "such a delicate subject" (Jäger 1996: 1) its ritual dimension was ignored, even though change and change of status, honour and dishonour are central elements within ritual processes (see Buck 1996).

Schneider was declared as fallen in Berlin (the document is dated 25th of April 1945) and then turned up in Lübeck under the name of Hans Werner Schwerte (this document is dated 2nd of May 1945) (Jäger 1998: 152). Schneider/Schwerte literarily staged a symbolic death and rebirth as a ritual of conversion. Schwerte's biography as an expression of social dynamics is legitimised throughout by ritual actions.[15] Various institutions awarded honours and decorations to Schwerte without knowing his true identity. Therefore, Schwerte was not authorised to accept these honours. Thus, the respective removal of distinctions (see Vogt 1997: 337–368) and re-conversions were performed after his unmasking.[16]

Regarding the case Schwerte/Schneider in terms of failure of ritual, the following observation can be made: the denial of ritual honours occurred because they had not been legitimised—even though they were valid. The institutions dissociated themselves from Schwerte/Schneider in a perfectly legal way. They no longer wanted to be part of his biography which is legally illegitimate but ritually legitimised. The official instructions for the awarding of academic titles and of orders of merit say that the present state of knowledge legitimises an honour which can be denied should compromising details subsequently become known.

ID=2049; date of last access 1/6/2004). In 1982, Schneider/Schwerte was made Honorary Professor of the University of Salzburg (Jäger 1998: 16). In 1985 he was awarded the decoration *Officier de l'ordre de la Couronne* by the Kingdom of Belgium. Between 1970 and 1973 he was principal of the RWTH Aachen (Jäger 1998: 15).

[15] It starts off with Schneider's symbolic death, which is performed by the widow as funeral ritual for the soldier who was killed in an unknown place. Then follows the rebirth as Schwerte which was ritually performed as a repeated initiation (university with its academic rituals of doctorate and habilitation), starting a family, which is ritually performed by the marriage with the widow Schneider, academic career with the respective rituals of consecration, legitimisation and honour for academic representation and international cooperation, establishment of political status.

[16] In connection with the *Internationale Germanistenlexikon 1800–1950* published on August 12th 2003, the membership of several professors well-known after 1945, became public. Comparable measures like those in the case Schneider/Schwerte were not taken.

This phenomenon applies to each system of rules: supposing that the interpretation-model 'mistake' is constitutive for the definition of normacy and normality, deprivation and legal sanctions would prevent the de-legitimised person from profiting from the symbolic and economic capital that he had gained by his ritual legitimisation. They do increase his indirectly effective agency, though, which gives him the power to define order and the corresponding normality. The mistake's power to influence the order of the respective institution increases proportionally to the mistake's significance and the possible sanctions.

e) *Peter Handke: his return of the Georg Büchner Prize to the donator*

An honour might be refused before its performance has taken place because the winner is afraid of negative consequences for his image. A ritual might be disturbed by an unknown interest group in order to use the forum of publicity to announce their own intentions. No matter what happens, all of the ensuing actions that have been motivated by a ritual confirm the latter's importance as a mediatory authority that is productive in the socio-cultural field of society. Thus, confirmation is given that the ritual is taken seriously as an organisational factor of social reality. The explication of a mistake boosts the importance of the ritual. This also applies to Peter Handke's return of the Büchner Prize, which was awarded to him by the *Darmstädter Akademie für Sprache und Dichtung* in 1973. In 1999, he returned the prize in response to the Western attitude towards the new organisation of former Yugoslavia. By so doing, Handke opened up a new dimension in the history of the Büchner Prize. On April 6th 1999, he explained and enacted the return of the prize by means of an autobiographical-programmatic declaration.[17]

[17] The letter has the following wording: "In his Easter message the pope condemns at the 12th day of the war against Yougoslavia the fractricidal war, but not the attaque of the NATO against a small nation. And on the first page of 'Le Monde' from Easter Sunday, 4th april 1999, following the banner headline 'The Nato strikes in the heart of Belgrad', begins a long commentary of the archbishop of Cambrai and President of the commission 'justice and peace' of the French episcopate, where the NATO-war against Yougoslavia is sanctioned. Citation: 'Today it's necessary to have some helicopters to put out the fire, yesterday a bucket of water would have been sufficient. The archbishop continues to speak of all Christians and all humans of good will for whom the arms never represent a solution—but for the moment it's urgent to disarm the aggressor. Never. But for the moment. And the President for the episcopal justice draws the conclusion. Citation: In this case there was only the choice between a non-activity—which was in the legal sense uncorrect—and an activity which was ethically necessary. War ahoy. Christian and human of good will. But me, the writer Peter

Even though Handke announced the return of the prize, it remained doubtful whether Handke could also return the honour that had been given to him on the occasion of the award. The ritual, as an act of individualisation (stigmatisation, charisma), is irrevocable. Only the portent of the symbolically formed alliance may change—not the alliance itself. Above all, it seems that Handke wanted to place a symbolic mark against Western culture. As a result, he left the Catholic Church in protest against the Pope's Kosovo declaration and returned the Büchner Prize money. Thus, by politically instrumentalising culture, he made the same mistake he accused the Church and the *Darmstädter Akademie* of making. He did however accept Serbian prizes.[18] Handke prepared his spectacular decision by publishing several literary articles in advance. In his articles he declared his unilateral solidarity for Serbia.

The Academy reacted with restraint. It pointed to the question of the technical realisation (cheque, money transfer) and the due interest rates.[19] The Academy believed that Handke's misunderstanding of the Büchner Prize as State Prize and the fact that the Academy did not declare its solidarity for Serbia—which no one could seriously demand—are the root causes for Handke's act of dissociation. Thus, the Academy does intervene when a mistake is perceived, and the decision to act is left to Handke. However, he did not succeed in gaining symbolic capital by trying to scandalise the academy. On the contrary, his reputation and his image were diminished—winged by repeated comparisons with Ezra Pound's engagement for Mussolini and Louis-Ferdinand-Celines' engagement for Hitler. Handke dissociated himself from his honour, which had been good for his career as a writer.

An important function of literary and cultural ritual—from which the author profits for his self presentation—seems to be highlighted

Handke, baptized and practising catholic, if possible, I declare that I am leaving this catholic church. Against every commission of ethics: Three cheers for justice. Another little thing: I give back the dotation for the Büchner-Prize in 1973 to the German Academy (fortunately only 10.000 DM): symbolically, as according to the Western media is the NATO-attaque in the heart of Belgrad, inevitable as according to all people the war of the world against Yougoslavia: in order not to lose my credibility. For everyman his credibility.'" (http://www.muenster.org/frieden/preis.html; date of last access 1/6/2004).

[18] Goldener Schlüssel von Smederevo 1998, Serbischer Ritter 1999 (see Güntner 1999).

[19] See "The President of the Academy: Handke is a case for psychiatry". In: *Berliner Morgenpost* 09/Apr/1999 (http://www.physiologus.de/komment/lit/hande1.htm; date of last access 1/6/2004).

by the opportunity to effectively stage the publication of political confessions and programmatics in the media. Handke's case prompted a discussion on EU policy on Serbia. On the occasion of the awarding of the *Friedenspreis des Deutschen Buchhandels* to the Turkish author Yasar Kemal in 1997, Günter Grass (1997) took the opportunity to present his opinions on immigration and peace politics during the eulogy.

The study of the system of rules und offences in modern times makes manifest the importance of distinguishing and limiting marks. Furthermore, it shows that, from the institution's point of view, social functional constellations have priority over the suggestions for innovation made by involved individual. Sartre, Rich and Handke turned down a ritual of consecration; or rather they dissociated themselves from a ritual which had already been performed because participation would undermine their political views. The border between their individual political positions and those of the institution would merge. The diagnosis of mistake is based on a moral obligation to an individual worldview for which the unity of speaking and acting functions as a border line of individual identity. If this line is overstepped, personal credibility will be at stake.

The failure of ritual illustrated by the awarding of a literary prize to Elfriede Jelinek in 1969 shows that the institution is also concerned about not overstepping the border.

> EJ is awarded the poetry-award of the Austrian student organisation. During the youth-culture week in Innsbruck in 1969 she gets both the prose-award (for an extract of 'wir sind lockvögel baby!' 'We are decoys baby') and the poetry-award. Already this first public appearance provokes a scandal which results in the fact that the competition is never repeated. In a parliamentary inquiry the FPÖ expresses the lack of understanding for the fact, that institutions award a prize to an author of pornographic texts (Stähli 2003: 50).

What the FPÖ perceived as a mistake was that the people who are responsible for the contest had not restricted the culture—which is supported by the public purse—to the appropriate limits that the party's values demanded. The FPÖ assumed that its party political definition of culture is accepted by the majority as a definition of general social validity. This argument does not concern the author herself. Its aim is rather to push through a cultural constellation which—according to the party—would be compromised by honouring Elfriede Jelinek or another cultural practice with a similar point of view. Considering the party's interpretation of the rules that are said to constitute official culture, the honouring of Jelinek's texts would be an offence against those rules. Had she participated in another contest, the scandal might not have occurred. Once again, the term mistake proves to be a relational one. Yet again, it turns out that a threat to the rules of an official institution sparks a debate on the limit of tolerance that restricts the values of this institution or order. Which means the definitional power of deviation is confirmed. The ritual establishes a relation of interdependence between institution and aspirant (prizewinner, actor, celebrated or honoured person). Even though the perception of a mistake (failure of ritual) marks the beginning of a process of dissociation and distinction, the aspirant continues to be bound to the institution on account of the explicit borderline that will be drawn in the course of the process mentioned above.

Fascination and refusal, membership and non-membership merely constitute different forms of relationship. One has to analyse each case on its own merits in order to see to what extent the forcing of limits and the ensuing official discourse about definition of norms, normacy and normality work as "Beschleuniger des Normenwandels" (Hondrich 2002: 28).

References

Baumgart, Reinhart 1972. "Rede auf den Preisträger [des Büchner-Preises Uwe Johnson]". In: *Jahrbuch 1971*, Deutsche Akademie für Sprache und Dichtung (ed.). Heidelberg: Lambert Schneider, 39–46.

Brössler, Daniel 2004. "Pithart brüskiert Bayern. Prager Staatschef verweigert Annahme der Europamedaille". In: *Süddeutsche Zeitung*, 06/May/2004.

Buck, Theo 1996. "Ein Leben mit Maske oder 'Tat und Trug' des Hans Ernst Schneider". *Sprache und Literatur* 77: 48–81.

Cohen-Solal, Annie 1988. *Sartre 1905–1980.* Reinbek: Rowohlt.

Dücker, Burckhard 2003. *Erlösung und Massenwahn. Zur literarischen Mythologie des Sezessionismus im 20. Jahrhundert.* Heidelberg: Synchron.

—— forthc. *Literatur als Handlungsprozess. Beiträge zu einer ritualwissenschaftlich fundierten Literaturgeschichte.* Heidelberg: Synchron.

Espmark, Kjell 1988. *Der Nobelpreis für Literatur. Prinzipien und Bewertungen hinter den Entscheidungen. Aus dem Schwedischen von R. Volz und F. Paul. Mit einem Nachwort von F. Paul.* Göttingen: Vandenhoek & Ruprecht.

Feuck, Jörg 2000. "Eklat: Autorin verteidigt zwei Nazi-Literaten". In: *Frankfurter Rundschau*, 16/Aug/2000.

Filser, Hubert 2001. *Nobelpreis. Der Mythos. Die Fakten. Die Hintergründe.* Freiburg et al.: Herder.

Foucault, Michel 1961. *Folie et déraison. Histoire de la folie à l'âge classique.* Paris: Gallimard.

Gladigow, Burkhard 2004. "Sequenzen von Riten und die Ordnung der Rituale". In: *Zoroastrian Rituals in Context*, Stausberg, Michael (ed.). Leiden & Boston: Brill, 57–76.

Grass, Günter 1997. "Die Literatur verkuppelt uns und macht uns zu Mittätern". In: *Frankfurter Rundschau*, 20/Oct/1997.
Grimes, Ronald L. 1988. "Infelicitous Performances and Ritual Criticism". *Semeia* 43: 103–122.
Güntner, Joachim 1999. "Ein Ritter ohne Preisgeld. Gibt Peter Handke den Büchner-Preis zurück?" In: *Neue Züricher Zeitung*, 09/Apr/1999.
Hartwig, Ina 2002. "Lieber Herr König". In: *Frankfurter Rundschau*, 16/Oct/2002.
Hjärne, Harald 1974. "Laudatio auf Carl Spitteler". In: *Nobelpreis für Literatur* 1917/1919/1920. Zürich: Coron Verlag, 15–20.
Hondrich, Karl Otto 2002. "Die Lust am Skandal". In: *Enthüllung und Entrüstung. Eine Phänomenologie des politischen Skandals*, Hondrich, Karl Otto (ed.). Frankfurt: Suhrkamp, 24–37.
Jäger, Ludwig 1996. "Editorial". *Sprache und Literatur* 77: 1–3.
—— 1998. *Seitenwechsel. Der Fall Schneider/Schwerte und die Diskretion der Germanistik*. München: Wilhelm Fink Verlag.
König, Helmut (ed.) 1998. *Der Fall Schwerte im Kontext*. Opladen & Wiesbaden: Westdeutscher Verlag.
Luhmann, Niklas 1971. "Öffentliche Meinung". In: *Politische Planung. Aufsätze zur Soziologie von Politik und Verwaltung*, Luhmann, Niklas (ed.). Opladen: Westdeutscher Verlag, 9–34.
Ohmer, Bernadette 2004. "Interview mit Andreas Maier vom 13.06.2003". In: *Geschichte und Funktion des aspekte-Literaturpreises*, Ohmer, Bernadette (ed.). University of Heidelberg: unpublished thesis.
Österling, Anders 1946. "Verleihungsrede bei der Überreichung des Nobelpreises für Literatur an Hermann Hesse am 10. Dezember". In: *Nobelpreis für Literatur* 1945/1946/1947, Zürich: Coron Verlag, 15–22.
Pasternak, Boris L. 1981. *Perepiska s Ol'goj Frejdenberg*. New York: Harcourt Brace Jovanovich Inc. (German translation used: *Briefwechsel 1910–1954*. Frankfurt: S. Fischer, 1986).
Rich, Adrienne 1997. "Why I refused the National Medal for the Arts". In: Los Angeles Times Book Section, 03/Aug/1997. URL: http://www.barclayagency.com/richwhv.html (date of last access 1/6/2004).
Rusinek, Bernd A. 1998. "Schwerte/Schneider: Die Karriere eines Spagatakteurs 1936–1995". In: *Der Fall Schwerte im Kontext*, König, Helmut (ed.). Opladen & Wiesbaden: Westdeutscher Verlag, 14–47.
Sartre, Jean-Paul 1964. *Les Mots*. Paris: Gallimard (English translation used: *The Words*. Trans. Bernard Frechtman. New York: George Braziller, 1964).
Schirrmeister, Albert 2003. *Triumph des Dichters. Gekrönte Intellektuelle im 16. Jahrhundert*. Köln & Weimar & Wien: Böhlau Verlag.
Stagl, Justin 2001. "Orden und Ehrenzeichen. Zur Soziologie des Auszeichungswesens". In: *Sinngeneratoren. Fremd- und Selbstthematisierung in soziologisch-historischer Perspektive*, Bohn, Cornelia & Herbert Willems (ed.). Konstanz: Universitätsverlag Konstanz, 177–196.
Stähli, Regula 2003. "Elfriede Jelinek: Chronik von Leben und Werk". In: *Programmheft Elfriede Jelinek: Das Werk. Burgtheater im Akademietheater Spielzeit 2002/2003*, Lux, Joachim & Gwendolyne Melchinger (ed.). Wien: Burgtheater GesmbH, 48–63.
Vogt, Ludgera 1997. *Zur Logik der Ehre in der Gegenwartsgesellschaft. Differenzierung Macht Integration*. Frankfurt: Suhrkamp.
—— 1998. "Aktivposten mit Dauerauftrag. Die Inszenierung von Werten—eine Fallstudie zur Alltagspraxis staatlicher Auszeichnungen". In: *Inszenierungsgesellschaft. Ein einführendes Handbuch*, Willems, Herbert & Martin Jurga (ed.). Opladen & Wiesbaden: Westdeutscher Verlag, 253–271.
Winch, Peter 1958. *The Idea of a Social Science*. London: Routledge & Kegan Paul Ltd.
Zimmermann, Alexandra 1993. *Von der Kunst des Lobens. Eine Analyse der Textsorte Laudatio*. München: iudicium.

DEALING WITH DEVIATIONS IN THE PERFORMANCE OF MASONIC RITUALS

Jan A.M. Snoek

To err is human. Therefore, the question is not whether deviations in the performance of rituals occur, but how they are dealt with. In most cases, deviations in the performance of masonic rituals will not result in a failed ritual. But there are many different strategies to prevent undesired escalation, resulting in a real failure. Since masonic Grand Lodges are autonomous and independent, and since roughly speaking each country has its own Grand Lodge, some of which are several hundred years old, each developed in the course of time its own style, also in respect to dealing with deviations. Little is documented about such issues, but being a mason myself now for over 30 years, I can report also from my own experience. What follows claims to be no more than a collection of examples, which could be extended *ad libitum*. I have grouped them under the headings 'Prevention of deviations', 'Correction of deviations', 'Acceptation of deviations at the level of the participants', 'Acceptation of deviations at an official level', 'What if there is something wrong with the candidate?', and 'Abolishing rituals, degrees or Rites'.

1. *The author's position*

Having specialised as a scholar in the research of masonic rituals, while being a mason myself, has forced me over the last two decades to constantly reflect conscientiously about my position as an outsider, yet also insider. To discuss such issues, the emic/etic-distinction, introduced by Harris in 1968, is useful. He defines these terms as follows:

> Emic statements refer to logico-empirical systems whose phenomenal distinctions or 'things' are built up out of contrasts and discriminations significant, meaningful, real, accurate or in some other fashion regarded as appropriate by the actors themselves (Harris 1968: 571).
>
> Etic statements depend upon phenomenal distinctions judged appropriate by the community of scientific observers (Harris 1968: 575).

It follows, then, that 'emic' and 'etic' are adjectives to qualify statements, formulated by someone in order to communicate with someone else.

Emic statements, then, are formulated by an insider in order to communicate with other insiders, whereas etic statements are formulated by a scholar in order to communicate with other scholars. I have therefore concluded elsewhere, that "an emic scholarly approach is a *contradictio in terminis*. Scholarly discourse is always etic and should therefore be conducted in etic terms" (Snoek 1987: 7). A scholar, thus, is in his scholarly work always obliged to translate emic statements into etic ones, no matter whether these emic statements are uttered by others, or thought out by himself. That is part and parcel of our profession. Since this article intends to be a scholarly one, I consciously choose an etic—that is, scholarly—position, rather than an emic—that is, insider—one. I am not writing here as a mason to other masons, but as a scholar to other scholars. Therefore, when I report about my own experiences as a mason, I do this as if I, a scholar, would have interviewed me, as a mason. For example, when I report on a change in a ritual which I once introduced myself, the fact alone that I do report this betrays an etic position: as a mason amongst masons, I would not normally disclose this, since among masons, one is generally not supposed to change the rituals: they are regarded to have "always been so", although it is well known, that this is in fact not the case.

However, being a mason, I can report what I know that masons, at an emic level, regard as ritual failures, mistakes or errors. Such a judgment is possible only at an emic level; from an etic perspective, one can only observe deviations, either between script and performance, or between different performances. And, as we shall see, such deviations need not be experienced, at an emic level, as failures.

2. *Prevention of deviations*

The performance of initiation rituals forms the heart of Freemasonry. Indeed, whatever Freemasons may further do in their lodges (and that differs from country to country and sometimes even from lodge to lodge), without these rituals it could not be considered Freemasonry. It is through these rituals that candidates become members, and members get a higher status. There is by definition no official interpretation of the meaning of these rituals, but the members are encouraged to seek for an interpretation which is meaningful to them personally. In the course of time, the form of these rituals has changed in different ways in different countries, resulting in different systems, generally referred to as Rites.

The Grand Lodges which follow the Swedish Rite have completely fixed the text to be spoken during the performance of the rituals, and also the action is prescribed in much detail. In the lodges belonging to these Grand Lodges, a copy of the ritual script is available for each functionary in the lodge, and everyone reads his text completely: nothing is spoken by heart. Even if the Master of the lodge leaves his place in order to perform some action for which he has to have his hands free, the Master of Ceremonies or someone else holds the text before him, so that he can still read it. Thus it is guaranteed in principle that the text spoken is exactly that which is prescribed. If someone should nevertheless deviate from it, he can be blamed with doing so intentionally. However, since these scripts are kept in the lodge, and no individual Brother is allowed to take a copy home, while furthermore no-one is urged to learn any part of the text by heart, I doubt that anyone would notice minor deviations.

Lodges following the English tradition, on the other hand, will generally forbid the presence of any booklet with the text of the ritual during its performance: everything is done by heart. There does not exist an officially sanctioned version of the text on paper, firstly because the traditional oath forbids writing the text down (Snoek 1998 [= Snoek 2003a]), and secondly there is the idea that no written text can fully describe the ritual, wherefore one can learn the true ritual only by copying the observed praxis (mimesis). Of course there do exist printed texts of the rituals, which are used to learn the text from, but they are not allowed to be used during a ritual performance. Obviously, that approach is prone to error. In order to reduce the chance of errors, there is typically not only an official lodge meeting once a month, but also a monthly 'Lodge of Instruction' when the ritual which is to be performed the next time is rehearsed under the guidance of an old experienced member until everyone knows exactly what to say and do.

Another mechanism to forestall errors is that in this system, the officers progress through the offices. That means that once one is elected to the function of Tyler (the guard, keeping watch outside the lodge room before its door), one knows that one will have the function of Inner Guard the next year, after which follow the functions of Junior Deacon, Senior Deacon, Junior Warden, Senior Warden, Master of the Lodge and Immediate Past Master. After that, one can be elected to such functions as Master of Ceremonies, Secretary or Treasurer. Generally speaking, one can say that the functions one performs in succession are increasingly more demanding, especially with respect to ritual performance. Thus one is gradually trained over a number of years, during which one is increasingly familiarised with the rituals, before one has to perform as Master of the Lodge—definitely the most demanding function.

Also, if the Master—especially if he was installed only recently—still feels unsure about his mastering of some of the larger charges, he can delegate most of these to other members, either Past Masters (who will still know those texts) or in particular young members who are eager to show their quality in such tasks.

In the United States of America, the high degrees (that is, the degrees 4 to 33) of the Ancient and Accepted Scottish Rite have since the second half of the 19th century been performed on stage, with the (large numbers of) candidates just watching the performances (e.g. Brockman 1994 and Hill 1994). Once this step was made, a logical second one was to use members with professional or amateur experience in acting as performers in these rituals. Although these performers are not professionally performing these rituals (i.e., they are not paid to do so), they do use their trained skills in these activities, which to some extent also decreases the chance of errors.

3. *Correction of deviations*

I already mentioned the measures which lodges—following the English system where texts of the rituals are banned from the lodge room during their performance—take to prevent deviations. If, during the performance, something nevertheless goes wrong, there are two members who will normally try to make corrections. The first one is the Immediate Past Master (i.e. he who was the Master of the lodge during the preceding year), who still knows the text of the rituals quite well by heart, often better than the current Master. The Immediate Past Master sits directly besides the reigning Master, and thus can prompt the latter without significantly disturbing the performance. The second person who can make corrections—not only in Anglo-Saxon lodges—is the Master of Ceremonies (always also a Past Master). His constant duty is to see that all goes well, and if not, to make corrections as he judges necessary. Obviously, both the Immediate Past Master and the Master of Ceremonies will always weigh whether it is worth making a correction, or whether it would disturb the ritual progress more than improve it.

Of course, a functionary can sometimes correct a mistake himself when he realizes he has made one. For example, in the Dutch or French traditions, if a Master becomes aware that a few minutes ago he had turned two pages of his text instead of one, and as a result has skipped a complete section of the ritual, he may insert that section at a later moment, if he judges that to be better than interrupting the ritual in order to go back to where the omission began.

4. *Acceptation of deviations at the level of the participants*

Generally, there is a great tendency to accept errors which are obviously made unintentionally. However, often it is only the one who made such a mistake who is aware of the fact; most others do not even notice that it has happened. This is the result of the fact that it is generally regarded more important to go on with the performance than to disturb it in order to make some clumsy correction. The candidate who is initiated does not know the ritual anyway, so he will hardly ever notice a mistake, as long as the performers behave as if what they do is as it should be done. And the impression the ritual makes on the candidate is regarded more important than anything else. Often, a Master will succeed in performing the ritual in such a way that hardly anyone will notice that he made an error. In such a case, when he afterwards tells the others that he is aware of having made this error, the others will usually compliment him on having done so in such a way that they did not notice.

Another situation occurs when one has the possibility of correcting or preventing a deviation, but decides—for example for the sake of the quality of the performance—not to do so, thus deviating intentionally from the script. While I was acting as Master of Ceremonies, I once saw that during the ritual opening of the lodge, the Master opened the Bible at the wrong place. I could have waited until a suitable moment and then walked up to the Bible and turned it to the right place, but on that occasion I decided that the correction would disturb the performance more than it was worth. On another occasion, while inspecting the lodge room immediately before the start of the ceremony, I discovered that a certain document which, according to the script of the ritual, should be handed out to the candidate, was not available. I discussed the situation with the Master and the Immediate Past Master, and we decided that we would just skip this rite. The alternative would have been that one of us would have gone home, fetched his own copy, made a photocopy of it, and brought that to the lodge in order to be handed to the candidate. However, that would have considerably delayed the start of the ceremony, so that it would have ended later and more Brethren would probably not have stayed for the ritual meal which followed the main part of the ritual. We decided that skipping the rite of handing out this document was in this case the lesser evil. Probably no one noticed the deviation, and if they did, they did not complain.

There are also cases where the deviation is apparently experienced as better than the usual practice. Once, while visiting another lodge many years ago, I saw that the Master of Ceremonies there made a particular gesture at a certain point, that was not in the script, but which I found at once highly attractive. Since I was at that time the Master of Ceremonies in my own lodge, I introduced it there the very next time, without giving notice in advance. Hardly anyone reacted afterwards, and the few Brethren who did were all quite positive. So I kept doing it as long as I held this function. Then, my successor followed in my footsteps, continuing the practice without any comment. And even today it is done that way. I once overheard one Brother asking another about the age of this custom, to which he received the answer that it had always been done that way in this lodge (which was founded in 1757!). This is a nice example of the invention of tradition (Hobsbawm & Ranger 1983), I think.

Not always are deviations accepted. I moved to Germany six years ago, and was elected Master of Ceremonies in a Heidelberg lodge three years later. Having internalised the Dutch ritual practice, as customary for my lodge in Leyden (The Netherlands), I at first had difficulty in performing my function in the Heidelberg lodge the way the Brethren there expected me to do. In the late 19th and early 20th century—as the result of theosophical influence—it became usual in many Grand Lodges, including both the German and the Dutch ones, for everyone in the lodge room to always walk around the centre in one direction only, viz. with the sun (to the right). In the 1970s and 1980s, many Dutch lodges—including my lodge in Leyden—recognized that in the 18th and most of the 19th century, there was no inhibition against walking counter to the sun (to the left), on the contrary: the alteration of the direction in which perambulations of the lodge were made was rediscovered to point to the way one walks through the traditional form of a labyrinth (a so called Trojan castle) (e.g. Pott 1984: 63–65), a form which has a high symbolic content. So, now even the Master of Ceremonies was supposed always to take the shortest route, in order not to unnecessarily disturb the flow of the performance. That was how I was trained. Even though I tried to behave as the German Brethren expected me to, I frequently made unintentional errors, especially on the first few occasions that I occupied the function. There were numerous vociferous complaints from the Brethren, so I tried even harder to do as they wished. And when I succeeded, I was praised by the same Brethren who had complained.

Also intentional deviations are not always accepted. One example is the occasion when a Brother, aspiring to be elected as the next Master of my lodge, was offered the opportunity to exercise that function during one ceremony in order to show if he was capable to do so. He used the opportunity to extensively present in those parts of the ritual where he was allowed to speak in his own words, his personal, somewhat unusual interpretation of the ritual. Now this runs counter to the basic principles of Freemasonry, which hold that no official interpretation of the ritual exists, and thus that interpretation cannot be part of the ritual. The result was that afterwards the Brethren openly criticized this behaviour and did not elect him as the next Master. Indeed, he never came to be elected as such. Clearly his performance failed to achieve his intentions.

5. *Acceptation of deviations at an official level*

Deviations are not only actually accepted, in some cases this is even officially declared. For example, the rituals published officially by the Dutch Grand Lodge[1] contain a preamble in which it is stated that "The following rites of the initiation[2] are declared binding:", after which follows a list of, for the first degree 9, for the second degree 8, and for the third degree 10 rites, each indicated by its shortest possible description. The whole list is in each case no more than about a dozen lines long. This, of course, implies that all the other rites described in the ritual are *not* obligatory! The laws of the Order furthermore state that

[1] I don't know when precisely these lists were introduced. The last edition I possess that does not yet have this preamble is from 1955, while the first edition I have that includes it is from 1961.

[2] In later versions: "of the ritual".

"in case of deviations [from this prescription], if any, the validity of a performed initiation [into the first degree], passing [to the second] or raising [to the third degree] nevertheless remains undisputed".[3] In other words, no matter how much one deviates from the prescribed form, the Order will always recognize the candidate in his new status once the ceremony has been performed. Here, as well as in other contexts, the rule is that one can be initiated in a particular degree only once in his life (Snoek 1987: 69, 133, 156f., 173, 177, 179f.). Even if someone gives up his membership of his Order, he remains initiated and, at least in some Grand Lodges, can occasionally be invited to participate in a ceremony (e.g. when a son or good friend is initiated). If he later decides to request re-admission into the Order, then—if that is granted—he is not initiated anew, but just inscribed as a member again.

6. *What if there is something wrong with the candidate?*

Candidates for initiation must generally fulfil certain requirements (Snoek 1987: 156f., 173). That is not different in Freemasonry. In the first printed version of the laws for the first Grand Lodge, Anderson's *Constitutions* of 1723, we read for example:

> The Persons admitted Members of a *Lodge* must be good and true Men, free-born, and of mature and discreet Age, no Bondmen, no Women, no immoral or scandalous Men, but of good Report. [And:]
> ... no Master should take an Apprentice, [...] unless he be a perfect Youth, having no Maim or Defect in his Body, that may render him uncapable of learning the Art, of serving his Master's Lord, and of being made a Brother, and then a Fellow-Craft in due time, [...] (Anderson 1723: 51).

These rules made sense, of course, as long as the Freemasons really worked freestone into sculptures. From the 18th century onwards, several of these rules were followed with diminishing strictness. For example, today it is absolutely acceptable for a blind candidate to be initiated, even though the light symbolism is extremely important in the rituals. Yet, some requirements will always remain, and problems may arise if the candidate does not meet them.

Probably the most extreme case is that when the candidate does not show up. I once came to a lodge meeting where two candidates

[3] Here too, I don't know precisely when this rule was introduced. My copy of 1952 does not contain it, while my copy of 1986 has it in Law of the Order I, Art. 18.

were planned to be initiated, but both were not there. One was ill, and the other had asked for some more time to decide if he wanted to be initiated into this degree. As a result, the whole initiation part of the ceremony was cancelled.

One of Anderson's criteria is that the candidate must be "of mature and discreet Age". As a rule, Grand Lodges require that candidates be at least 21 years old. However, probably all of them do grant dispensation if that is requested for a somewhat younger candidate. And if he is a 'Lewis', that is, a son of a Freemason, then he may often be initiated as soon as he is 18. In the 18th century, the majority of the members of my lodge in Leyden were students, often from abroad. Hardly anyone of them was 21 when initiated. Consequently, this lodge used to request and to pay for dispensation to initiate candidates younger than 21 during the whole next year, at the same time when the yearly subscriptions to the Grand Lodge were paid.

Another requirement which Anderson formulates is that the candidate be "no Women". Yet, today there are numerous mixed and female masonic Orders. The first lady who is supposed to have been initiated into Freemasonry was Elizabeth St. Leger (1693–1773). In 1713 she married Richard Aldworth, and thus is commonly known as the Hon. Mrs. Aldworth. Before her marriage, she lived at the castle of her father, Arthur St. Leger, first Viscount Doneraile of Doneraile Court, County Cork, Ireland. Her father held lodge in his manor from time to time, with his sons and some friends. On one of these occasions, Elizabeth hid herself in a place that gave her a good view of what happened without being seen. Once the lodge meeting was over, she tried to get away, but stumbled and fell, which made a noise that the men heard. They caught her and deliberated as to what to do with her. Basically there were only two options: to kill her or to make her swear to keep secret what she had seen and heard. Eventually they decided for the last option, and thus made her take the traditional masonic oath, which is how she became a Freemason. Although the description of how she got initiated was only published, with the authority of the family, in 1811, the claim that she was initiated is generally believed to be correct. There also exist other versions of this story, which, however, are generally regarded as less reliable.[4] Surely, her sex was a grave deviation of the tradition.

[4] The full report of 1811, as well as two other versions, are quoted in Mackey 1966, sub Aldworth, 49–50. For a more romantic version of the story see Mellor 1982: 13–28 [= Mellor 1985: 1–13].

Interestingly, remarkably similar stories occur in two so-called early French exposures: *La Franc-Maçonne*[5] and *Les Francs-Maçons Ecrasés*[6] (although the name of Lady Aldworth is not mentioned there) at the time that in France the first so-called adoption lodges developed, i.e. lodges, adopted by a male lodge, in which women were initiated by a team of officers composed of women and men. The rituals of the adoption lodges were different from those in use in the male lodges, however, and the initiated women were not allowed entrance into the male lodges, whereas the men had free access to the adoption lodges. Although the 'Grand Orient de France' regularised the adoption lodges in 1774, the English Grand Lodges always forbade its lodges from having adoption lodges.

Only at the end of the 19th century were a few women initiated in male lodges using the male rituals. The most influential case is that of Maria Deraismes. Refused by the 'Grand Orient de France', she asked the lodge 'Les Libres Penseurs' to initiate her. In May 1881, 'Les Libres Penseurs', founded only 13/8/1880, decided that it wanted to initiate women. It asked permission to do so from the 'Grande Loge Symbolique Ecossaise', to which it belonged. On 12/9/1881, that permission was refused. On 28/9/1881 'Les Libres Penseurs' asked permission to withdraw from the 'Grande Loge Symbolique Ecossaise', which was granted 9/1/1882. On 25/11/1881 Maria Deraismes was proposed as a Candidate by seven Master-Masons of 'Les Libres Penseurs', voted upon, and accepted. On 14/1/1882 'Les Libres Penseurs' then initiated Maria Deraismes (first degree only), while being an unattached lodge ('loge sauvage'). However, finding itself completely isolated, 'Les Libres Penseurs' decided to return to its original Grand Lodge: on 7/8/1882, the lodge was re-integrated into the 'Grande Loge Symbolique Ecossaise', without Maria Deraismes, and on promising not to initiate any further women. Thus, this experiment too could have been regarded a failure, had not in 1893, Georges Martin, a member of the lodge 'La Jérusalem Ecossaise' of the 'Grande Loge Symbolique Ecossaise', together with Maria Deraismes, created the first mixed masonic Order, working with the male rituals. In a few decades, this Order developed into a world-wide organization, and it is still the largest mixed Order in existence. Although nothing proves that she ever received the 2nd

[5] Brussels 1744: 29ff. English translation in Carr 1971: 131ff.

[6] Amsterdam 1747: xxvii–xxviii. Regrettably, this passage is skipped in Carr 1971.

and 3rd degree herself, Maria Deraismes conferred these degrees once 'Le Droit Humain' was founded.[7]

One may contemplate what went wrong here in who's perspective. In the view of the existing male Freemasonry, the sex of the candidate Maria Deraismes was surely an unacceptable deviation in the performance of her initiation ceremony. The other way round, the fact that 'Les Libres Penseurs' returned to its Grand Lodge without Maria Deraismes, and on promising not to initiate any further women, can hardly be interpreted otherwise than that what both the members of that lodge and Maria Deraismes had hoped to accomplish with her initiation had failed.

Not only the physical properties of a candidate must satisfy certain conditions, the ritual procedure also requires the cooperation of the candidate on certain issues. Sometimes the candidate concerned is, however, incapable or unwilling to do so. An interesting example occurred in the 1920s in the British federation of the mixed Order 'Le Droit Humain'.[8] In order to understand what happened here, one has to know that in the masonic tradition, a candidate for initiation into the first degree is requested to hand over all his 'metals', which is normally interpreted to refer to his money and his jewels. It is taken to be a symbol, indicating the death of the candidate as a 'profane' person; later during the ceremony, he will be reborn as a Freemason. Although it is nowhere written, it seems to be a very old tradition that one's wedding ring is exempted from this directive, on the one hand because it is not seen as a material possession, and on the other hand quite simply because wedding rings are often difficult to remove. For Annie Besant, however, being at that time not only the Grand Master of the British Federation of 'Le Droit Humain', but also a serious theosophist, such symbolism was charged with magic. Therefore, she would prefer such directions to be taken literally. This is for example seen when she "... expressed it as her personal opinion that a candidate having no legs wearing artificial ones containing metal, cannot be admitted if wearing them during initiation ...".[9] That, indeed, was her personal

[7] Rognon 1994: 51; Benchetrit & Louart 1994: 25–30; Hivert-Messaca & Hivert-Messaca 1997: 221–253; Jupeau-Réquillard 2000: 122–125; Prat et al. 2003: 15–24.

[8] All documents referred to concerning this case are in the archive of the 'Human Duty Lodge' within the archives of the British Federation of 'Le Droit Humain'. I thank the Most Puissant Grand Commander, Brian Roberts, for kindly giving me access to that archive. For full quotes of the texts concerning this case, see the appendix.

[9] *Draft Minutes of the 31st Meeting of the Lodge of Installed Masters, Human Duty, No. 6,*

opinion. However, apparently she had turned it into a rule in a letter of 1921, but then overruled that rule herself in one particular case in 1926. What is interesting here is that the candidate concerned *refused* to remove the ring, rather than that she physically could not remove it. Counter to what might seem logical, taking a principle stand like that could impress Annie Besant. Yet in the eyes of others, this behaviour of hers might indeed seem absolutely arbitrary. And this was dangerous: soon a substantial number of members left the Order, precisely because of the autocratic and arbitrary way in which she ruled it. It is not surprising, therefore, that a vote was taken on January 17th, 1927, that can only be interpreted as a clear vote of no-confidence against Annie Besant, based on the Wedding Ring case. In order to settle the matter, a meeting took place with Annie Besant on July 18th, which seems to have restored the peace between her and the Order. Regrettably, this is about where the archives I found on this case stop, so I did not find out what the final decision was concerning the question whether this woman had to be re-initiated, so I am not sure if the initiation of this woman, wearing her wedding ring during her initiation, failed or not (i.e. if her initiation eventually was declared invalid). But it certainly came close to a failure. It also came close to a failure for Annie Besant, who almost lost control of her Order.

In the appendix, I present the material which I found on this case in full, because it is quite unusual to see such a problem discussed so explicitly, and also because the sources, though printed, are not readily available to most theoreticians of rituals.

7. *Abolishing rituals, degrees or Rites*

So far we have examined examples of deviations in performances in masonic rituals. There are, however, also more dramatic cases when rituals (in the sense of prescripts), degrees, or even whole Rites are abolished or rejected. The Netherlands are a nice example of the first two possibilities, while Germany and France have some famous cases of the last kind.

---

held on 20th June, 1927, p. 3, as corrected in the *Draft Minutes of the 32nd Meeting... held on 3rd October, 1927*, p. 2. This statement shows that what Annie Besant found unacceptable about a candidate wearing a wedding ring was not that it symbolises a bond other than the one to be created during the initiation, but genuinely that it is made of metal.

All efforts to come to standardised rituals for the 'blue' degrees (Entered Apprentice, Fellow Craft, and Master Mason) for the Dutch Grand Lodge in the 18th century failed. It was only in 1820 that the first official rituals could be printed (Snoek 1997). Under Prince Frederik as Grand Master from 1816 to 1881 (e.g. Van Peype 1997), the situation remained stable until 1865, when new rituals were adopted. However, these new rituals were not to the liking of all. In 1878, Brother A.S. Carpentier Alting published his own ones. They must have been received rather positively, since a second edition was still published c. 1910. The Board of Grand Officers apparently regarded this phenomenon also sufficiently significant to react. They appointed a committee which had to come up with proposals for new official rituals, and appointed Carpentier Alting as its secretary. The proposal was published in 1880, but rejected by the Grand East (the yearly meeting of representatives of all the lodges of the Grand Lodge). The Board of Grand Officers now decided to come up with their own proposal. In 1901 they proposed to drop the three degree system and replace it by only one degree. The ritual for that one degree was based on what they then thought to have been the ritual of the Mithras mysteries in the Roman times. Again the Grand East rejected the proposal, and all the Grand Officers stepped down. Eventually, a new proposal by the Board of Grand Officers in 1928/29 was accepted. But such rejection of proposed rituals for a masonic Order is in fact quite normal.

Dutch freemasonry also offers an interesting example of a case of dropped degrees (Snoek 1996). After several failed efforts to standardize the rituals of the so called 'higher' degrees during the 18th century, the French occupation of the Netherlands and the threat of a take-over of Dutch freemasonry by the French 'Grand Orient', brought success in 1803. The 'Order of the High Degrees' was founded, and its Rite and rituals established at the same time. The Rite would exist of four degrees (above the 'blue' ones) only, viz. (4) Selected Master (Maître Elu), (5) Scots Master or Knight of St. Andrew, (6) Knight of the Sword and the East, and (7) Sovereign Prince of the Rosy Cross (Rose Croix). Because of the explicitly Christian character of the last degree, it was decided that it would be forbidden to confer this degree other than 'by communication'. That is: it was not allowed to perform its ritual, although that ritual was established to the same extent as those of the other three degrees. This interdiction lasted only three years: in 1806 the chapters of the Order were allowed to decide themselves if they wanted to confer this degree ritually or 'by communication'.

In less than 50 years, however, the feelings with respect to the degrees of this order completely reversed, and thus in 1854 it was decided that from now on, the Rose Croix degree *had to* be conferred ritually, while the 'Intermediate Degrees' were only allowed to be conferred by communication! For over a century, the Brothers who possessed these 'Intermediate Degrees' hardly knew their names, so, effectively, this decision abolished them.

The French 'Rite Ecossais philosophique' is a double example, changing several times the degrees which composed it from 1774 to the middle of the 19th century, when the Rite was abolished out of lack of interest.[10] All in all, there seem to have been no less than five different, successive lists of degrees composing the Rite. On several occasions, the transition from the older to the newly adopted list involved dropping one or more degrees. For example, in 1776 the degree of 'Chevalier Maçon dit de l'Orient' was replaced by two degrees: the 'Rose-Croix' and the Freemasons "being so fortunate as to be decorated with the three colours" or 'Académie des Vrais Maçons'. And in 1815, when the third system was replaced by the fourth, the 'Rose-Croix', 'Chevalier du Phoenix', and 'Sage Vrai Maçon' disappeared. When finally in 1843 the last version of the Rite is reported, no less than four degrees of the previous version had gone: 'Maître Parfait', 'Chevalier Elu Philosophe', 'Grand Ecossais', and 'Chevalier de l'Anneau Lumineux'. The Rite was a highly exotic one, comprising degrees which reenacted themes from classical mythology, as well as the extremely alchemical 'Académie des Vrais Maçons'. The extreme erudition required from its candidates made it unsuitable for the later 19th century. It seems to have just faded out between 1844 and 1849.

But a Rite can also be actively killed. Some famous examples are to be found in Germany. There, the Order of the Strict Observance, founded in 1751 by Karl Gotthelf, Reichsherr von Hund und Altengrotkau (1722–1776), had grown in about thirty years to be the single largest masonic Order in Europe, having ca. 10,000 members of its 'blue' lodges and ca. 1,375 in its higher degrees. Most German lodges belonged to it. In 1772, Jean-Baptiste Willermoz had introduced the Strict Observance in France, but he grew increasingly unhappy with the Rite. This consisted, since it had merged with Starck's Clerics, of

[10] See for this example Snoek 2003b, esp. 65–71 ("Appendix II: The development of the Rite Ecossais philosophique").

seven degrees; after the usual three 'blue' ones came (4) Scots Master, (5) Novice, (6) Knight (*Eques*), and (7) *Eques professus*. The problem for Willermoz in France was that the Rite claimed to be directly descended from the Knight Templars. Those were in the past abolished by the French king, who had then also confiscated their possessions. In other words: whoever claimed in France to be the legal descendant of this Order would give the French king the uneasy feeling that a claim on these possessions might sooner or later come. Since the relation between the king and freemasonry had been an ambivalent one at best in France, Willermoz had no interest in challenging his king in this way. Furthermore, he was a Martinist. So he reformed the Strict Observance into a new system: his Rectified Scottish Rite, which did not claim a relation with the historical Knight Templars, and which was thoroughly Martinist. In 1782, at the Convent of Wilhelmsbad, he succeeded in convincing the leaders of the Strict Observance to abolish their Order, and to offer its lodges to adopt the Rectified Scottish Rite. Some did, others did not. Many German masons were not attracted by the French Christian mysticism of the Martinist Rite.

In fact, this move promoted a drift of members to another young German masonic Order: the Illuminati of Bavaria, founded in 1776 by Adam Weishaupt (1748–1830). In 1780, the experienced freemason Adolph Freiherr von Knigge (1752–1795) had joined that Order and created a new system of high degrees for it, one of the most complex masonic Rites ever constructed. In 1782, one of those who moved from the Strict Observance to the Illuminati was Johann Joachim Christoph Bode (1730–1793). He promoted the Order in all the German speaking countries and recruited in a short time a large amount of new members, including Goethe, Herder, and Nicolai. In fact, the Order attracted actively and intentionally only the political and cultural elite, but of those it soon incorporated most. Thus it was unavoidable that in a particular political conflict, there would be Illuminati on both sides. The conflict arose when, after the death of the Kurfürst Max Joseph of Bavaria, this state was inherited by Karl Theodor, Kurfürst of the Palatinate. Karl Theodor had just built a new palace in Mannheim, and did not want to move to Munich, the capital of Bavaria. Emperor Joseph II of Austria, on the other hand, was quite interested in Bavaria. He was willing to exchange it for the Austrian Netherlands (Belgium) plus an interesting sum of money. Two people, however, did not like this idea: the widow of Max Joseph (who wanted Bavaria to remain German) and the future successor of Karl Theodor (who wanted Bavaria for himself). As it happened, it was some Illuminati who, not as such but as individuals, asked Prussia to intervene and to prevent Austria from taking possession of Bavaria, which happened. Obviously Karl Theodor was not pleased. Despite the fact that other Illuminati had supported the exchange, he now punished those who had worked against him by forbidding the Order in Bavaria. This happened in 1784. The next year the Order was officially abolished in all of Germany. So here we have a second example of a flourishing Order which was abolished as a result of active intervention, this time not from inside, but from outside. Interestingly, however, the Illuminati in fact continued after 1785! Bode became the new leader of the Order. First priority was a reform of the system. When Bode died in 1793, Reinhold took over. The Order was now re-christened the 'Bund des Einverständnisses'. Together with Schröder, Herder, Goethe, Hufeland and others, Reinhold continued the reform-project, which eventually resulted in the famous Schröder Ritual of 1801, which was of great influence on German freemasonry. Schröder's 'Engbund', which continued until 1868, can be regarded as the last continuation of the original Order of the Bavarian Illuminati.[11]

8. *Summary*

Deviations in the performance of masonic rituals do occur. Different traditions have different strategies to prevent them as far as possible, and also have different ways of correcting them if necessary, but there is a high level of acceptance of deviations, both by participants and by the official masonic institutions (Grand Lodges), though not everything is accepted. Rarely, however, will mere deviations be allowed to escalate into the failure of the ritual. What seems a more problematic issue are candidates who do not satisfy the official requirements. Here too there is some tolerance, but the masonic world remains divided over, for example, the acceptability of initiating women.

Furthermore, rituals can be replaced by new ones (whereby the old ones become automatically abolished), but also newly designed rituals are often rejected. Which one of the two rivalling rituals wins or loses depends on which one the members feel satisfies their needs

[11] On this example see: Bernheim 1998; Schüttler 1997; Te Lindert 1998.

and those of potential members best. The same mechanism also holds for rivalling degrees within a Rite. Eventually, even a whole Rite can become outdated, loosing it from others which are better adapted to the needs of their time. Interesting to see is the case of the Order of the Illuminati of Bavaria, which was officially abolished under external pressure, but managed nevertheless to survive. Clearly, this product was not yet outdated.

Appendix: texts concerning the 'wedding ring case'

R[ight] W[orshipful] Brother John B. Philipp, 30° ([from lodge] No. 38), referring to paragraph 2 of the Report of the Board of General Purposes adopted at the 26th meeting, with which the National Consistory had (P.F.29) indicated its concurrence, said he was informed that a departure from the strict observance in regard to the divestiture of m[etals] and v[aluables], in the preparation of a candidate for initiation, had occurred in circumstances which were felt by some R[ight] W[orshipful] B[rethren] to call for enquiry; according to his information a candidate, who had already been refused initiation because she was unable or unwilling to remove her wedding ring, had since been initiated in the same lodge, the M[ost] P[uissant] G[rand] C[ommander] [i.e. Annie Besant] (a member) having taken the Chair and performed the ceremony, without her (the candidate's) having strictly fulfilled the requirements. The R[ight] W[orshipful] Brother, on being pressed, said that he was given to understand that the incident had occurred in lodge No. 760. The R[ight] W[orshipful] Brother therefore moved, and the R[ight] W[orshipful] Secretary seconded "that it be referred to the Board of General Purposes to consider and report on the alleged departure from a ruling of the Lodge, which is in question." The Deputy Chairman of the National Consistory (R[ight] W[orshipful] Brother Besant-Scott, 33°, M.S.C. &c. &c.), a Past Master of the lodge in question, who was present on the occasion mentioned, said that the M[ost] P[uissant] G[rand] C[ommander] was, she considered, entitled in virtue of her inherent powers to act as she had and, for reasons which seemed to her sufficient, to override on occasion her own previous decrees in the matter. The President of the Board of General Purposes (R[ight] W[orshipful] Brother Lockwood, 32°) said that she considered that investigation of the incident was desirable, as the Lodge ought to know in what manner and circumstances such departures from custom and rule were to be held allowable; part of the M[ost] P[uissant] G[rand] C[ommander]'s letter containing her ruling on the matter (dated 10th August, 1921; K.B. 33) was read. R[ight] W[orshipful] Brother Blackmore, 31° ([a member of the lodges] Nos. 24, 728, and 817) question[s] the propriety of this Lodge's questioning the actions of its R[ight] W[orshipful] M[aster] [i.e. Annie Besant again!], the M[ost] P[uissant] G[rand] C[ommander]. The position of other private lodges in such cases was the subject of enquiry and discussion on the part of several R[ight] W[orshipful] B[rethren]; an amendment directing the Board to give definite instructions as to the method of appeal in such cases was moved by R[ight] W[orshipful] Brother Clifford, 30° ([from lodge] No. 706), but after discussion was withdrawn; a closuring amendment "to adjourn discussion *sine die*" was ruled to be out of order. After considerable debate the motion before the Lodge was put, and was carried by a considerable majority.[12]

In accord with the instructions of the L[odge of] I[nstalled] M[asters] the Board enquired into the case of the initiation of a Candidate while still wearing her wedding ring. The R[ight] W[orshipful] M[aster] of the Lodge in question was invited to attend and give an account of what took place. It appears that on the first occasion when the Candidate refused to remove the ring, the ceremony did not take place. Later the M[ost] P[uissant] G[rand] C[ommander] was approached, and at first "saw no reason why the usual conditions should be dispensed with." However, on being approached, she decided to take the ceremony herself, that being the only way in which the usual conditions could be dispensed with.

It would thus appear that in certain cases the M[ost] P[uissant] G[rand] C[ommander] is prepared to grant dispensation from the rule, in some circumstances, and under certain conditions, but that she alone has power to deal with such cases.

The Board wishes to point out that should any R[ight] W[orshipful] M[aster] wish to bring any such case before the M[ost] P[uissant] G[rand] C[ommander], he should send a full statement of the case to the Board of General Purposes, for initial consideration, when the further appropriate procedure through the Lodge of Installed Masters

---

[12] *Draft Minutes of the 28th Meeting of the Lodge of Installed Masters, Human Duty, No. 6, held on 4th October, 1926*, p. 2f.

and the National Consistory for approaching the M[ost] P[uissant] G[rand] C[ommander] will be followed.[13]

R[ight] W[orshipful] Bro[ther] Cohen proposed and R[ight] W[orshipful] Bro[ther] Meyer seconded, that all incidents in this case be sent to [the] M[ost] P[uissant] G[rand] C[ommander] as an appeal against the recommendation of the Board of General Purposes, Many R[ight] W[orshipful] B[rethren] affirming that the M[ost] P[uissant] G[rand] C[ommander] had already given a ruling on the matter of wearing the wedding ring at initiations, R[ight] W[orshipful] Bro[ther] Philipp proposed, and R[ight] W[orshipful] Bro[ther] Stanley Clarke seconded, an amendment that the Supreme Council be approached through the proper channels to give a ruling as to whether the removal of the wedding ring is (1) a landmark of Freemasonry, (2) a regulation of the Supreme Council or (3) a regulation of this Federation. After further discussion this amendment was carried and subsequently passed as a substantive motion.[14]

WEDDING RING. WITH regard to the removal of the wedding ring before initiation, the injunction of the M[ost] P[uissant] G[rand] C[ommander] is imperative that it must be removed. However, it appears that in certain cases the M[ost] P[uissant] G[rand] C[ommander] is prepared to grant dispensation from this rule, in some circumstances, and under certain conditions, but that she alone has power to deal with such cases. Should any R[ight] W[orshipful] M[aster] wish to bring any such case before the M[ost] P[uissant] G[rand] C[ommander], he should send a full statement of the case to the Board of General Purposes, for initial consideration, when the further appropriate procedure through the L[odge of] I[nstalled] M[asters] and the National Consistory for approaching the M[ost] P[uissant] G[rand] C[ommander] will be followed.
(*L[odge of] I[nstalled] M[asters]*, 21*st June*, 1926, *and* 17*th January*, 1927).[15]

---

[13] "Report of the Board of General Purposes" in the invitation for the 29th Meeting of the Lodge of Installed Masters, to be held January 17th, 1927.
[14] *Draft Minutes of the 29th Meeting... held on 17th January*, 1927, p. 2f.
[15] *Digest of Rulings [of the Lodge of Installed Masters Human Duty No. 6] To the 31st March, 1927.*

[S]he [i.e. Anny Besant] was not in any way laying down the law but in her opinion a blind candidate cannot be admitted as he is unable to fulfill his O[bligation] to answer signs. In reply to a request for further guidance, the R[ight] W[orshipful] Master [Annie Besant] expressed it as her personal opinion that a candidate having no legs wearing artificial ones containing metal, cannot be admitted if wearing them during initiation, nor can any paralysed person unable to make the signs from physical disability, but if able to make the signs intelligibly she considered he could be initiated.[16]

[S]he referred to the resolution passed by the Lodge on 17th January, 1927, to be sent through her to the Supreme Council with regard to the initiation of a candidate wearing a wedding ring. She expressed her willingness either to present this resolution herself or to allow it to be sent to the Supreme Council through any other channel, but she suggested in order to make it more intelligible that the following wording be substituted for that already passed.

"Since all m[etal] and v[aluable] articles must be removed before initiation, can a wedding ring be retained?"[17]

The Board finding it impossible to accept the suggested alteration in the form of the resolution regarding the removal of the wedding ring passed by the L[odge of] I[nstalled] M[asters] in January last, approached the M[ost] P[uissant] G[rand] C[ommander] asking her to meet certain members of the L[odge of] I[nstalled] M[asters] for consultation on the matter. The meeting took place on July 18th last, and the result will be communicated by the R[ight] W[orshipful] Deputy Master.[18]

The Report of the Board of General Purposes was then presented by the R[ight] W[orshipful] Deputy Master in the unavoidable absence, through illness, of R[ight] W[orshipful] Bro[ther] Lockwood, 32°, President of the Board.... He then asked the Secretary of the Board,

---

[16] *Draft Minutes of the 31st Meeting... held on 20th June, 1927*, p. 3, as corrected in the *Draft Minutes of the 32nd Meeting... held on 3rd October, 1927*, p. 2.

[17] *Draft Minutes of the 31st Meeting... held on 20th June, 1927*, p. 2/3, as corrected in the *Draft Minutes of the 32nd Meeting... held on 3rd October, 1927*, p. 1.

[18] "Report of the Board of General Purposes" in the invitation for the 32nd Meeting of the Lodge of Installed Masters, to be held October 3rd, 1927.

R[ight] W[orshipful] Bro[ther][19] Bird, 30°, to read the Minutes of the Board Meeting with regard to the report of the interview granted by the R[ight] W[orshipful] Master [Annie Besant] to some members of the Board. She read as follows: "The report was entirely satisfactory, the M[ost] P[uissant] G[rand] C[ommander] receiving the deputation with kindness and sympathy. She expressed herself in agreement with the Board as to the adherence to the points in her letter to the Order, and stated she would write another communication to be read at the Lodge of Installed Masters which she hoped would clarify the position."

R[ight] W[orshipful] Bro[ther] Fores, 18°, proposed, and R[ight] W[orshipful] Bro[ther] Stanly Clarke, 30°, seconded the adoption of the Report which was then passed unanimously.[20]

References

Anderson, James 1723. *The Constitutions of the Free-Masons*. London: Printed by William Hunter, for John Senex at the Globe, and John Hooke at the Flower-de-luce over-against St. Dunstan's Church, in Fleet-street.

Benchetrit, Karen & Carina Louart 1994. *La Franc-Maçonnerie au feminine*. Paris: Belfond.

Bernheim, Alain 1998. "La Stricte Observance". In: *Acta Macionica* 8: 67–97.

Brockman, C. Lance 1994. "Catalyst for Change: Intersection of the Theater and the Scottish Rite". *Heredom* 3: 121–146.

Carr, Harry (ed.) 1971. *The Early French Exposures*. London: The Quatuor Coronati Lodge No. 2076.

Harris, Marvin 1968. *The Rise of Anthropological Theory. A History of Theories of Culture*. London: Routledge & Kegan Paul.

Hill, Lawrence J. 1994. "Beyond the Scenery: Effects Used to Enhance Scottish Rite Ceremony". *Heredom* 3: 147–158.

Hivert-Messaca, Gisèle & Yves Hivert-Messaca 1997. *Comment la Franc-Maçonnerie vint aux femmes. Deux siècles de Franc-Maçonnerie d'adoption, féminine et mixte en France: 1740–1940*. Paris: Éditions Dervy.

Hobsbawm, Eric & Terence Ranger (ed.) 1983. *The Invention of Tradition*. Cambridge: Cambridge University Press (Past and Present Publications).

Jupeau-Réquillard, Françoise 2000. *L'Initiation des femmes, ou le souci permanent des francs-maçons français*. Monaco: Rocher (Franc-Maçonnerie, Humanisme et Tradition).

Mackey, Albert G. [9]1966. *Encyclopedia of Freemasonry*. New York: Masonic Publishing.

Mellor, Alec 1982. *Histoire des scandales maçonniques*. Paris: Pierre Belfond (English translation used: *Strange Masonic Stories*. Richmond: Macoy Publishing, 1985).

Pott, P.H. 1984. *'. . . Om met U te werken . . .'. De traditionele arbeid in de Loges in Nederland in de tweede helft van de twintigste eeuw; een aanzet met een verantwoording*. Den Haag: Maçonnieke Stichting Ritus en Tempelbouw.

[19] Within the British Federation, the appellation of female members has shifted back and forth between Sister and Brother. As the next sentence reveals, Brother Bird is a woman.

[20] *Draft Minutes of the 32nd Meeting . . . held on 3rd October, 1927*, p. 3f.

Prat, Andrée et al. 2003. *L'ordre maçonnique le Droit Humain*. Paris: PUF (Que sais-je? 3673).

Rognon, Francois 1994. *Chronique des Origines de la Grande Loge de France*. Le Mans: Editions du Borrégo.

Schüttler, Hermann 1997. "Karl Leonhard Reinhold und die Illuminaten im Vorfeld der Französischen Revolution". In: *Der Illuminatenorden (1776–1785/87). Ein politischer Geheimbund der Aufklärungszeit*, Reinalter, Helmut (ed.). Frankfurt: Peter Lang, 323–350.

Snoek, Jan A.M. 1987. *Initiations: A Methodological Approach to the Application of Classification and Definition Theory in the Study of Rituals*. Pijnacker: Dutch Efficiency Bureau.

—— 1996. "De Rozekruisgraad en het probleem van de blasfemie". *Het Rozekruis* 70.2: 19–32.

—— 1997. "Le développement des rituels maçonniques aux Pays-Bas de 1734 à nos jours". *Acta Macionica* 7: 283–294.

—— 1998. "Oral and Written Transmission of the Masonic Tradition". In: *Acta Macionica* 8: 41–52 (reprinted 2003a).

—— 2003a. "Printing Masonic Secrets—Oral and Written Transmission of the Masonic Tradition". In: *Alströmersymposiet 2003. Fördragsdokumentation*, Bogdan, Henrik (ed.). Göteborg: Frimureriska Forskningsgruppen i Göteborg, 39–56 (reprint of Snoek 1998).

—— 2003b. "Swedenborg, Freemasonry, and Swedenborgian Freemasonry: An Overview". In: *New Religions in a Postmodern World*, Rothstein, Mikael & Reender Kranenborg (ed.). Aarhus: Aarhus University Press, 23–75.

Te Lindert, Wilgert 1998. *Aufklärung und Heilserwartung: Philosophische und religiöse Ideen Wiener Freimaurer (1780–1795)*. Frankfurt: Peter Lang.

Van Peype, Dirk C.J. 1997. "Prince Frederik (Grand Master 1816–1881) and the Higher Degrees in the Netherlands". *Ars Quatuor Coronatorum* 110: 91–105.

PERFECTION AND MISHAPS IN VEDIC RITUALS

Axel Michaels

karmopapātaḥ prāyaścittam (*Kātyāyanaśrautasūtra* XXV.1.1)
For mishaps in rituals [there is] the (ritual) atonement.

1. *Introduction*

Nobody is perfect, but Vedic ritual is—at least according to the Vedic ritualists. After all, the ritual is made by the gods. Everything within the ritual is consecrated, thus non-human. Whatever gets into the sacrifice has to be sacrosanct; otherwise it pollutes and destroys the ritual. Nothing is natural, everything is ritual. Even the elements are not pure in themselves; even they have to be consecrated. For the air could be polluted by insects, water by excrements, the holy fire could mix with the profane etc. (see Negelein 1915: xxii).

Thus, it is men who make mistakes, not the ritual. That is why the *brāhmaṇa* priest—not really being human any more and thus perfect—has to be silent in Vedic rituals. The *śūdras*, in contradistinction, are regarded as defective, incomplete or 'fallen' because they have separated from the Vedic ritual. The question for ritualists, thus, is: how can the ritual be protected against the imperfections of human beings?

Looking at Vedic and Hindu material from various sources I propose the following answer: Vedic ritual has to be protected[1] and it is finally protected by two rather non-ritualistic notions: knowledge and faith, *vidyā* and *śraddhā*. I will first present several examples of mishaps in *śrauta* rituals, then elaborate on ancient methods of healing the mistakes, and finally try to show how the rather technical methods of healing and means of rectifying mishaps in ritual lead to a certain notion of internalization and autonomy of the ritual that is, I propose, more or less necessary for any kind of ritual thinking. Rituals, I argue with Don Handelman (2004), are to be seen as dynamic events in their own right that cannot really fail on the doctrinal level.[2]

[1] *yajñasya aghātāya* (*Taittirīyabrāhmaṇa* III.8.9.4).
[2] On the distinction between efficacy on the doctrinal and on the operational level, see Moore & Myerhoff 1977: 10ff.

2. *Mishaps in Vedic rituals*[3]

Vedic rituals aim at a certain result. If mishaps or obstacles arise the consequences could be serious: "Dans ce dédale de prescriptions minutieuses l'erreur est aisée et les conséquences en sont terribles," writes Sylvain Lévi (1898: 123). Indeed, mishaps could severely harm the sacrificer and his family. The fear of failure was therefore great. The sacrifice was regarded as an achievement of perfection, something that is without any harm. One of the many Sanskrit terms for 'sacrifice' is *ma-kha* which the *Gopatha-Brāhmaṇa* (II.2.5) explains to be a compound of *mā* and *kha*, i.e. 'without any hole'.

Thus, we read in the *Śatapathabrāhmaṇa* (XI.5.3.8ff., see *infra*) that the householder (*gṛhapati*) would die if the *gārhapatya*, the domestic sacrificial fire, were to go out; or that the cattle would die if the *anvāhārvyapacana* fire were to go out; or that the family would be without heirs if all sacrificial fires were to go out; or that the sacrificer would see unpleasant things in this and the next world if the fires were to go out even if there were no wind.

Almost any mishap could lead to far-reaching results; it could even destroy the whole country. The loss of the horse in the horse sacrifice (*aśvamedha*), for example, would cause a war. The range of mishaps is even more than the impressive list of ritual failures compiled by Ronald L. Grimes (1988) and Peter von Moos (2001), e.g. misfire, abuse, ineffectuality, violation, contagion, opacity, defeat, omission, misframing etc. The number of possible mishaps is almost infinite.[4] Murphy's law can be easily applied for what could go wrong apparently did go wrong. The Vedic ritualists had been fully aware of what could fail. *Āśvalāyana-Prāyaścittāni* 1b, for example, lists what could eventually be subject to errors: the sacrificial material, place and time of the ritual, the sacrificial fees, the priest and his wife. To mention only a few examples of mishaps in ritual:[5]

---

[3] See Thite 1975: 161ff., from which most of the following examples are taken.

[4] See, for example, *Śatapathabrāhmaṇa* XII.4.1.1ff. for a list of possible mistakes during the *agnihotra* ritual.

[5] For further references see Negelein's index to the *Atharvaprāyaścittāni* and Kane 1968ff. vol. 4: 58.

- Problems with the fire: the sacrificial fires are contaminated by each other or by the village fires or the forest fires (*Aitareyabrāhmaṇa* VII.6–8); there is the sudden extinction of the sacrificial fires (*Śatapathabrāhmaṇa* XI.5.3.8ff.).
- Misbehaviour: the Brāhmaṇa might break his silence (*Śatapathabrāhmaṇa* I.7.4.20) or recite a hymn or verse wrongly. A famous example is *Ṛgveda* I.32.6 which has long been used to demonstrate the importance of correct accentuation for if *indraśatruḥ* is recited with the wrong accent it means the opposite of the 'Indra's defeater' and thus destroys the ritual effect.
- Spoiled meals and food: the sacrificer could lose his off-spring, cattle or even his house if milk is allowed to fall down during the ritual, if it is touched by worms, or if it is not poured into a mould (*Taittirīyabrāhmaṇa* III.7.2.1–5); the sacrificer would suffer from leprosy or would get piles (*arśas*) if rain dropped on milk that is offered in the sacrifice (dto.); the sacrificial meals could become sour, fermented or burnt; the sacrificer might eat the food of a woman with child (*Aitareyabrāhmaṇa* VII.9).
- Polluting animals: a dog which goes between the fires breaks the sacrifice (*Taittirīyabrāhmaṇa* I.4.3.6). The horse of the *aśvamedha* might couple with a mare (*Śatapathabrāhmaṇa* XIII.6.8.1), a donkey could make unpleasant noises nearby; a crow, considered a messenger of death, could fly down on the sacrificial arena; the sacrificial animals could run away, break down, become sick, roar etc. Animals of the night, e.g. mice or ants could show up; crows or vultures which are regarded as birds of death, could appear und thus pollute the sacrifice.
- Destruction of sacrificial items: charcoal could fall from the fire; the sacrificial post (*yūpa*) to which the animals are bound could fall, break or start to bud.

In general, Vedic sacrifice is seen as a body that embodies truth and salvation. Often the sacrificial altar has the form of a human or animal body. Thus, mishaps can hurt it, can literally wound or break it (*Śatapathabrāhmaṇa* XII.6.1.2), separate it or make holes (*chidra*) in it (*Aitareyabrāhmaṇa* III.11). The sacrifice can even be killed or run away. Thus the utmost care and diligence is required in avoiding mistakes. If they happened, the sacrifice would have to be restored. For this several methods were used.

3. *Restitutio in integrum*

Elsewhere I have tried to show the methods for alterations and variations in a (Newar) death ritual (*sapiṇḍīkaraṇa*) which allows for a considerable reduction in the strictness and formality claimed by most definitions of ritual (Michaels & Buß forthc.). Basically, I proposed the following methods: substitution, alteration, omission, fusion, reduction, repetition and invention. Some of these and other methods such as recitation or donation can be traced to Vedic origins. They all make for a *restitutio in integrum*, i.e. they help to heal the ritual and rectify any mishap that might occur.

The most widespread Sanskrit term used for ritual atonement is *prāyaścitti* or *prāyaścit(ta)*,[6] which is defined by a commentator of the *Āpastambaśrautasūtra* (IX.1.1) as follows: "*prāyaścitti* is a (ritual) act which has the purpose of removing (any) mistake".[7] The Vedic ritualists have composed extensive texts, called *prāyaścittāni* etc., in which the casuistry as well as rules and remedies to rectify mistakes in ritual are listed.[8]

Thus, the method of substitution (Skt. *pratyāmna*) is very common in Vedic rituals. If, for instance,[9] the sacrificial spoon (*juhu*) splits during the sacrifice it can be placed on the *āhavanīya* fire and replaced by another spoon (*Aitareyabrāhmaṇa* VII.5). If in the *aśvamedha* the horse gets lost, it can be replaced by another horse; significantly, this substitution is called *prāyaścitti* in the *Śatapathabrāhmaṇa* (XIII.1.6.3). If the *soma*-plant is not available, it can be substituted by the *pūtikā*-plant; if this plant is not available, the *arjuna*-plant can be taken etc. (*Taittirīyamahābrāhmaṇa* IX.5.3.ff.). If sacrificial material is spoiled it can be exchanged with pure material (*Śatapathabrāhmaṇa* XII.4.1.2). If a priest fell sick, if the wife of the sacrificer became impure, or if the householder died, in all these cases substitutes could be given.[10] Similar material, ghee and butter for instance could substitute for each other, and long lists declare what had to be regarded as equal or similar. Basically, the material means of expiation—water, fire, *kuśa* grass, gold, the *brāhmaṇa* etc.—are identical and exchangeable.

The method of alteration is a variant of the *substitutio* for it anticipates the alternatives performed during the rituals. From the early Brāhmaṇa texts onwards we find such alternatives mentioned, for instance, through the references to other schools or regional practices (*deśadharma*: see Wezler 1985).

---

[6] For the etymology of *prāyaścitti* or *prāyaścitta* as well as a general discussion of the term, see Stenzler 1876, Bonnerjea 1931, Gampert 1939: 23–29, Kane 1968ff. vol. 4: 59, Thite 1975: 163f.

[7] *doṣanirharaṇārthaṃ karma prāyaścittam*, quoted from Negelein 1915: xii.

[8] See also the *Śatapathabrāhmaṇa* XII.4, *Aitareyabrāhmaṇa* 32.2–11, *Mānavagṛhyasūtra* I.3, *Hiraṇyakeśigṛhyasūtra* I.5.1–16, *Āśvalāyanaśrautasūtra* III.10.

[9] For more examples see Thite 1975: 166, and Negelein 1915: xi–xx.

[10] For references and further examples see Negelein 1915: xxxviii.

Similarly, the method of omission is a necessity for coping with unforeseen infelicities, shortages or negligence on the part of the ritual participants in the supply of sacrificial material.

The method of (gradual) reduction (Skt. *tantreṇa*) has been applied in several cases. Thus, if the sacrificer was about to die within the next twenty-four hours, the elaborate *soma* sacrifice could also been performed within one day (*ekāha*; see *Atharvaprāyaścittāni* 3.9).

Moreover, mishaps or mistakes could often be rectified by repetition or renovation. If, for example, the fire-pan (*ukhā*) is broken, another is prepared, and this ritual act of making another fire-pan is again called *prāyaścitti* (*Śatapathabrāhmaṇa* VI.6.4.7f.).[11]

Besides these and other methods, further ways of rectifying mishaps can be found in the Vedic material. Thus, often mishaps can be cured by recitations of hymns or verses from the Vedic *saṃhitās*. When for instance the cart by which the *soma* is brought into the sacrificial arena makes creaking noises, a verse[12] is to be recited; this is itself the *prāyaścitti* (*Śatapathabrāhmaṇa* III.5.3.17f.). If the *agnihotra*-cow makes a noise while being united with the calf and being milked, one should recite *Ṛgveda* I.164.10 (*sūyavasād bhagavatī*...) (*Aitareyabrāhmaṇa* V.27).

A seemingly simple but effective way of healing a broken sacrifice is the use of three utterances (*vyāhṛti*) *bhūḥ*, *bhuvaḥ* and *svaḥ* which are also regarded as 'all-*prāyaścittis*'.[13] As proposed by Negelein (1915: vli) this rite originally was a means of substituting the complicated and complex ritual atonements with just one rite: ghee or another offering had to be given into that fire which was related to a *saṃhitā* which was recited falsely. Later the *vyāhṛti* formula was combined with a simple offering of ghee in the *āhavanīya* fire with the words: "Whatsoever ritual mistake has been done, this alone is (i.e. the rite) the total accomplishment (*kḷpti*), the all-*prāyaścitti*."[14] It became a universal means to cure mishaps in the ritual recitation of the Veda. These holy syllables are also often preventively used for unknown mishaps. According to a myth from the *Jaiminīyabrāhmaṇa* (I.357f.), the three *vyāhṛtis* were created by Prajāpati as an essence or condensation of the three Vedas since the gods had asked him for remedies to heal mistakes in the sacrifice. Thus, the

[11] For further examples see Negelein 1915: XV, with note 257.

[12] *svaṃ goṣṭham avadātam: Vājasaneyisaṃhitā* V.17.

[13] *Sarva-prāyaścitti* or *-prāyaścitta, Aitareyabrāhmaṇa* V.27, cp. Thite 1975: 167 with further references.

[14] *yat kim cāvidhivihitaṃ karma kriyate tasyaiṣaiva sarvasya kḷptiḥ sarvasya prāyaścittiś ceti hi śrutir bhavati* (*Atharvaprāyaścittāni* 3.8).

vyāhṛtis are explicitly understood as means to join the broken sacrifice: "These *vyāhṛtis* are internal fastenings of the Vedas; just as one may unite one thing with another or joint with a joint or with a cord unite an object of leather or something which has come apart, so with this one unites whatever in the sacrifice has come apart (broken)".[15]

One of the most common means to overcome any violation of ritual rules are donations, especially gifts to gods or priests. Both, then, act as healers of the spoiled ritual: "for whatever joint of the sacrifice fails, that breaks; and whichever then is the deity in that (part of the sacrifice) through that deity he heals the sacrifice, through that one makes the sacrifice complete again" (*Śatapathabrāhmaṇa* XIII.6.1.2, transl. Eggeling). Thus, if the horse of the *aśvamedha* falls sick, a pap (*caru*) is given to Pūṣan since this deity rules over the beasts (*Śatapathabrāhmaṇa* XIII.3.8.2), and if any eye-disease befalls the horse, a *caru* is donated to Sūrya, since the body moves (√*car*, 'to move') through eyes (*Śatapathabrāhmaṇa* XIII.3.6.4).

Seen from the point of view of ritual practice smaller mishaps had to be overlooked and disregarded. If, for example, a crow would come into the sacrificial arena but immediately fly away no ritual atonement had to be performed: "His *gārhapatya* is this (terrestrial) world, his *anvāhāryapacana* (or southern fire) the air world, and his *āhavanīya* yonder (heavenly) world; and freely, indeed, birds, both combined (*yukta*) and single, pass to and fro in these worlds; and even if a whole crowd were to pass through between his fires, let him know that no harm and no hurt will come to him" (*Śatapathabrāhmaṇa* XII.4.1.3, transl. Eggeling).

To sum up: Vedic ritual literature, especially the Brāhmaṇa and *prāyaścitta* texts, is fully aware that mishaps in rituals happen. It differentiates between various types of ritual failure, considers various causes and offers various means to resolve the problems depending on the type of mishap or mistake.

The Brāhmaṇas do not yet refer to personal guilt but only to ritual failure. However, the cover term for the treatment of ritual failure and personal guilt, *prāyaścitta*, later becomes common to both cases. In Hindu classical law it became necessary to differentiate between actions undertaken with and without intent in order to know which of the two results—those which are caused by intentional (*kāmata* or

[15] *Aitareyabrāhmaṇa* V.32, transl. Thite, 1975: 167; cp. also *Jaiminīyopaniṣadbrāhmaṇa* III.4.4.4.

jñāna) sins or those caused by unintentional (*akāmata, ajñāna*) sins—are destroyed by penances.[16]

> Wise men know that a restoration is for an evil committed unintentionally; some say, on the evidence of the revealed canon that it is also for one done intentionally. An evil committed unintentionally is cleansed by reciting the Veda, but one committed intentionally, in confusion, (is cleansed) by different sorts of particular restorations. A twice-born man who has incurred the need for restoration, through fate or by an act committed in a former (life), should not associate with good people until restoration has been completed (*Mānavadharmaśāstra* 11.45–47).[17]

The logic behind this is that only intentional acts count ritually. The distinction between intentionally and unintentionally committed offences has to do with the nature of ritual actions. For any ritually valid act must be performed with a *saṃkalpa* (see Michaels 2005), which must be formulated (a) prior to the ritual, (b) consciously, and (c) verbally; it must (d) also mention the purpose of the ritual and should be (e) accompanied by certain ritual gestures. Thus, a decision to take a religious vow must not only be well articulated and formulated prior to the performance of the ritual, it must also be consciously declared—usually but not necessarily in a public and audible form. This is what Humphrey & Laidlaw (1994: 88ff.) have called the ritual commitment. Indeed, only if such a formal decision has been made and expressed in words are the ritual acts religiously valid. Unintentional actions, therefore, are ritually less valued and thus easier to exempt from penitential punishments.

4. Prāyaścitta *and knowledge*

Any mishap 'breaks' the ritual and the methods mentioned help to join or put it together again. This all looks very technical as if everything in Vedic rituals were very strict, as if rules had to be strictly observed to avoid ritual failure. However, two points must be made which help to understand why Vedic and Hindu rituals seldom really fail.

Firstly, the agency of the *brāhmaṇa* priest should not be underestimated. It was he who had to supervise the ritual, to intervene if mishaps happened, to recite the correct *mantras*, to guide the other priests. He had to separate the important from the unimportant und thus guarantee

---

[16] Kane 1968ff. vol. I: 63ff., 75, 80, Rocher 1980, Day 1982: 215.

[17] See, for instance, *Mānavadharmaśāstra* 11.45–46, *Yājñavalkyasmṛti* 3.226, *Gautamadharmasūtra* 19.3ff.

the success of the ritual. As mentioned before, he is often compared with a healer and doctor.

Secondly, even though mishaps in the rituals were considered to harm the people involved, and even though all possible methods to rectify ritual mistakes had to be applied, the Brāhmaṇa texts sometimes mention that one should not be too afraid of mishaps. The *Śatapathabrāhmaṇa* even declares mistakes and incompleteness to be helpful:

> 8. Then, as to the successful issue of the sacrifice. Now, whatever part of the sacrifice is incomplete (*nyūna*) that part of it is productive for him; and what is redundant in it that is favourable to cattle; and what is uncertain (*saṃkasuka*) in it that makes for prosperity; and what is perfect in it that is conducive to heaven.
> 9. And if he thinks, "There has been that which was incomplete in my sacrifice," let him believe "That is productive for me: I shall have offspring produced (in men and cattle)."
> 10. And if he thinks, "There has been that which was redundant in my sacrifice," let him believe, "That is favourable to cattle for me: I shall become possessed of cattle."
> 11. And if he thinks, "There has been that which was disconnected in my sacrifice," let him believe, "That makes for my prosperity: prosperity, surrounded by splendour, fame and holy lustre, will accrue to me."
> 12. And if he thinks, "There has been that which was perfect in my sacrifice," let him believe, "That is conducive to heaven for me: I shall become one of those in the heavenly world." This then is the successful issue of the sacrifice; and, verily, whosoever thus knows this to be the successful issue of the sacrifice, by him offering is made by a wholly successful sacrifice (*Śatapathabrāhmaṇa* XI.4.4.8–12, translation follows partly Eggeling).

According to this passage, one had not necessarily to be afraid of the mishaps, and rituals are not only governed by the rigidity of ritual rules. What also counts is both the rule and the spirit or knowledge of the ritual agents. *Prāyaścitti* and *vidyā* ('knowledge') go together, are sometimes even used as synonyms.[18] If there is no knowledge, there would also not be efficacy with regard to ritual. This also means that knowledge alone can sometimes rectify the mishaps in rituals, and that in the end knowledge alone can substitute ritual. All this, of course leads to the widespread notion of the inner (*mānasa/ī*) ritual and ritual criticism of the Upaniṣads.

This argument seems to be in contradiction to the fact that rituals can mostly be efficacious even if they are performed ignorantly, out of

[18] See, for instance, *Śatapathabrāhmaṇa* XI.5.3.8ff. or *Gopathabrāhmaṇa* I.3.13; cp. Thite 1975: 171.

confusion (*bhrantyā*) or absent-mindedly (*vismaraṇāt*), for it is generally accepted that the ritual works independently of the sacrificer's or priest's mind if the prescribed rules are followed. This is why ritual atonement is necessarily independent of the guilt of the ritual agents.

However, the Vedic ritualists apparently were aware of a general problem mentioned in the beginning. How can imperfect men perform perfect rituals? If it would only be the action *per se* then animals could also sacrifice and get the reward (*puṇya*) of ritual action, and this was again and again stressed by opponents of rituals. The fishes which always take a bath in the holy water, somebody who would innocently step on cow-dung, the birds flying around a temple and thus doing a *pradakṣiṇā* or a ritual circumambulation around the holy place are standard examples of such satirical ritual criticism (see Michaels 2004).

The Vedic ritualists therefore stressed the importance of knowledge and faith. Thus, it was regarded as a bad omen if rain dropped on the sacrificial spoon and thereby increased the *agnihotra*-milk, for the rain had not been consecrated und could therefore not be integrated in the sacrificial arena. Such mishaps and other similar ones apparently could be counteracted not by actions but by bona fides, i.e. thoughts alone:

> They also say "If it were to rain upon (*upariṣāt*) any one's Agnihotra-milk when it has been ladled into the offering-spoon, what rite and what expiation would there be in that case?" Let him know "Light (or sap) has come to me from above (*upariṣāt*); the gods have helped me: I shall become more glorious;" and let him by all means make offerings therewith. This, then, is the rite performed in that case (*Śatapathabrāhmaṇa* XII.4.2.20, transl. Eggeling).

Another example from the Brāhmaṇa texts for the stress on right knowledge is the initiation of Śauceya Prācīnayogya. When in the process of it the priest Uddālaka Āruṇi asked his student about the details of the *agnihotra* ritual, he also says:

> If thou hast offered the Agnihotra knowing this, then it has indeed been offered by thee; but if (thou hast offered it) not knowing this, then it has not been offered by thee (*Śatapathabrāhmaṇa* XI.5.3.4, transl. Eggeling).

Then, the teacher instructs him in the esoteric meanings of the *agnihotra*, and afterwards the student asks his *guru* about the knowledge of how to counteract various mishaps with regard to the sacrificial fires, e.g.:

> Sauceya, thus instructed, said: "I would yet ask thee a question, reverend sir."—"Ask then, Prācīnayogya!" he replied. He said, "If, at that very time, the Gārhapatya fire were to go out, dost thou know what danger there is in that case for him who offers?"—"I know it," he replied; "before

> long the master of the house [i.e. the sacrificer himself] would die in the case of him who would not know this; but by dint of knowledge I myself have prevailed."—"What is that knowledge, and what the atonement?" he asked.—"The upward breathing has entered the breath of the mouth—this (is the knowledge); and I would make the offering on the Āhavanīya—this would be the atonement, and I should not be committing that sin".—"This much, then reverend sir, we two (know) in common," said (Sauceya) (*Śatapathabrāhmaṇa* XI.5.3.9, transl. Eggeling).

Interestingly, the term used for knowledge here is *prāyaścitti*. The ritual action alone cannot prevail over mishaps, but along with the right, esoteric knowledge mistakes cannot really endanger the ritual.

In passing I should mention that the problem of ritual perfection was discussed in a much more sophisticated form by the Mīmāṃsakās or specialists in the interpretation of Vedic rituals.[19] Jaimini, for example, was fully aware of the basic problem that imperfect men cannot create perfect rituals. He discusses all relevant aspects: the relationship between the first archetypical performance and its ritual repetition, prototype and realization, main (*prakṛti*, *pradhāna*) and subsidiary (*śeṣa*, *aṅga*) actions, divine and human agency (*adhikāra*), material and action, as well as the methods of substitution and the problem of efficacy (*apūrva*). However, for him, the way out of the paradoxical situation was not the 'protestant' interiorisation of the ritual but its conversion into an absolute entity. It is the ritual itself that has its own agency independent of those who perform it.

5. *Conclusion*

What does all this mean for ritual theory? Caroline Humphrey and James Laidlaw rightly remarked (that): "Ritual is prescribed action, you have to get it right, and yet sometimes it seems that so long as you try, so long as you accept the ritual commitment, it is almost impossible to get it wrong" (Humphrey & Laidlaw 1994: 128). Indeed, as was already observed by Julius Negelein, the seemingly stereotyped and fixed (Vedic) ritual was always and quickly adapted to the practical needs of the priests and sacrificers: "Es war also für alle Fälle Vorsorge getroffen. Das scheinbar so starre Ritual paßte sich den praktischen

[19] I am especially thankful to Francis X. Clooney, S.J., for an illuminating seminar on such questions he held in the summer term 2004 at the South Asia Institute; see also his brilliant study *Thinking Ritually* (Clooney 1990).

Bedürfnissen mit wunderbarer Geschmeidigkeit an" (Negelein 1915: xxxix). Thus, rituals despite being formal, repetitive and stereotyped are full of dynamics, and this is basically due to the methods aiming at a *restitutio in integrum*, especially *substitutio, alteratio, iteratio, ommissio, reductio, repetitio, inventio* as well as *recitatio* and *donatio*. It is by these methods that a failed or even messy performance does not inevitably invalidate the ritual as a whole (see Grimes 1988). Thus, ritual facilitates change rather than obstructs it.

Moreover, ritual is always subject to mishaps or mistakes, it can always fail or be criticised. Ritual—one could perhaps say—is the imperfect realisation of the idea of perfection. However, as Humphrey and Laidlaw also remarked, "if you abandon the assumption of perfect order and perfect repetition, imperfection and variation become illuminating, rather than being noise that a well-honed interpretation dampens down and edits out" (Humphrey & Laidlaw 1994: 130).

All that has been said before supports the idea of 'ritual in its own right' as proposed by Don Handelman in a recent issue of *Social Analysis* (2004). Rituals are indeed to a certain extent autonomous and have their own integrity by which they create the capacity of self-healing. The methods mentioned above precisely serve that purpose.

References

Sources

Aitareyabrāhmaṇa. Ed. and transl. by M. Haug. Bombay: Government Central Book Depot, 1931.

Āśvalāyanaśrautasūtra: The Śrauta-Sūtras of Āśvalāyana. With the Commentary of Gārgya Nārāyaṇa. Ed. by Rāmanārāyaṇa Vidyāratna. Reprint of the edition Calcutta 1864–1874. Osnabrück: Biblio-Verlag, 1982.

Gautamadharmasūtra. In: *Āṣṭādaśasamṛtayaḥ*. Ed. by Khemarāja Śrīkṛṣṇadāsa. Bombay: Veṅkateśvara Stīma Yantrāyala, no date.

Gopathabrāhmaṇa: Das Gopatha-Brāhmaṇa. Ed. by Dieuke Gaastra. Leiden: Brill, 1919.

Hiraṇyakeśigṛhyasūtra: The Gṛhyasūtra of Hiraṇyakeśin with extracts from the commentary of Mātṛdatta. Ed. by J. Kirste. Vienna: Hölder, 1889.

Jaiminīyabrāhmaṇa: Jaiminiya-Brahmana of the Samaveda. Complete Text critically edited for the first time by Prof. Raghu Vira and Dr. Lokesh Chandra. Nagpur: International Academy of Indian Culture, 1956.

Kātyāyana-Śrautasūtra and other Vedic texts. Ed. by Lokesh Chandra. New Delhi: International Academy of Indian Culture, 1982 (Śata-Piṭaka Series 304).

Mānavadharmaśāstra. V.N. Mandlik (ed.). Bombay: Nirṇaya Sāgara Press, 1933.

Mānavagṛhyasūtra: Das Mānava-Gṛhya-Sūtra nebst Commentar in kurzer Fassung. Ed. by Friedrich Knauer. St. Petersburg: L'Academie Impériale des Sciences 1897.

Śatapathabrāhmaṇa. Ed. by A. Weber. Berlin: Ferd. Dümmler's Buchhandlung; London: Williams and Norgate, 1849.

Taittirīyabrāhmaṇa. 3 vols. Poona: Ānandāśrama, 1979 (Ānandāśrama Sanskrit Series 42).

Vājasaneyisaṃhitā: Yajurvedasaṃhitā. Ed. and English transl. by R. H. Griffith. Delhi: Nag Publishers, 1990 (reprint).

Yājñavalkyasmṛti with the commentary Mitākṣara of Vijñāneśvara. Ed. by W. Laxman Shāstri Pansīkar. Bombay: Nirṇaya Sāgara, 1918.

Secondary literature

Bonnerjea, Biren 1931. "*Prāyaścitta*, or Hindu ideas on the expiation of sin". *Indian Antiquary*. August and September.

Clooney, Francis X. 1990. *Thinking Ritually. Rediscovering the Pūrva Mīmāṃsā of Jaimini*. Vienna: Institute for Indology.

Day, Terence P. 1982. *The Conception of Punishment in Early Indian Literature*. Waterloo, Ontario: Canadian Corporation for Studies in Religion.

Eggeling, Julius (trsl.) 1882–1900. *The Śatapathabrāhmaṇa*. Oxford: Clarendon (The Sacred Books of the East 12, 26, 41, 43, 44).

Gampert, Wilhelm 1939. *Die Sühnezeremonien in der altindischen Rechtsliteratur*. Prague: Orientalisches Institut.

Grimes, Ronald L. 1988. "Infelicitous Performances and Ritual Criticism". *Semeia* 43: 103–122.

Handelman, Don 2004. "Introduction: Why Ritual in Its Own Right? How So?" *Social Analysis* 48.2: 1–32.

Humphrey, Caroline & James Laidlaw 1994. *The Archetypal Actions of Ritual. A theory of ritual illustrated by the Jain rite of worship*. Oxford: Clarendon Press.

Kane, Pandurang V. [2]1968ff. *History of Dharmaśāstra*. 6 vols. Poona: Bhandarkar Oriental Institute.

Lévi, Sylvain 1898. *La doctrine du sacrifice dans les Brāhmaṇas*. Paris: Leroux.

Michaels, Axel 2004. "Hāsyamārga—Zur Komik ritueller Förmlichkeit". In: *Ritualdynamik: Kulturübergreifende Studien zur Theorie und Geschichte rituellen Handelns*, Harth, Dietrich & Gerritt Schenk (ed.). Heidelberg: Synchron Verlag, 405–418.

—— 2005. "Saṃkalpa: The Beginnings of a Ritual". In: *Words and Deeds. Hindu and Buddhist Rituals in South Asia*, Gengnagel, Jörg & Ute Hüsken & Srilata Raman (ed.). Wiesbaden: Harrassowitz (Ethno-Indology. Heidelberg Studies in South Asian Rituals 1), 45–64.

Michaels, Axel & Johanna Buss forthc. "The dynamics of ritual formality: Contextual and textual variations in a Newar death ritual".

Moore, Sally Falk & Barbara G. Myerhoff 1977. "Introduction. Secular Ritual: Forms and Meanings". In: *Secular Ritual*, Moore, Sally Falk & Barbara G. Myerhoff (ed.). Assen & Amsterdam: Van Gorcum, 3–24.

Moos, Peter von 2001. "Einleitung. Fehltritt, Fauxpas und andere Transgressionen im Mittelalter". In: *Der Fehltritt. Vergehen und Versehen in der Vormoderne*, Moos, Peter von (ed.). Cologne & Weimar & Vienna: Böhlau, 1–96.

Negelein, Julius von (ed.) 1915. *Atharvaprāyaścittāni: Ein Beitrag zur Entstehung des Schuld- und Sühnegedankens im ältesten Indien*. New Haven: The American Oriental Society.

Rocher, Ludo 1983. "Karma and Rebirth in the Dharmaśāstra". In: *Karma and Rebirth in Classical Indian Traditions*, O'Flaherty, Wendy Doniger (ed.). Delhi & Patna & Varanasi: Motilal Banarsidas, 61–89 (repr. of 1980).

Stenzler, Adolf Friedrich 1876. "On the Hindou doctrine of expiation". In: *Transactions of the second session of the International Congress of Orientalists held in London in September 1874*. London: Trübner, 205–212.

Thite, Ganes Umakanth 1975. *Sacrifice in the Brāhmaṇa-Texts*. Poona: University of Poona.

Wezler, Albrecht 1985. "Dharma und Deśadharma". In: *Regionale Traditionen in Südasien*, Kulke, H. & D. Rothermund (ed.). Stuttgart: Franz Steiner Verlag, 1–22.

'ALL THE KING'S HORSES AND ALL THE KING'S MEN': THE 2004 RED MATSYENDRANĀTHA INCIDENT IN LALITPUR[1]

Christoph Emmrich

Humpty Dumpty sat on a wall;
Humpty Dumpty had a great fall;
All the king's horses, and all the king's men,
Couldn't put Humpty together again.

1. *Introduction*

On Sunday, April 25, 2004 at 9.30 p.m. local time on the second leg of its procession through Lalitpur, Nepal, the ceremonial chariot carrying the so-called 'Red Matsyendranātha' fell on its side and its crown touched the ground. This necessitated the recovery of the god from the chariot and the interruption of the procession for one entire month due to the complete rebuilding of the vehicle followed by the necessary rituals of atonement and exculpation. Experiencing the daily clash of party supporters with the King's security forces and with the Maoist threat looming larger than ever, people and press were quick to establish sinister links: after 1934, when the Kathmandu Valley was hit by one of its worst earthquakes in recorded history, 1990, when the citizens of Nepal took to the streets in a popular uprising against autocratic rule, and in 1999, when almost the entire royal family was

[1] This article originally appeared in *Indologica Taurinensia* 32 (2006). It could not have been written without the invaluable help of my dear colleague Nutan Dhar Sharma, M.A., to which my thanks go in the first place. Furthermore, I would like to thank my teacher Laxmi Nath Shreshta for unfolding for me the world of Nepālī newspapers, Rajesh Shrestha from the South Asia Institute Branch Office Kathmandu for helping to collect the press coverage, Anil Bajracharya for introducing me to the procession as well as his brother Arun for calling late on April 25 and making sure I had not been hurt during the dramatic events. I would like to further extend my thanks to all the Guṭhiyārs involved in the procession's performance whom I talked to, whose collaboration I cherish and whose work I admire. I greatly thank Niels Gutschow, Axel Michaels and Alexander von Rospatt for critically reading the first draft of this paper, as well as Martin Gaenszle, David Gellner, Roland Hardenberg and Hermann Kulke for remarks and fruitful discussions.

wiped out in a palace massacre, this year's incident has been the last in a long line marking the country's troubled fate. The article will try to analyse what exactly happened during this year's crash against the background of popular belief, the history and practice of the rite, and how the damage was assessed by the lay folk as well as by the ritual specialists, which measures where recommended and how and for what purpose they were applied. Keeping in mind the two interpretations of the incident as offence against the godhead or as portentous omen, this is an enquiry into whether in this context there is any appropriate place for or, from the participants' perspective, any acceptance of a notion such as 'mistake' or 'failure'. The recorded actions and testimonies, on the contrary, suggest it might be far more appropriate to explore the possibilities and opportunities of re-enacted, or rather pre-enacted and thus calculated catastrophe inherent in this particular ritual, which happens at a moment of crisis, enables the performance of a breakdown, restoration to a pristine state, forgiveness and well-being. However, if we really would have to talk about the fall of the Red Matsyendranātha in terms of failure, we would have to say: the ritual cannot fail, because, under the current circumstances, it has to fail, in order for the crisis to be overcome.

2. *The procession in history*

The current worship of the deity, which culminates in its annual procession, reveals multiple layers of different divinities and cults.[2] The earliest identifiable layer probably belongs to the cult of Buṃgadyaḥ and can be connected to the local cult of Buṃgamatī, possibly an originally female goddess[3] at the centre of an annual fertility rite inviting the first rains to ensure a rich harvest.[4] At a later stage a Bodhisattva cult was probably superimposed and subsequently fused with Śaiva royal cult, affiliated with Lalitpur Newar kingship under the Malla dynasty. The latest layer is constituted by the cult of the Nāth Yogi Matsyendranātha (Nep. *Macchindranātha*)[5] which developed out of North Indian Śaiva ascetic movements, supported by the so-called Nāth Yogis, and was

---

[2] Analysed by Lienhard 1978, Locke 1973 and 1980 and Vergati 1985.

[3] Its temple is referred to as the 'bride's paternal home' (*māitī*). See Locke 1973: 8.

[4] On this aspect of the procession see Vergati 1985.

[5] In this article only Nepālī (Nep.) and Nevārī (Nev.) terms given in brackets are identified as such. All other terms in brackets are in Sanskrit.

itself in turn eventually integrated into a Gorkhalī and Indo-Parbatiyā and finally pan-Nepalese royal state cult.[6] Today the Matsyendranātha Jātrā is referred to as a 'national festival', while maintaining in popular belief its strong connections to the agricultural cycle. The to-date most popular legend connected with the deity testifies to the Nāthyogic layer. Here too, Matsyendranātha is connected with rain as he was brought from Kāmarūpa by a Bhaktapur king, a Brahmin, viz. Buddhist priest (*vajrācārya*) and a farmer (Nev. *jyāpu*) to the Kathmandu Valley, which was suffering from a severe drought, to have his pupil Gorakhnātha, who had sat down blocking the rain-bestowing serpent deities (*nāgas*), rise and pay reverence to his teacher, thereby allowing it to rain again.[7]

The important chronicle Gopālarājavaṃśāvalī suggests that the procession was originally introduced by King Narendradeva of Bhaktapur for a divinity called Śrī Bugma Lokeśvara not much prior to 984 CE (Locke 1980: 300). The Tibetan monk Dharmasvāmin in his account of his visit to Nepal in 1226 describes the rite of reconsecration of a deity called Ārya of Bu kham and mentions that its festival includes a round of visits to the homes of people, recalling a monastic begging round (Roerich 1959: 54f.). However, it takes until 1558 (678 N.S.) for the chariot (*ratha*) to be mentioned in a grant. First regulations regarding the rite seem to be laid down in an inscription from February 16, 1673 (793 N.S.) by King Śrīnivāsa Malla at the Tabāhā in Lalitpur (Tevārī 1963, 10: 1–7). Related rites are subsumed under the term 'Four Sisters', which includes possibly again pointing at the equivocal gender of the deity, besides the Rāto Matsyendranātha of Lalitpur the Rāto Matsyendranātha of Cvabhāra, as well as the Seto (White) Matsyendranātha of both Kathmandu and of Nālā. The other three chariot festivals seem to be off-springs of the Lalitpur one (Locke 1980: 243). The rites of the Matsyendranātha of Bhaktapur include a procession together with a host of other local deities. The New Year's celebrations in Bhaktapur, the Bisket Jātrā, involve a procession of the chariots of the divine couple Bhairava and Bhadrakālī as well as the hoisting of a giant wooden pole (*liṅga*). This latter feat is undertaken in such a way that it takes at least a whole day to accomplish the task. Repeated incidents during the lifting of the pole regularly lead to injury

[6] For an extensive study of the relationship of the cult with Newar and Indo-Parbatiyā kingship see the excellent study by Bruce M. Owens 1989.
[7] Locke 1980: 280–296.

and death, which are, in urn, said to be ominous for the coming year. In April 2004 four men died and half a dozen were injured. Finally, it is possible to draw parallels to the procession of the famous Jagannātha of Puri. It is said there that the collapse of the chariot would be a sign of the dissolution (*pralaya*) of the world. However, although falls are recorded from the past, nowadays nobody seems to remember any fall.[8]

3. *The procession in practice*

To put the incident into perspective I will at least briefly sketch the procession and its narrative.[9] The deity (*deva*, Nev. *dyaḥ*) Red Matsyendranātha (Nep. Rāto Matsyendranātha)[10] spends six months of the year in the village Buṃgamatī, six miles south of Lalitpur, and six months at Tabāhā in Lalitpur itself. Every 12th year the procession (*yātrā*, Nep. *jātrā*) is conducted from Buṃgamatī to Lalitpur and back. All the other years it starts at Tabāhā and ends in Buṃgamatī. The god's face is renovated every year before the beginning of the procession in an installation rite (*jīvanyāsapūjā*). During its renovation its spiritual essence is removed from the image and kept in a water pot (*kalaśa*).[11] The god's set life-cycle rites (*daśakarma*) are performed, after which he is placed in the entrance of the central temple at Tabāhā for worshippers to pay reverence (Nep. *darśana linu*).

The procession starts with the ascension of the god onto his chariot (*rathārohaṇa*) to which he is brought on a palanquin, accompanied by the king's chief adviser's (*rājaguru*) guard, the Sarduljang platoon (or Nep. *gurujuko paltana*). The ascension of the chariot is performed at a place called Phulchowk, next to the Eastern so-called 'Aśoka Stūpa', as a temple consecration rite which inaugurates the worship by the local populace as well as pilgrims from all over the country. Besides Matsyendranātha a host of other images, including one of the Buddha Dīpaṃkara, said to be of deities, whose processions where suppressed

---

[8] For the relevant literature see Mishra 1971 and Macdonald 1975.

[9] For detailed ethnographies see Locke 1973: 17–38, and 1980; for a brief sketch of the procession see Anderson 1971: 53–61.

[10] So called by Hindus and outside Lalitpur; also called *bodhisattva* Avalokiteśvara (Nev. Laskadyaḥ), Āryalokeśvara, Padmapāṇi Lokeśvara (Lokanātha), or Karuṇāmaya by the Buddhists, which form the majority of Lalitpur's inhabitants, and Nev. Buṃgadyaḥ (Skt. Buṅgadeva) by all Newars.

[11] See Owens 1995. For the relative rites performed for the restoration of the Svayambhūcaitya see von Rospatt 2000.

by incorporation into the current cult, are placed on the chariot. On the fourth day the chariot is set into motion by young men pulling ropes attached to it. It is welcomed by a second, smaller chariot of Mīnanātha (Nev. Cākudyaḥ), pulled only by male children, who leads the Red Matsyendranātha into what may have been the original core Lalitpur. They stop at a locality called Gābāhā. Two days later the chariot proceeds to a place called Sundhārā, this time preceding the smaller chariot and passing the royal palace, where it usually stops for an hour or two. After a period of again two days the procession sets off to the southernmost tip of Lalitpur close to the so-called 'Southern Aśoka Stūpa' at Lāgaṃkhel. Here the chariot circumambulates the god's mother's shrine thrice and is left standing in an open lot for a day. The chariot is finally pulled to a place nearby called Poḍe and left there for about a month in which period the Lāgaṃkhel Jātrā is celebrated. This festival includes the casting of a coconut into the crowd from the top of the chariot (hence its more popular Nep. name Narivala Khasalne Jātrā), to be caught by a man who is said to become father of a son within the next year, the celebration of the Rāto Matsyendranātha's clan deity (*kuladevatā*) as well as the establishment of the right time (*muhūrta*, Nep. *sāita*) for the beginning of the second phase of the procession by astrologers. Within the next two weeks the chariot will be led to a place called Jawalakhel (Nev. Jyāhulākhyaḥ) where a member of the governmental trust (Guṭhi Saṃsthāna) will show the gods jewel-spangled vest (Nep. *bhoṭo*, Nev. *bhvata*) to the crowd, the king's chief adviser's guard and the king himself, who is also present and pays his homage to the god. After this the god is taken from the chariot and is brought back to Buṃgamatī, where he is verbally abused by the local populace for his long absence before being welcomed and purified and finally returning to his temple, an event which is celebrated in a festival attracting pilgrims from all over Nepal.

4. *The chariot as palanquin and temple*

Closely connected with the technical aspect of the rite and its disruptions is the architectural construction of the chariot (Nep. *ratha*, Nev. *khaḥ*) itself.[12] The castes responsible for its construction are people from

[12] Studies on the architectural aspects of the chariot have been done by Niels Gutschow in Gutschow 1979 and Gutschow & Kölver & Shreshtacharya (ed.) 1987: 103–106.

the carpenter caste (Nep. *vaḍhaīs*), who take care especially of the lower part of the chariot including wheels, chassis and cabin, and people from the construction worker caste (Nep. *yānvalas*; Nev. *yaṃvaṃs*), who work on the upper part, i.e. the dominating spire. The chariot in its core is made entirely of wood and is assembled without the use of metal, including nails or screws, resorting entirely to cane (Nep. *bet*, Nev. *pau*) cut in Indian forests near Susta and Siliguri[13] and kept flexible by placing it into a large water tank near the place of the chariot's assembly at Phulchowk. The chariot is thus 'sown together' by using a cane as a 'needle'. A lower deck (Nev. *ghaḥkū* or *hyamvak*) consisting of planks is fixed to a base consisting of two axes and supported by four wheels (made of a wood called Nep. *sānadāna*, Nev. *naṣiṃ*), rimmed by re-inforcing metal rings and covering 18 hand spans (Nep. *hāta*) with each rotation. Between the platform and the axes a huge roughly hewn pole (Nev. *ghaḥmāḥ*) 18 hand spans long (made of a wood called Nep. *saura*, Nev. *ghaḥmāḥ*) is inserted from the front of the chariot, its front end curving up above the height of the deck. It is identified with the *nāga* Karkoṭaka who is supposed to have helped carry Matsyendranātha on the expedition from Kāmarūpa. This and the wheels, which ought to be replaced every 12 years, are the only pieces that can be utilized more than just once. Across the two axes two further poles are placed on the lower platform on both sides of the *ghaḥmāḥ*. These poles, which function as the main bases of the lower deck, bear the whole upper structure. On them the upper deck, the 'god's place' (Nep. *bimāna khata*, Nev. *dyaḥkhaḥ*, made, as the rest of the scaffolding, of a wood called Nep. *lākurī*, Nev. *sūsiṃ*), measuring 1.6 × 2.3 metres, is placed, rimmed by a railing. It is a special shrine (Nev. *buikaḥ*), built open to four sides with a flat roof. This place, where the god is seated, is claimed to be the part of the chariot to which the strictest rules of construction apply (Adhikari 2004). The Nep. *khata* or Nev. *khaḥ* (the Nev. expression designating also the entire chariot), of which there are nine, vertically constituting the entire chariot, refer not only to the deck's plane, but to the whole scaffold including the deck up to the next level. The roof of the shrine carries a wickerwork of branches (Nev. *soraḥ hate*), fixed to the shrine's roof on a level called (Nev. *phviṃkhaḥ*) tied together by creepers assembled to form a slender spire, called 'the pole [which is Mount] Meru' (*meru-daṇḍa*), i.e. mountain-shaped axis mundi of South

[13] For the use of rattan in the chariot's construction see Amatya 1997: 18–22.

Asian cosmology, which takes the total height of the vehicle to 18 hand spans. In a second working phase the chariot is decorated. The wheels are painted by applying three eyes, their corners oriented towards the axis, whereby they become four Bhairavas which in the Nāthyogic legend function, like the giant *nāga*, as demonic bearers of the palanquin enclosing Matsyendranātha on his way to Nepal. Hence, it may be helpful to conceive of the chariot as a palanquin turned vehicle and the procession as centred round a palanquin-bearing core, remnants of which are still conserved in the preliminary procession of the priests (Nev. *pāṃjus*) bearing the deity from its temple at Tabāhā to the chariot at Phulchowk. The wheels, in their identification with the Tantric Bhairava,[14] whom blood sacrifices are offered, are regarded as dangerous as they might crush participants in the procession.[15] At the protruding front end of the pole the bronze-cast face of a demon called Vetāla, who usually carries the celestial Akāśa Bhairava, is applied, meant to lead and guide the travellers. Metalwork is applied to the platform's railings and especially to the shrine above whose openings bronze tympanums (*toraṇas*) depicting the Five Buddhas (*pañcabuddhas*) are fixed, a ritual which is carried out during the consecration of temples. Green branches of conifers are applied to the spire giving it the semblance of a forest giant. Finally, a wheel-shaped object termed 'parasol' (Nep. *gajura*, Nev. *byamo*, made of a wood called Nep. *phalauṭa*), is fixed horizontally at the axis on top of the spire together with three cotton flags and two long bandanas in the colours of the Five Buddhas (red, blue, white, green, yellow) which reach down two thirds the length of the spire and resemble the gilt strips on temple roofs. On completion, the ideal vertical orientation of the spire carrying the so-called 9th floor (Nev. *yakaḥkha*), which should stand at 90° to the ground plane, very often ends up at a tilt of about 5°–15°. This, as was pointed out to me by the supervisor of the construction Dil Kumar Badhai, is due to its

[14] According to a Vaḍhaī I asked, also the relative parts of the axes are part of that identification.

[15] They require a special consecration which takes place after the mounting of the chariot by Matsyendranātha and after sunset (in this case, 7.45–8.15 p.m., on April 21, 2004), involving the sacrifice (*balipūjā*) of a sheep below the right front wheel of the chariot and the sprinkling of all four wheels with its blood. On that occasion witnesses said that the Bhairavas might draw blood during the procession if it was not given to them in advance. For the parallels to the Jagannātha of Puri and the connected sacrifices s. Mishra 1971.

non-rigid but relatively loose connection to its base[16] and the relatively mobile web of branches and creepers which have ample space to move and resettle. For foreign observers who see the chariot for the first time, the degree of inclination in relation to is base is frighteningly precarious. However, as the spire is made out of relatively light materials, and with its volume and twig and leaf covering hiding a relatively porous interior, the unbalanced look is deceptive. The total netto weight of the chariot, according to the construction worker, amounts to roughly 2 tons with the spire making up only 1/4 of the total weight. To this one has to add the weight of an average of 20 people who travel on it during the passage, including the deity, its decor as well as materials for the daily ritual. To my questions about the considerable inclination of the spire this year my informants replied that this was totally within the norm of a chariot constructed according to the rules. When asked about the danger of toppling they said that the danger lied not in the construction of the chariot, but in the way it was handled on the way, especially how skilfully it was steered.

Essential for the movement of the chariot are four ropes attached to the pole and the platform, which extend over a distance of 25 metres in front of the chariot. Young men pull the ropes while one of them sits right in front on top of the *nāga* inciting the pullers and synchronizing the pulls with the call of "A-ste! A-ste!" As the chariot is equipped with no inbuilt steering mechanism, and as the action of rope-pulling does not provide any control to the path of the chariot on an often sloped and almost always uneven terrain. Hence, men called Nev. *ghakūs*, usually older than the pulling youths, apply appositely manufactured wedge-like wooden brakes (Nev. *ghaḥ mā*) made out of conical blocks half a metre in length with thin sticks of a metre's length pierced through them to handle the wedges which are kept at ground level, to the turning wheels in such a way as to alternately block them thereby determining the direction in which the chariot moves. As this involves working close to the wheels while the chariot moves, this activity is regarded not only the most important for the safe passage of the deity but also as the most dangerous.

[16] An informant compared the spire to a very big basket tied on to a car ("*gāḍīmā lagāeko ḍālo jastai*").

5. *The history of incidents*[17]

The first date mentioned in reference to a breakdown of the chariot is 1618 (738 N.S.) when apparently several such incidents resulted in the removal of the deity and its placement in a rest house (Nep. *pāṭi*) for the duration of the repairs to the chariot (Regmi 1965–66; vol. 2: 905). In 1631 (751 Nepāla Saṃvat)[18] the chariot was blocked for a number of days until the king's chief counsellor (*rājaguru*) ascended it, thereby getting it to move again.[19] In 1654 the Buddhist Wright's Chronicle mentions several breakdowns (Wright 1877: 240f.). In 1656 (776 N.S.) just after his first rice feeding (*annaprāśana*), which happens when children are about six months old, a child climbed onto the chariot, was possessed by the god and complained that the king had built a temple that was taller than the chariot, after which the god left the child and did not talk again (Wright 1877: 242). Ill omens persisted during the following year culminating in the theft of jewels from the vest of the deity (Wright 1877: 243). In 1662 (782 N.S.) because of the death of the Kathmandu king Pratāpa Malla no instruments were played during the procession—which led to the death of the prince, a major storm and damage to Lalitpur. The king of Lalitpur went to Cvabhāra to perform an exculpation rite (*kṣemapūjā*) on the day of the solar eclipse.[20] In 1676 (797 N.S.) the paint coating on the god's face came off in blisters. The god had to be taken from the chariot and the re-consecration rituals of face painting had to be repeated before the chariot could move on.[21] The deterioration of the paint seems to have been a frequent and important occurrence as it is mentioned as having happened in 1714 (834 N.S.) on day two of the bright half of the month of Caitra (Paudel et al. 2020–2023 II: 74) as well as in 1818, (N.S. 938), when an earthquake rocked the valley as the god was being taken back to Buṃgamatī (Sharma 1969: 6, 18), when the chariot passed a place called Thati on day twelve of the dark half of

[17] I have so far not been able to include here the details given in the still unpublished Nevārī Matsyendranāthavaṃśāvalī dated 1654 (N.S. 774), Ms. A 922/7 in the catalogue of the Nepal German Manuscript Preservation Project, an important text for the history of the incidents surrounding the chariot, on which I am currently working.

[18] This local era beginning in CE 879 was used particularly in the period of Newar Malla rule in the Kathmandu Valley (Slusser 1982: 389).

[19] Padmagiri's chronicle in Hasrat 1970: 69.

[20] Thapa 1970: 10, 3; Paudel & Lansāl 2020–2023 II: 65.

[21] Rajvamsi 2020: 10.

the month of Vaiśakha. In 1681 (N.S. 801) one of the beams of the chariot broke before leaving Buṃgamatī and four days of exculpation rites had to be performed, but the chariot broke down repeatedly on its way. In 1682 (N.S. 802) the chariot got stuck and an animal sacrifice (*balipūjā*) had to be performed three or four times by a local priest. This having had no effect, a priest was called from Buṃgamatī, but his sacrifice (*balipūjā*) failed too. Finally, a Brahmin from Lalitpur was called to read out texts and this got the chariot moving again (Regmi 1965–66 III: 92). An inscription dating 1690 (N.S. 810) states that this year the chariot fell at Yaṃpibāhā and the god had to be taken out (Tevārī 1963ff.; vol. 10: 14). Later chronicles[22] comment that an architectural item in gold had to be added to the chariot at the request of the deity who spoke through a boy who had just undergone initiation (Nev. *bare chuyegu*). Here we have the first source referring to the righting of the chariot with the help of ropes. In 1691 (N.S. 811) the chariot fell over at Būbāhā. There were big difficulties in saving the god who was severely damaged. But repairs were made and the procession continued.[23] 1693 (813 N.S.) saw several breakdowns and the chariot apparently even fell into a hole.[24] In 1705 (825 N.S.) the main pole broke more than once and each time the exculpation rites could not be performed at the right time. At that time King Yoganarendra of Lalitpur died and King Śrī Śrī Bhaskara Malla of Kathmandu temporarily appropriated the throne.[25] In 1708 (828 N.S.) a man who climbed on top of the chariot's pinnacle fell and died.[26] 1717 (837 N.S.) seems to have been a particularly bad year as the chariot's main pole cracked 31 (sic) times and the chariot of Mīnanātha burnt to the ground. Subsequently, an epidemic broke out in Lalitpur and King Ṛddhinarasiṃha died (Regmi 1965–66; vol. 2: 352). In 1724 (844 N.S.) a dog touched the god while being taken down from the chariot. On arrival back in Buṃgamatī the divinity came in contact with a pig and extensive atonement rites (*prāyaścittapūjās*) had to be performed.[27] In 1741 (861 N.S.) the chariot toppled twice and King Rājyaprakāśa Malla performed *kṣemapūjās* at the main Śaivite shrine of Paśupatinātha (Regmi 1965–66; vol. 2: 190).

[22] Paudel & Lansāl 2020–2023 II: 72; Thapa 1970, 10: 7.
[23] Regmi 1965–1966 III: 35.
[24] Regmi 1965–1966 III: 97f.
[25] Regmi 1965–1966 III: 52.
[26] Vajracarya 1975/1976: 29.
[27] Paudel & Lansāl 2020–2023 II: 75.

1747 (867 N.S.) had a minor goddess or fairy (*devatā*) touch the chariot to set it going again, after it got stuck.[28] In 1760 (880 N.S.) appeared Matsyendranātha in his temple in Lalitpur to King Viśvajita Malla with his back turned towards him. A riot broke out because of the king's mistress and Viśvajita committed suicide.[29] 1833 (953 N.S.) and 1856 (976 N.S.) had terrible earthquakes which damaged the shrine or disrupted the procession.[30] In 1862 (982 N.S.) during the reign of Surendra Vikrama Śāha the chariot fell over while being pulled from Buṃgamatī had to be dismantled. Two weeks later another chariot was ready. This suggests that if the criteria for rebuilding were the same as today, the 'parasol' had touched the ground. It is worth noting that records of falls which resemble the present one, i.e. in which either the position of the fallen chariot or a reconstruction of the chariot is described do not reach back to the Malla period. Whatever the reason may be, it is conspicuous that contemporary journalism[31] and popular memory[32] connect the beginning of a history of falls with the Śāha dynasty, neither take into account the dramatic breakdowns during the Mallas, nor consider it an event which has to be mentioned in connection with the procession from its onset. In 1833 during the circumambulation of the shrine of Matsyendranātha's mother a fire broke out on the chariot that lasted for two hours and damage was done to the god, which had to be repaired after removing the image through appeasement rites (*śāntisvastipūjās*).[33] The same happened four years later, this time including the chariot of Mīnanātha, but without damage to the image. In 1875 the chariot broke apart near modern day Maṅgalbajāra (Nev. Maṃgaḥ). Also this occasion must have been similar to the incident of 2004, because a new chariot was constructed. During the continuation of the procession King Surendra died, which brought the festival to a standstill lasting 13 days.[34] In 1934 an earthquake

[28] Paudel & Lansāl 2020–2023 II: 78.

[29] Thapa 1970: 10, 11; Regmi 1965–66 II: 362.

[30] Rana 1992; Sharma 1969, 6: 25.

[31] Adhikari 2004 gives 1802 (V.S. 1858), which falls in the reign of Gīrvaṇayuddha Bīra Bikrama Śāha (1797–1816), as the first date of a fall comparable to the one in question. Anonymous 2004c follows Adhikari in this.

[32] Gīrvaṇayuddha Bīra Bikrama Śāha (1797–1816) was mentioned to me twice when asking about the first such incident. Many interlocutors however, as vague as they may be, point out that such incidents had not always occurred and had become more frequent in recent times.

[33] Sharma 1969, 6: 25.

[34] Sharma 1968, 5: 28.

levelled an extensive number of buildings in the Kathmandu valley including the temple of the god at Tabāhā. During that year's subsequent procession the chariot fell over.[35] In 1970 and 1971 (Vikrama Saṃvat[36] 2026 and 2027) the chariot fell over in Nakkhu and Saugaḥ respectively, completely breaking apart both times and even with the 'parasol' touching the ground on the second occasion (see picture 1): in early 1972 King Mahendra passed away (Sangraula 2004; Adhikari 2004b). In 1980 (V.S. 2036), when a controversial referendum was held, first only the chariot's spire broke, leaving the 'parasol' undefiled, but then the chariot fell on its left side and had to be reconstructed (see picture 2).[37] In 1990 (V.S. 2046) the chariot fell. That same year the democracy movement toppled the one-party Pañcāyata system.[38] In 2001 (V.S. 2057) the chariot fell at a place called Naḥ, just after leaving Phulchowk, allegedly breaking up entirely (Adhikari 2004) and within a month, on June 1st the massacre of the royal family took place (Maharjan 2004). The last time Matsyendranātha fell was as recent as last year, 2003 (V.S. 2060), again a couple of hundred metres after the start at Phulchowk. Leaving aside the ongoing political crisis, no exceptional political event was remembered to have been connected to the incident.

As we have no handbooks dealing with the prescribed ritual of the procession as a whole, these sources help us shed some light on the possible development of aspects of the ritual. Certainly, what we have here are reports from a variety of heterogeneous sources, the value of each single one would have to be assessed according to its place, time and author. However, the voices we hear are in all but the more recent ones chronicles which generally tend to try to explain certain events at the royal court, be it political decisions or changes in power, and seem to connect them with events surrounding complications in the transfer of the chariot or the state of the god's image. On the

---

[35] However, Adhikari 2004 also refers to falls in the years 1944 (V.S. 2001), 1951 (V.S. 2008), 1955 (V.S. 2012), 1969 (V.S. 2026).

[36] Era of Indian origin beginning 57/56 BCE and in use in the Kathmandu Valley since the beginning of the Śāha period (Slusser 1982: 384–385).

[37] Sangraula 2004. A photograph in my possession documents a crash in 1984 (V.S. 2040) when the chariot apparently came off the road and crashed into a house under construction, though remaining intact and with the parasol way above the first floor.

[38] Sangraula 2004; Adhikari 2004. Again, according to Adhikari the chariot also "completely gave away" in the years 1992 (V.S. 2048), 1996 (V.S. 2052), while it "broke down three times" in 1994 (V.S. 2050).

other hand, we also find explanations of changes in ritual which may indirectly allow speculation on a possible political background to the community of ritual specialists and the groups in charge of the cult. What is interesting is that the toppling of the chariot seems not always to have been the major worry of the practitioners of the cult, as it is today. The dangers facing the god on its journey seem to have been much more diverse in the past. The chariot on the whole seems to have been more frail, if one believes the numbers of breakdowns during one procession in several years. Yet, it is not to be excluded that these figures were influenced by current historiographical and political motives. Damage through fire, ritual pollution through animals and the deterioration of the god's paint coating seem to have been major threats, which the few people I asked today were unable to recall such an incident having occurred during their lifetime. On the other hand it is remarkable that this year's incident and the subsequent measures taken, to be mentioned below, though not described in detail, seem to have been no novelty.

6. *The 2004 incident and its assessment*

On Sunday, April 25, 2004 (13 Vaiśākha), 9.30 p.m. the chariot toppled at a place called Calāchem̊, 200 metres before reaching its prescribed halt at Sundhārā, falling to its right and crashing onto the ground just between the Nārāyaṇa temple and a small Gaṇeśa shrine, slightly damaging the latter (see picture 3). Eight people including two policemen, two priests and four 'locals', i.e. people from the neighbourhood, were injured, two of them seriously (Maharjan 2004). The image of Matsyendranātha was hardly damaged at all, whereas materials for worship and the images of the other deities on board were scattered all over the ground and had to be collected and safeguarded by the priests. The number of people present at the site was said to be in the thousands (Ojha 2004). The Chief of Lalitpur District Police was quoted as saying that "the chariot had started leaning from Saturday" (Ojha 2004) already, from which one would assume that a trained eye might have been able to observe a change in the structure—an assumption for which I was unable to get any independent confirmation. On Monday, April 26 workers started preparing to raise the chariot again which on the same evening was re-erected with the help of two cranes and left standing at the site when it had crashed (Rāsasa 2004a).

Speculations as to the reason for the fall shot up the same night. They generally could be divided into three lines of argument, one seeing faults in the construction of the chariot, the other in the way it was handled and in the continuation of the procession after dark, and the last in religious shortcomings during the entire process.[39] What lends weight to the first assumption is the fact that since V.S. 2050 there have been repeated incidents of the structure of the chariot giving way, though without always leading to a fall. However, apparently on-the-road repairs had become much more frequent than before.[40] The few voices I heard directly accused the Vaḍhaīs and Yānvalas of not doing their job properly. Prakriti Adhikari, correspondent for the government-owned paper *The Rising Nepal* reports on the more serious accusation of the groups in question actually bagging profits, to which the response was that everyday orders were far more profitable than the construction of the chariot—which was considered mainly for its religious merit (Adhikari 2004). A member of the Guthi Saṃsthāna, who wanted to remain unnamed, favoured the line of faulty construction and disagreed, saying that the reason for the frequent breakdowns lay rather in the employment of young inexperienced artisans and in the lack of engagement in supervising the basic fitting work by the elders. When asked by the press whether the materials used by the artisans had been checked by the Guṭhi Saṃsthāna, the director of its Lalitpur branch Hari Prasad Joshi declared that he would prefer to leave these decisions to the artisans themselves.[41] The arguments and the officials' reactions identify this position as one which intends to put the blame on the Guṭhi Saṃsthāna. This may partly be motivated by the intention of certain groups, particularly the people living between Maṅgalbajāra and Sundhārā directly affected by the crash, to make claims and push for negotiations.

The second position connecting the fall with the chariot's handling

[39] E.g. Adhikari 2004: "The reason for the eventful fall this time was neither of the two mentioned here, it was because those dragging the huge structure did not deter in their ordeal despite the darkness that prevailed till late night. The enthusiastic participants in the chariot procession went on pulling the chariot in the same direction encountering an eventual accident."

[40] Adhikari 2004. S.M. Amatya mentions that the accident presumably of 1994 was explained to have happened due to the poor quality of the rattan employed (Amatya 1997: 20).

[41] Adhikari 2004. Here H.P. Joshi is quoted as not wanting to engage in speculations about the reason of the crash: "I am least aware about the reasons that lead to the falling down of the chariot."

was by far the most frequent. Alcohol consumption by those who pulled, physical and mental exhaustion and the practice of continuing after dark, i.e. after 9 or even 10 p.m., were the reasons mentioned, also adding the fact that the group straightening the spire had been working from the housetops.[42] The most widely favoured explanation was that the coordination between the group responsible for braking and steering the chariot and the group conducting the straightening of the spire became increasingly difficult due to the above mentioned reasons, which resulted in both a final conflicting steer and pull which had the chariot topple.[43] People I talked to referred to an existing rule of stopping the chariot at sunset even when the prescribed destination has not been reached, which has been almost entirely abandoned in recent years. The president of Lalitpur's powerful Farmers' Caste Society, the Jyāpu Samāja, Chiri Babu Maharjan was the strongest public spokesperson in favour of prohibiting the procession after dark.[44] Another argument mirroring the argument of faulty construction, and brought up twice on the streets of Lalitpur, but which I was not able to find in the press, was that the group responsible for moving the chariot had been newly engaged for that purpose, was inexperienced and underpaid, which sounds like yet another shot aimed at the Guṭhi Saṃsthāna. Another opinion I heard and read was that the chariot was pulled down on purpose by parts of the crowd involved. That hooliganism and ill-will of certain groups may also be a factor is a minority view[45] that probably overstretches and polarises the facts, but it touches upon an important point and shows that explaining the accident as a mere technical failure of an otherwise competent, focussed, coordinated and success-oriented group fails to do justice to the complexity of this event.

The third line of argument, finally, combines both previous lines. It claims that over the last years things have been going wrong, both during the construction of the chariot and during the procession. Tari Babu Dangol, the elder (Nep. *thakāli*) of the Yānvala Guṭhi (Adhikari 2004), denied any faulty assembly and—adopting the perspective of the Brahmin elite, with their emphasis on wrong and right and their

[42] Ojha 2004. Ojha adds that "the road was bad, still was being pulled." After looking at the place of the crash I would discard this additional cause.

[43] Maharjan 2004.

[44] Adhikari 2004. Currently, discussions are being conducted on how to enforce this proposition.

[45] One of the two Brahmins travelling on the chariot this year, Prakash Dhar Sharma, is quoted by Adhikari 2004b.

insistence on mistakes—maintained that these days the rules of conduct (Nep. *ācārako niyama*) which apply to those who work on the construction site until the completion of the chariot, such as abstaining from garlic, meat and sex, are not followed any more. Similarly, Tari Babu points out that during the procession many of the youngsters pulling the chariot fail to take off their leather belts. His most vitriolic attack is directed towards those riding the chariot: "People ride on the chariot carelessly, so the god is angry and then the chariot dilapidates suddenly." Additionally, he mentions that women are more and more frequently seen on the deck of the chariot.[46]

In this context the question of the cause is closely connected with the question of the effect. The most immediate effect was the injury of the eight people mentioned in the reports. As I was told by the Guṭhi Saṃsthana, demands of reimbursement of the treatment costs of the hospitalized was the most manifest and pressing consequence. The above criticism directed towards the construction and handling has to do with a genuine personal pain, with venting a general anger at the authorities and at raising the stakes and increasing the chances of pushing through financial demands. Also in this incident the deeply ingrained reflex of blaming the authorities and making demands in such diverse cases as natural disasters, rebel violence, electrocution or road accidents—against the backdrop of a state on the verge of financial meltdown and shackled by widespread corruption—shows that the self-paternalising attitude in political matters among much of the public persists unbroken within the religious setup. On the other hand, it also shows the strong resistance to an elite which claims the monopoly on determining what is right and wrong, in condemning and possibly punishing trespassers,—resistance which does not take the form of refuting that claim, but retaliates with the counter-claim that the elite, which is expected to take care of the people's well-being, must compensate for not living up to the expectation of being omnipotent. The conflict of the elite and the non-elite is a main feature of this event, which can only be understood if one does not adopt the perspective of one party, but listens to their polyphony. To adopt the elite-centred discourse of right or wrong, success or failure precludes polyphony. A second almost immediate effect to be witnessed the next morning was

[46] Adhikari 2004 refers to three women who rode on the chariot in 1994 (V.S. 2050) and caused it to break down thrice that year.

a general despondent feeling among people I met, among acquaintances, neighbours, shopkeepers and people on the street, with the crash being the major topic of discussion. This was especially true for the neighbourhood, the quarter of Calāchem̊, but also in a broader sense for the community between Gābāhā and Sundhārā, and ultimately for Lalitpur. This concentric expansion of damage becomes clear when one speaks to people from other parts of Lalitpur who sympathize with the inhabitants of Calāchem̊ as having experienced a setback regarding the merit they would have received if the chariot had passed successfully, and which now had turned into a negative premonition. Exactly what concrete effects the fall could or would have was never explicitly stated, merely that it was bad for the people living there and that something had to be done immediately. Further, a frequent complaint by people from other parts of town was about the delay in completing the procession, which now would be likely to finish a month behind schedule. A neighbour referred to the present situation as if "he had to take a deep breath" (Nep. *malāī thulo sāsa linuparthyo*) until the procession would resume. References to the Kathmandu Valley, the country as a whole and even to the monarchy were comparatively rare and were much more frequent in the press of those days (Maharjan 2004; Sangraula 2004). However, first reactions to the crash were full of allusions to the current state of the country, and criticism of the king's as well as the parties' and even the Maoists' policies. The strikes called by both Maoists and political parties, as well as the demonstrations above all by the student's unions in the weeks after the incident, leading to the resignation of Prime Minister Thapa who had been the year before installed by the king, were continuously read and referred to in the light of the fall of the Rāto Matsyendranātha. These, however, are readings which I only heard from people who are not ritual specialists and not involved with the organization or performance of the event. They seemed to refer to the event as if it confirmed something which they had already known or feared anyway, and expressed their pessimistic attitude towards political and social affairs by calling on a divine event. It seems as if those outside the ritual responsibility for it referred to the event from the perspective of inverted prophesy and stressed in a more deterministic way the connection of the fall that occurred with events that also had just happened or were just taking place.

It is interesting to note that in opposition to that view, ritual specialists seem to downplay the necessity of a link between the fall and current or past political events, or even of bad effects on the local community close to the accident. Bageshwar Rajopadhyaya, a Brahmin of Lalitpur whom I asked about his view on the matter, and especially whether he considered the fall of the deity an ill omen for the neighbourhood, Lalitpur, the country and the crown, dismissed these views as wrong and bad. He said that it could not be that the whole country should suffer just because some people had pulled the chariot badly and made it fall. Instead, he said that the necessary measures would be taken to make sure that the damage done to the deity and to the chariot was repaired, and that the safe passage of the chariot during the remaining part of the procession was guaranteed. He added that there are obstacles (*vighna*) on every journey (Nep. *jātrā*) and that with the help of the knowledge of the priests and engineers and the financial contribution from the responsible authorities the enterprise would be led to a successful conclusion. Different from the non-specialists' view of seeing the past accident as cause for past or present political trouble, he seemed rather to have his eye on the possible future dangers which have to be avoided on the god's journey.[47] As we will see below, this is also the view of the chief astrologer employed for planning the new start of the procession. However, there the focus will be on both appeasing the inimical planetary deities who keep the chariot blocked and smoothing the way to ward off future obstacles. The talk of obstructions seems to be the common way to denote the incident among ritual specialists, because Nucheman Shakya, senior member of the priest body from Buṃgamati, also speaks of 'obstructions or accidents' met by the deity on its way (Sangraula 2004). Both the reaction of Bageshwar as well as of Prakash Dhar Sharma, quoted above, seem to follow the strategy of transposing the cause for the disruption outside the ritual. It is an external impediment, the wrong handling by simply ignorant of willingly disruptive elements[48] alien to the know-how and the inner ritual core of the performance. It is the Puraṇic and Sanskritic narrative of the dark and demonic *asuras* who disrupt the gods' activities. This transposition of responsibility and the elite's use of the categories good and bad, right and wrong, is still mirrored in the opinion of the chief supervisor of the construction who cites the non-dharmic behaviour of

[47] Axel Michaels points at the conflict within the Brahminical tradition that the pilgrimage as journey must include and take into account the dangers of defilement implied when leaving the ritual arena of the house (Michaels 1994: 306).

[48] Often also called 'miscreants' in the Nepalese press (personal communication by Niels Gutschow) in line with post-colonial South Asian official parlance.

his collaborators as responsible for the incident. He as supervisor and carrying the moral authority of the elder remains detached from the wrongdoings by knowing the right conduct and bemoaning the downfall. Interestingly, however, in his case the group of people or rather the ensemble of actions that undermine the efforts is allowed to penetrate far more into the core of the ritual performance, including those who ride on the chariot and those who put it together.

According to the local office of the Guṭhi Saṃsthāna, its first reaction was to issue a report of the incident to the central office of the Guṭhi Saṃsthāna with a carbon copy sent to the Royal Police. According to §8 of the Saṃsthāna's statute,[49] it is for the board of directors (Nep. *saṃkṣāla samiti*) to decide which further steps to take. It is supposed to nominate a specialised committee (Nep. *vidvat samiti*) of seven members, this year chaired by Dr. Madhava Bhattarai, the Deputy Royal Priest (Nep. *nayaḥ badagurujyu*), and co-chaired by the Royal Astrologer Angur Baba Joshi and five people of high social standing. Conspicuously, this year Buddhists were missing from the list, as I was told by the officer in charge. The directors board would commission a report, to be delivered to the Royal Palace by the board of experts, demanding information as to the condition of the chariot, the amount of new materials needed, the time employed for rebuilding, what kind of rituals would be necessary and what changes the board of experts would suggest. The board of experts convened on Friday, April 30, consisting additionally of Rudra Kumar Shrestha, an influential member of the city council of Lalitpur, representatives of the Ministries of Home, Law and Culture, and the Director General of the Departments of Land Reform and Management. The results were sent to the central office, announced immediately and published the day after (Rāsasa 2004c and 2004d). The reason given for the crash was darkness, and carelessness on the part of those pulling the chariot. Six people had been injured by the collapse of the structure, three seriously and still hospitalized with a leg fracture, a spine fracture and severe concussion respectively. Some ornaments of the chariot were found to be missing. The most important decision, however, whether the chariot would have to be rebuilt before the procession could continue or not, remained undecided. Instead, it was advised that one consult old local residents, knowledgeable people

[49] Śreṣṭha 2053: 196–228.

(Nep. *vidvat*) and heads of local Guṭhis (Nep. *guṭhiyārs*) and have the matter discussed. As the officer at the branch office told me, there are no texts available for these situations. Instead, one relies on personal advice founded on the oral transmission of precedents. Rebuilding would entail the sorting out the reusable from the non-reusable parts, which would have to be discarded. Furthermore, it transpired that the Guṭhi Saṃsthāna considered allowing metal parts to be used in building future chariots. This proposal, which has been brought up before (Adhikari 2004), came among complaints that the kinds of materials—especially wood required for certain parts of the construction—were hard to find, and amidst speculations that the replacement of some parts by unsuitable materials could have led to the crash. However, this push for allegedly safer construction techniques was said to have been opposed by traditionalists who felt that "any deviation from tradition in the way the chariot is built would violate religious norms."[50]

After premature reports that the procession would continue, on Tuesday, April 29 (Rāsasa 2004b) it became clear that the 'parasol' having touched the ground made it necessary to disassemble most of the chariot and have it rebuilt before continuing the procession.[51] The decisive document in this matter, which was made accessible to me, is a letter in Nepālī[52] from the astrologer Kirti Bharata Joshi, chosen to present the decisive diagnosis, to the Head of the Guṭhi Saṃsthāna of Lalitpur (Nev. *śrīmāna pramukha jyū*), Hari Prasad Joshi, dating May 14, 2004 (Jyeṣṭha 1, V.S. 2061) giving an astrological analysis of the time of the fall, giving the correct timing (*sāita*) for the repeated ascension of the deity onto the chariot (*punaḥ rathārohaṇa*) for Friday, May 21, 2004 (*jyeṣṭha* 8, *śukravāra*, V.S. 2061) on page one and on the following eight recommending the procedures for the appeasement rite (*śāntisvāsti*). The letter states that the chariot happened to have fallen pointing south (*dakṣiṭarpha palṭiekovare*) in Calācheṁ̊ near Sundhārā on the sixth day

[50] Ibid. Adhikari 2004 quotes a *jyāpu* elder, Chiri Kaji Maharjan, who objected especially to the shape of the chariot being altered, as well as Cheto Nath Sharma, whom Adhikari calls 'cultural scientist', as supporting a modification of the chariot's shape "to ensure security and to save tradition."

[51] "Because of the chariot's 'parasol' (*gajura*) touching the ground they thought this to be a serious matter. [...] According to their tradition, after the chariot's parasol has touched the ground, a whole new chariot has to be built" (*yasapāli rathako gajurale bhuiṃ nai choekolāī unīharule jhan gambhīra māneko chan*. [...] *unakā anusāra, yasarī rathko gajurle bhuiṃ choepachi pheri nayāṃ ratha nai banāunuparcha*.) Maharjan 2004.

[52] This letter is couched in a highly Sanskritic Nepālī, so I have refrained from specifying the language of terms or phrases.

(*ṣaṣṭhān-tithi*) of the light half of the month Vaiśakha N.S. 1124, viz. V.S. 2061, under the lunar mansion (*nakṣatra*) of *ārdra* or *punavarsu* (sic),[53] the conjunction (*yoga*) *sukarma*,[54] the lunar division of the day (*karaṇa*)[55] being *kaulava* or *taitila*,[56] the day Sunday, Vaiśākha 30, the planetary deities having been visible in an inauspicious way (*gṛha aśubha dekhie-kole*) Mars (*maṃgala*), Mercury (*budha*), Saturn (*śani*), the lunar eclipse deities Rāhu and Ketu, the Moon (*candramā*), the Sun (*sūrya*) and so on (*-ādi*), meaning possible other relevant deities not mentioned. The instructions for the offering to the planetary deities repeat the timing, mention the astrological 'location' (*gṛhasthāna*) of the chariot's fall as bad and foresee bad consequences (*vividha duṣṭsaphalnivaraṇa*) for country and king if these rites are not carried out. In order to achieve pleasure (*sukha*) and blessing (*aiśvarya*) and in order to complete the procession without prior obstacle (*nirvighna pūrvaka*), offerings have to be made to the obstructing deities—as given in the subsequent list. The letter then mentions the other rites required for the complex appeasement ritual which further include a fire sacrifice (*homa*), worship (*pūjā*) dedicated to Kumbheśvara (the form of Śiva to which Lalitpur's biggest Śaivite temple is dedicated), the virgin goddess Kumārī, Paśupati (the form of Śiva at his most revered temple in the Valley), his consort Guhyeśvarī, Śrī Macchindranātha (sic) himself, Bhairavanātha including a sacrifice (*bali*), Mahākāla, Gaṇeśa the deity of beginnings, ways and obstacles, 'and others' (*-ādi*). Further text reading (*pāṭha*), chanting (*japa*), and a concluding exculpation rite (*kṣemapūjā*) are required.

7. *Re-instalment and appeasement*

On Thursday, April 29 the *Annapūrṇa Poṣṭ* published a note reporting that, in their first public appearance since the incident the king and his queen together with the crown prince and his wife had gone to a visit to the shrine at Dakṣiṇakālī and offered to the goddess, protector of the royal family, as prescribed by the texts.[57] Comments by acquaintances

---

[53] Skt. *ārdra* being the fourth and *punarvasu* the fifth of seven lunar mansions.
[54] The seventh of the 27 yogas, in which the joint motion in longitude of the sun and moon amounts to 13°20'.
[55] An astrological unit by which the day is divided in 11 parts, measuring the waxing and waning of the moon.
[56] The third and fourth astronomical daily period respectively.
[57] *Śāstrokta vidhipūrvaka dakṣiṇakālī bhagavatīko pūjā-ārcanā garibaksyo.* Rāsasa 2004b.

of mine pointed to a connection between this visit and the event, stressing its gravity for the crown. According to the Nichaya Raja Shakya, representative of the Lalitpur Buddhists during the procession and in charge for the last 21 years, the time window for the reconstruction of the chariot would be till June 4.[58] After that the next window would be from August 31 to September 5 (*Himalayan News Service* 2004). Hari Prasad Joshi stated that reconstruction would cost NEPR 600 000,—and that the government had given permission to procure the necessary choice of timber (*Himalayan News Service* 2004).

On Wednesday, May 5 between 8.00 and 8.10 p.m. a rite was celebrated to inaugurate the reconstruction (*ratha punaḥnirmāṇa*) of the chariot. In front of the chariot, already depleted of the spire and the shrine, four holes had been dug in which four beams were to be stuck serving as tyre jacks (Nev. *hākī*) for the vehicle for the time of its dis- and reassembly. One woodworker and three scaffolding workers performed the ritual called Nev. *hāṃvo pujā*, which is done before beginning any kind of construction work. On Thursday, May 6, between 10.30 a.m. and 12.30 p.m. the chariot was lifted by means of 18 men and four jacks. Skipping the time during which the chariot was being rebuilt, on Friday, May 21 at 8.56 a.m. at the astrologically determined time (Nep. *sāita*) the reconstruction of the chariot by Vaḍhaīs and Yānvalas under the direction of Senior Engineer (Nep. *variṣṭha injiniyara*) Saroj Thapaliya was declared completed. A group of 10 Rajopādhyāyas and two Jośis under the direction of Shri Kavijananda Rajopadhyaya of Pakutva, Lalitpur recited verses (*japa*) and texts (*pāṭha*) from 9.10 to 11.30 a.m. at the small temple of Vaṃśagopāla at Sundhārā, in accordance with the directions prescribed in the astrologer's letter. At 9.30 a.m. the bronze-cast face of Akāśa Bhairava was brought to the chariot and fixed to the *nāga's* tip. At 10.09 a.m. the king's adviser's guard arrived at Sundhārā joined by the sword-holder of the king and fired two rounds of salute. At 10.14 a.m. the Rāto Matsyendranātha was taken from the rest house in a procession, with the platoon leading the way, followed by a sweeper (Nep. *poḍe*, Nev. *pvaṃ* or *pvaḥ*) with his broom, people laying a strip of white cloth for the god to tread on, two people carrying bells, two sword bearers, another sweeper with his broom, a woman

[58] By contrast, repairs to the Bhaktapur chariot during Bisket, being much smaller, can usually be done within a day, even in the case of a broken axis. The chariot has three days to cover a much shorter distance and always reaches its destination (personal communication by Niels Gutschow).

offering flowers to the deity, a fly whisk (*camara*) bearer, the main priest, the palanquin of Matsyendranātha carried by four priests, the Buddha Amitābha or Dīpaṃkara carried by a priest, and a man carrying the silver box in which the foot piece (*pādukā*) of the deity is kept. The procession took a direct route to the chariot reaching it in seven minutes (i.e. 10.21 a.m.),[59] after which Matsyendranātha and Dīpaṃkara were hoisted and placed into the chariot's shrine. Immediately after, at 11.44 a.m., three Vajrācāryas, all of Buṃgamati, namely the seniormost Surya Muni (officiating as Nev. *thāypāṃju*), the second seniormost Punya Raja (officiating as *mūlācārya*) and finally Kapila Muni (officiating as *upādhyāya*) started the exculpation rite (*kṣemapūjā*), the patron (Nep. *jajamāna*) in this case being a Śreṣṭha from Pūrṇacāṇḍī. They were assisted by the staff of the Guṭhi Saṃsthāna and the seniormost priest had a photocopy of the astrologer's letter which he would use to cross-check. The rite started with the *mūlācārya* accepting the cow's gift (*godāna*) including a calf, after which he celebrated a flask worship (*kalaśārcana*). At 12.11 p.m., with the assistance of the *upādhyāya*, he began the central offering to the Nine Planetary Deities (*navagrahadāna*). Throughout this rite the *thapaju* recited the Grahamātrikāpāṭha, the Ganeśapāṭha as well as the Pratyangirapāṭha. To conclude the *kṣemapūjā*, the patron performed the worship of all the deities present on the chariot (Nev. *cakapujā*), after which the members of the Guṭhi Samṣthāna present offered their financial contribution (*dakṣiṇā*) to the priests, and the entire event was wrapped up by 12.41 p.m.

On Saturday, May 22 preparations for the remaining rites started at 10.30 a.m. It was 11.18 a.m. when the diagrams (*yantras*) where drawn on the ground, after which the entire priestly staff of the chariot from Buṃgamatī, i.e. seven Vajrācāryas and 14 Śākyas read and performed the Guṇakaraṇḍavyūha, one after the other. The fire sacrifice (*homa*) was performed by the same *mūlācārya* from the day before, Punya Raja Bajracharya, assisted by the *upādhyāya* Kapila Muni Bajracharya who also performed the protective rite called *pañcarakṣa*. Thereafter, the *thapājū* Surya Muni Bajracharya celebrated the standard set of life-cycle rites in their reduced version and necessary in the consecration and empowerment of religious artefacts, the *daśakarma*, while the other two

[59] The mounting of the chariot by the deity had been prescribed for the time between 8.56 and 9.11 a.m. after the completion of an exculpation rite (*kṣemapūjā*). The deviation from this time could not be explained to me.

Vajrācāryas sang Tantric songs (*caryāgīti*), and two other Vajrācāryas performed sacrifices to four of the Eight Mother Goddesses (*aṣṭamātrikābali*) and the according to the tradition most effective one, the *mahābali*. Again, as on the preceding day, the patron was the Śreṣṭha from Pūrṇacāṇḍī, Lalitpur. The *daśakarma* came to an end at 1.00 p.m. and the performers relaxed after having had a meal called Nev. *pañcāku* (Skt. *pañcakuśa*) consisting of five kinds of buffalo meat, which is said to be the favourite dish of the goddess[60] and in this case accompanied by pastry, wine and beer. 1.45 p.m. was the time for the sacrifices, whose texts had been read beforehand: a ram for the Sacrifice for the Eight Mother Goddesses, another ram for the Great Sacrifice dedicated to the Bhairavas of the four wheels and axes, as well as a buffalo for the Bhairava of the pole in front. While the chariot was sprayed with powerful spurts issuing from the tied-up buffalo's aorta, the priests in charge of tending to Matsyendranātha covered the entrance to the holiest with a red curtain, thus protecting the Bodhisattva from the gushing blood.[61] The meat of all three animals was divided up among the Vajrācāryas. The *homa* was resumed at 2.25 p.m. and was rounded off by the prescribed offering of a full ladle of ghee into the fire (*pūrṇāhuti*) and the offering of a coconut. An hour later two rams stemming from Buṃgamatī were sacrificed in a rite dedicated to the successful execution of the entire ritual regarding the chariot (*viśvakarmabali*) and the meat distributed among the staff of the Guṭhi Saṃsthāna present. Finally, one last ram was offered to the wheel and axis Bhairavas and given to the members of the Guṭhi responsible for the braking and steering of the chariot, the Ghaḥkhu Guṭhi. At that time it was 4.00 p.m. The entire series of rituals can be read as an alternation of rites which repeat those undertaken on the first occasion, i.e. at the beginning of the procession, and of those which intervene, thus taking into account the crisis and helping to solve it. The ascension onto the chariot is repeated (*punar rathārohaṇa*), after which the planets are appeased and the obstacle which is still blocking the chariot at its place is removed. After that the consecrating life-cycle rites of the god are repeated and concluded with an exculpation rite which purifies the travelling god and makes him fit for accomplishing his task. The people, eager to resume the pulling of the chariot, would

[60] "The goddess' blessed food" (Gellner 1992: 286).

[61] Owens has convincingly described the role of sacrifice in a cult centred on a deity which abhors killing (Owens 1993: 265f.).

have to wait until the fourth day counting from Friday, i.e. Monday, May 24 to accomplish what would have been done almost a month earlier if the Red Matsyendranātha had not fallen.[62]

8. *Getting it done*

What does it mean, if we, being researchers of ritual, talk in this case to Newar ritual specialists and non-specialists about ritual mistake or failure in a Newar ritual? Reactions to my inquiries were very often characterized by politely cloaked irritation. My interlocutors usually not only denied that there was any such thing as a 'mistake' (Nep. *galti*; Nev. *dvaṃgu*) or failure (Nep. *asaphaltā*; Nev. *suthām̐ malāḥgu* or simply *phela*). Rather, the strategies for explaining the incident all resembled the ones depicted above and none would find the term 'mistake' fitting, neither for the breakdown of coordination among the pulling parties, nor for the moral conduct of the participants to explain what had happened. The irritation was less veiled and quickly mutated to outright bemusement when I inquired about failure. Replies ranged from assurances that all the parties involved were working at it to bring the procession to a happy ending, "as they do every year," to the reaction of a student, Vikash Maharjan, who said to me in English: "Failure is when I fail my exam. When there is no rain or when the king and the Maoists fight, it is not failure, it is very, very worse" (conversation on August 31, 2004).

However, another reaction, which transcends the terminological question and which is much more subtle, was one of indignation. Leaving aside the uneasiness which accompanies discussions of the dark and dangerous sides of events or the impression that people would object to washing their dirty linen in public, both of which I experienced little of, not a few interlocutors, especially those who knew me better, and one Brahmin who did not know me at all, asked me, half, if at all, jokingly, who I thought I was talking to them about 'mistakes' and 'failures'. The point raised by this reply is not so much that this might be an attempt to deny me the right to formulate my critique, but the

[62] Rāsasa 2004e and 2004f. It may be of relevance for the continuation of the procession after the incident that after arriving at Sundhārā, the stop it had failed to reach on April 25, the chariot would have to be turned on the spot to face West: [...] *rathlāī sohī paścima diśātarpha muhāra moḍera* [...] (Anonymous 2004b).

far more fundamental point about which identity I take on when I talk about ritual in such a way. The problem here is the status one acquires and the role one plays or, even worse, the opportunities one forfeits when speaking as a European Indologist and field researcher about 'mistakes' and 'failures' in a ritual context. While searching for an 'indigenous' way to assess what is going on in a Nepalese ritual, the danger is that one takes over the position of the Parbatiyā Brahmin, Newar Rājopadhyāya or Vajrācārya or one which is very similar to these, because it is they who are associated with an authority and a competence which one pretends to have when asking questions of this kind. Discussions with Parbatiyā and Newar ritual specialists about rituals they have witnessed of other practitioners, or in which they collaborated are generally marked by the focus they put on the mistakes the other did. This is markedly the case when the Newar talks about the 'mountain Brahmin's' (Nep. *parbatiyā bāhun*) performance and vice-versa, reflecting a complicated and historically loaded adversarial relationship. The dangers of the assimilation of the Western researcher to the specialised elite and the limitations of doing research while turning into a 'White Brahmin' are well-known and it is necessary to reduce rather than re-enforce them. The voices documented above show that even when speaking with ritual specialists about the breakdown of this ritual, which is essentially run by Newars and thoroughly embraced by other ethnic groups, there was practically no mention of a particular mistake or an overall failure. Rather, the discussion seems to be much more interested in causes which lie beyond or have made their way into the inner core of the rite. This means that even the Nepalese ritual elite, when faced with different challenges, may have very different ways of speaking about different rituals, whereas the Euroamerican academic conducting ritual criticism would start by applying the categories of mistake and failure to a much larger range of cases. The Brahmins that we try to be might turn out to be more 'white' than 'Brahminical'.

Is it at all helpful to ask about ritual mistake and failure for the understanding of what has happened during the annual journey of the Red Matsyendranātha? It might be. I am not so interested in arguing that we produce the mistakes and failures we are looking for in an environment that allegedly does not know what we are talking about. This may even be the case and doing so might even produce interesting results. Instead, I would like to close by raising the slightly more disturbing point that by probing for mistakes and failures and turning ourselves into the referees of the ritual match we take over the role of one ritual group, narrowing down the perspective on what is actually going on and giving up the advantage of being able to access the event through different social and ethnic groups. Additionally, and even more problematically, by taking over that dominating perspective we assimilate and thereby claim to be those who are in the position to judge what good and what bad rituals are. We do this without actually having to negotiate ourselves what is good and what is bad within a certain ritual or social setup, which the practicing ritual specialist inevitably has to do. We take over the knowledge and claims of the Brahmin without taking over his duties, constraints and the pressures he faces to compromise and find solutions. In order to find out more about the performance, instead of rating it along the lines of right/wrong, good/bad, successful/failed, which we, the performer, the ritual specialist or the broader public might have taken over from a ritual handbook or a group which we have found do be in sync with our own, it would be much more fruitful to measure the performers' work both according to the expectations of the various performers themselves and of their more or less specialized public composed of bystanders, the audience of radio and TV, newspaper readers, artisans, political authorities and ritual specialists. In other words, one would have to let all those who interact in and thereby create the ritual event speak and choose their own categories. The interviewed partners should be the ones not only to tell us under which conditions something is good or bad, but also whether a certain act can be good or bad at all, and, most importantly of all, who is entitled to call something good or bad, right or wrong, a success or a failure. While in the field of the everyday criticism of art self-entitlement comes easy, as field researchers we should be very wary of self-entitlement regarding partners on whose behalf we tend to speak much too easily. The functioning of art and ritual might have a much larger design which eludes us if we try to speak in the language of only one group, the language of mistakes and failures being such a language. In contrast, I would plead for the event in its untidiness, for the competing voices issuing from it, to speak and to be listened to.

Accordingly, the journey of the Red Matsyendranātha, in my view, should not be seen as an event ruled by the obsession with 'getting it right' that allows for the occasional mistakes and failures to which the ritual critic may condescendingly grant the dubious honour of being tools for a better understanding of ritual. Instead, is about trying to manage in an imperfect world, in which no harvest can be rich enough to feed the mouths of the hungry, in which the onset of the rainy season is always a time of crisis, of hope and preoccupation, where the activities of government, military and rebels are not conducive to peace and prosperity, in which it is a rule that things go other than planned—though not for good, because there is always a chance for recovery, a way to salvation, and there is always time to pick oneself up and remove the obstacles. What happens is not the mistake of a single person, not even of a single group. At the most, diverse groups are said not to have acted according to the norm, but even more so, the world's condition is such that it is this aberrant behaviour that is the norm, not the exception. And it is this condition which both creates the obstacle and demands its removal. The god's fall is no sign which the gods send from above, because the god is at the centre and reaches out to create the periphery and the whole. It is the god who gets angry and throws himself to the ground and he does so because the people act in a way that gives him reason to fall. The god throws himself to the ground and is brought to fall at the same time. The god cannot do otherwise than interrupt the circle of his journey. The drama of breakdown is part of the ritual event and it is in this ritual that the broken can be mended. Nothing goes wrong because everything has already gone wrong. Nobody makes a mistake because almost everybody is potentially messing up all the time anyway. Except in the eyes of a few people, this ritual is neither about getting it wrong or getting it right, it is about getting it done. It is the striving for completion and completeness of the incomplete in serving the god and in competing for his favours that brings about a better life. And, as we have seen, it takes all the king's horses and all the king's men to show that man can get things done, can, so to speak, put Humpty Dumpty together again in a world where things tend, almost inevitably, to break. This year, on the morning of Friday, April 23, two days before the ill-fated day, my neighbours in Cākupāṭ pointed out to me that rain had fallen last night. The Red Matsyendranātha's journey had been successful even before it could fail.

Picture 1: 1971 (courtesy C. Emmrich)

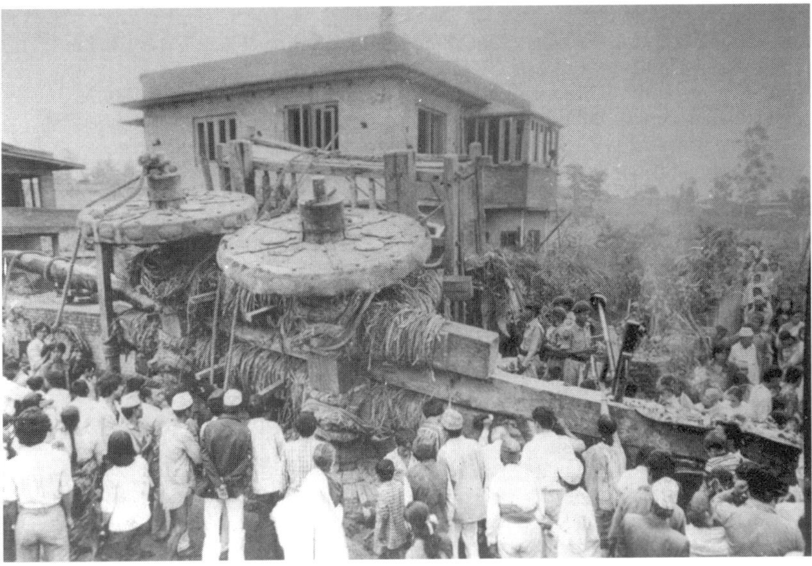

Picture 2: 1980 (courtesy C. Emmrich)

Picture 3: 2004 (copyright Min Bajracharya and the Himal Press)

References

Adhikari, Prakriti 2004. "Rato Machhindranath Chariot. The Mystery Behind The Fall: Know It". In: *The Rising Nepal*, 18/Jun/2004: 9.

Amatya, Swoyambhu Man 1997. *The Rattans of Nepal*. Kathmandu: IUCN (IUCN Nepal Biodiversity Publication Series 2).

Anderson, Mary M. 1971. *The Festivals of Nepal*. London: Unwin & Allen.

Anonymous 2004a. "Macchindranāthako nayā ratha banaine". In: *Nepāla Samācār Patra*, 24/Apr/2004: 2.

—— 2004b. "Ratha ṭaldā arko pūra". In: *Ceṣṭā Saptāhika*, 28/Apr/2004: 1.

—— 2004c. "Bigrieko ratha punaḥnirmāṇ kārya samāpta". In: *Gorakhpatra*, 21/May/2004: 3.

Bagchi, Prabodh Chandra 1934. *Kaulajnanah Nirnaya and Some Minor Texts of the School of Matsyendranatha*. Calcutta: Metropolitan Publishing House.

Briggs, G.W. 1953. *Gorakhnath and the Kanphata Yogis*. Calcutta: YMCA Publ. House.

Gellner, David 1992. *Monk, Householder and Tantric Priest. Newar Buddhism and its Hierarchy of Ritual*. Cambridge: Cambridge University Press.

Grimes, Ronald L. 1988. "Ritual Criticism and Reflexivity in Fieldwork". *Journal of Ritual Studies* 22: 217–239.

Gutschow, Niels 1979. "Ritual Chariots in Nepal. Mobile Architecture in Asia: Ceremonial Chariots, Floats and Carriages". *Art and Archeology Research Papers* 16: 32–38.

—— & Bernhard Kölver & Ishwaranand Shresthacarya (ed.) 1987. *Newar Towns and Buildings. An Illustrated Dictionary Newārī-English*. Sankt Augustin: VGH Wissenschaftsverlag.

Hasrat, Bikrama Jit 1970. *History of Nepal*. Hosiarpur: Hasrat.

Himalayan News Service 2004. "Rato Machhindranath's Chariot Undergoing Repairs". In: *The Himalayan Times*, 08/May/2004: 4.

Jośi, Rajalāla 2004. "Ratha ṭalepachi ani a hune bhayale buṭāpākā cintita". In: *Annapūrṇa Poṣṭ*, 27/Apr/2004: 3.
Lienhard, Siegfried 1978. "Religionssynkretismus in Nepal". In: *Buddhism in Ceylon and Studies on Religious Syncretism in Buddhist Countries*, Bechert, Heinz & Richard Gombrich (ed.). Goettingen: Vandenhoek & Ruprecht, 146–177.
Locke, J.K. 1973. *Rato Matsyendranath of Patan and Bungamati*. Kathmandu.
—— 1980. *Karunamaya: The Kult of Avalokitesvara-Matsyendranath in the Valley of Nepal*. Kathmandu.
Macdonald, Alexander 1975. "Juggernaut Reconstructed". In: *Essays in the Ethnology of Nepal and South Asia*, Macdonald, Alexander (ed.). Kathmandu: Ratna Pustak Bandhar, 27–60.
Maharjan, Indra 2004. "Pheri ṭalyo Macchindranātha". In: *Himāla*, 28/Apr/2004: 32.
Michaels, Axel 1994. *Die Reisen der Götter. Der nepalische Paśupati-Tempel und sein rituelles Umfeld*. Bonn: VGH Wissenschaftsverlag.
Mishra. K.C. 1971. *The Cult of Jagannatha*. Calcutta: K.L. Mukhopaddhyay.
Ojha, Kedar 2004. "Rato Machhindranath Chariot Topples. Eight Injured, Five of them Serious". In: *The Kathmandu Post*, 26/Apr/2004: 2.
Owens, Bruce McCoy 1989. *The Politics of Divinity in the Kathmandu Valley: The Festival of Bungadya/Rato Matsyendranath*. New York: Columbia University PhD Thesis.
—— 1993. "Blood and Bodhisattvas: Sacrifice among the Newar Buddhists of Nepal". In: *The Anthropology of Tibet and the Himalayas*, Ramble, Charles & Martin Brauen (ed.). Zürich: Völkerkundemuseum der Universität Zürich, 258–269.
—— 1995. "Human Agency and Divine Power: Transforming Images and Recreating Gods among the Newar". *History of Religions* 34.3: 201–240.
Paudel, Nayanāth & Devīprasād Lansāl 2020–2023. *Bhāṣāvaṃśāvalī*. 2 Vols. Kāṭhmāṇḍu.
Rājvaṃsī, Śaṃkaramān (ed.) 2020. *Aitihāsika kuṇḍalī*. Kāṭhmāṇḍū: Purātatva Vibhāga.
Rana, J.B. 1992. *Nepālko Mahābhūkampa*. Kāṭhmāṇḍū.
Rāsasa 2004a. "Chariot of Red Machhindranath lifted again". In: *Rising Nepal*, 27/Apr/2004: 3.
—— 2004b. "Rajdampatibā a pūjārcanā". In: *Annapūrṇa Poṣṭ*, 29/Apr/2004: 4.
—— 2004c. "Rāsasa. Red Macchindranath chariot to be rebuilt." In: *Rising Nepal*, 01/May/2004: 2.
—— 2004d. "Matsyendranāthako nayā ratha banāine". In: *Annapūrṇa Poṣṭ*, 01/May/2004: 2.
—— 2004e. "Rāsasa. Chariot Procession of Red Machhendranath Resumes Today". In: *The Rising Nepal*, 24/May/2004: 3.
—— 2004f. "Macchindranāthako ratha tāniyo". In: *Kāntipur*, 25/May/2004: 2.
Regmi, D.R. 1965–66. *Medieval Nepal*. 4 vols. Calcutta: Mukhopadhyaya.
—— [3]1969. *Ancient Nepal*. Calcutta.
Roerich, G.N. 1959. *Biography of Dharmasvāmin. A Tibetan Monk Pilgrim*. Patna: K.P. Jayaswal Research Institute.
Rospatt, Alexander von 2000. *The Periodic Renovations of the Thrice-Blessed Svayambhūcaitya of Kathmandu*. Leipzig: Habilitation thesis.
Sangraula, Bikash 2004. "Rato Machhindranath Topples: Divine Will or Simple Physics?" In: *The Kathmandu Post*, 26/Apr/2004: 7.
Sharma, Bal Chandra (ed.) 1968–1969. "Kāṭhmāṇḍū Upatyāko Ek Rajavaṃśāvalī". *Ancient Nepal* 4 (1968): 1–15; 5 (1968): 1–17; 6 (1969): 1–29.
Slusser, Mary Shepherd 1982. *Nepal Mandala. A Cultural Study of the Kathmandu Valley*. Princeton: Princeton University Press.
Śreṣṭha, Gyanendra Bahadur (ed.) 2053. *Guṭhi Saṃsthāna Aīn 2033*. Kathmandu: Paravi Publishers.

Tevārī, Rāmjī I. (ed.)1963. *Abhilekh Sangraha.* 12 vols. Kathmandu: Itihāsa saṃśodhana maṇḍala.
Thapa, Ramesh Jung (ed.) 1969–1970. "Vaṃśāvalī Rājabhogmālā". *Ancient Nepal* 7 (1969): 1–24; 8 (1969): 1–24; 9 (1969): 1–24; 10 (1970): 1–24; 11 (1970): 1–17.
Vajrācārya, Gautmavajra 1975/1976. "Aprakāśit Thyāsāphu". *Pūrṇimā* 12: 22–39.
Vergati, Anne 1985. "Le roi faiseur de pluie: une nouvelle version de la légende d'Avalokiteśvara rouge au Népal". *Bulletin des Etudes Françaises de l'Extreme Orient* 74: 287–303.
Wright, Daniel 1877. *History of Nepal with an Anthropological Sketch of the Country and People of Nepal.* Translated from the Parbatiya by Munshi Shew Shunker Singh Pandit Shri Gunanand. Cambridge (reprint: Madras Asian Educational Services, 1993).

PREVENTIVE MEASURES AND "QUALITY CONTROL"

As demonstrated in the previous section, most traditions are not only aware of the inherent riskiness of ritual performances but also provide for strategies to avoid negative consequences arising from errors or mistakes in ritual. On the one hand, it seems that most traditions develop such strategies, but on the other no two of these strategies are alike: here, again, the context determines the concrete form of the measures. Although traces of such strategies are discernible in many traditions dealt with in the contributions to this volume,[1] the two papers presented here especially concentrate on such preventive measures and modes to ensure a ritual's 'quality'.

In Johanna Bus's case study, as in many other textual traditions, the possibility of mistakes and consequently 'doctrinal (i.e. postulated) failure' is excluded through reparation or atonement rituals, which are part and parcel of the rituals proper. As 'meta rites' (rituals that work on other rituals), they aim at correcting, undoing, or transforming some other rite.[2] It is however noteworthy that these 'meta rites' are governed by rules that equal those rules for the ritual performance proper. In her article "The Sixteenth *Piṇḍa* as a Hidden Insurance Against Ritual Failure" Johanna Buss deals with a death ritual in Nepal that is supposed to transform the deceased from the helpless (but dangerous) condition of a ghost into the safe state of a forefather. However, even though this ritual should ensure the safe passage of the deceased, as a part of that ritual yet another 'ball' is offered "to the sorrowful deceased", dedicated collectively to any member of the own family who might have faced

[1] In addition to atonement rituals as method of excluding mistakes and failure, Michaels in this volume argues that in Vedic ritual systems the rituals' inherent riskiness is dealt with by the internalisation of the entire ritual process. Snoek's case study even lists an instance where it is explicitly stated that the validity of the ritual remains undisputed even if the ritual rules are not adhered to. Another means to cope with the riskiness of rituals is the 'incorporation' of deviations in ritual by attributing them to superhuman agency and thus considering them as part of the ritual process (see Weinhold, see also Emmrich).

[2] Thus Grimes in his "Response" to the contributions presented on the occasion of the panel 'Ritual Mistakes and Failure of Ritual' during the AAR conference, held in 11/2004 in San Antonio, Texas (unpublished).

the destiny of not being transformed into a forefather. Buss concludes that there exists an awareness that the ritual can fail and the deceased has to stay in his wretched condition. Every deceased is potentially an unpacified spirit even if he has been transformed into an ancestor through the appropriate ritual. The fear of ritual failure in the described case—and the performance of the relevant 'insurance-ritual'—is thus not so much a fear of making a specific mistake, but the awareness of the principle of disorder which might especially come to mind in connection with an actual case of death.

Eftychia Stavrianopoulou's paper "Ensuring Ritual Competence in Ancient Greece. A Negotiable Matter: Religious Specialist" focuses on the connection between the possibility of flawed performance and the definition of 'competence' with regard to ritual specialists in Ancient Greek cults. In her case study the interface of doctrinal and operational efficacy seems to be the notion of ritual competence. The evidence makes clear that priestly authority and expertise has been strategically defined. Given the importance of ritual in mediating relations between humans and nonhuman powers, its performance was not only crucial to its efficacy, but also to the evaluation of the abilities of the ritual specialist. An emphasis on the correctness of performance promotes and maintains expertise, but it does not rule out the right of other groups to judge the performance's correctness. Such groups are the general audience, i.e. the public attending the rituals, or the central political institutions. In that way the political community became not only part of the construction of the ritual specialist's authority, but also of the confirmation of his competence. Stavrianopoulou thus shows how in Ancient Greece the quality of the rituals is ensured right from the start: the ritual specialist was the central figure, and the risky situation was managed by writing down and revealing the ritual regulations to the public on the one hand, and by assigning nearly unlimited performative expertise to the ritual specialist on the other. The ritual is only then to be considered a failure when the person equipped with ritual expertise is ignored and a third party carries out the ritual: the specialist's infallibility as well as the rituals' quality was thus ensured.

THE SIXTEENTH *PIṆḌA* AS A HIDDEN INSURANCE AGAINST RITUAL FAILURE

Johanna Buss

1. *Introduction*

Already in the earliest ritual texts, the ritual specialists of India had provided different means of preventing or rectifying mistakes in ritual (see Michaels in this volume). For the actual performance of a Hindu ritual, there are options for alteration, such as the substitution, repetition or shortening of ritual sequences, or the substitution of materials to be used in the ritual (Michaels & Buss forthc.), all of which reduce the danger of mistakes by allowing certain—though not arbitrary—variations within a ritual. After all, for remedying the noticed and unnoticed mistakes in ritual, there are atonement rituals (*prāyaścitta*,[1] see Gampert 1939 and Kane 1991: 57–86, and Michaels in this volume).

In the following discussion, no specific occurrence of a mistake in ritual or failure thereof shall be dealt with. Instead, the focus is on a ritual whose performance generally questions the validity of earlier performed rituals by assuming their failure, and aims at eliminating the results of this assumed failure. Although its function seems to be similar to the atonement rituals, it cannot be regarded as one. From the emic point of view, it is not termed or perceived as such. Moreover, the feared results of an assumed failure of an earlier ritual are implicitly adjusted, but not the mistakes of a specific ritual which are rectified explicitly, as is done in the *prāyaścitta*.

This shall be explained with the example of the Newar death ritual (Nev. *latyā*), performed on the 45th day after death. The specific performance of a *latyā* in Bhaktapur shall be described on the basis of a film by Christian Bau (Gutschow & Michaels 2005) of the *latyā*, as performed on 22nd August 2002. Within this ritual sequence, a special offering is made for those who are deceased but could not enter the secure state of 'forefatherhood' for various reasons. The assumption of the existence of these ghosts implicitly questions the efficacy of

[1] If not marked as Nevārī (Nev.) all terms written in italics are Sanskrit.

earlier death rituals held for them, and thus reveals the uncertainty of whether these rituals were efficacious. With the help of personal handbooks, serving not so much as strict prescriptions but more as a kind of memory aid for the performances and especially for the recitations of the officiating priest, this special offering shall be analysed. Additionally, the *Pretakalpa* of the *Garuḍapurāṇa* (hereafter referred to as *Garuḍapurāṇa*) and the *Garuḍapurāṇasāroddhāra* shall be considered in order to illustrate the importance of some of the concepts discussed within Hinduism.[2]

It will be argued that the general fear of failing to achieve a desired religious aim, which could lead to questioning ritual action as such, is met by rituals; it does not mean that the efficacy of the ritual as a mode of action is questioned. On the contrary, the possibility of failure strengthens the importance of the ritual act. Different external factors are held responsible for failure, but not the ritual itself, which in this way can effectively serve as a means of coping with exceptional situations of crisis and disorder.

2. *The sixteenth ball* (piṇḍa)

Nevārī *latyā* literally means '45' and denotes the rituals that are carried out on the 45th day after death. Hindu death rituals are not over with the actual funeral, and usually continue for one year after death. After this period the deceased is no longer remembered individually but honoured collectively in ancestor rituals, which are performed at fixed times during the year (see Gutschow & Michaels 2005). Nowadays Hindus execute most of the rituals during the first twelve days after death, anticipating the end of the year on the twelfth or thirteenth day with the performance of the *sapiṇḍīkaraṇa*, the 'creating of the *piṇḍa*-community'.[3] This also means that many of the rituals to be performed during the year are carried out within the days leading up to *sapiṇḍīkaraṇa*. The same is true of the Newar rituals, where the ritual

---

[2] I refer the reader to material and discussions given in my doctoral thesis (Buss 2006).

[3] Due to the divergence in the concept of Hinduism and the manifold creeds which have been subsumed under this term, it is hardly possible to make any statement that is valid for the whole of Hinduism. Thus, if not referring to the special example of a Newar death ritual, I use the term Hindu or Hinduism relating to Purāṇic and Dharmaśāstric concepts or the Hindu practice according to these concepts.

climax is reached on the 45th day. According to the *Garuḍapurāṇa*, the deceased has to pass through different stages until he safely reaches his three immediate forefathers (*pitaras*), i.e. father, grandfather and great-grandfather. Because the soul is bodyless after cremation, the deceased needs at first a new body for covering the year-long journey through the underworld. This body is provided by his descendants by offering ten or more sacrificial balls made from rice or wheat (*piṇḍas*), each of which represents a limb of the newly created body (see Knipe 2005, Gutschow & Michaels 2005: 11, 103). It is believed that within the first year after death, the deceased has to travel through sixteen different cities of the underworld until he reaches the city of the god of death, Yama. Besides other gifts, the deceased also receives offerings of water and a sacrificial ball at each of the cities. The sixteen stations correspond to the twelve months and four additional points of time within the first year.[4] The journey is dangerous, and the helpless deceased suffers from hunger and thirst on his way. He is only relieved through the offerings of his descendants during this time. His condition is also believed to be very fragile since he is totally dependent on his offspring. If they neglect the rituals he will stay in this condition. He doesn't belong anymore to the world of the living and is not yet a member of the next world. In this liminal stage the deceased (*preta*) is vulnerable and dangerous, trying to get back to the living. It is feared that if he is not satisfied, he will harass his family, causing misfortune and misery. After the lapse of one year, the deceased shall be united ritually with his forefathers (*pitaras*) in a rite called 'creating the *piṇḍa*-community' (*sapiṇḍīkaraṇa*). The main purpose of the *sapiṇḍīkaraṇa* is to transfer the deceased (*preta*) from the helpless and fearful condition of a ghost to a safe state among his forefathers (*pitaras*). The death rituals thus serve different purposes: to take care of the deceased and help him to reach a happy and safe state, but also to exclude him from the world of the living and prevent his return, mirroring the ambivalence of death,[5] as well as restructuring the social community of relatives.

In the following, I give a short account of the rituals which took place on 22nd August 2002 in Bhaktapur/Nepal, with an emphasis on the parts that shall be discussed afterwards.[6]

---

[4] For the timings, see Michaels & Buss forthc.; and for an interpretation of number sixteen, see Buss 2005a.

[5] For an investigation of this ambivalence in Hindu death rituals see Evison 1989.

[6] For more details concerning the death rituals in Bhaktapur/Nepal and a broad

In the early morning of the 45th day, members of 39 related families brought materials to be used during the rituals. The priest, Mahendra Sharma,[7] prepared the floor of a room on the ground floor in the house of mourning. After smearing it with cow dung for purification purposes, he drew ritual designs (*maṇḍalas*) with rice powder on the floor. The ritual was performed by him and the chief mourner, Narain Kumār Svāgamikha, who is the father of the deceased. This was an exception, as usually these rituals have to be performed by the eldest son of the deceased. In this case, however, he had died at the age of 35, and his own son was too young to perform the rituals. Most of the time, the two main agents of the ritual were crouched opposite one another on the floor, performing the rituals together on the small ritual arena between them. Mahendra Sharma guided the chief mourner in almost all respects. Other family members were present but scarcely active, except for the cousin of the chief mourner, who assisted him in providing materials.

At first, Mahendra Sharma installed the regular deities on the left side of the ritual arena, which were to stay present until the family left the house to perform the gift of a bed (*śayyādāna*) outside the house. These deities were Gaṇeśa, food for the cow (*gogras*), Kumārī or Aṣṭamātṛkā, Sūrya, Nārāyaṇa, Sadāśiva, Gṛhalakṣmī, the personal deity (*iṣṭadevatā*) or the lineage deity (Nev. *dugudhaḥ*), and also a black ammonite (*śālagrāma*) representing Nārāyaṇa. Then Mahendra Sharma and the chief mourner invoked and worshipped five gods in small water jugs, namely Sūrya, Nārāyaṇa, Gaṇapati, Sadāśiva and Varuṇa. Afterwards, the chief mourner kneaded dough for the sacrificial balls, using flour, water, milk, a banana and some wet rice. He shaped fifteen equally-sized round balls. Mahendra Sharma covered them with black sesame seeds, which are an integral part of death and ancestor rituals because they represent the sweat of Viṣṇu, and are thus a means of purification. Mahendra Sharma directed the chief mourner to place fourteen of the fifteen sacrificial balls on a diagram, which he had previously drawn, and consisted of fourteen square fields in three rows (the upper and lower rows with

description of the *latyā* and other rituals see Gutschow & Michaels 2005, which this account relies upon.

[7] Since this account is based on a more detailed description that I gave in Gutschow & Michaels 2005, I also follow the policy of the authors of the book not to leave the persons concerned in the description as anonymous objects of research, but to perceive them and refer to them as acting subjects and thus give the original names of the agents and places. See Gutschow & Michaels 2005: 3f.

four fields, the middle row with six fields). These fourteen balls belong to a set of sixteen sacrificial balls, which serve as nourishment for the deceased on his way through the underworld. The first ball of this set had already been given on the tenth day, so the next fourteen counted as numbers two to fifteen of the sixteen balls. During the placing of the balls one by one on each of the square fields, Mahendra Sharma recited their dedication as food for the deceased. The last one of the fifteen, which the chief mourner had already prepared, is not counted as the sixteenth, and is placed silently on top of the other fourteen. According to the priest, this ball is dedicated to the unknown deceased. Afterwards, these balls were worshipped like Hindu gods in a *pūjā* with ritual services (*upacāras*) such as flowers, incense, lamp, a sacred thread, libations of water and offerings of unhusked ritual rice (*akṣata*). After this worship they were put back in the brazen bowl, in which the dough had been prepared and kept aside. The ritual arena was then partially wiped clean and newly prepared by Mahendra Sharma, who drew new diagrams (*maṇḍalas*). Again the regular deities—still present on the left side of the ritual arena—were worshipped. Then, on a newly drawn diagram representing the ocean (*samudra*), the priest offered water libations from three tiny water cups (*arghapātra*) to the deceased (*preta*), the forefathers (*pitaras*) and the ancestor-gods (*viśvedevāḥ*, lit. 'all-gods'), which is a special class of gods that must be worshipped at every ancestor ritual (*śrāddha*).[8] Again the chief mourner prepared new dough for the next sacrificial balls, out of which he shaped five balls. The first of them was called *vikalapiṇḍa*, to be translated as 'ball for the deprived' or 'ball for the sorrowful [deceased]', and was offered and worshipped separately. According to the local priest, the *vikalapiṇḍa* is dedicated to the miscarriages of the family or to the unknown deceased for whom a proper death ritual had never been performed. After this offering, the actual *sapiṇḍīkaraṇa* was performed. First the chief mourner formed the three balls for the father, grandfather and greatgrandfather. Mahendra Sharma covered them with black sesame seeds and the chief mourner placed them on the ritual area, then both of them worshipped the forefathers in the form of the balls with ritual services. The ball for the deceased (*pretapiṇḍa*) was slightly bigger and had an oval shape

---

[8] For a discussion of the identification of the pre-greatgrandfather generation with the *viśvedevāḥ*, as it has been proposed by Knipe 1977 and subsequently by Michaels 2004: 143, see Buss 2006.

in contrast to the round balls of the forefathers. The unification of the deceased with his forefathers is achieved by dividing the ball of the deceased into three parts and merging each with one of the balls of the forefathers. Thus, the unification of the deceased with his forefathers is performed very vividly. The forefathers and the deceased are not conceived of as simply represented by the balls but as actually being present in the *piṇḍas*. This could be concluded from Mahendra Sharma's instruction to handle the balls carefully; otherwise the ancestors might be hurt. In the Hindu tradition, the importance of the *sapiṇḍīkaraṇa* is greatly stressed as the ritual which transforms the deceased into a forefather, a revered god-like being. The ritual thus helps him to enter the heavenly world (*divyaloka*), or the world of Viṣṇu (*viṣṇuloka*; see also Knipe 1977). The three balls were again worshipped and kept aside. Now Mahendra Sharma received two water jugs, money and other gifts. Outside the house on the street a bed was prepared and given to Mahendra Sharma and his wife along with more gifts, each of which regarded as a gift for the deceased to help him on his journey through the underworld. After Mahendra Sharma and his wife had left, the chief mourner and three more family members carried the previously offered balls to the nearby Hanumante river where they were discarded. Finally the chief mourner worshipped a Śivaliṅga at the bank of the river.

As this account shows, the sacrificial balls generally play an important role in death and ancestor rituals. And being somewhat 'multifunctional', they serve as food for the deceased, the ghosts and the forefathers; they are used to build a new body for the soul after the physical body has been cremated; and ultimately they are perceived as manifestations of the deceased and the forefathers that they are offered to, and in this function they are worshipped like Hindu gods. Therefore, it is not possible to confine the balls to one function.

For the problem I wish to discuss, the sixteenth ball is of special importance: it is not quite clear which ball is to be counted as the sixteenth. The 'first to the fifteenth' balls are easy to identify, as described above. Yet, there are two balls which could be the sixteenth: the *vikalapiṇḍa* or the *pretapiṇḍa*. As the function of the balls varies, it is not problematic that the *vikalapiṇḍa* is not dedicated to feed the deceased—as is the function of the other fifteen balls, but rather to release the ghosts of miscarriages or 'unknown deceased'. Moreover, this dedication would fit very well with the dedication of the "*mantra* for the gift of the sixteenth ball" in handbook HB_2 belonging to Mahendra Sharma's brother-in-law, Aishvaryadhar Sharma, translated below. HB_2 does not mention a *vikalapiṇḍa*, but only the sixteenth ball. The other possibility is that the *pretapiṇḍa* has to be counted as the sixteenth, which is supported by the view of the local priests as well as by some pan-Indian, Hindu ritual treatises (Kane 1991: 518–520 and Müller 1992: 197), so it is also possible to link the below cited *mantra* with the *pretapiṇḍa* as the sixteenth. The position of the *mantra* in the handbooks clearly supports the second interpretation.

3. *The* mantra *for the gift of the sixteenth ball* (piṇḍa)

For the described ritual, the priest Mahendra Sharma used two handbooks (HB_1 and HB_3), which are not very elaborate concerning the procedure of the ritual, but contain some of the verses to be recited during the ritual and served as a kind of memory aid for Mahendra Sharma. After presenting the order of the timings for offering the sacrificial balls over one year for the deceased, and after presenting the recitations for the offering of the three balls for the three preceding generations, HB_1 and HB_3 provide the *ṣoḍaśakalāstotra*, the 'praise of the sixteenth of sixteen (balls or *śrāddhas*)'. In HB_1 the *mantra* reads: "Through mc, o Lord, the pretahood concerning the *preta* will become pitṛhood. Through the grace of the grandfather he (the deceased) goes to the realm of Viṣṇu".[9] This *mantra* clearly refers to the *pretapiṇḍa* and is given in HB_1 as the last *mantra* in the *sapiṇḍīkaraṇa*, just before the recitations for the gift of a bed (*śayyādāna*). There is no reference to the *vikalapiṇḍa* in HB_1 or HB_3, although Mahendra Sharma offered the *vikalapiṇḍa*.

The following *mantra* is not included in Mahendra Sharma's handbooks, but has been taken from the personal handbook (HB_2) of the brother-in-law of Mahendra Sharma, Aishvaryadhar Sharma. He has compiled many verses and occasionally prescriptions for the death rituals. The verses and prescriptions found in his handbook generally follow the same pattern as Mahendra Sharma's performance described above. The above-cited verse is given with slight variations in Aishvaryadhar Sharma's notes, under the heading "characteristics of (gaining) the same (status like the forefathers)" (*samānaviśeṣa*) together with other *mantras* recited at the *sapiṇḍīkaraṇa* (HB_2 Aishvaryadhar Sharma: 43). Then

[9] For a transcription of HB_3 and a translation and edition of HB_1, compare Gutschow & Michaels 2005: 153–175.

another long *mantra* follows, covering several pages with the name '*mantra* for the offering of the sixteenth ball' (*ṣoḍaśīpiṇḍadānamantra*), reading:

1. *Oṃ*, for all of those who died in our family and cannot reach a happy state, for the sake of releasing them I give this ball.
2. Whoever died in the family of my maternal grandfather...[10]
3. Whoever died in a related family...
4. Whoever died (as a child) before getting teeth and also those who have been afflicted in the womb, for the sake of releasing them...
5. Those who have been cremated and others who have not been cremated, and those who have been killed by lightning or thieves, I give this ball to them.
6. To those who have died in a forest conflagration and those who have been killed by a lion, tiger, biting animals or horned animals, I give this ball.
7. Those who hung themselves, who died through poison or weapons, or who killed themselves (in any way), to them I give this ball.
8. Those who died on a forest path, in the forest, who died through hunger and thirst, who were killed by *bhūta*, *pretas* and *piśācas*,[11] to them I give this ball.
9. Those who have gone into (the hells) Raurava, Andhatamiśra and Kālasūtra, for the sake of releasing them I give this ball to them.
10. And to those who have gone into (the hells) Asipatravana or the terrifying Kumbhīpāka, for the sake of releasing them...
11. To those who have gone into the womb of cattle, or (are reborn as) a small bird or a creeping animal or have been reborn as trees, to them I give this ball.
12. For those who bear multiple torments and have been led away on the order of Yamas (i.e. the god of death), for the sake of releasing them...
13. For those who bear the innumerable torments and those who have gone into the pretaworld,[12] for the sake of releasing them...
14. Those who have to wander through thousands of different rebirths

[10] The missing parts in the verses have to be completed with either "for sake of releasing them I give this ball" or "to them I give this ball."
[11] These are three different types of ghosts.
[12] I.e. the sphere or world of the unpacified ghosts.

by virtue of their own deeds, and for whom it is difficult to be reborn as a human, to them I give this ball.

15. Those who stayed in the hells and bore the torments, for the sake of releasing them…
16. Those who are staying in heaven, the intermediate sphere, and on the earth, forefathers, relatives etc., and those who have died without being ritually prepared, to them…
17. Those of my forefathers (*pitaras*) who remain in the form of unpacified ghosts (*preta*), all of them should always be satisfied through the offering of the ball.
18. Those relatives who are not related, and those relatives in other rebirths, for them I give the ball, it should fall indestructably to their share.
19. Whoever died in the lineage of (my) father (*vaṃśa*) and mother, or teacher, father-in-law and other relatives who have died…
20. Whoever died in my family, and whose balls were lost (*luptapiṇḍa*), those who are without son and wife, those whose (death) rituals have been destroyed, and those who are blind from birth and also the lame…
21. Those who are miscarriages, known and unknown in my family, for them this ball has been given through me. It should fall indestructably to their share.
22. Those who were born in my father's lineage since the beginning of creation, and descendents of my mother's lineage, those who were servants in both of my lineages, those who are to be supported and nourished…
23. Friends, pupils, cattle and trees,[13] respectable persons and their dependants, those who have gone into another rebirth, to them, *svadhā*,[14] I give the ball.

(HB_2: 46–50)

After this *mantra* follow the *mantras* for dividing the *pretapiṇḍa* into three parts (*tripiṇḍa*).

It is not quite clear to which *piṇḍa* the *mantra* has to be related. Although the local priests consider the *pretapiṇḍa* to be the sixteenth *piṇḍa*,

[13] The enumeration of animals and trees conveys that all kinds of living beings shall be included.

[14] *Svadhā* is a special invocation used only for the forefathers.

it seems quite unlikely to link the above cited *mantra* with this *piṇḍa*, since the *pretapiṇḍa* has a special position and meaning as a representation of the deceased. Anyhow, the earlier-stated multifunctionality of the *piṇḍas* also allows such an interpretation. And after all, the view of the local tradition should not be ignored. Furthermore, the position of the *mantra* just before the dividing of the *pretapiṇḍa* supports this interpretation. In case the *pretapiṇḍa* is taken as the sixteenth, this stresses once more the family relations, which are especially strengthened and re-established at death rituals.[15] This is also expressed in the terminology, using the word *piṇḍa* as a category of kinship: the patrilinear lineage, which is obliged to perform death rituals for each other, is called *sapiṇḍa* 'having the same *piṇḍa*'. This term, as Parry states, pertains to a concept of sharing the same body particles (Parry 1994: 204). Thus the *pretapiṇḍa*, if considered to be the sixteenth, is not only offered as a means of transferring the deceased into a happier state, but it also represents the whole (deceased) family, which is trying to be released.

On the other hand, the *mantra* fits very well to the function of the *vikalapiṇḍa* as an offering for the 'unknown deceased'. Nevertheless, it is not to be decided here with which ball the *mantra* has to be linked, but rather to interpret the contents of the *mantra*.

4. *The infallibility of ritual*

The first verse of the *ṣoḍaśīpiṇḍadāna mantra* can be read as the essence of the whole *mantra*: all family members who might have faced an unhappy destiny after death are taken care of and should be liberated from their condition. This theme is taken up and varied in the following verses, where all kinds of relatives are listed, including enumerated examples of different conditions in which they may suffer after death, as well as the possible reasons for their state. This list seems to be a sort of 'general template', covering every possible reason for staying in the unhappy condition of an unpacified ghost (also called *preta*), in a bad rebirth or even in one of the countless hells. The reasons are also

[15] Nevertheless, Gutschow stresses the fact that in Bhaktapur the feeling of obligation to participate in death rituals is nowadays decreasing due to different reasons, e.g. the conversion of family members to other, anti-ritualistic religious sects, and thus abandoning the old rituals. Additionally, it is due to the increasing mobility of urban people, which sometimes makes it impossible to take part in the death rituals. See Gutschow & Michaels 2005: 198–201.

wide-ranging, from: a 'bad death'[16]—such as suicide, a violent death or murder, death through wild animals, weapons or poison—, an early death as a child or even in the mother's womb, to one's own bad deeds (*karma*), or the incorrect performance of death rituals. At the end of the list, friends and other members of the household are also mentioned; the main emphasis, however, is on the relatives. Four different reasons pertaining to ritual mistakes are mentioned:

- In verse 16, those who had died yet weren't prepared ritually (*mṛtā asaṃskṛtā ye ca*) are named. This pertains to those death rituals which ideally begin before death, so that the dying person can perform atonement rituals and then die on the ritually prepared ground, listening or reciting the names of gods or holy verses.[17]
- In verse 20, at first those family members are mentioned whose ball was lost (*ye me kule luptapiṇḍāḥ*). This clearly pertains to a disturbance of some kind in the death ritual, and for the procedure of which balls are an integral part. It could denote the simple loss of a ball, but it more likely denotes a robbed ball, which is another connotation of the word *lupta*. This relates to the unpacified ghosts, who are always hungry and thirsty and therefore constantly trying to steal balls and ritual offerings. For that reason they are either chased away by a *mantra* at the beginning of the rituals or they receive their own share—as in the case with the *vikalapiṇḍa*. Therefore, the offering of the *vikalapiṇḍa* performs a double function, namely to protect the current ritual from being disturbed by hungry ghosts and to help those hungry ghosts by feeding or releasing them.
- Again in verse 20 those deceased are mentioned who do not have a son or a wife (*putradārāvivarjitāḥ*). This situation is perceived as causing a ritual failure, or—in the terms of Grimes (1988b: 116)—an omission of ritual since the son has to perform the death ritual for his parents. Those who do not have a son or family member to perform the death rituals have to suffer permanently as ghosts, as e.g. the story of King Babhruvāhana in the seventh chapter of the *Garuḍapurāṇasāroddhāra* illustrates: the king meets an unpacified ghost who is suffering from a 'bad state' simply through not having had a family member or friend perform the death rituals for him.[18]
- Finally in verse 20, those deceased are named whose rituals have been destroyed (*kriyālopagatā ye ca*), and generally signifies a failure of the ritual.

---

[16] For the concept of the 'bad death', see Sell 1955.
[17] *Garuḍapurāṇasāroddhāra*, chapters 8–9.
[18] Cp. Buss 2006, where this story and other versions in the *Pretakalpa* of the *Garuḍapurāṇa* are compared and analysed.

Thus, the *mantra* includes different reasons for ritual failure. This list clearly indicates that Hindu tradition itself is aware of the possibility of mistakes or failure, and moreover provides a means of dealing with them.

Furthermore, the *mantra* tries to cover the whole range of deceased who might suffer in any bad condition. The exhaustiveness of the list, covering each and every person who might be in a bad condition after death, and not only those whose rituals have failed, leads to the question of why there are—even though hypothetically—so many unpacified ghosts and unhappy deceased in the family, and why the offering of the sixteenth *piṇḍa* is carried out together with the *latyā*, which itself serves to pacify the deceased and transfer him into a peaceful state.

The purpose of offering the sixteenth ball seems clear: to pacify those ghosts who might constantly hover around, hungry and thirsty or eager to steal those offerings meant for the latest deceased family member. It is helpful to reflect in which ways rituals can be efficacious. Moore & Myerhoff (1977: 10ff.) point out that there are different levels of efficacy in religious rituals. They distinguish between doctrinal and operational efficacy, with the former referring to a system of religious beliefs:

> The religion postulates by what causal means a ritual, if properly performed, should bring about the desired result. [...] Doctrinal efficacy is a matter of postulation. As the intrinsic explanation, it need merely be affirmed. It lacks the dimension of outcome or consequences which is attributed to operational efficacy.

Under operational efficacy they subsume the social or psychological effects of a ritual. It is evident that doctrinal efficacy is not in the same way empirically testable as operational efficacy (see Buss 2005). But that does not mean that it is without consequences. On the contrary, in the case of a Hindu death ritual, this statement has to be modified. Those doubts or fears of failing the desired religious effect, namely to transfer the deceased into a safe state, are not only a question of personal belief or simple affirmation, but can be a severe threat to the family or the community. Those deceased who are stuck between the worlds of the living and the ancestors are feared to come back to their family and cause trouble, such as through accidents, illnesses or the possession of family members. These fears have to be understood quite literally in Hindu culture, and thus it is a question of cultural perception and interpretation of these phenomena. Insofar as the subjective experience and the cultural patterns of interpretation are concerned, the failure of the doctrinal efficacy is at least negatively testable: if a ritual is considered to have failed, severe consequences can follow (see Freed & Freed 1993, Schömbucher 1993). Therefore, in this case it is appropriate to assume the possibility of failure on the level of doctrinal efficacy.

Going back to the empirical level, it is not very likely that so many deceased in the family have been so badly neglected or left without rituals. Even those who have died a bad death and therefore have been pacified with special rituals, such as the 'offering for Nārāyaṇa' (*nārāyaṇabali*), identifying the deceased directly with the Viṣṇu in his form as Nārāyaṇa, have not been left in their miserable state. Where, then, does this fear of ghosts originate? Rituals treating the 'unhappy deceased' reveal a special fear of what Hasenfratz called the 'acosmic dead':

> Wer dagegen im Unfrieden mit der Gemeinschaft (etwa als Delinquent und Über-Treter gemeinschaftlicher Norm) oder als Betroffener eines außer-ordentlichen Ereignisses (etwa durch Un-Glück, Un-Fall, Un-Tat) stirbt, ist vom Leben der Gemeinschaft, damit von personalem Sein abgeschnitten (Opfer von Un-Fall oder Un-Tat sind—auch ohne "eigenes" Verschulden—wesenhaft mit dem Un-Heil verbunden, das über sie hereinbricht). Ein solcher Toter ist ein akosmischer Toter, denn er rechnet als Un-Person zur un-weltlichen Zone des Nicht-Lebens außerhalb der Gemeinschaft und ihrer Normen (Hasenfratz 2001: 234).

Thus the acosmic dead belongs to the sphere or principle of disorder, to which everything belongs that challenges or threatens the order (of the living). Therefore, it includes not only ritual failure, but anything challenging the social or cosmic order, such as moral misconduct or a bad death, which can be perceived as a 'death-failure' in terms of not dying 'correctly'—in a good and (ritually) prepared death. That is also why other kinds of unhappy states are mentioned in the *mantra*.

So far my analysis has been conducted from an etic point of view, extracting these concepts out of the textual tradition combined with the single performance of a death ritual. However, on a certain level this is also reflected in the minds of the participants of the ritual. Although, most probably, few of the participants understand any of the Sanskrit verses or let alone are familiar with the theological concepts, there is awareness that there are unpacified ghosts in the family. In addition, the answer most often given as to whom these balls are offered is that they are for the 'unknown *preta*', the unknown (unpacified) ghosts who have not received a proper funeral. The connection of ghosts with the assumption of failure or omission of a proper ritual reveals a fear of them residing in a threatening and dangerous acosmic state.

One of the main functions of ritual is to create and recreate the social and cosmic order. In this function, rituals do not serve as an economic means to an end, but as modes of action to cope with disorders such as crises or transitional stages—be it the social stages accomplished in the life cycle rituals (Turner 1969) or the seasons in calendrical or other cyclic rituals. Due to the processuality of life and cosmos, there is a perpetual dialectic process between order and disorder, which the ritual helps to cope with. The fear of ritual failure in the described case is thus not so much a fear of making a specific mistake, but the awareness of the acosmic sphere or the principle of disorder which might especially come to mind in connection with an actual case of death. That demonstrates that the ritual is important to help handle the disorder, and thus the performance of a single ritual does not mean that it is not effectual, but that the result is not static.

The perpetual threat occurring out of this dialectic process leads to the suspicion of whether everything was done correctly when a disorder or crisis had occurred, something which can easily be attributed to the mistake of a human or non-human agent within the ritual. Factors not linked with the ritual process can as well be held responsible, e.g. one's own misdeeds or certain bad deaths. Thus, the ritual is not so much a means of creating a singular effect by a single performance, but a performative means of handling a crisis or some (life) threatening disorder. And as such, it is not questioned as a mode of action. But any possible influence which might lead to a failure of the ritual is attributed to external factors: the ritual itself is always efficacious in the sense of providing people with a means of handling situations of crisis and disorder.

It has to be taken into consideration that I am dealing with different kinds of rituals here. The *sapiṇḍīkaraṇa* is a life-cycle ritual which is to be performed only once for a person. The offering of the sixteenth *piṇḍa*, however, is repeatedly performed within each new *sapiṇḍīkaraṇa*, and thus belongs to a different category of ritual.

The dialectic process of structure and disorder makes it necessary to 'update' certain kinds of ritual regularly (to borrow a computer metaphor); this necessitates that 'anti-virus' programs be regularly updated, otherwise the disorder in the form of viruses will threaten to destroy the (computer) cosmos. Likewise, rituals need to be 'updated' to account for the latest environmental, social and mental changes in human lives. Nevertheless, this only pertains to certain kinds of rituals, such as calendrical or cyclic rituals, and usually not to once-only life-cycle rituals. But—and this might be a special case with Hindu death rituals—when associated with the death of a person, there might be a special fear of death, dissolution and disorder. Ghosts and ancestors are demanding beings: they threaten their offspring if they are not fed and honoured. If neglected, they belong to the same acosmic sphere, and the difference between hungry forefathers and hungry ghosts becomes marginal. By assuming the re-appearance of disorder in the form of ghosts, the effect of the life cycle ritual is implicitly doubted. That does not mean that every deceased is feared to stay a ghost, it only suggests that there is an awareness of disorderly elements which might threaten the ritual. Since the performance of the death ritual can only be executed once, there have to be other rituals to cope with these threats. These other rituals, however, negate on a certain level the effects of the *sapiṇḍīkaraṇa*. Thus, the ritual needs 'updating' to handle all new challenges, but that updating means the negation of an earlier ritual, at least in the case of the *sapiṇḍīkaraṇa*. That is the very reason why it is necessary to attribute failure to a ritual, and thus the option of failure—at least in the above discussed case—is an integral part of ritual.

References

Sources

GP *Garuḍapurāṇa*, Uttarakhaṇḍa (Pretakalpa). Ed. by J. Vidyāsāgara. Calcutta, 1890 (trsl. and annotated by a board of scholars. 3 vols. Delhi 1978–1980).

GPS *Garuḍapurāṇasāroddhāra*. Publ. by Tukaram Javaji, Bombay: Nirnaya Sagara Press, 1912.

HB_1 *Personal handbook* of Mahendra Raj Sharma, Bhaktapur, dated [vikrama] saṃvat 1997 phālguṇa śudi 10 roja 7, i.e. 1940 CE. Nepālī paper, 31 foll., no title.

HB_2 *Handbook of Aishvaryadhar Sharma*, Patan, no date, no title.

HB_3 *Personal Handbook of the priest Mahendra Sharma*, Bhaktapur. A collection of main *stotras* used during the *latyā* ritual; no date, no title.

Secondary literature

Buss, Johanna 2005. "Gieriger Geist oder verehrter Vorfahr? Das 'Doppelleben' des Verstorbenen im newarischen Totenritual". In: *Der Abschied von den Toten. Trauerrituale im Kulturvergleich*, Assmann, Jan & Franz Maciejewski & Axel Michaels (ed.). Göttingen: Wallstein, 181–198.

—— 2005a. "Continuity in the change of rituals: the sixteen *śrāddhas*". *Chakra* 4/5.

—— 2006. *Pitṛ, Preta und Piśāca. Mythische und Rituelle Totenbilder im Garuḍapurāṇa und Garuḍapurāṇasāroddhāra*. University of Heidelberg: unpublished dissertation.

Evison, Gillian 1989. *Indian Death Rituals. The Enactment of Ambivalence.* Oxford University: unpublished dissertation.

Freed, Ruth S. & Stanley A. Freed 1993. *Ghosts: Life and Death in North India*. Seattle: Univ. of Washington Press.
Gampert, Wilhelm 1939. *Die Sühnezeremonien in der altindischen Rechtsliteratur.* Prag: Orientalisches Institut.
Grimes, Ronald L. 1988a. "Ritual Criticism and Reflexivity in Fieldwork". *Journal of Ritual Studies* 2.2: 217–239.
—— 1988b. "Infelicitous Performances and Ritual Criticism". *Semeia* 43: 103–122.
Gutschow, Niels, & Axel Michaels, with Buss, Johanna & Nutan Sharma and a film on DVD by Christian Bau 2005. *Handling Death. The Dynamics of Death and Ancestor Rituals Among the Rural Newars of Bhaktapur, Nepal.* Wiesbaden: Harrassowitz.
Hasenfratz, Hans-Peter 2001. "Totenkult". In: *Handbuch religionswissenschaftlicher Grundbegriffe*. Vol. 5, Cancik, Hubert (ed.). Stuttgart: Kohlhammer, 234–243.
Kane, Pandurang Vaman [3]1991. *History of Dharmaśāstra.* Vol. 4. Poona: Bhandarkar Oriental Research Institute.
Knipe, David M. 1977. "Sapiṇḍīkaraṇa: The Hindu Rite of Entry into Heaven." In: *Religious Encounters with Death: Insights from the History and Anthropology of Religions*, Reynolds, F.E. & E.H. Waugh (ed.). University Park: Pennsylvania State University Press, 111–124.
—— 2005. "Zur Rolle des 'provisorischen Körpers' für den Verstorbenen in hinduistischen Bestattungen". In: *Der Abschied von den Toten. Trauerrituale im Kulturvergleich*, Assmann, Jan & Franz Maciejewski & Axel Michaels (ed.). Göttingen: Wallstein, 62–81.
Michaels, Axel 2004. *Hinduism. Past and Present.* Princeton: Princeton University Press.
—— & Johanna Buss forthc. "The dynamics of ritual formality: Contextual and textual variations in a Newar death ritual".
Moore, Sally Falk & Barbara G. Myerhoff 1977. "Introduction. Secular Ritual: Forms and Meanings". In: *Secular Ritual*, Moore, Sally Falk & Barbara G. Myerhoff (ed.). Assen & Amsterdam: Van Gorcum, 3–24.
Müller, Klaus-Werner 1992. *Das brahmanische Totenritual nach der Antyeṣṭipaddhati des Nārāyaṇabhaṭṭa.* Stuttgart: Franz Steiner Verlag.
Parry, Jonathan 1994. *Death in Banaras*. Cambridge: Cambridge Univ. Press.
Schömbucher, Elisabeth 1993. "Gods, Ghosts and Demons: Possession in South Asia". In: *Flags of Fame. Studies in South Asian Folk Culture*, Brückner, Heidrun et al. (ed.). Delhi: Manohar, 239–267.
Sell, Hans Joachim 1955. *Der Schlimme Tod bei den Völkern Indonesiens*. S'Gravenhage: Mouton & Co.
Turner, Victor 1969. *The Ritual Process, Structure and Anti-Structure*. New York: Aldine Publishing Company.

ENSURING RITUAL COMPETENCE IN ANCIENT GREECE. A NEGOTIABLE MATTER: RELIGIOUS SPECIALIST

Eftychia Stavrianopoulou

"Anyone is good enough to be a priest", claimed the Attic orator Isocrates (II *Nikokles*, 6) in the 4th century BCE, and meant that the functions of the priestly office required no particular talent, in contrast to the office of a King.[1] The same criticism and mistrust of the role of ritual specialists in ancient Greek cults, which one can detect in this statement,[2] can be observed in the research literature since the publishing of Jules Martha's book on the Athenian priesthood in 1882. Most of the scholars speak denigratingly of Greek priests and priestesses, while at the same time pointing to the high reputation they had in the society of that time as well as their role as executors of rituals.[3]

For Walter Burkert the Ancient Greek religion is "a religion without priests."[4] For, alongside those persons who can be considered

---

[1] Cf. Demosthenes, *Prooimia.* 55, p. 1461.

[2] Cf. also the statement in Xenophon, *Cyropaedia* 1, 6, 2: "[...] For I had you taught this art on purpose that you might not have to learn the councels of the gods through others as interpreters, but that you yourself, both seeing what is to be seen and hearing what is to be heard, might understand; for I would not have you at the mercy of the soothsayers, in case they should wish to deceive you by saying other things than those revealed by the gods [...]."

[3] Martha (1882: 10): "Le culte dans l'antiquité, est un service administratif et le sacerdoce un office public. Le prêtre est un des agents de l'authorité souveraine"; Stengel (1920: 33): "Ein eigentlicher Priesterstand hat in Griechenland nie existiert. Es gab keinen Religionsunterricht, keine Predigt, und je mehr ängstlicher Aberglaube schwand, desto seltener bedurfte man eines Vermittlers zwischen sich und der Gottheit"; Ziehen (1913: 1411): "Nach der bis in die neueste Zeit herrschenden Ansicht hat es bei den Griechen ein Priestertum im eigentlichen Sinne dieses Wortes nicht gegeben." See also *infra.*

[4] Burkert (1985: 95): "Greek religion might almost be called a religion without priests: there is no priestly caste as a closed group with fixed tradition, education, initiation, and hierarchy, and even in the permanently established cults there is no *disciplina*, but only usage, *nomos*. The god in principle admits anyone, as long as he is willing to fit in to the local community; [...] among the Greeks, sacrifice can be performed by anyone who is possessed of the desire and the means, including housewives and slaves." See further Rüpke 1996: 245f. (who points out that our image of religious specialists in the Graeco-Roman antiquity was rather formed by Christianity); Jameson 1997: 175f.; Sourvinou-Inwood 2000: 39f.; Gordon 2001. For a discussion on the term "religious specialist" see Turner 1972; cf. also the collective reflections in the volume of Beard & North 1990 on the religious specialists in the Ancient World.

specialists in ritual (priests, exegetes, oracle interpreters), the ability and the right to perform a ritual were also accorded to both magistrates and private persons.[5] The head of the family was permitted to carry out sacrifices at home himself; the 'traditional sacrifice' (*thysiai patrioi*) was conducted by the heads of a clan, for the community it was very often the demarch (the head or mayor) and for the state partly the magistrates who were responsible for these sacrifices; private persons were permitted to perform purifications and atonements. Moreover, the Greek specialists in ritual do not appear to have corresponded to the image of an intermediary between god and the people,[6] for no special training and no special knowledge were necessary in order to hold the office of a priest.[7] In addition, many priests only remained in office for a short time, having received it through the drawing of lots or even by purchase, and even among those in whose families the priesthood was hereditary there were many who held other positions in the state besides that of priest.[8]

This rather confusing picture on the role of Greek priests contrasts with the special interest on the correct performance of a ritual action as revealed from a group of epigraphic sources known summarily as 'sacred laws' in the research literature on ancient history.[9] Detailed descriptions of sacrificial rituals, the exact planning of processions, lists of purity commandments and regulations governing ritual specialists make up the contents of these so-called sacred laws. They represent the written fixation of old and new regulations and alterations, and especially the visible announcement of them to the entire religious community.

The peculiarity of the sacred laws for us lies in the fact that they are, in their majority, the result of a political process of discussion, i.e.

---

[5] For the complexity of the relations between priests and magistrates see Gschnitzer 1989.

[6] Cf. Stengel 1898: 32: "... auch die Griechen, wie andere Völker, geglaubt haben, gewisse Personen stünden den Göttern näher als die andern, hätten von ihnen besondere Kräfte und Fähigkeiten erhalten und seien deshalb geeignet und imstande, auch andern die Gunst der Gottheit zu verschaffen und zu sichern. Dann aber mußte die Folge sein, daß man ihnen die Vermittlung zwischen dem Gotte und der Menge überließ, sie mit der Ausübung des Kultes [...] und dessen Formen und Gebräuche sie allein kannten und richtig zu üben verstanden, betraute."

[7] On the different opinions in scholarship upon the ritual competence of Greek priests see Garland 1984: 114f. and 1990: 73–91; Gladigow 1997: 103–118; Chaniotis forthc.

[8] Stengel 1920: 34–37; 40–42; Turner 1983: 141–173.

[9] For discussions on this problematic term see now Parker 2004 and Lupu 2005: 4–9.

decisions made by the political leadership of a community. As decisions, they were ratified and recognised as laws by the political institutions of the council and the assembly, following the corresponding motion by one or more individuals and subsequent discussion. Religious matters were thus considered political and were supervised as such, since only the orderly course of religious life could guarantee an orderly course of individual life for the *politai* (citizens) and the *politeia* (the community of citizens).[10] There is thus no distinction made between religion and politics, since both are regarded as one process for supporting the well-being of all.

The lack of such a differentiation may explain the fact that ritual practice was not left only to specialists and may thus justify the ambivalent judgements of scholars on their ritual competence.[11] On the other hand the effects of such a blurring between religion and politics have still to be considered. How was the ritual competence of a priest in ancient Greek ritual and cult defined, mediated and confirmed? Was a ritual performance endangered, if an incompetent or only partly competent ritual specialist carried it out? What were the means used by the community in order to minimize the risk of a ritual's failure? Or to put it in another way, how could the efficacy of a ritual be guaranteed despite the incompetence of the specialist? In the following I will try to trace some answers concerning the profile of a Greek priest as well as the interactions between the religious specialists, the cult participants and the community as a whole.

1. *An example: the priest of Isis in Priene*

The city of Priene, located in Asia Minor on the south side of the Mykale mountains has yielded a fragmentarily preserved inscription dating from about 200 BCE, which contains regulations for the cult of the Egyptian gods Isis, Sarapis, and Anubis. The temple of the Egyptian gods, the foundations of which were uncovered at the eastern edge of

[10] Cf. the reflections on that crucial point of Sourvinou-Inwood 1999 and 2000. An obvious example of the lacking boundaries between politics and religion can be observed in the fact, that in two of the four monthly meetings of the Assembly of the People in Athens the laws required "that three cases of sacred matters [*hiera*] are to be dealt with, three audiences for heralds and embassies [*kerykes kai presbeiai*], and three cases of secular matters [*hosia*]" (Aristotle, *Athenaion Politeia Pol.* 43.6).

[11] See above n. 7.

the town, is dated to the 3rd century BCE. The cult of Isis, Sarapis, and Anubis must have been introduced in consequence of the integration of Priene into the sphere of influence of the Hellenistic ruling house of Egypt, the Ptolemaic dynasty, in the course of that century. Although the temple and the finds made there do not give us any clear indications of the 'Egyptian' character of the cult, being rather reminiscent of the structures of Greek shrines, both the epigraphic evidence and the votive statuettes of Isis found in private houses are witnesses to the undoubtedly wide popularity of the cult in Priene. The inscription discussed below placed originally in the colonnade of the temple refers to the efforts of those responsible for the cult to regulate not only the course of the rituals, but also their perfect performance:

> [...] The priest shall sacrifice two of the doves prescribed to Sarapis [...] and Isis, and shall place them upon the altar. He shall also carry out the other sacrifices for Sarapis and Isis and the other gods honoured with them, and the torchlight procession dedicated to Isis, as is proper. The priest shall also provide the oil prescribed for the torchlight procession, in sufficient quantity for the two lamps to the extent of one talent each. The priest shall sacrifice to Apis at the times prescribed. [...] The priest shall also order the Egyptian who is to carry out the sacrifice in the manner of those versed in this. No person not versed in these things shall be permitted to carry out the sacrifice for the goddess, excepting only the priest. If anyone not versed in these things should carry out the sacrifice, he shall be fined 1000 drachmas and he shall be charged before the magistrates (Sokolowski 1955, no. 36, lines 9–16; 20–25).

The sacrifices and festivals, the actions of the cult personnel, instructions and sanctions for disregard of these, form the contents of this text. The text reads like a ceremonial book, in which it has been set which rituals are to be performed, how, when, and by whom. Attached to a part of the temple colonnade, the inscription was to serve as a reminder to visitors and initiates of the rules obtaining in this cult centre. In the surviving part of the inscription the yearly sacrifice for Isis and Sarapis on the 20th of the month Apatourion is mentioned, a date corresponding to the Osiris festival in Egypt at the beginning of November. The second great festival, the torchlight procession, took place in honour of the goddess Isis: the priest was to provide the oil needed for this.[12] In addition, the text also mentions further sacrifices,

[12] In other temples dedicated to Egyptian deities, whether Greek or Roman, large numbers of oil lamps have been found, while literary texts and inscriptions mention a festival at night for Isis, in which only such oil lamps were used.

such as the sacrifice of two doves for Isis and Sarapis, which the priest is to deposit upon the sacrificial table. Here, the preparation of a meal for the deities corresponds evidently to the Egyptian ritual of daily 'hospitality'. Altogether, the descriptions of the ritual, which can be indirectly drawn from the text, give the impression that much effort was expended to continue to preserve the "authentic," i.e. Egyptian, character of the newly introduced cult.[13] These efforts are also underlined by the requirement of an Egyptian, in other words a "true specialist of this cult." The priest of the Egyptian deity in Priene is obliged to order an Egyptian priest of Isis for the purpose of performing the sacrifice. The latter is obviously to ensure and supervise the correct performance of the rituals. His role in the ritual and his qualifications for it are paraphrased in the text with the word 'versed'. In the following sentence, however, the possibility that no 'versed' Egyptian priest might be at hand for the sacrificial festival of Isis is also taken into consideration. In this case only the local priest among the "unversed" is to be permitted to perform the sacrifice. Disregard of this regulation has a fine and a public charge before the magistrates as a consequence.

The key word, connected most closely with the successful performance of the sacrificial ritual and, not least, with the efficacy expected of this ritual, is, without any doubt, the word 'versed' (ancient Greek *empireia*). But what is the meaning of this word in general, and especially in this specific context? What effect did the irregular presence of a versed or experienced religious specialist, and, contrariwise, the regular presence of a non-versed religious specialist, have on the practice of the cult and its rituals? By what means was the inexperience of the local cult specialist compensated for, an inexperience that could be a factor of instability and a possible source of error? Who, finally, decided whether the ritual had been carried out correctly or incorrectly?

Two types of priest are juxtaposed in the text: the 'versed' Egyptian and the 'inexperienced' local Greek priest as given in that text. The profile of the local priest can be regarded as typical for a Greek priest: he is appointed to certain deities and to a certain temple, and he is to carry out the ritual actions in the proper fashion. He lacks, however, any special training. Indeed, in the classical Greek cults such training was neither a prerequisite nor a characteristic for holding office as a

---

[13] For the introduction of the cult of Isis and other cults of Egyptian deities in Greek cities cf. Roussel 1916; Magie 1953; Vidman 1970; Dunand 1973; Baslez 1977.

priest. But it is a regular feature of Egyptian priests. Experience here means reflexive knowledge,[14] comprehension of the matter, command of the technique and adroitness in execution, close acquaintance with the content of a ritual and how to perform it. All these aspects belonged to the training of a cult specialist in Egypt. In this, the Egyptian priest of Isis differs from the Greek priest of Isis: the Greek priest of Isis can be classified, in this regard, as inexperienced and cannot function *a priori* as a guarantee that the cult will be preserved and, as a consequence, be perceived from the outside in a positive way.

The Egyptian cult specialist invited to this ritual was on the other hand capable of guaranteeing the correctness of the ritual and therefore its efficacy. His competence was perceived as authentic by the cult participants in Priene, who will hardly have known either the Egyptian language or the course of the ritual. This surely contributed to the intensity of the religious experience. Although (or because) the constant presence of an Egyptian priest could not be ensured, his actions constituted all the more not only the climax of the ritual, but also the yardstick against which the religious community measured the local priest. The local priest of Isis was seemingly in a difficult and, above all, precarious position. It seems that his authority, conferred upon him by his office, was limited by the irregular presence of an experienced colleague—or, rather, this is the conclusion drawn by a modern observer. The text tells us a different story.

If the structure of the text is considered, the regulation in question is somewhat 'buried' in its middle. It forms the end of the first part of the text, which deals with the description of the various sacrifices, and stands before the beginning of the second part, in which the gifts of honour for the cult personnel are listed. Thus the textual part concerning the presence of an Egyptian priest requires some attention and patience on the part of the reader to be noticed. Conversely, the active person in all sections is the local priest: he is the one responsible, the one sacrificing, thus the local experienced cult specialist. He is the one who, like his Egyptian colleague, interprets the stars to decide when the sacrifice for a deity (Apis) is to be carried out. In that way ritual competence is attributed to him, although this does not correspond to the same level of especially knowledge and training that an Egyptian

[14] For the distinction between practical knowledge, which is learned mainly in mimetic processes, and reflexive knowledge see Wulf 2006. See also Jennings 1982.

priest would have. In his case experience would primarily mean technique and dexterity, enabling him to conduct a perfect ritual.[15]

The local Greek priest of Isis may be inexperienced compared with the Egyptian priest, but he is the experienced one compared with the local cult personnel and the participants in the cult. As competent he is the sole guarantor for the correct performance of the rituals. This authority, which rests primarily upon his office, compensates for the lack of experience and thus avoids the danger of erroneous performance: the sacrificial ritual can only go wrong if someone other than the priest carries it out. This means, however, that the reasons for the success or failure of the ritual are not to be sought, or at least not primarily to be sought, in the manner of execution of the ritual, but solely in the person responsible. Consequently, evaluation of how and when the ritual has failed becomes simpler, for it can only fail through the actions of a not designated person. Transgression of this rule will be punished by means of a fine and particularly by laying public charges. In this manner the limitation of potential causes of failure to one single factor enables on the one hand the clear rectifying of a failed ritual, visible to all participants through this double punishment. On the other hand it promotes the authority of the Greek priest towards the one of the Egyptian specialist. The public acknowledgement of the ritual actions as well as of the rules concerning their violation generates a common level between ritual specialists and cult participants. On that level the cult participants claim ritual competence equal to the one of an Egyptian priest and that of the inexperienced-experienced Greek priest.

2. *Interlude: a second example*

At the temple of the god of healing and cures, Asclepius, in the city of Pergamon in Asia Minor, it was the regulation for the ill supplicants to sacrifice three cakes prior to their stay in the temple (the so-called 'incubation'): outside, on the altar, two sacrifices for Tyche, 'success', and Mnemosyne, 'remembrance', had to be made, in the *abaton* of

[15] Cf. the efforts on the part of Greek priests of Egyptian deities to obtain special knowledge and the emphasis on such knowledge in the epigraphic testimonies from Delos (IG XI 4, 1290) and Anaphe (IG XII 3, 247).

the temple one for Themis, 'right'.[16] Three sacrifices in two different spatial areas, inside and outside, outdoor altar and *abaton*:[17] outside, in the surroundings of a temple accessible to all, the stone stelae with the cult regulations for the cult in question were set up, so that everyone could read them; outside, too the sacrifices, were made, in the presence of the cult participants; inside, in the Holy of Holiest, only the priest was permitted to enter, as only he was responsible for 'right and custom' and only he could transmit this 'right and custom' to the audience and guarantee it.

Tyche, Mnemosyne, Themis: this *triptychon* reflects the connection between the success of the ritual, the remembrance of the ritual itself and its rules and regulations, and the ritual specialist. All three elements are mutually conditioned and had the goal to preserve the 'right and custom' in the cult of Asclepius. Through the sacrifice to Mnemosyne the remembrance of past rituals is evoked. Further it is intended to trigger the remembrance of those regulations, which are to be observed in performing the ritual. Whether ritual specialist or participant, both must adhere to these if they wish to contribute to the success of the ritual.[18] It can thus be said that Mnemosyne stands for the remembrance of the practice and for remembrance through practising.

Remembrance can contribute to the success of a ritual and help to avoid the danger of a ritual mistake or even the failure of a ritual. Successful remembrance and a successful ritual guarantee 'right and custom' and constitute them at the same time.[19] In this connection

---

[16] Wörrle 1969: 185–187. The inscription dates from about 160 BC, however it repeats the content of an older version (*ibid.*).

[17] For the *abaton*, the area to which entry for cult participants or visitors was normally forbidden, see Parker 1983: 167, note 132 with references.

[18] Cf. the example of the conviction of a high priest of the temple of Demeter at Eleusis in court for impiety and offering sacrifice contrary to the ancestral rites (Demosthenes 59, *Neaira* 116). Among the charges brought against him was that at the feast of the harvest he sacrificed on the altar on behalf of a woman, although it was prohibited to offer sacrifices on that day, and the sacrifice was not his to perform, but the priestess. Another example (Philostratus, *Vita Apollonii* 1, 10) from the cult of the healing god Asclepius shows that the misconduct of a supplicant could lead to the failure of the ritual. Before approaching the god and in order to receive healing dreams people had to perform certain rites like purifications of the body and sacrifices. When a wealthy Cilician supplicant sacrificed after his arrival at the temple on "such a magnificent scale before he has gained anything from this god", the god refused to help him and bade him leave the sanctuary because his conduct was not "that of a votary, but rather of a man who is begging himself off from the penalty of some horrible and cruel deeds" (Edelstein & Edelstein 1945: 292f. [T. 517]).

[19] See the heading of the public documents evocating the 'good luck' or 'good

the role of the priest as the one who alone may represent 'inside' and 'outside' and who may participate both in the 'remembrance' and the 'success', as well as in 'right and custom', is of fundamental importance. The difference between him and the other people participating in the cult is recognisable in the fact that he alone is permitted and able to represent the 'inner part' of the cult.

3. *The negotiability of priestly ritual competence*

In our first example we have outlined the different ritual competences and the problem of the 'holding in tutelage' of the ritual specialist by the community. The core of the matter is the difference between the ritual competence of the Greek priest and that of the other participants in the ritual. That this needed to be established is clearly shown by the ambivalence of the roles of specialists and laymen in the fields of 'remembrance' and 'success' of a ritual. The communal institutions (council and assembly) impart to the members of the political community in general and the members of the cult of Isis in particular the framework of the ritual, the ritual actions, and the role of the one carrying out the ritual.

But what does this manner of imparting signify, so visible to all participants in the cult? The decision, engraved in stone, is to serve memory. It is to be a help in remembering, a yardstick as well as a reminder: by having the regulations written down—in every detail too—all participants in the cult are informed of the regulations to be obeyed in this cult, they are simply accessories. Accordingly, all are transformed into active and passive bearers of the success or failure of the ritual in question. They have to remind themselves again and again of the regulations and to adhere to these, for disregard of the regulations by a participant in the ritual would endanger the ritual, indeed, direct the anger of the gods at the entire community.[20] But they should also always remember the regulations when carrying out the corresponding ritual, for execution of the ritual by any other than the nominated persons, or the sacrifice of other than the selected animals, would also endanger the ritual's success. As a consequence the participants in the

fortune', i.e. the success of the ratified text (remembrance), in order to endorse the civic order.

[20] On divine anger see Parker 1983: 241–243 and 257–280.

cult were trained to be bearers of ritual knowledge and to be critical observers in particular.[21]

This last point contains a certain danger, for the revelation of the ritual's course makes the position of those performing it more difficult, or places their ritual competence in question. If all participants in the cult were to contribute towards the success of the ritual, it is nonetheless true that the text is clear about conducting the ritual: the Egyptian priest and the local Greek priest are the only ones permitted to do this. The first-named had unlimited ritual competence, while the competence of the local priest first had to be constituted or justified, respectively. The distinctive characteristic dividing the participants in the cult from the priests is called experience. Experience in this case can also be taken to mean remembrance of the practice and remembrance through practice, but also comprises remembrance by carrying out the practice. For this reason the remembrance on the part of a priest is not only more perfect in comparison to that of a participant, it is actually the guarantee for the success of a ritual action and the preservation of 'right and custom'. Only when the proper performance of the prescribed actions has been accomplished, their expert and competent execution can be assured and renewed in accordance with 'right and custom'.

It comes as no surprise that 'right and custom', i.e. the success of communication between deity and participants by means of the rituals, stands at the centre of a cult. But the role of the political representatives in the affair is noteworthy. They are the ones who evoke this transparency, who support the ritual authority of the local priest, and who make the difference in competence between the participants in the cult and the ritual specialist visible to the outside. While the political representatives enable the cult participants to gain a look into the ritual actions, thus designating them as sharing responsibility, they also explicitly point out the limitations of their participation: carrying out the ritual is the sole preserve of the priest. Any disregard of this regulation is punished twice, namely with a large fine and a public laying of charges. This interconnection between politics and religion again becomes evident. One would expect divine punishment for any transgression of cult regulations, such as a curse or exclusion from the cult. The threat of public charges, in my opinion, can only be explained from the identification of the whole community with its cults.[22]

---

[21] See Wulf 2006.

[22] See also Parker (2004: 65) who accepts that secular sanctions imposed by the

The cults practiced in every Greek *polis* are a part of the identity of the *polis*. They contribute to the construction of an artificial, unique 'topography'. Carrying out the sacrificial rituals was not only for the good of the participants in the cult, but also for the good of the *polis*. First the sacrifice provided by the city is made, and then the other sacrifices follow. Priests and magistrates often work together in performing the rituals.[23] In this fashion the *polis* has a direct, even vital interest in preserving the cults. Mistakes in the rituals of the city cults can negatively affect the lives of all citizens, for the wrath and revenge of the gods will not be limited to the persons directly responsible for the mistakes. The interference of political instances in cult matters must be seen in this light. To enforce and not to weaken the authority of the priest in his office is one strategy within such preventive measures. The focus on one factor as the only possible 'sources of error' for the failure of a ritual is another one.[24]

4. *Negotiating ritual competence = negotiating ritual failure*

"For pious thoughts towards God there will always be thankfulness without stint," says one oracle of Apollo. Pious thoughts and pious actions, one must add. This responsibility was to be borne by all participants in the cult of the Egyptian deities in Priene. The political heads of the community were most certainly aware of the danger represented by inaccurate performance for the efficacy of the rituals and the reputation of the cult in general. In this context the person of the ritual specialist was not only the central figure, but also the most impugnable. Management of this problematic and risky situation was carried out by means of the dialectic scheme of 'remembrance—success → right and custom'. By writing down and revealing the ritual actions and regulations the participants in the cult and the ritual specialists were made supervising agents, although with different degrees

general assembly reveal the strong commitment of the *polis* to maintaining religious conformity and avoiding the anger of the gods; see also Latte 1920: 48–61.

[23] See Gschnitzer 1989.

[24] The central political authority trying to minimize the mistrust in the competence of the specialist—expressed through gossip (e.g. Sokolowski 1955: nos. 3–5; 79) as well as through bringing forward motions in the assembly—used several measures on various levels such as taking the oath from the whole body of civic magistrates (e.g. Sokolowski 1955: no. 13) or the publication of the relevant decree in several sites inside and outside of the city (e.g. Sokolowski 1955: nos. 3, 13) or even the rejection of any proposal referring to the status of a specialist (e.g. Sokolowski 1955: nos. 3–5).

of ritual competence. While both groups were required to contribute both actively and passively to the success of the rituals, only the ritual specialist could give form to this success and transform it into 'right and custom'. The competence of the ritual specialist is based upon his threefold 'remembrance', the practical ritual knowledge, the reflected knowledge on ritual practice based on previous ritual performances as well as the experience of carrying out a ritual, and thus differs from that of the competence of the participants in the cult, which was located only on the first two levels.

Ritual competence is therefore founded on the performance of the ritual and is of considerable significance for the efficacy of the ritual.[25] The bearer of this competence can give form to its execution at his own discretion, within the limits set by tradition, without endangering the efficacy of the ritual. The ritual is only then to be considered a failure when the person equipped with this specific ritual competence is ignored and a third party carries out the ritual.

A clearly structured situation, easy to control: all possible mistaken actions and situations, which could ruin the ritual and the cult involved, are prevented right from the start. The execution of the rituals by someone other than the designated specialist was now regarded as having failed. The participants in the cult were to concentrate on and supervise this aspect. Their contribution to the success of the rituals was thus shifted, for their critical eye was to be on all participants, no longer just the person of the ritual specialist and his actions. The correct performance of the rituals was declared a common matter in this fashion both by the ritual specialist and by the participants.

The focus on this one single point led to a strengthening of the position of the ritual specialist and equally to a strengthening of the position of the participants as a controlling instance. In addition, the focus on a transgression of the rules visible to all enabled a rapid re-instatement of cult order by means of a sanction also visible to all. The fact that this sanction corresponded to profane law may surprise the modern observer, but this was the more pragmatic route for an Ancient Greek religious community to prevent further transgressions, a community which was at the same time a political community and as such was the instance that regulated and set norms. With this in mind, the conditions, under which the rituals in a cult could be performed, were dependent on public consent and acknowledgement: there was

[25] See Schieffelin 1996. On efficacy see now Podemann Sørensen 2006.

no mystery about the rules, how a ritual could be efficacious, but also how a ritual could fail.[26]

References

Sources

Aristotle, *Athenaion Politeia.* Rackam, Harris (transl.), *The Athenian Constitution.* London: Harvard University Press (Loeb Classical Library), 1931.
Demosthenes, *Prooimia.* Clavaud, Robert (ed., transl.), *Démosthène, Prologues.* Paris: Les Belles lettres, 1974.
Demosthenes, *Neaira.* Blass, Friedrich (ed.), *Demosthenes, Orationes.* Leipzig: Teubner, 1891.
IG. *Inscriptiones Graecae.* Berlin: De Gruyter, 1873–.
Isocrates, *Nikokles.* Blass, Friedrich (ed.), *Isocrates, Orationes.* Leipzig: Teubner 1891.
Philostratus, *Vita Apollonii.* Jacobs, Friedrich (ed.), *Flavius Philostratus, Vita Apollonii.* Leipzig: Teubner, 1832.
Xenophon, *Cyropaedia.* Miller, Walter (transl.), *Xenophon, Cyropaedia,* London: Harvard University Press (Loeb Classical Library), 1960.

Secondary literature

Baslez, Marie-Françoise 1977. *Recherches sur les conditions de pénétration et de diffusion des religions orientales à Délos.* Paris (Collection de l'École Normale Supérieure de Jeunes Filles 9).
Beard, Mary & John North, (ed.) 1990. *Pagan Priests. Religion and Power in the Ancient World,* London: Duckworth.
Bourdieu, Pierre 1990. *The Logic of Practice.* Stanford: Stanford University Press.
Burkert, Walter 1985. *Greek Religion: Archaic and Classical.* Oxford: Oxford University Press (German orig.: *Griechische Religion der archaischen und klassischen Epoche.* Stuttgart: Kohlhammer [Die Religion der Menschheit 15], 1977).
Chaniotis, Angelos forthc. "Priests as Ritual Experts in the Greek World". In: *Practitioners of the Sacred: Greek Priests from Homer to Julian,* Dignas, Beate & Kai Trampendach, (ed.), Cambridge Ma.
Dunand, Françoise 1973. *Le culte d'Isis dans le basin oriental de la Méditerranée I.–III.* Leiden: Brill (Études préliminaires aux religions orientales dans l'Empire romain 27).
Edelstein, Emma L. & Ludwig Edelstein 1945. *Asclepius: Collection and Interpretation of the Testimonies I–II.* Baltimore: Johns Hopkins Press.
Garland, Robert 1984. "Religious Authority in Archaic and Classical Athens". *Annual of the British School at Athens* 79: 75–123.
—— 1990. "Priests and Power in Classical Athens". In: *Pagan Priests. Religion and Power in the Ancient World,* Beard, Mary & John North, (ed.), London: Duckworth, 73–91.
Gladigow, Burkhardt 1997. "Erwerb religiöser Kompetenz. Kult und Öffentlichkeit in den klassischen Religionen". In: *Religiöse Kommunikation—Formen und Praxis vor der Neuzeit,* Binder, Gerhard & Konrad Ehlich (ed.), Trier: WVT (Stätten und Formen der Kommunikation im Altertum VI), 103–118.
Gordon, Richard L. 2001. "Priester". In: *Der Neue Pauly. Enzyklopädie der Antike 10,* Cancik, Hubert & Helmuth Schneider (ed.). Stuttgart: Metzler, 319–322.

[26] As Bourdieu 1990: 238 notes, it is "the group that *creates and designs its own actions* through the work of official recognition, which consists of *making each practice collective,* in that it is *made public, delegated and synchronised*".

Gschnitzer, Fritz 1989. "Bemerkungen zum Zusammenwirken von Magistraten und Priestern in der griechischen Welt". *Ktema* 14: 31–38.
Jameson, Michael 1997. "Religion in the Athenian Democracy". In: *Democracy 2500? Questions and Challenges*, Morris, Ian & Kurt Raaflaub (ed.). Dubuque: Kendall/Hunt (Archaeological Institute of America. Colloquia and Conference Papers No. 2), 171–195.
Jennings Jr., Theodore W. 1982. "On Ritual Knowledge". *Journal of Religion* 62: 111–127.
Latte, Kurt 1920. *Heiliges Recht*. Tübingen: Mohr.
Lupu, Eran. 2005. *Early Greek Law. A Collection of New Documents*. Leiden: Brill (Religions in the Graeco-Roman world 152).
Magie, David 1953. "Egyptian Deities in Asia Minor in Inscriptions and on Coins". *American Journal of Archaeology* 57: 163–187.
Martha, Jules 1882. *Les sacerdoces athéniens*. Paris: Thorin.
Parker, Robert 1983. *Miasma. Pollution and Purification in Early Greek Religion*. Oxford: Oxford University Press.
—— 2004. "What are Sacred Laws?" In: *The Law and the Courts in Ancient Greece*, Harris, Edward M. & Lene Rubinstein (ed.). London: Duckworth, 57–70.
Podemann Sørensen, Jørgen 2006. "Efficacy". In: *Theorizing Rituals I: Issues, Topics, Approaches, Concepts*, Kreinath, Jens & Jan Snoek & Michael Stausberg (ed.), Leiden: Brill (Numen), 523–543.
Roussel, Pierre 1916. *Les cultes Égyptiens à Délos du IIIe au Ier siècle av. J.-C.* Paris: Berger-Levrault.
Rüpke, Jörg 1996. "Controllers and Professionals: Analyzing Religious Specialists". *Numen* 5: 242–262.
Sokolowski, Franciszek 1955. *Lois sacrées de l'Asie Mineure*. Paris: Boccard (École française d'Athènes IX).
Sourvinou-Inwood, Christiane 1990. "What Is Polis Religion?". In: *The Greek City From Homer to Alexander*, Murray, Oswyn & Simon Price (ed.). Oxford: Oxford University Press, 295–322.
—— 2000. "Further Aspects of Polis Religion". In: *Oxford Readings in Greek Religion*, Buxton, Richard (ed.). Oxford: Oxford University Press, 38–55.
Stengel, Paul ³1920. *Die griechischen Kultusaltertümer*. München: Beck (Handbuch der klassischen Altertumswissenschaft 3).
Turner, Victor W. 1972. "Religious Specialists". In: *International Encyclopedia of the Social Sciences* 13, Sills, David L. (ed.), New York: Crowell Collier & Macmillan, 437–444 (= In: *Magic, Witchcraft, and Religion. An Anthropologicqal Study of the Supernatural*, Lehmann, Arthur C. & James E. Myers [ed.], 1985, 81–88, Palo Alto: Mayfield Publishing Company).
Turner, Judy Ann 1983. *Hiereiai: Acquisition of Feminine Priesthoods in Ancient Greece.* Ph.D. University of California, Santa Barbara: UMI.
Vidman, Ladislav 1970. *Isis und Sarapis bei den Griechen und Römern: Epigraphische Studien zur Verbreitung und zu den Trägern des ägyptischen Kultes*. Berlin: de Gruyter (Religionsgeschichtliche Versuche und Vorarbeiten 29).
Wörrle, Michael 1969. "Die Lex sacra von der Hallenstraße (Inv. 1965, 20)". In: *Die Inschriften des Asklepieions*, Habicht, Christian (ed.). Berlin: de Gruyter (Altertümer von Pergamon 8.3), 167–190.
Wulf, Christoph 2006. "Praxis". In: *Theorizing Rituals I: Issues, Topics, Approaches, Concepts*, Kreinath, Jens & Jan Snoek & Michael Stausberg (ed.), Leiden: Brill (Numen), 395–411.
Ziehen, Ludwig ²1913. "Hiereis". In: *Paulys Realenzyklopädie der klassischen Altertumswissenschaft*. Vol. VIII. Stuttgart, 1411–1424.

CONTINGENCIES AND EMERGENCE

A central difference between 'ritual failure' and 'mistake' is that failure refers to the efficacy of a ritual whereas a mistake refers to the procedural performance and as such is closely related to competence and agency. However, both notions are contingent: rituals are actions and are, as any other human action, never free of contingencies. While the contingencies or 'risks' lying in a ritual's performance is concentrated on in the section on "Mistakes, Procedural Errors and Incorrect Performances" in this volume, the contributions to this section mainly focus on the uncertainty of the outcome of a ritual, that is, a ritual's efficacy.

In many cases it is a ritual's efficacy which determines whether the action counts as 'success' or as 'failure'. However, 'efficacy' (or lack of efficacy) denotes a wide range of phenomena: the effects of a ritual postulated on a doctrinal level, its (immediate or long-term) social consequences, the fulfilment of individual expectations, empirically detectable effects, unexpected outcomes, and so on.[1] The case studies presented here clearly show that a ritual's efficacy cannot be reduced to one of these aspects (see also Grimes 1988: 105; Tambiah 1979). The articles in this section therefore reflect on the diverse ways in which the rituals can be efficacious—or fail to produce the expected or wanted results.

In Karin Polit's contribution "Social Consequences of Ritual Failure: a Garhwali Case Study" the 'doctrinal' (postulated or believed) efficacy of a ritual—if performed successfully—is identical with the expectations of the participants and performers: the patient was to 'overcome' her infertility. However, since the ritual failed to produce the expected result, 'emergent' aspects constituted the effects of the ritual: in that situation, the question of who or what is responsible for the failure was negotiated. As Polit argues, a long-term emergent effect of these kinds of 'failed' rituals is that they can serve as social mediators, even if they have negative social consequences for certain individuals or groups involved. The 'final failure' of rituals aiming at enabling the woman to conceive

[1] For a detailed discussion of these diverse 'modes of efficacy' see the article "Ritual Failure and Ritual Dynamics" by Hüsken concluding this volume.

children ended a long situation of suffering for two families but at the same time had negative consequences for the individual patient.

Brigitte Merz's article "When a Goddess Weeps—Ritual Failure or Failed Performance? A Case Study from Nepal" clearly shows that it is of utmost importance to throw light on an event from diverse angles in order to determine whether a ritual performance is 'effective' or not. From the audience's point of view the ritual described by Merz was 'flawed' or at least it went on not as smoothly as the participants had hoped, because the medium either 'overdid' her performance or the goddess was extraordinarily upset. From the perspective of the ritual's initiator it remains unclear whether the ritual counted as success: since she wanted to ensure the gods' blessings for her son's future enterprise the success (or failure) of this enterprise will have determined her final evaluation of the performance. And finally, from the medium's point of view, what emerged out of this performance can be interpreted as a success, because her attempt to reorganise the hierarchical structures among the mediums succeeded in the long run. Here, as in Polit's case study, it is rather the 'emergence'—sometimes even the long-time repercussions—which determines the assessment(s) of the ritual.

Maren Hoffmeister in her article "Change of View: the Ritual Side of Serial Killings and the Conditions for Fortunate Failure" vividly demonstrates that analysing 'ritual failure' helps to understand ritualised actions that are not culturally defined as 'ritual' (see Grimes 2000: 26, 28, *et passim*). Hoffmeister metaphorically categorises 'serial killings' as 'ritual'. Rather than 'murder *is* ritual' she analyses 'murder *as* ritual'. She looks at the conditions which make the 'ritual' fail by juxtaposing the motivations and intentions of the murderer ('personal script') with those ascribed to him by the society ('social script'). Hoffmeister's paper convincingly shows how analysing a failed ritualised activity as 'failed ritual' helps to understand underlying patterns and structures. She uses the notion 'ritual failure' as a tool for revealing collectively shared ideas and the way in which they were 'superimposed' on the performers.

References

Grimes, Ronald L. 1988. "Infelicitous Performances and Ritual Criticism". *Semeia* 43: 103–122.

—— 2000. *Deeply into the Bone. Re-inventing Rites of Passage*. Berkeley & Los Angeles & London: University of California Press.

Tambiah, Stanley J. 1979. *A Performative Approach to Ritual. Radcliffe-Brown Lecture*. London: British Academy.

SOCIAL CONSEQUENCES OF RITUAL FAILURE: A GARHWALI CASE STUDY

Karin Polit

In the field of ritual studies, ritual failure has been explained from many different perspectives. In his description of a "ritual which failed to function properly", Geertz (1973: 146) describes failure of function as a natural result of social change. Distinguishing culture as a framework of beliefs from the social world as interactive behaviour, he attributes the failure of ritual to a growing discontinuity between the community's cultural framework of beliefs and the actual patterns of social interaction. Bell harshly critiques this assumption because "we are led to assume that successful rituals are those in which these terms or forces are 'perfectly congruent'" (1992: 34) so that a failed ritual necessarily leads to change. Meanwhile, other scholars have argued that ritual failure results from failure in a flawed performance, in the sense that the ritual specialist failed to perform a convincing ritual (Grimes 1985; Schieffelin 1996), or that the subject of the ritual failed to perform what was expected of her as an initiate (Laderman 1996). In this volume we see another collection of reasons why a ritual can fail. Some look at the performative aspects of ritual (see Merz in this volume), some look at rituals that need an audience to be successful (see Brosius in this volume), some focus on the emic view of ritual failure (e.g. Weinhold), others give us an insight into rules and regularities made to prevent failure (see Stavrianopoulou in this volume). In contrast, this paper will not be concerned with why a ritual has failed or how to prevent failure, but with the consequences of ritual failure.

In line with the arguments of Geertz (1973), Bell argues that rituals and ritual practices "are themselves the very production and negotiation of power relations" (1992: 196). If we take this seriously, then rituals are to be seen not only as related to social realities and power relations in the social and political world, and therefore processes that are constantly adjusting to these realities in the social world (Drewal 1992), but also as powerfully influencing people's lives with real social consequences. Therefore, ritual failure should not only be seen as an effect of ritual dynamics and ritual change, but also as a factor leading to social change and social consequences.

Most Garhwali people believe that a properly performed ritual cannot fail. Therefore, if a ritual fails to produce the expected results, they often explain this in terms of human error: impurity, mistakes by the priest or the sponsor in preparing and implementing the ritual, or other human errors. Rappaport (1979: 2–10) relates such unfalsifiability to the 'sacral' aspect of a ritual. He argues that since the rituals are so closely connected to deities, it is impossible for practitioners to think that a ritual should contain the risk of failure. In this view, the only explanation for the failure or inefficacy of a ritual is human failure. The divine is divine exactly because it does not make mistakes. This unfalsifiability of rituals was discussed at length by Evans-Pritchard (1937), and also by scholars such as Skorupski (1976), Krausz (1989), and Morris (1987). They all have postulated that in the emic view of people performing a ritual, a ritual is a divine action; a divine action is divine because it is by definition perfect, therefore no ritual can fail. What is important for the following case study is that in Garhwal the factors leading to ritual failure or ineffectiveness of a ritual are seen as 'technical' factors, but the efficacy of a properly performed ritual is rarely questioned. This view of ritual can have severe social consequences for people involved in a ritual that has failed, as I will show on the following pages.

Garhwal is a former princely state in the central Himalayas of India, the population is mostly rural, and religious rituals are part of people's everyday life. Different rituals are performed to ensure village and family welfare, or to avoid failure of the crops and similar problems that are believed to occur when village or family deities are neglected. Also common are healing rituals, performed to cure afflictions brought on by deities, demons, and ghosts (see Sax 2004, Polit 2006). If such a ritual is performed, but does not achieve the expected results, cure of the affliction, the failure is usually explained in terms of ritual mistakes: the ritual was not performed properly, the priest or the sponsors made mistakes or some polluting element disturbed the ritual and made it ineffective (see Sax & Polit 2002).

As in many ritual traditions, it is not expected in Garhwal that every ritual follows a certain, well-defined structure (see also Schechner 2002: 45–77). There are always common elements in these healing rituals, but every ritual specialist has his own style. He alone is expected to know how the ritual is to be performed. Therefore, a ritual hardly ever fails during the preparation or during the ritual practice. Whether such a ritual was successful or not is therefore judged by its efficacy. If the expected results do not occur, the ritual is retrospectively defined as 'failure'. Then people in Garhwal start looking for the reasons of the failure of the ritual. Who will be identified as being responsible for this failure and will thus have to suffer the social consequences is the result of a complicated social discourse. People are seen as responsible for the ritual failure, and people suffer social consequences as a result. Different social strategies are applied to identify the culprit. In the end, usually power relations within and among the family and community lead to the identification of somebody or something responsible for the failure. In the course of this article, I will discuss the case of a Garhwali woman for whom a number of unsuccessful healing rituals were performed, who was subsequently defined as being herself responsible for the failure of the rituals and who suffered severe social consequences.

By the time I met her, Bimla was around 38 years old, married for 22 years and still childless. She and her family members told me the following story during several interviews and conversations. She was born as the oldest daughter of a very poor Dalit family. The term Dalits is usually used for activists of the low castes or scheduled castes in India. The term refers to the situation of the low caste people as oppressed, marginalised and underprivileged. In Garhwal, low caste people are often referred to as Harijans, a Gandhian term for people of the lowest castes. This term is more and more seen as discriminating and the local people prefer to call themselves Dalits. This is the reason why I, too, use this term when I refer to the lowest castes of the region.

At the time Bimla was born, her father had just lost his job in the army and returned home, jobless and penniless. Nevertheless, the family was happy at the time she was born. She was ten years younger than her brother and people were happy about her birth because her mother had not had any children within the past ten years, and Bimla was very pretty. Everybody adored her during childhood, people used to call her the prettiest girl in the village. Her parents found a suitable husband for her when she was sixteen and married her off to a village about one hour away from their home. After marriage she moved to her husband's house. He was the second of three brothers. At first Bimla lived with the older brother of her husband and his wife (*jeth* and *jethani*) in peace. Her mother- and father-in-law had already died at the time of her marriage, which meant that her *jeth* was the head of the household and her *jethani* was responsible for managing the work in the house and the fields. Later, her husband's younger brother (*devar*) got married, too, and a third woman joined the family home. After the other two women had each given birth to two children, they started picking on Bimla about her childlessness, the villagers started gossiping, and people began calling her names. Finally, her *jeth* decided to consult an oracle about her childlessness.

Oracles are very popular in the Garhwal region. They are men or women who are the chosen vehicles of certain local deities. In oracular sessions, the deity uses their bodies to be in contact with devotees, to talk to them, and to bless them. During an oracular session, a deity will talk to the client, define his or her problem, and give advice about a solution. Often, the solution is a ritual, performed by a ritual specialist who learned this art, often from his father, and who controls the deities through his ritual powers. In contrast to the oracles, the ritual specialist or *guru* never gets possessed during his rituals (see Sax 2004: 5–10).

After Bimla had not given birth to a child within the first years of her marriage, her husband's elder brother got worried and went to an oracle to find out about her problem. The oracle said that she had been afflicted by a local demon from her husband's village and that this affliction was the reason why she was still childless. That is why the family arranged for the appropriate ritual, the *chal puja*, to be performed. A goat and a chicken were sacrificed, the deity was pacified and the demon was told to go back to where he had come from. The ritual was performed, but nothing happened. This first time, the family simply assumed, without further discussions in the village or with the ritual specialist, that the ritual specialist must have made a mistake. For this reason, they consulted another oracle and repeated the ritual with another ritual specialist. When this ritual did not have any effects, either, they tried different solutions to the problem: they repeated the ritual, went to another oracle, worshipped the family deity, the village deity, gave a feast in honour of her father's family deity, built a shrine for this deity in her husband's village, and so on. Still nothing happened. Bimla did not become pregnant and the tension in her household and her parent's house was getting worse and worse with every passing day. The women in the village were harassing her and her family members gradually increased the pressure on her. In Garhwal, or rural India in general, a childless woman is not considered a complete woman. Fertility of her body and fertility of the land as well as the health and well-being of her family are very closely associated with each other. If a married rural woman has no children at all, she will lose her femaleness, will no longer be considered a valuable part of society and will be pushed to the margins of her world, where people associate her with Hijras (transvestites) and other marginal people. Furthermore, if a woman does not bear children for her husband, it is considered his right to find himself another wife and ensure the reproduction of his family. As Berreman (1963: 144–145) explains, the duty of a Pahari woman is to comfort her husband and to ensure the fertility of his land and his family. Childlessness is a problem for Garhwali Hindu men, and Hindu men in general, as they expect their sons to take responsibility for their important death rituals: "Specifically it is thought that only what has been given in life and at these ceremonies will be available to the spirit for livelihood in the afterlife" (Berreman 1963: 130). Therefore, it has been common until today that a man will take a second wife if his first wife remains childless.

In Bimla's case, there was a very strong bond between husband and wife, and therefore they tried every possibility they saw to have children together. They had numerous rituals performed, went together to allopathic practitioners, and had all sorts of expensive treatment. They performed yet more rituals. He took her with him when he moved to work in a city in Uttar Pradesh. He made it possible for her to stay in the city, away from the family that was torturing her for her childlessness, and he did everything he could to make her material life comfortable. However, after 22 years of hope and disappointment, her husband gave up. He finally started considering a new marriage. Two years before I met them, he had proposed to Bimla and her family to marry her younger sister. This was considered to be a very gentle and honourable move on his side. Her family was reassured that he honoured the relationship he had with her and the family ties that had been established through their marriage. In proposing to marry her sister, he not only wanted to reinforce family ties, but he also gave her the opportunity to take part in the new family life as more than the first, childless wife. As Berreman has noted, "the first wife is especially likely to be jealous or vindictive if the second wife has been taken to make up for her own failure to bear children, for in such a situation she may feel threatened" (1963: 171). Since the children of a Garhwali women's sister are structurally her own children, this proposal also meant that her family and her husband tried to find the best possible solution for all involved. However, Bimla refused. She threatened to kill herself and curse them all before she would die. Such a death curse is thought to be very powerful in Garhwal, endangering the whole family for generations. Her husband obeyed her wishes and her sister got married to another man. Within a year she had a son.

I met Bimla first at the engagement party of her niece, the daughter of a middle sister. She was playing with a young baby, her younger sister's child, that very child that could have been her husband's, all day, seemingly enjoying the time with the child. A couple of days later, she asked me about the oracle and ritual specialist I was working with at that time. She had heard about his great powers and asked me to take her to him one day. Maybe, she said, he could help her to save her life. Therefore, one morning a few days later, Bimla, her brother's wife and I mounted my motorcycle and set off to visit this famous ritual specialist, hoping that he could perform the miracle. During the initial oracular session there, the deity said that she was possessed by a powerful demon called *shaitan*. This demon had fallen in love with her when she was an unmarried young girl. In her dreams, he had married her and to him, she was his wife. Therefore, when her parents married her to her 'real' husband, he sealed her body so that she would not be able to conceive a child from this other, 'illegitimate' man. The demon continued to visit her in her dreams, and in this dreamworld they lived together and made love as husband and wife. The ritual specialist suggested a treatment including daily ritual healing sessions for over two weeks and a bigger ritual in the end of these sessions. She agreed to come for this treatment for initially ten days. In the end, we visited him almost daily for four weeks. Every day she had to bring a mixture of rice and black lentils she had put under her tongue over night. The ritual specialist swept the bad influences out of her body with feathers and leaves, dropped them into the rice-lentil mixture and told us to dispose of the dangerous mixture into the river below his house. He also talked to her intensively about her dreams and her well-being. Sometimes he asked about her menstruation, sometimes about pains, sometimes about her dreams of the demon. At the end of the treatment he performed a long and elaborate ritual at the river bank. It included more sweeping, more *mantras* and the sacrifice of a chicken.

To Bimla and her natal kin, this was her last chance. During the treatment, everybody was hopeful, but people had also already started talking about the consequences if the ritual failed this time. It was clear to everybody that this would be an important decision in Bimla's life. Either, so they said, she would become pregnant, or she would have to agree to her husband's getting married a second time. It was clear to all her natal kin that no woman could be so selfish as to keep her husband from having children just for the sake of her own, personal happiness. This was considered to be unacceptable behaviour that could not be tolerated any longer. She was rather ambivalent about her hopes and fears. When she talked about the possibility that the ritual might fail, the only option she saw was to kill herself. All she wanted was to be happy with her husband, and in her view, they should be content with each other, she was still not ready to let an intruder enter their relationship.

> If my husband marries again, what will I do in his house? He will start loving this new, young woman more than he loves me. She will then get all the affection and I will become a housemaid. I could not live in a house like that. I cannot go back to my parents, either. This is shameful, and how will they feed me? They can hardly feed themselves. If he gets married again, I will kill myself.

Her husband did not know what she was doing at the time she had the ritual treatment. He had left her in her natal home after her niece's engagement party and had gone back to work. The ritual treatment lasted longer than she had expected. He was very angry with her by the time it was finished and she was finally ready to go home. Her brother accompanied her to her husband's house and I did not hear from her for another three months. Then, she said, she became pregnant but lost the child in her third month. Confused, desperate and aching with grief, she called up her family to go and ask the ritual specialist what had gone wrong. The specialist said that he had bound the demon for three months and that he had told her to come back after that to perform another final ritual that would then rid her of the demon. Since she had not come for this final ritual, he said, the demon had been set free again and had destroyed her child.

That was the moment when social negotiations about responsibilities, consequences and duties started between her, her husband, her natal kin and the ritual specialist. More important for these social negotiations than whether anyone had actually made recordable mistakes during the ritual performance, or whether the ritual specialist's statement about the incomplete ritual was true or not, was the web of power-relations, social and cultural expectations connected to gender related behaviour, and a complicated play of individual desires and cultural and social restraints. It is not uncommon in Garhwal that a ritual specialist is blamed for the failure of a ritual. As we have seen earlier, if a small ritual does not show any effects, the ritual is simply repeated with another ritual specialist. This decision is usually made without long discussions, and only adds to the bad reputation of the ritual specialist, which in turn can lead to less people consulting him. In this case, however, nobody questioned the ritual specialist's explanation. Instead, people blamed Bimla for the failure of this and all the previous rituals. I assume that this can be attributed on the one hand to the popularity of the ritual specialist at that time, which has been increased by my constant presence at his oracular and healing sessions, and on the other hand to Bimla's long history of inefficacious rituals in the past as well as to the notion that she was behaving in an unacceptable way as wife and daughter. As a consequence, she should finally give in and let her husband marry again. By the time I saw her again four months later, she looked much older than the year before and had clearly given up hope for herself. "What am I supposed to do? There is no hope for me. I am a withered old flower. I will not have any children. I will have to live with that". When I asked her about her husband, she ground her teeth and said: "I don't know. He will not live like that. Perhaps he will, because he is growing old, too. But I think he will marry another woman." She had stopped talking about killing herself. The will to fight her family, her husband's family and her husband had left her, along with the will to threaten them with deadly curses.

Thus, the ritual itself had served as a social mediator. Its failure had ended a long situation of suffering for two families and finally brought a solution. However, its failure also had severe social consequences for Bimla. While the ritual specialist's explanation of her childlessness restored her femaleness—the demon possessed her and prevented her from having children exactly because she was such a desirable female—her failure to rid herself of this demon now forced her to give in to her husband's second marriage. Even though the ritual clearly failed to fulfill Bimla's and her family's expectations and hopes, it did exercise its transformative power on Bimla in a very unexpected way. The power of the ritual brought her 'back in line' with socially acceptable behaviour, thus ending an unbearable and shameful situation and protecting both families' honour.

References

Bell, Catherine 1992. *Ritual Theory, Ritual Practice.* New York: Oxford University Press.

Berreman, Gerald D. 1963. *Hindus of the Himalayas: Ethnography and Change.* Delhi: Oxford University Press.

Drewal, Margaret 1992. *Yoruba Ritual.* Bloomington: Indiana University Press.

Evans-Pritchard, Edward E. 1937. *Witchcraft, Oracles and Magic among the Azande.* Oxford: Clarendon.

Geertz, Clifford 1973. *The Interpretation of Cultures.* New York: Basic Books.

Grimes, Ronald L. 1985. *Research in Ritual Studies.* Washington D.C.: University Press of America.

Krausz, Michel (ed.) 1989. *Relativism: Interpretation and Confrontation.* Notre Dame: University of Notre Dame Press.

Laderman, Carol 1996. "The Poetics of Healing in Malay Shamanistic Performances". In: *The Performance of Healing*, Laderman, Carol & Marina Roseman (ed.). New York & London: Routledge.

Morris, Brian 1987. *Anthropological Studies of Religion: An Introductory Text.* Cambridge: Cambridge University Press.

Polit, Karin 2006. "The Effect of Marginality on People's Well Being: An Ethnographic encounter among Dalits of the Central Himalayas". *Anthropology and Medicine* 12(3). Special Issue: *The Ills of Marginality*, Ecks, Stefan & William S. Sax (ed.). London: Carfax, 225–237.

Rappaport, Roy 1979. *Ecology, Meaning, and Religion.* Richmond: North Atlantic Books.

Sax, William S. 2004. "Heilrituale der Dalits im indischen Zentral-Himalaya". In: *Ritualdynamik: Kulturübergreifende Studien zur Theorie und Geschichte rituellen Handelns*, Hart, Dietrich & Jasper Schenk (ed.). Heidelberg: Synchron.

—— & Karin Polit 2002. "The Cult of Bhairav: A Healing Cult of Resistance?" Paper given at the conference for Dalits' studies in Pune, 12–14/Dec/2002.

Schechner, Richard 2002. *Performance Studies: An Introduction.* London & New York: Routledge.

Schieffelin, Edward L. 1996. "On Failure and Performance. Throwing the Medium Out of the Séance". In: *The Performance of Healing*, Laderman, Carol & Marina Roseman (ed.). New York & London: Routledge, 59–89.

Skorupski, John 1976. *Symbol and Theory.* Cambridge: Cambridge University Press.

WHEN A GODDESS WEEPS—RITUAL FAILURE OR FAILED PERFORMANCE? A CASE STUDY FROM NEPAL

Brigitte Merz

The Newars, the indigenous populace of Kathmandu Valley in Nepal, celebrate a wide range of festivals throughout the year, in which domestic and cosmic rituals have a great place of importance. In the course of everyday life, household and temple deities are worshipped, life cycle rites (*saṃskāras*) are conducted, and on special days particularly elaborate rituals (such as *jātrā, vrata* etc.)[1] are performed. Every life stage is determined by clearly defined rituals, beginning with rites to guard the unborn child, to the last rites and death rituals. While performing these numerous rituals, there is always the possibility that at some time, something will go adrift, that a mistake will slip in or, in the worst case, a ritual will prove a failure. The Newars generally respond to a 'mistake' (Nep. *galti*; Nev. *dvaṃgu*)[2] during a ritual by a means also found in the rest of the Indian subcontinent (see Hüsken 2006; Michaels, this volume): they perform special exculpation rites that serve to excuse the mistakes or errors that have been made. These rituals are termed *kṣamā pūjā* and they will always be conducted when one wishes to restore the original order, ask for forgiveness for doing something wrong (Parish 1994: 109), or to apologise when it proves necessary to disturb the deities (as, for instance, when one has to climb onto a temple during restoration work). In the context of my research among female healers who have established themselves as mediums of a deity, typical mistakes or errors are, for instance, when the seam of the sari of a *pūjā* participant touches the water vessel that was used in the ritual, or if somebody steps barefoot into a specific ritual area. However, these were not seen as a serious mistakes. Mostly they were quickly excused by the mediums, especially if they happened unintentionally. In certain ritual

---

[1] *Jātrā* (Skt. *yātra*) comprise public processions performed as part of religious celebrations and "journeys" undertaken by gods during a designated period; *vratas* are vows made to a god to adhere to certain rules regarding sleep, meals, washing etc. in veneration of the god or in order to have the god grant them a long cherished wish.

[2] In the present article, Nepali (Nep.) and Nevāri (Nev.) terms are given in brackets. All other terms are in Sanskrit.

contexts it suffices to perform a *kṣamā pūjā*[3] or a exculpation rite just once a year, and in this manner apologise in general to the deities for any unintentional mistakes made during the previous twelve months. In the case of smaller, personal rituals an additional *kṣamā pūjā* is often performed a few days after the ritual has been conducted in order to apologise for any mistakes that may have occurred. In this way the dangers that might arise from 'mistakes' committed during the ritual are largely warded off, and the 'failure' of a ritual becomes virtually impossible. However, even though a ritual as such cannot fail, there are many ways in which participants of a ritual can commit mistakes and the way they can be perceived and interpreted may have a negative effect on the ritual itself, the mediums and the participants. The case examined below shows that not only the mediums and their bodies are affected by the participants' care in the preparations for the ritual, but also that, at times, the ritual space provides a space for negotiation of power and status between the mediums themselves and that both aspects appear interconnected.

1. *A healing cult of the goddess Hāratī in Nepal*

The case in point concerns a ritual that was conducted within a healing cult devoted to the goddess Hāratī in Nepal.[4] Ritual possession by the goddess is generally considered to be a fairly recent phenomenon (Coon 1989: 1; Gellner 1994: 42f.) that has become more widespread over the past forty or so years, or at least been brought more strongly to public awareness in recent years.[5] After a sometimes longer sometimes shorter initiation period, men but above all women become regularly possessed by the goddess Hāratī[6]—a former smallpox deity whose main temple is

[3] A *pūjā* is a religious service performed for a deity. For an etymology of the word *pūjā* see Thieme-Breslau (1939: 104–125).

[4] The field reserach was mainly conducted between 1993 and 1996 in the Kathmandu Valley, as well as in South and West Nepal. I would especially like to thank Shamsher B. Nucchhen Pradhan, who for many years worked as my field assistant and as a 'door opener' to many Newar families. I am likewise very grateful to the mediums, their family members and their devotees, with whom I was able to raise the issue of how to conduct a ritual properly and of behaviour in general during rituals.

[5] For further articles on spirit possession in Nepal see Berglie (1976, 1982), Devkota (1984), Dietrich (1998), Durkin-Longley (1982), Gellner (1992, 1992, 1994) and Iltis (2002); on Shamanism in Nepal see Desjarlais (1992), Hitchcock & Jones (1976), Höfer (1974a, 1974b) and Maskarinec (1995).

[6] For details about the goddess Hāratī in Nepal and the etymology of her name see Merz (1996, 2004).

located at the Buddhist *stūpa* Svayambhunath in Kathmandu—as well as by her six children, her sisters, and further deities. While possessed the mediums (Nev. *dyaḥmāṃ*) heal and allow the devotees (*bhaktas*) to worship the deities they embody. The chief protagonists in the present case are three women who are all mediums of the goddess Hāratī of many years standing, and who normally perform their healing sessions at their own homes. During these séances they treat physical ailments and tend to various personal concerns, such as forthcoming exams, disputes over inheritances, wishes for marriage or children, and the like. On occasion, however, the three women meet at one of their houses and conduct a joint *pūjā*. Although it is quite common for other ritual specialists like shamans to join for a séance (see Desjarlais 1992, Kendall 1996, Levi-Strauss 1991, Mascarinec 1995 and Schieffelin 1996), in the general context of the Hāratī cult it is rather unusual that mediums jointly conduct a *pūjā*. Nevertheless, the three mediums in question had a history of conducting *pūjās* together, although I was told that it happened much less frequently then some years back. The general purpose of these *pūjās* in which all three mediums are present is to allow the devotees the opportunity to give thanks to the deities for passing an exam, for a smoothly conducted wedding, for the birth of a son, or such like. In the present case the initiative for this 'thanksgiving *pūjā*' came from Surya Shrestha, a member of the cult who, since becoming a widow several years ago, runs a transport company together with her two sons and her daughter. She wanted not only to give thanks for the restoration of her younger son's health after a prolonged illness, but also to ask for the goddess's blessings for a new enterprise that her elder son wished to set up. The congregation further consisted of a number of spectators and participants whose main wish was to worship the various gods and goddesses who manifest in the mediums during such *pūjās*, which can take up to 12 hours.

2. *The ritual*

The *pūjā* began shortly before 11 a.m. after the three mediums had taken their designated seats (*āsana*). The women were Raj Kumari Shakya, a woman in her early fifties and the oldest of the three, Laksmi Shrestha, a woman in her mid-forties, and Chandika Shrestha, a woman in her late thirties. It is important to note briefly the hierarchical relationship between the three if the ensuing ritual is to be properly understood: Raj Kumari was not only the eldest woman; she also had initiated the other two into the cult and was regarded as their teacher or *guru*. Laksmi had received her initiation a number of years ago, followed a few months later by Chandika. As for the actual possession by the deities, Raj Kumari—the oldest of the mediums—was chiefly possessed by the goddess Hāratī herself, whilst Laksmi was mostly possessed by Hāratī's eldest daughter, Dhana Maiju, and Chandika—the youngest of the three—was chiefly possessed by Hāratī's youngest son, Jilan Bhāju. This constellation also reflects the internal hierarchy of the deities within the cult, in which Hāratī comes at the apex and the children are assigned descending positions on the basis of age.

The *pūjā* began with Surya, the "initiator" of this *pūjā*, going to one deity after another—as manifested in the mediums—, sitting before each in worship and giving thanks for her son's recovery. As she finished she was followed by the other participants, who numbered around a dozen. After about 90 minutes Surya sat down once again before Laksmi, who at the beginning of the ritual was possessed by Dhana Maiju, the oldest of Hāratī's daughters. Surya presented the goddess with various offerings, consisting primarily of various foodstuffs (Nev. *ame*), rice spirit (Nev. *aylāḥ*; referred to in the ritual context as *pātra*), and small coins, and struck up a song of praise. At the end of the song Dhana Maiju remained quiet. She studied the offerings in her hand and finally remarked that something was wrong with the rice spirit she had been given, it didn't taste good. With that she cloaked herself in pregnant silence. The eldest of the mediums, Raj Kumari, at all the time still possessed by the goddess Hāratī, who was sitting beside her, immediately intervened and consoled the perplexed devotees by assuring them that everything would be restored to order ("In the end there will be no mistake, child."). The ritual proceeded and Surya shifted her place closer to Chandrika, who was possessed by Hāratī's youngest son. In the meantime Dhana Maiju's mood had visibly darkened. She began criticizing various points relating to the other participants, finally listing the individual errors that had been made prior to the ritual. According to her, a number of things were being done incorrectly at Surya's home. Her sons did not remove their leather belts when they entered the kitchen during the preparation of the food for the *pūjā*, they failed to perform the annual death rites for their father at the proper time, and Surya herself wore the wrong shoes while preparing the food. Surya humbly apologised to the goddess, promising that she would wear her straw shoes while in the kitchen and use her influence on her children. The *pūjā* continued. The deities were worshipped one after the other by the members of the congregation. But Dhana Maiju, who is normally known for her jokes, behaved differently on this occasion and remained unusually silent. When my turn came, she complained that on one occasion I had entered this *pūjā* room on the fourth day of my menstruation, something that was only permitted after the seventh day. A woman who had arrived somewhat later was accused of entering the room after previously having eaten boiled rice. Another married woman was taken to task for wearing a kind of trouser suit normally worn by younger women instead of a Sari. And still the *pūjā* continued. But some five hours after the commencement of the *pūjā* Dhana Maiju suddenly began to weep. The participants and spectators were shocked and dismayed not least because of the amount of the emotion she showed. To understand the participants' reaction to Dhana Maiju's tears, it is important to realize that in Newar society, loud and/or visible sobbing in public is essentially reserved for the death of a relative or someone in the immediate family. Moreover, only women will weep out loud, visibly, in public during the mourning period, and only at set times of day. They only weep "at the right time in the correct place" (Emmrich 2005: 232). Apart from a few exceptions, men will weep during the procession to the cremation site and during the cremation of the deceased, and not in public (see also Emmrich 2005: 228f., Gutschow 2005: 164ff.). These restrictions on weeping during the mourning period are also accounted for with reference to a ritual text that states, "in cases of mourning the deceased is forced to eat the tears and mucus of the weeping relatives" (Buss, forthc.). In order not to hinder the departure of the dead spirit, people should not mourn out loud after the 45th day following the bereavement (Gutschow 2005: 165f.). Even if a *pūjā* is not performed in public in the same way as mourning ceremonies before the house of the departed or during a funeral procession, the audience and participants at a *pūjā* give it a certain public character in which emotional outbursts are met by surprise and dismay. In addition, in the present case it is a goddess that is weeping. And this could mean that someone had committed an error and if the worst comes to worst, may have drawn the wrath of the god to them. It is understandable, then, that not only the audience was dismayed, but in particular Surya, who has initiated the *pūjā*, was very upset. She repeatedly asked the goddess for forgiveness (*kṣamā*), but Dhana Maiju would not stop crying and called among her sobs for first her mother and then her father. Only with great difficulty did Raj Kumari, the older medium who was sitting by her side and who at that moment was possessed by Hāratī, manage to placate the goddess's eldest daughter. She poured drops of holy water onto Dhana Maiju, talked with her in the 'gods' language' (Nev. *dyaḥ bhāy*), and finally sang a little song and danced while seated until Dhana Maiju finally calmed down.

Shortly after, Laksmi—still possessed by the goddess Dhana Maiju—began to explain her behaviour, telling the participants at the ritual that although she had learned from her 'mother' (the goddess Hāratī) and been under her protection for a long time, she was now an adult and thus could take her mother's place when it came to complaining about the mistakes in the preparations for the *pūjā*. She backed up her accusations by once again listing all of the mistakes that had been made prior to and during the ritual. But for all her attempts to explain herself, the goddess did not succeed in dispelling the feelings of uncertainty and confusion that reigned among the participants. In a further attempt, made a few minutes later, she jokingly remarked (still possessed by Dhana Maiju) that "Children must cry sometimes, otherwise they don't feel good". And some time after that she explained to the still bemused participants that they shouldn't think that it was Laksmi who had wept, for it had been she herself, i.e. the goddess Dhana Maiju, who had wept.

After about another hour, during which the three mediums were possessed by further deities, the *pūjā* came to an end and all of the participants who remained sat down together in the *pūjā* room for a meal. The atmosphere during the meal seemed relaxed, with people chatting and joking. Laksmi also joined in the conversations, but she pointed out that she had a headache.

3. *The immediate and long-term repercussions of this ritual*

Despite the errors that Dhana Maiju said had happened during the preparations for the ritual, and despite the incorrect behaviour of some of the participants during the ritual, the ritual was not stopped or pronounced a failure. So is it true, as tentatively assumed at the beginning of this article, that a ritual in the context of the Hāratī cult can hardly fail? This impression gradually deepened during a number of conversations conducted with the participants and mediums. Although certain rules (Nev. *niyam*) must be adhered to, there are several possibilities for 'making up' when these are infringed out of ignorance or lack of experience, i.e. when a mistake is made. These seem to be a phenomenon that can be found all over South Asia. Humphrey & Laidlaw (1994), for example, show that mistakes during the performance of a ritual in a Jain temple are often simply ignored and become "non-actions". As such, it is not possible to get something wrong: the worst thing that can happen in the Jain context is that one has not performed a ritual at all. The emphasis in this case study however is on mistakes that are made unwittingly—such as when someone who has come for the first time enters the *pūjā* room after having eaten boiled rice, unaware as they are of the relevant rule. Although the deity may grow angry or get annoyed (Nev. *kopa*), he or she will nevertheless be placated when the guilty person asks for forgiveness (*kṣamā*) and assures them that their incorrect behaviour had been unintentional. Generally speaking the mediums' rules (Nev. *niyam*) are largely concerned with avoiding pollution. A mourner, for instance, is prohibited from entering a medium's *pūjā* room during the stipulated period of mourning, as are men and women from a house where a birth has just taken place, women during the first seven days from the onset of menstruation, and families in which (Nev.) *bare teyegu* (the ritual seclusion of pre-pubertal girls) is being conducted. Since these taboos also play similar roles in other ritual contexts among the Newars and are well known, there is little problem in adhering to them in the context of the Haratı mediums and their cult. The matter is more complicated when it comes to restrictions that are not generally known, but that are of particular importance to the mediums. These include for instance the prohibition on eating chicken eggs or chicken meat prior to visiting a medium. If someone nevertheless enters the *pūjā* room after eating eggs or chicken, this amounts to a grave error with serious consequences—not for the ritual itself but for the medium concerned. A medium's reaction to such a breach of the rules may manifest itself by her immediately feeling unwell, or later feeling ill—even to the extent of vomiting throughout the ensuing night. So interestingly, the pollution involved in such infringements of the rules does not affect the ritual, nor the ritual's sponsor, but solely the medium. In answer to my question whether a ritual has ever failed or had to be discontinued, I was told that this had never occurred and would only happen if the person who officiated at the *pūjā* died during the process. But even then that would not be an error in the conducting of the ritual, so the ritual would not have failed but simply have been discontinued for obvious reasons.

But to return now to the case in point. What occurred? A ritual was conducted, errors were ascertained in the preparations as well as incorrect conduct during the ritual by several of the participants, yet regardless of this the ritual was not discontinued. Nevertheless, there was a disturbance during the ritual when one of the mediums, possessed by the goddess Dhana Maiju, suddenly began to weep. The errors which the medium identified as such, did in fact have an effect, albeit not on the ritual but on the medium, and as a further result on some of the participants. Looking first at the effect on the medium, we see that after the ritual was over Laksmi complained of a headache during the meal they ate together. It was assumed by both the participants and the mediums that the reason for this could have laid on the one hand in the food and *pātra* that Surya had brought as her offering, which had presumably been polluted by her children's conduct, and on the other hand in the mistakes made by various participants during the ritual. Both of these elements would have constituted a pollution that in the final count affected the medium and led to her feeling unwell and having a headache. As already mentioned, this is not uncommon in the context of these mediums, and is a phenomenon that can similarly be observed among other mediums of this cult. In most cases the feeling of uneasiness or illness is attributed to the fact that the goddess has been disregarded and the medium has to suffer. This raises the question, however, as to why this medium was affected and not the other two, for they had both eaten the same food and same rice during the *pūjā*, and sipped the same rice spirit.

But what effects did the ritual have in the present case on the participants? Initially it was a ritual like many others in which they had previously attended. Perhaps it was slightly more important than usual, because three mediums were involved and more gods manifested than is customary, and the *pūjā* was considerably longer than normal. But otherwise it did not differ initially from the rituals that the mediums conduct every day. The participants worshipped the deities; here as in the rites of worship at the temples the main concern is with seeing the god and being seen by the god (*darśan*), and the exchange of food—offering food and receiving it back in consecrated form (*prasād*) from the deity. But in order to become fully involved in this process it is essential that the participants believe that the deities are genuinely present in the bodies of the mediums, and believe in their authenticity. According to Claude Levi-Strauss, Pierre Smith, and Pascal Boyer, performative rituals "rest on a simulation, a half-believed fiction that some unseen supernatural event really happens as they are performed" (Humphrey & Laidlaw 1994: 8). According to Smith, for example, men try to convince women and children about the presence of a divine being by putting on masks, changing their voices, acting, playing instruments, and so on. "The central theme in the collective initiation of young men is their passage from the second group into the first, and it involves the exposure of the simulation" (Smith 1982: 105). But astonishingly, this does not affect the belief of the people. Levi Strauss (1991) uses the example of the shaman as a trickster, who can still be an effective healer. Boyer (1994) claims (following Kapferer 1983) that the possession of the exorcist is merely mimed, while people believe him to be possessed. And yet there is much discussion after the ritual about the authenticity or "reality" of the trance, and the validity of the ritual depends on the results of this discussion. What, therefore, is important in "performative-centred rituals" (as Humphrey & Laidlaw—following Atkinson 1989—term shamanic rituals and initiation ceremonies as opposed to "liturgy-centred rituals" like the daily *pūjā* of the Jains they studied) is to convince the audience, or at least to make the audience act as if they were convinced. It is not necessarily so important that a certain sequence or number of actions is enacted. Atkinson, for example, says that a performative ritual cannot be described or analysed as a preordained progression of delineated steps to which ritual practitioners and congregants collectively conform. It is rather a repertoire of ritual actions available to performers acting independently in the ritual arena (1989: 15). Likewise shamanic success is not defined by the ability to control disease and affliction, as it is always possible to find an excuse or an alternative diagnosis when a patient dies. It is more a matter of establishing personal shamanic power through a discourse with the audience, or in point of fact the main actor "must convince the audience and maintain this conviction" (Hüsken, this volume, p. 348).

So it is of the utmost importance in the present situation that the participants are convinced that it is the gods who speak to them and give them advice. As in the example given by Atkinson, where it is important for the success of the séance that "the powers of performing shamans should never be doubted (1987: 347) the participants of the *pūjā* should not have a shred of doubt and must have faith in the mediums' ability to represent the gods in a worthy manner. Whether we are involved here with a 'willing suspension of disbelief' (Coleridge 1967: 169; see also Schieffelin 1996: 79) or an unconscious action must remain an open question. But in the ritual described here a moment arose in which this faith, this 'suspension of disbelief' was questioned. It was the moment in which Laksmi, possessed by Dhana Maiju, began to weep. Although the participants were upset and dismayed by this during the *pūjā*, after the ritual—in some instances only several days later—they ventured mild doubts as to Dhana Maiju's authenticity during the ritual. Even if these doubts were never explicitly formulated, the fact that a deity had wept was mentioned time and again in various asides and passing remarks. The doubts related paramountly to the fact that the goddess wept almost uncontrollably and for a very long time. Was this genuinely Dhana Maiju ("but how can gods weep like that?"), or could it have been Laksmi who had wept? The latter possibility would suggest, however, that she was using her tears as a strategic device, because as already pointed out above, normally as a Newar woman she would only be allowed to wail like this at the time of mourning. Neither of which was the case here.

Either way, it is not surprising that the spectators and participants reacted the way they did. In particular, the *pūjā* had already been going on for over five hours prior to Dhana Maju's outburst of tears, and a high degree of shared involvement had developed among the participants during that time. Schieffelin (2006) refers to this state variously as "being-in-the-situation", "the mode of participation", or simply "deep participation", adding that it is distinguished by "deep focus, deep commitment, and intensity", and can be achieved, for instance, by dancing or playing rhythmic music together. In the present case study, the songs that are constantly sung during the *pūjā*—hymns of praise for the goddess Hāratī that the majority of participants know by heart—help to produce this atmosphere of deep involvement. Usually there is no place within this framework for doubts about the "authenticity" of the divine presence. The question that must be asked is whether Dhana Maju's sudden, loud sobbing, which did not fit into the framework, broke this deep participation among some or all of the participants. And further, whether—as with the shamans described by Levi-Strauss, who discerned a disappearance of social consensus among their patients as a result of their failures (1991: 198)—the tears did not sow seeds of doubt about the "authenticity" of the medium's performance in a number of the participants at the *pūjā*. Similar to the case reported by Schieffelin (1996) of a shaman who lost his credibility in the eyes of his visitors because he failed to convince them during a séance, for some participants the medium's tears resulted in such a lasting erosion of her credibility that they turned their backs on her. For a number of visitors the tears meant that they were no longer able to maintain the necessary 'suspension of disbelief' (Schieffelin 1996: 79). Deviations in the course of a ritual must not necessarily led to doubts being cast on the ritual itself or on the performer, as Brückner has shown in her example from South India, in which mistakes are allowed as long as everyone involved can live with them and the ritual as a whole keeps a balance: "...the main criterion for success, in spite of deviation, or failure, is the acceptability of the deviation by other performers and supposedly the deity, as also by the dignitaries and the larger audience" (1991: 322). In the case of Dhana Maiju, perhaps none of the participants would have expressed doubts if the goddess's weeping had been more restrained. But the intensity of Dhana Maiju's weeping, which was more reminiscent of someone wailing over the departed, evidently made it difficult for some of the participants to remain any longer in a state of "suspension of disbelief." The doubts of the devotees and her 'contested' status did not remain hidden from Laksmi. One month after the memorable *pūjā* she returned to the event during a healing session at her home. Possessed—this time by Hāratī—she explained in retrospect that Dhana Maiju had done the right thing at the time: "While my daughter was crying and started asking for her father I also felt very sad. But I tried my best to hide it." Here Hāratī is actively supporting her daughter, a thing that she did not do as such on the ritual occasion concerned.

4. *Not ritual failure but failed performance?*

In all this it should be remembered that a *pūjā* is always seen as an opportunity for the mediums to renegotiate their status. For their status never remains the same, and can alter from time to time during a medium's career. If at the outset a medium is mainly possessed by 'lower' gods, as for instance Hāratī's children, strict adherence to the rules (*niyam*) may lead to her body being considered sufficiently 'pure' that after a couple of years, 'higher' deities such as the goddess Hāratī will manifest in it. Consequently, a ritual of the kind described above can also be understood as a cultural performance, as a unique means for conveying messages (Belliger & Krieger 1998: 14) that not only allow the participants' social structures and religious views to be confirmed and reproduced, but also to be renegotiated and reconstrued. This is not however simply a matter of the representation of social reality, but above all of the negotiation of the status, recognition and honour of the individual mediums. It would appear that Laksmi Shrestha had a certain adeptness in using the ritual we have examined as a forum for her own person. As the goddess Dhana Maiju she not only showed that she is now adult and can step out of the shadow of her mother (the goddess Hāratī), and speak and act in her stead, but also signalled that she is stricter than her 'mother'. Hierarchically speaking, she attempted to assume a position on a par with Hāratī and to no longer be reduced to the role of a 'girl'. In practice—as revealed one month after the ritual in question—Laksmi Shrestha has already risen in the hierarchy because now Hāratī in person manifests more frequently in her.

The long-term repercussions of the ritual only became apparent months later. The assumed mistakes in the preparations for and during the ritual did not lead to its failure. But they prompted the goddess Dhana Maiju to weep, which for a number of the participants was and is so unbelievable that it led to a drop in the medium's perceived authenticity. And here lies the essential difference: a ritual in the context of Hāratī's mediums cannot fail—but there is nothing to stop the performance of a medium from failing (as was the case with Schieffelin's example—this was not a case of 'ritual failure' but 'performative failure'; Schieffelin 1996: 62). This having been said, instances of performative failure can nevertheless afford us much insight into the dynamics of rituals, into the personal aspirations and belief structures of the performers and the participants, the speed and acceptance of change in hierarchies, as well as the possibilities for changing the forms of expression in a ritual. Although it may be acceptable for gods to weep occasionally, as sometimes happens, they shouldn't overstep the mark. So if we assume that Laksmi's intention in the ritual was to signal her medium's maturity in respect to her *guru*, then we have to admit that this performance failed during this particular ritual and might have damaged the medium's reputation. But as we have just seen, in the long run it proved successful because a rise in status did actually occur. Consequently, a model like the one given by Schieffelin (1996) could be extended further so as to embrace such developments. The performance may end in failure, but ultimately there may be success even in such failures because there are many more factors to be taken into account in and outside of the ritual.

References

Atkinson, Jane Monning 1987. "The Effectiveness of Shamans in an Indonesian Ritual." *American Anthropologist* 89.1 (March): 342–355.

—— 1989. *The Art and Politics of Wana Shamanship*. Berkeley, Calif.: University of California Press.

Belliger, Andréa & David J. Krieger 1998. *Ritualtheorien. Ein einführendes Handbuch.* Opladen & Wiesbaden: Westdeutscher Verlag.

Berglie, Per Arne 1976. "Preliminary Remarks on some Tibetan 'Spirit Mediums' in Nepal." *Kailash* 4 (1): 85–108.

—— 1982. "Spirit-Possession in Theory and Practice: Séances with Tibetan Spirit-Mediums in Nepal." In: Holm, Nils G. (ed.), *Religious Ecstasy. Based on Papers read at the Symposium on Religious Ecstasy held at Åbo, Finland, on the 26th–28th of August 1981*, Stockholm: Almgvist & Wiksell, 151–166.

Boyer, Pascal 1994. *The Naturalness of Religious Ideas: A Cognitive Theory of Religion.* Berkeley, Calif.: University of California Press.

Brückner, Heidrun 2001. "Fluid Canons and Shared Charisma: On Success and Failure of Ritual Performance in a South Indian Oral Tradition". In: *Charisma and Canon: Essays on the Religious History of the Indian Subcontinent*, Dalmia, Vasudha & Angelika Malinar & Martin Christof (ed.). New Delhi: Oxford University Press, 313–327.

Buss, Johanna forthc. *Preta, Pitṛ und Piśāca. Rituelle und mythische Totenbilder im Pretakalpa des Garuḍapurāṇa, dem Garuḍapurāṇasāroddhāra und der Pretamañjarī* (PhD dissertation, Heidelberg 2006).

Coleridge, Samuel Taylor 1817 (repr. 1967). *Biographia Literaria, or Biographical Sketches of my Literary Life and Opinions.* Watson, George (ed.). Reprint London et al.: Dent.

Coon, Ellen 1989. "Possessing Power: Ajima and Her Medium". *Himalayan Research Bulletin* 9: 1–9.

Desjarlais, Robert R. 1992. *Body and Emotion. The Aesthetics of Illness and Healing in the Nepal Himalayas.* Philadelphia: University of Pennsylvania Press.

Devkota, P. L. 1984. "Illness Interpretation and Modes of Treatment in Kirtipur." *Contributions to Nepalese Studies* 11: 11–20.

Dietrich, Angela 1998. *Tantric Healing in the Kathmandu Valley. A Comparative Study of Hindu and Buddhist Spiritual Healing Traditions in Urban Nepalese Society.* Delhi: Book Faith.

Durkin-Longley.... 1982. *Ayurveda in Nepal: a Medical Belief System in Action.* PhD dissertation, University of Wisconsin

Emmrich, Christoph 2005. "Ujyā—Ein letzter Ritus der Vajārcāryas von Lalitpur," In: Assmann, Jan & F. Maciejewski & A. Michaels (ed.), *Der Abschied von den Toten. Trauerrituale im Kulturvergleich.* Göttingen: Wallstein, 223–234.

Gellner, David N. 1992. *Monk, Householder and Tantric Priest. Newar Buddhism and its Hierachy of Ritual.* Cambridge: Cambridge University Press.

—— 1994. "Priests, Healers Mediums and Witches: the Context of Possession in the Kathmandu Valley, Nepal". *Man* (N.S.) 29: 27–48.

—— & Uttam Sagar Shrestha 1993. "Portrait of a Tantric Healer: a Preliminary Report on Research into Ritual Curing in the Kathmandu Valley." In: Toffin, Gérard (ed.), *Nepal: Past and Present.* Paris: CNRS Éditions, 135–147

Gutschow, Niels 2005. "Totenrituale in Bhaktapur, Nepal. Trauer und Klage als Phasen von Reinigung und Reintegration." In: Assmann, Jan & F. Maciejewski & A. Michaels (ed.), *Der Abschied von den Toten. Trauerrituale im Kulturvergleich.* Göttingen: Wallstein, 151–180.

Hitchcock, John T. & Rex L. Jones (ed.) 1976. *Spirit Possession in the Nepal Himalayas.* Warminster: Aris and Phillips.

Höfer, András 1974a. "A Note on Possession in South Asia." In: v. Fürer-Haimendorf, Christoph (ed.), *Contributions to the Anthropology of Nepal*, Warminster: Aris & Phillips, 159–167.

—— 1974b. "Is the Bombo an Ecstatic? Some Ritual Techniques of Tamang Shamanism." In: v. Fürer-Haimendorf, Christoph (ed.), *Contributions to the Anthropology of Nepal*, Warminster: Aris & Phillips, 168–179.

Hüsken, Ute 2006. "Pavitrotsava. Rectifying Ritual Lapses." In: *Jaina-itihāsa-ratna. Festschrift Gustav Roth zum 90. Geburtstag gewidmet*, Hüsken, Ute & Petra Kieffer-Pülz & Anne Peters (ed.). Marburg: Indica et Tibetica Verlag (Indica et Tibetica 47), 265–282.

Humphrey, Caroline & James Laidlaw 1994. *The Archetypal Actions of Ritual. A Theory of Ritual illustrated by the Jain Rite of Worship.* Oxford: Oxford University Press.

Iltis, Linda 2002. "Knowing all the Gods. Grandmothers, God families and Women Healers in Nepal." In: Rozario, Santi & Geoffrey Samuel (ed.), *The Daughters of Hāratī. Childbirth and female Healers in South and Southeast Asia.* Routledge: London, New York, 70–89.

Kapferer, Bruce 1983. *A Celebration of Demons: Exorcism and the Aesthetics of Healing in Sri Lanka.* Bloomingtion, Ind.: Indiana University Press.

Kendall, Laurel 1996. "Initiating Performance: The Story of Chini, A Korean Shaman". In: *The Performance of Healing*, Laderman, Carol & Marina Roseman (ed.). London: Routledge, 153–176.

Levi-Strauss, Claude 1991 (1958). "Der Zauberer und seine Magie". In: *Strukturale Anthropologie I*, Frankfurt a.M.: Suhrkamp, 182–203.

Maskarinec, Gregory G. 1995. *The rulings of the night. An ethnography of Nepalese Shaman oral texts.* Madison: University of Wisconsin Press.

Merz, Brigitte 1996. "Wild Goddess and Mother of Us All. Some Preliminary Remarks on the Cult of the Goddess Hāratī in Nepal." In: Michaels, Axel & Cornelia Vogelsanger & Annette Wilke (ed.), *Wild Goddesses of India and Nepal.* Frankfurt, New York (u.a.): Peter Lang, 343–354.

—— 2004. *Bhakti and Shakti: göttliche und menschliche agency im Kontext des Heilkults der Göttin Hāratī in Nepal.* Universität Heidelberg: dissertation. URL: http://www.ub.uni-heidelberg.de/archiv/4599 (date of last access: 21.08.2006).

Parish, Steven M. 1994. *Moral Knowing in a Hindu Sacred City. An exploration of mind, emotion, and self.* New York: Columbia University Press.

Schieffelin, Edward L. 1996. "On Failure and Performance. Throwing the Medium out of the Séance". In: *The Performance of Healing*, Laderman, Carol & Marina Roseman (ed.). New York & London: Routledge, 59–89.

—— 2006. "Participation." In: Kreinath, Jens & Jan Snoek & Michael Stausberg (ed.), *Theorizing Rituals: Classical Topics, Theoretical Approaches, Analytical Concepts*, Annotated Bibliography. Leiden: Brill.

Smith, Pierre 1982. "Aspects of the Organisation of Rites." In: Izard, Michel & Pierre Smith (ed.), *Between Belief and Transgression: Strucuralist Essays in Religion, History and Myth.* Chicago: University of Chicago Press.

Thieme-Breslau, Paul 1939. "Indische Wörter und Sitten". *Zeitschrift der Deutschen Morgenländischen Gesellschaft* 39: 104–137.

CHANGE OF VIEW: THE RITUAL SIDE OF SERIAL KILLINGS AND THE CONDITIONS FOR FORTUNATE FAILURE

Maren Hoffmeister

I. *Introduction*

More than three homicides in a row are normally called a 'serial killing'. But this has not always been the case. At least in Germany, from the 1920s to the 1950s, the term commonly used was *Lustmord*, i.e. a killing for lust. In the 19th century the phenomenon was referred to as a 'ritual murder' (*Ritualmord*) and often was used to justify pogroms against the Jewish population. Scientific progress in medicine and psychology evoked a semiscientific explanation for these murder cases in terms of the sexual drive. Calling the phenomenon *Lustmord*, was thus a modern development. All these terms 'ritual murder', *Lustmord* and 'serial killing' indicate the same phenomenon, albeit, each in a different historical context. In my opinion, there are good reasons to study the phenomenon from the perspective of 'Ritual Studies', taking the concept of 'ritual' in its widest sense, as has become common since the 1970s.

II. *Ritual-theoretical considerations*

1. *Ritual theories*

Before 1970, it was generally assumed that rituals are an enactment of social or psychological subtexts and that they can be analysed on the basis of their scripts, which could be uncovered by studying the performances of the rituals. In other words, it was believed that there was always a reason to perform them, outside the rituals themselves. For Durkheim, this was the need to create social solidarity; for Freud, the necessity to suppress traumatic experiences, and for Malinkowski, the intention to influence the environment (Bellinger & Krieger 1998: 7). So, the ritual had both a meaning and a function which could be uncovered by the observer.

It was largely the achievement of Ronald L. Grimes, who heavily relied on the theory of Austin, that rituals have to be studied as such, apart from these extrinsic influences (Grimes 1996). While Austin shifted the perspective from the truth of language towards its ability to create reality, Grimes similarly shifted the focus from motives outside the ritual towards the ability of ritual to create a specific reality and how its various elements function.

The parallel between ritual and language is questioned however, when one assumes that rituals are intrinsically non-intentional acts (Humphrey & Laidlaw 1994: 35). Staal, for instance, believes that rituals are not only "without meaning" but also "without goal, or aim" (Staal 1996: 487). Refocusing on the performative force of the ritual provides an additional advantage: one no longer has to decide whether those participating in the ritual believe in it or not—a differentiation which Schechner thought central to the distinction between ritual and theatre (Schechner 1974).

Following Grimes, the term 'ritual' is no longer used exclusively for religious practices. Instead, it is broadened into a category of forms which can also be found in other social contexts such as sport, politics, the mass media, the arts, theatre, and jurisdiction (Fischer-Lichte 2004: 35). Such forms are distinguished from others by structural characteristics and conditions, but show at a performative level similarities to religious rituals.

The secularisation of the concept of ritual has brought about new definitions of the term. However, these alternate between a metaphoric use ('like a ritual') and an analytic category ('as ritual') (Wulf & Zirfas 2004: 18f.).

Some theoretical approaches take the concept of 'communitas' as a characteristic of rituals, that is, they focus on the importance of an experience shared by several participants (Turner 1989: 73). From this point of view, it seems rather implausible to apply the term 'ritual' to serial killings, for the killer acts alone and the interaction is limited to two persons, the killer and the victim. However, if we follow Bourdieu's concept of 'habitus' (Bourdieu 1999: 103f.), and Wulf's theory of mimesis and ritual, which suggest that the individual incorporates rituals by participating in them (Wulf & Göhlich & Zirfas 2001: 265), we see that the individual is not only shaped by society but also shapes or enacts society. The crime he commits is tightly bound to the society in which he lives and plays with social binaries such as strong—weak, moral—amoral, woman—man, life—death.[1] In other words, his crime lies in stagings as well as performative subversions of social norms. On the level of performance, the attacker, the victim, and the person discovering the corpse all share a knowledge of the situation they find themselves in, a knowledge of the action that has just taken place and that might take place again.

The term 'serial killer' carries in itself the threat of further violence, thus emphasising the element of repetition which is often regarded as a significant characteristic of rituals. Not every repetition indicates a ritual, though. Grimes suggests we should differentiate between traditional rituals and non-traditional rituals, calling the former 'rites' and the latter 'ritualisations' (Grimes 2000: 26). However, I will not follow this distinction, because I believe that Grimes's ritual criticism—or to be more precise, an analysis of the failure of the performance of killing—offers us sufficient opportunity to understand the killing as a ritual.

A number of authors have tried to determine rituals by using characteristics (e.g. Kreinath & Snoek & Stausberg 2006). The different points of emphasis depend however on the subjects of the individual studies. Wulf, for example, not only emphasises the dealing with differences in the context of rituals, but also stresses the performative surplus of rituals which goes beyond the performance of symbolical actions (Wulf & Zirfas 2004: 18f.); Michaels emphasises a feeling of timelessness and the evocation of a particular mood that he terms 'religio' (Michaels 1999); Staal underlines the absence of meaning in rituals (Staal 1996).

Many of these approaches share, however, the following convictions:

- rituals are symbolic and extremely powerful actions;
- rituals concern the community, i.e. they affect society;
- rituals are defined by a temporal as well as a spatial frame;
- rituals show an autonomous logic;
- rituals are repetitive;
- the action is always accompanied by a certain atmosphere or mood, which can be described as religious, magical or transcendental.

[1] For the society, the so-called lust murder proves to have great potential for being interpreted as a symbolic action, since on the one hand it makes no sense as an action in its own right, while on the other hand the repetition of sequences from the action, as well as the fact that it transgresses the bounds of life, suggest that it should have some meaning. Thus it demands to be attributed a meaning. This corresponds to Langer's central thesis that a symbol is even stronger if it contains less meaning (Langer 1942).

Snoek demonstrates that most of these features are fuzzy and are also found in other forms of action. According to him, it is mainly a matter of choice whether an action is regarded as ritual when only some, but not all of the typical characteristics apply to it (Snoek 2006). Due to the complexity of the particular actions and the variety of rituals, it is impossible to delineate a fixed definition for the ritual.

2. *The ritual failure approach*

Grimes demonstrates how one can analyse ritualistic elements and rituals by looking at the ways in which they can fail (Grimes 1996: 288). By looking at cases of attempted murder that were broken off by the attackers, a number of significant preconditions could be specified. Attacks were often broken off when the attacker failed to push a person into the role of victim and thus could not establish himself properly in the role of the culprit (misinvocation); if the temporal and spatial setting was misframed; if there were flaws in the distribution of the roles; and if the particular mood or atmosphere intended by the attacker—which can often be reconstructed by analysing the theatrical effect of the crime scene—is undermined ('flops' or 'insincerity').

There is a social script for the murders which is based on general assumptions in society about what action of the culprit towards the victim is motivated by what intention. According to Foucault, such concepts as 'ritual murder', 'killing for lust', or 'serial killing' are supported by their inclusion in discourses that give them their efficacy (Foucault 1992: 48f.). The interpretation of certain phenomena, first as 'ritual killings', and then as 'lust murders' makes visible certain historical shifts of power in society. Such concepts become modes of interpretation when they operate as independent agencies. They are very powerful, moulding the expectations that people have of the phenomena labelled in this specific way. Indeed, they distort our interpretations and presentations of the actual facts, so as to fit the ideas we have based on these concepts. In other words, these concepts function as models for, and of, the phenomenon. In the following, this shall be called the 'social script' of the ritual.

The actions of the murderer are read through the glasses of general assumptions about serial killers (e.g. as *Lustmord*). Analysing the failure of murders, however, enables us to distinguish between a general social script and the personal script of the culprit. For instance, the act of killing is not necessarily the climax of every culprit's 'performance'—

although according to the social script it ought to be. The killing may, for example, be only a peripheral part of a sequence of actions which can be understood as a ritual. The analysis of failed murder attempts can help to identify which actions, in the context of a killing, are framed as a ritual. Of course, in the following the phrases 'ritual of a homicide' or 'the ritual of a killing for lust' do not refer to the older concept of 'ritual murder' (Kohut 1913).

Since the culprit is a member of society, he would know this social script, whether consciously or unconsciously. However, he may have a number of reasons to construct his own script, if only to mislead the authorities in order not to be apprehended. Therefore, the potential culprit will also develop a personal script for his first homicide. At their first killing, however, 'successful' serial killers will typically be quite flexible, adapting their course of action to the circumstances as they appear. When, however, they succeed this first time in reaching their personal goals without being caught, this successful first time will itself tend to become the script for their further homicides. This mode shall be called the 'personal script' of the culprit.[2]

My intention is not to find an exclusive truth based on an understanding of the cases as rituals. Instead, this approach makes it possible to go beyond the common stereotypes and to show that the sequences of actions which comprise a particular murder may differ, perhaps considerably, from the expectations offered by these stereotypes. Differentiations between the personal script and the social script, and marking how the social script influences the personal script, help us to understand the dynamics of a series of murders.

III. *Serial killings interpreted as* Lustmord

In what follows, the historical development of the *Lustmord* interpretation of such crimes shall be briefly outlined, and the weakness of that interpretation demonstrated. In addition, a number of attempted murders will be presented, as committed by serial killers from the 1920s, 1930s, and 1960s, which did not lead to an actual homicide in all cases. These will be analysed as cases of 'failed rituals'.

[2] In terms of Jennings one could as well call it the acquisition of ritual knowledge in ritual actions (Jennings 1998: 157–172).

Lustmord was a pattern of interpretation that became popular in Germany in the 1920s. The term describes the murder of a female victim, committed by a perverted man who kills in order to satisfy his sexual desire. Today, such crimes are described as serial killings, a term which no longer indicates the motivation of the crime but implies rather that in a number of crimes, the murderer is one and the same person.

Lustmord replaced an earlier model of explanation for brutal and gruesome crimes, which found its motive in ritual practice. Even as late as the early years of the 20th century, such crimes were ascribed to Jewish rituals or blood rites.[3] At that time, criminal investigators sought to determine how much blood had been extracted and whether the crime had been committed according to a certain ritual; these examinations were carried out without a deeper knowledge of the rituals of the culture to which they were ascribed (Anonymous 1892). A secret meaning was attributed to the overkill—the action going beyond the killing—so that only an expert, well-informed about the rituals, was able to decode them. The need to understand the culprit's intentions guided the enthusiastic search for an explanatory system. This explanatory framework identified and classified patterns in the performance of the crime in order to determine the motivation for the murder. What this older concept 'ritual murder' could not explain, however, was the internal motivation of the individual perpetrator. As late as in the first decade of the twentieth century, for example, criminal justice experts witnessed a debate between two legal and criminalistic scholars over the extent to which 'ritual murders' were motivated by sincere superstitious belief or by a psychopathic delusion.[4] The new concept *Lustmord* offered a pseudo-scientific explanation for motives in such cases. It was a superficial application of Freud's 'theory of the sexual drive' (*Triebtheorie*) that had become popular by the 1920s. The concept was based on an

[3] In the case of the perception of a Jewish blood rite, such a ritual never existed. Since the first appearance of this lie in 1235, the existence of such a blood rite has always been denied by the popes and the kings. But the notion was strong enough to persist in the commonality even when revealed as a lie by the council. This council, which was organized by King Frederick II., consisted of baptised Jews (*Taufjuden*) from all over Europe. The reasoning based on Torah and Talmud showed that there are no blood rites at all in the Jewish religion because blood is regarded as impure. This perception is a misjudgement of the Jewish religion and a transfer of the wine taken at the Last Supper (Eucharist) (Smith 2002: 103; Nonn 2002: 55f.).

[4] Hellwig 1908 and 1910; Nussbaum 1907.

exaggeration of the significance of ultimately secondary aspects of the murders, such as the rape of the victim or the dismemberment of the victim's body.

A significant influence on the development and widespread acceptance of the *Lustmord* interpretation in the 1920s was the work of the crime expert Robert Heindl. In order to analyse the category of criminals he turned his interest to the 'professional' criminal (*Berufsverbrecher*; Heindl 1927). He developed the idea of a criminal who always uses the same *modus operandi*, or special strategy to commit the crime. According to Heindl, in order to earn a living the professional criminal would repeatedly use the same *modus operandi*, as long as it was successful. In Heindl's system, crime was always related to something commercial. This concept is still known in criminology under the term 'perseverance'. The careers of such criminals were catalogued in a large database of criminal acts which could be cross-referenced in order to identify a perpetrator. As a means of identifying criminals, this system remains controversial because it relies exclusively on the criminal repeatedly committing the crime in a similar fashion. With regard to the development of the *Lustmord* interpretation, however, the system was of key importance, even though *Lustmörder* or sex offenders were not included in Heindl's categorization of criminals.

Some 'killings for lust' seemed to uphold Heindl's ideas, because the police listed them systematically according to their similarities. As a result, police officials were often successful in determining that a series of murders had been committed by the same perpetrator. But their system was less successful in helping them to determine the identity of the perpetrator; often, as in the case of Fritz Haarmann or Peter Kürten, the apprehension of the murderer was only possible through pure coincidence rather than 'scientific' police work. The data base approach is not impartial, because criminologists often knew in advance what kind of murder case they had to solve. The data were adjusted to the expected motive, some aspects were emphasized. So there were two weak points. One was to establish 'perverted sexuality' as a motive for the culprit. The criminologists looked for sperm, sexual attacks or a kind of fetish (blond hair…), in order to reveal a connection between the victims. If they were unable to find anything, that was also regarded as evidence for the special perversion of the culprit. The other weak point was to construct a script for the killer, in which the target of each single homicide was the most violent criminal act ascribed to this specific killer by the police. Thus, the crime which was most horrifying to the criminologists served as the goal and benchmark for the other less cruel murders committed by the same perpetrator. In this way there emerged three different scenarios in each case: society's homogeneous labelling of the cases as *Lustmord*, the heterogeneous individual homicides by the culprit, and the definition of one integral goal by the police. The last two scenarios may be very close to each other, but not necessarily, because there may not be an integral goal to all of the murders. Moreover, the culprit's goal may also be an unattainable fantasy which therefore remains invisible in the deeds.

This is an important parallel to the phenomena described in ritual theory. Repetition and rigidity are also attributed to rituals. In well-known rituals we only see what we expect. In reality, however, they expose dynamic differences in their performances. Rituals differ and change in each repetition, because of the performative surplus (Wulf & Zirfas 2004: 29).

Lustmord was a category to account for bloody killings that made no 'rational' sense under any other schema. A close analysis of court documents such as psychological reports suggests that the motivations for the deeds might have had their roots in family conflicts rather than in a perverted sexual drive.[5] One can argue that the victims were executed instead of somebody or something else (Girard 1992). *Lustmord* is rather more evident in the area of cultural imagination than on the level of the culprit's motivation, which is interspersed with aggressions, confused ideas, and feelings of guilt. Despite the lack of explanations, a number of ritualised and repeated elements can be found when the individual homicides are analysed. The interplay of various factors which influence the beginning and the course of the killing can be analysed especially successfully with the help of documented cases of failed murder attempts by known 'serial' murderers/lustmurderers. Interrogations of the culprits regarding these deviations from the personal scripts reveal the ways in which these scripts were acted out as rituals.

1. *The selection of the victims*

The murderers under discussion here selected their victims on the basis of details or minor phenomena which caught their attention, such as the driving of a bicycle or, in the case of young men, the lack of body

[5] Sace Elder also shows the connection with domestic violence in the case of Grossmann from the 1920s, who is labelled lustmurderer (Elder forthc.).

hair. The behaviour of the attacked person was as important as his or her outward appearance. This can be shown clearly in the case of Jürgen Bartsch (1969).[6] Cheeky or disrespectful children who contradicted Bartsch or laughed at him escaped his violence. Straight and obedient ones did not.[7] Rather than selecting his victims according to a special sexual attraction, Bartsch chose children of a particular age who could easily be handled and manipulated. Adolf Seefeld (1935),[8] like Bartsch, preferred to murder boys (wearing sailors' suits) who gave a well-behaved impression. Moreover, for their crimes Seefeld and Bartsch lured the victims to their favourite scenes. It is not possible to make any generalisations about the way serial killers choose their victims. Peter Kürten (1931)[9] did not show any standard criteria in his selection of victims that could be attributed to their appearance. The secluded scene of the crime and the possibility to kill with a high degree of cruelty were the critical factors in his decisions. Consequently, the only factor his victims had in common was the fact that Kürten regarded them as easy to subdue. The case of a drunken worker is a good example.

The selection of the victim depends on the perpetrator. There are no common attributes which define a victim. Thus the murderer acts according to a personal script. As a result, the ritual depends on different factors which build the frame of the ritual performance.

2. *Location, atmosphere, and metamorphosis of the perpetrator*

The atmosphere is of major importance for the killings. Although in modern ritual research, ritual is no longer exclusively restricted to the domain of the holy or religion, a special atmosphere is often thought to surround many rituals.[10]

Clearings, forest paths, and caverns were among the scenes of the crimes. Bartsch needed equipment charged with ritual meaning—candles, fire, cords, and knives—in order to create an appropriate atmosphere in a cavern. He placed his equipment at the scene in advance, in

[6] Landgericht Wuppertal, Aktenzeichen 2 Kls 6/67; Jugendkammer des Landgerichts Düsseldorf, Aktenzeichen VII–61/70 jug/5 Kls 4/70.

[7] Bartsch wrote educational directives for mothers during his term in jail.

[8] Schwurgericht Schwerin, Aktenzeichen Ks. 33/34.

[9] Schwurgericht Düsseldorf, Aktenzeichen 15 K1/31.

[10] Köpping & Rao refer to Caillois, who emphasises ecstasy (*Rausch*) as a constitutive element of a ritual. Caillois 1982 (1958); Köpping & Rao 2000: 4; Michaels 1999: 36.

order to avoid the risk of the action remaining incomplete. The victim had to be alive at the beginning of the deed, preferably unsuspecting. The beginning of the script was marked by a violent act intended to both shock and terrify the victim. Far from deterring Bartsch from his criminal acts, his victims' cries for help were obviously part of the atmosphere he desired and were thus part of his personal script. For Kürten, too, an essential component of the murderous script was the element of surprise. Whether overpowering his victims unaware from behind or turning from a harmless companion into a brutal attacker, as if suddenly possessed by a demon, Kürten sought to see his own power in the astonished eyes of his victims (Berg 1939: 326). The distribution of power installed in this performance relies on the atmosphere in order to guarantee the orderly completion of the action to follow.

A parallel between the murder and traditional rituals can be deduced here. Disturbing the atmosphere may also destroy the traditional ritual (see also Weinhold, this volume). The absence of important ritual accessories can also ruin the ritual action. These aspects belong to the conditions of several categories claimed by Grimes as types of infelicitous performances, such as 'omission', because an action cannot be performed if the important objects are missing, or 'flop', because a special appropriate mood cannot be produced, for example, if the candles can't be lit on Sabbath dinner (Grimes 1996: 288).

3. *Failure resulting from a disturbance of the atmosphere*

The murderers under consideration here sought to separate the ritual space, their victim and themselves from the rest of society for the course of the action. The separation was not only convenient but also had symbolic significance for the perpetrator. A failure or interruption of the deed sometimes came about if super-ordinate powers—divine or governmental—emerged. In the case of Kürten, the invocation of God or the mentioning of hell by the victims several times troubled the atmosphere, so that Kürten spared their lives. Similarly, when Bartsch was asked by one of his victims if he would go to jail, he interrupted his performance and tried unsuccessfully to save the victim's life. The first crime of Johann Eichhorn (1939)[11] was interrupted because the attacked woman pronounced his name aloud. Thus we see that the

[11] Landgericht München, Aktenzeichen 1Js-So 1059/39.

subordination of the culprit to an accepted social or divine order may lead to an interruption of the action.[12]

The distribution of power was also disturbed when, as in the case of Eichhorn, enthusiasm replaced the fear of the weapon, or, in the case of Bartsch, laughter or even a threat came from a potential victim.[13] Mistakes like these were grave enough to keep the culprit from continuing the violent action. This is not only a 'misinvocation' in the sense of Grimes. It is also a 'lack of the requisite feelings' and a 'flop' in producing the appropriate atmosphere.

4. *Development of the personal scripts as a result of failures*

While criminologists tried to reconstruct the script of the crime, assuming the worst part of it (e.g. the horrifying mutilation of the body) to be its goal, a different reality can be observed when we look at the actions of certain culprits. The start of the action was often very difficult for Eichhorn, because the attacked persons successfully defended themselves or their behaviour did not show the desired effects, i.e. of being horrified or surprised. In one case an attacked woman did not even defend herself at all and Eichhorn broke off after pushing her and putting her into a foetal position. After these failures, he developed a new personal script. In all four cases heard in court, the shooting of the victim started the performance carried out on the person. The possibility of the victim reacting was minimised by a firm grip to the throat and a shot following immediately. The killing was not the aim of the action, but it guaranteed an undisturbed atmosphere. The resulting distribution of power enabled the culprit to perform his actions on the unconscious or dead body. In this way the belief in the action and the power of the culprit could not be questioned by the victim. According to the social script labelled as *Lustmord*, however, the killing should mark the end of a series of violent actions. In the final speech for the prosecution, this 'mistake' was successfully ignored and the violent actions of the culprit were put in the 'right' order.

---

[12] According to Schechner, in order to call something a ritual it is important that the participants believe in the ongoing performance, otherwise he would rather call it theatre (Schechner 1974: 473).

[13] Bourdieu writes about patterns which exist and which can be used by participants of the same culture (*Habitus*) (Bourdieu 2000: 143). In these cases the prospective victims do not behave according to the expected patterns.

As in the case of Eichhorn, Bartsch's course of action reveals a process of learning from experience. For example, the scope of Bartsch's actions gradually narrowed. He developed an idealised course of action—cutting up the body and finally holding the beating heart in his hands. The victim was supposed to be conscious throughout the action, experiencing everything he did. His intention was to create a maximum of pain. Therefore he developed, based on his experience gained from preceding deeds, a certain ritualised order of cuts and violations. Additionally, he improved his strategy by luring children into a cavern without having to injure them or to strike them down in advance. In contrast to Eichhorn's case, the course of the deed follows the social script of *Lustmord* because the killing takes place at the end. Both Eichhorn as well as Bartsch show the development of a certain script which, afterwards, could be made compatible with the script of *Lustmord*. But what happens in the case of a murderer who shows neither the motivation for *Lustmord* nor any other stereotype?

While society's understanding of such a crime coined the idea of the *Lustmord* in the Weimar Republic, the case of reference at the time—Peter Kürten, regarded as the 'king of the sexual criminals' (Wehner 1937: 131)—reveals a different motivation. His actions were based on an urge to revenge earlier unjustified prison sentences and maltreatment. A confused idea of a balance of power made him believe that a cruel killing of innocent victims would increase the guilt of his former oppressors, and as a consequence he was pleased by the panic he spread within society. His personal script strongly depended on his experience gained from previous interactions and therefore remained dynamic. Kürten did not form target groups for his homicides, but killed people of different age and sex. He varied the weapons used in order to increase the horror within the community and to make the police look for more murderers than necessary: one killer per weapon. Even if he did not really know the data base approach of the police, he shared the conception that a killer usually performed one particular trick, such as always using a knife in a certain way or always killing with a hammer. He used this existing expectation about the culprit in order to mislead the police. Newspaper reports and articles were of great importance for Kürten because they determined the efficacy of his actions. The lack of reports about a corpse made him send sketches and letters to the police and eventually to newspapers, because he only regarded a deed as accomplished if the corpse had been found. The lack of a newspaper report constituted, according to his concept, a mistake which caused the failure of his performance. His deeds clearly show that we are dealing here with a highly dynamic concept which depended on its effects on society.

It is questionable whether one can speak of a ritual in the case of Kürten, or whether it would be better to call it 'try-out'. Analysis of his failed cases shows the ritual and ritualised character of the beginning and the end of the deeds. The beginning also depended on finding a victim and evoking a special atmosphere. One victim said that he would go to hell if he murdered her, another one started to invoke Jesus Christ. Kürten was stopped in his action by these references to Christian religion. In the witnesses' statements, some of them observed that Kürten abruptly transformed into a completely different person: they could not recognise him any more. Kürten described the situation as a sudden obsession by a demon, but the fact that he planned the deeds as well as the use of certain weapons revealed this to be an element of his defence strategy. He therefore dropped it and emphasised the idea of revenge on society. The course of the deeds, however, remains dynamic, with Kürten trying to stage an emotional event in order to create a highly horrifying impact on society. This forms a great contrast to the case of Bartsch, who aimed at maximum emotional effect within the setting of his actions for himself and consequently, being both author and addressee, developed a highly ritualised form for his homicide cases.

Kürten broke the fundamental rules of the *Lustmord*-script that existed in the cultural imagination of his society. He not only murdered women but also children, one man, and even animals, varying the weapons he used and the courses of his action. Furthermore, he set buildings on fire and combined arson and murder by setting fire to a corpse. According to Kürten, a number of these attempts were aimed at increasing the horror he caused within society. In Kürten's case, deviations from the script *Lustmord* can be found at every level: the selection of victims, the varying ways of committing a crime, and the absence of the presentation of himself as a dangerous pervert. Depicted as the 'king of sexual criminals', deviations from the imagined concept were ascribed to his universal sadistic drive. The authoritative experts ascribed his intention to kill to his assumedly being suddenly overwhelmed by his perverted drive. When his actions were compared with the social script, this seemed to be a mistake the performer made while committing the crime. But in fact it did not contradict his personal script. Defacto, personal script and social script would lead to two completely different deeds if executed, but in these cases they were presented by the experts as resulting in the same performance. Nevertheless, these discrepancies confirmed the authority of the experts because they were able to interpret and judge the crimes as evidence of a powerful, flexible and universal sadistic drive.

The way Adolf Seefeld (1935) killed lacked the bloodiness, or at least the physical violence carried out by the culprit's own hands which is ascribed to the *Lustmord*, and consequently the criminologists and jurists changed his personal script from somebody who poisons to somebody who strangles his victims without leaving conspicuous traces (social script). This happened although there were hints that he always tried to dispose of the sexually abused victims, using the same trick of killing the children with poison and staging them and the place where he left them in such a way that the children seemed to have frozen to death while sleeping. In this way he tried to conceal that a crime had happened. The killing was not the paramount goal.

IV. *Conclusions*

Although Heindl's theory proved to be useful because it was possible to ascribe the homicide cases to one culprit on the basis of the use of one particular strategy, the interpretation of the crimes—especially by applying the script of the *Lustmord*—obscured the sequence of events and the characteristic ritual context of each single killing because of the serious simplification involved and the assumption that all homicides committed by the same culprit would be identical.

After considering the scene of the crime and the senselessness of the deed, the members of society, including journalists, criminologists, psychologists, and lawyers, believed they knew the inner thoughts, feelings, and motivations of the culprit. The motive 'murderous sexual drive' was both the reason behind the killings and a threat of future crimes. From the medical point of view the crimes happened under a compulsion based on the drive of the culprit and, therefore, always had to follow the same pattern. The juridical point of view accepted the repetitive pattern as well, but ascribed it to intention and planning. All of these readings of the crime focused on a certain ritual structure which included a special beginning of the deed, a special atmosphere of fear and violence, a certain place and time of action, a special course of events and an expectation of the deeds to follow. This social script had such a cultural power that it extended beyond the criminal justice system, reinforcing as it did the widespread notion of sexual danger for women travelling alone and the idea that children should be carefully guarded.

During the interrogation and with the help of physicians, the culprit developed a biography which set him apart from society as an abnormal individual and qualified his performative identity. He adjusted his interpretation of the deeds to the social script. The motive was related to his perverted sexuality, which could only be satisfied by a bloody killing. The crime scene was interpreted as resulting from a sexually ecstatic condition of the murderer, and not as a result of his rage. Also, no attempt to investigate the culprit's actual emotional involvement was made. Culprits of the 1920s and 1930s deviated from the script of the *Lustmord* in their crimes by killing boys or even men instead of women, discrepancies which were neglected by referring to the abnormality of the drive. The preparations for the court hearing consisted in the search for further homicide cases. The prosecution tried to bring the cases in line with the script of the *Lustmord*. This meant producing an appropriate motive, an appropriate identity (based on a perverted drive), and a biography leading to a climax in the culprit's perverted development.

In court, the social script overwrote the personal script of the perpetrator. What the perpetrator articulated in the crime and afterwards about his motivation was heard only in so far as it supported the social script. These trials can be understood as anti-rituals (*Gegenrituale*) insofar as society here overwrote the powerful rituals of the culprits.[14] The culprit had to regret his deeds, had to admit that his actions were wrong, had to accept his own abnormality, his total difference. Society, on the other hand, conceptualised itself as civilised, never capable of committing equally cruel crimes. Performatively it erased the existence of these deeds—and the ritual knowledge the culprit gained[15]—from their society. Freedom from violence as a goal functioned as constitutive element of society, the exertion of violence marked its boundaries.

The public perception of ritual is always based on a social script. The differences between personal and social scripts fade unless the ritual shows significant failures. Thus, the dynamics of traditional ritual also vanish and the participants always seem to take part in the same

[14] Hoffmeister 2003: 423–442; Winn 1998: 449–470. Ritual as a ritual opposition in: Bergesen 1998: 273.

[15] Jennings 1998: 157–172.

performance. This mechanism produces a consistency in action which obscures the fact that history and time have passed by and body, identity and culture have been modified.

Ritual is a scientific construction which allows us to look at the homicide cases without relaying on such constructive explanations as *Lustmord* or 'Jewish Ritual Murder'—as in the early 20th century. The analysis of the 'failed ritual', the attempted murders, shows the determinants which would have been needed in order to complete the murderous action. Such elements as the lack of candles or the crying of the victim, a lack of self-defence or the refusal to accept the power of the perpetrator on the part of the victim, may abort the action. Such 'failures' can be found on different levels. The event of 'murder' can itself be a 'mistake' from another ritualised action. The determinants of the homicide depend on the personal script of the perpetrator. The script is not a fixed text, it is interchangeable, developing step by step in the course of the actions. It exists and makes progress only on the performative level. It can be read as a dynamic ritual. Seen in this way, the differences between the social script of the deed and the individual script become comprehensible. Interpreting such 'serial murders' in terms of rituals provides fertile ground for a more precise and illuminating method of understanding the criminals and their crimes.

For ritual studies the subdivision between personal and social script is interesting because it shows the polysemantic traits of the performed ritual. It shows how open the ritual is to interpretation, highly different personal intentions, and symbolic actions, which require an explanation. On the basis of a social script, society agrees beforehand on the interpretation of the 'ritual' as *Lustmord*, almost completely independent of what actually happens in the performance or which symbols are used in the execution of the personal script of the killer. It is only important that these actions are performed in a symbolic mode. The agreement about whether there is ritual failure or how to interpret a particular ritual is a question rather of the distribution of power in society than of the correct use of its symbols.

References

Anonymus 1892. *Der Xantener Knabenmord: Der Prozeß Buschhoff. Verhandlungen vor dem Schwurgericht zu Cleve vom 4. Juli–14. Juli 1892.* Crefeld: J.B. Klein'sche Buchdruck.

Belliger, Andréa & David J. Krieger (ed.) 1998. *Ritualtheorien. Ein einführendes Handbuch.* Opladen: Westdeutscher Verlag.

Berg, Karl 1939. "Der Sadist". *Zeitschrift für die gesamte gerichtliche Medizin* 17: 245–347.
Bergesen, Albert 1998: "Politische Hexenjagd als Ritual". In: *Ritualtheorien: Ein einführendes Handbuch*, Belliger, Andrea & David J. Krieger (ed.). Opladen & Wiesbaden: Westdeutscher Verlag, 265–284.
Bourdieu, Pierre 1999. *Sozialer Sinn: Kritik der theoretischen Vernunft*. Frankfurt: Suhrkamp (German translation of: *Le sens pratique*. Paris: Édition de Minuit, 1980).
—— 2000. *Zur Soziologie der symbolischen Formen*. Frankfurt: Suhrkamp (reprint of 1970).
Caillois, Roger 1958. *Les jeux et les hommes: Le masque et le vertige*. Paris: Gallimard (German translation used: *Der Mensch und die Spiele*. München: Ullstein, 1982).
Elder, Sace forthc. *Murder Scenes: Criminal Violence in the Public Culture and Private Lives of Weimar Berlin*.
Fischer-Lichte, Erika 2004. *Ästhetik des Performativen*. Frankfurt: Suhrkamp.
Foucault, Michel 1992. *Archäologie des Wissens*. Frankfurt: Suhrkamp (German translation of: *L'archéologie du savoir*. Paris: Gallimard, 1969).
Girard, René 1982. *Le bouc émissaire*. Paris: Grasset (German translation used: *Ausstoßung und Verfolgung. Eine historische Theorie des Sündenbocks*. Frankfurt: Fischer Taschenbuch Verlag, 1992).
Grimes, Ronald L. (ed.) 1996. *Readings in ritual studies*. London: Prentice-Hall International.
—— 2000. *Deeply into the Bone: Re-Inventing Rites of Passage*. Berkeley: University of California Press.
Heindl, Robert [4]1927. *Der Berufsverbrecher: Ein Beitrag zur Strafrechtsreform*. Berlin: Pan-Verlag Heise.
Hellwig, Albert 1908. *Verbrechen und Aberglaube. Skizzen aus der volkskundlichen Kriminalistik*. Leipzig: Teubner.
—— 1910. "Blutmord und Aberglaube: Tatsachen und Hypothesen". *Zeitschrift für die gesamte Strafrechtswissenschaft* 30: 149–174.
Hoffmeister, Maren 2003: "'Ich konnte nicht anders'. Ritual als Zwang". *Paragrana* 12.1–2: 423–442.
Humphrey, Carolin & James Laidlaw 1994. *The Archetypal Actions of Ritual. A Theory of Ritual Illustrated by the Jain Rite of Worship*. Oxford: Clarendon Press.
Jennings, Theodore W. 1998. "Rituelles Wissen". In: *Ritualtheorien: Ein einführendes Handbuch*, Belliger, Andrea & David J. Krieger (ed.). Opladen & Wiesbaden: Westdeutscher Verlag, 157–172.
Kohut, Adolph 1913. *Ritualmordprozesse. Bedeutsame Fälle aus der Vergangenheit*. Berlin-Wilmersdorf: Basch.
Köpping, Klaus Peter & Ursula Rao 2000. *Im Rausch des Rituals. Gestaltung und Transformation der Wirklichkeit in körperlicher Performanz*. Hamburg: Lit-Verlag.
Langer, Susanne K. 1942. *Philosophy in a New Key; A Study in the Symbolism of Reason, Rite, and Art*. Cambridge, Massachusetts: Harvard University Press.
Michaels, Axel 1999. "'Le rituel pour le rituel?' oder Wie sinnlos sind Rituale?" In: *Rituale heute. Theorien—Kontroversen—Entwürfe*, Caduff, Corinna & Joanna Pfaff-Czarnecka (ed.). Berlin: Reimer, 23–48.
Nonn, Christoph 2002. *Eine Stadt sucht einen Mörder*. Göttingen: Vandenhoeck und Ruprecht.
Nussbaum, Arthur 1907. "Der psychopathische Aberglaube". *Zeitschrift für die gesamte Strafrechtswissenschaft* 27: 350–375.
Schechner, Richard 1974. "From Ritual to Theatre and Back: the Structure/Process of the efficacy-entertainment Dyad". *Educational Theatre Journal* 26: 455–480.
Smith, Helmut Walser 2002. *The Butcher's Tale. Murder and Anti-Semitism in a German Town*. New York & London: Norton.
Snoek, Jan A.M. 2006. "Defining 'Ritual'". In: *Theorizing Rituals. Topics, Approaches, Concepts. With an Annotated Bibliography*, Kreinath, Jens & Jan A.M. Snoek & Michael Stausberg (ed.). Leiden & Boston: Brill (Numen-Bookseries).

Staal, Frits 1996. "The meaninglessness of ritual". In: *Readings in Ritual Studies*, Grimes, R.L. (ed.). Upper Saddle River, New Jersey: Prentice Hall, 483–494.
Streng, Franz 1978. "Brandstiftung und Sexualität". In: *Sexualität und soziale Kontrolle*, Hess, H. & Hans Udo Störzer & Franz Streng (ed.). Heidelberg: Kriminalistik-Verlag, 41–61.
Turner, Victor Witter 1989. *Vom Ritual zum Theater*. Frankfurt & New York: Campus.
Wehner, Alex 1937. "Plädoyer". In: *Die Kunst der Verteidigung. Sechs große Verteidigungsreden*, Güldenagel, Karl (ed.). Berlin: Hermann Sack Verlag, 131–154.
Winn, Peter A. 1998. "Rechtsrituale". In: *Ritualtheorien: Ein einführendes Handbuch*, Belliger, Andrea & David J. Krieger (ed.). Opladen & Wiesbaden: Westdeutscher Verlag, 449–470.
Wulf, Christoph & Jörg Zirfas 2004. *Die Kultur des Rituals. Inszenierungen, Praktiken, Symbole*. München: Fink.
Wulf, Christoph & Michael Göhlich & Jörg Zirfas (ed.) 2001: *Grundlagen des Performativen*. München: Fink.

COMPETING PERSPECTIVES: THE DISCURSIVE PRODUCTION OF RITUAL

"The enactment of all ceremonial (or theatrical) performances is inherently risky [since] the ritual performances are necessarily subject to the variable competencies of the major performers, the competing agendas and ongoing evaluations of all the participants, as well as unforeseen contingency and blind luck", says Schieffelin (1996: 80). The existence of 'competing agendas' or intentions of the participants implies that within the tradition(s) explicit critique and accusing others that they have made mistakes is the rule rather than the exception. While the scholar has to be very careful regarding the vocabulary he uses when it comes to deviations, those contributions to this volume dealing with conflicting assessments of rituals within certain traditions show that there is little hesitation in accusing other members of the same tradition of 'getting it wrong.' Diverse assessments of ritual events can exist side by side: varying perspectives result in diverse evaluations of what counts as 'mistakc' or as successful performance. In this section competing perspectives within certain ritual traditions or social settings are unfolded. In many cases, these rituals are not a means to conflict resolution but are objects of conflicts themselves. The contributions to this section clearly show that these conflicts refer to the realm external to the ritual: not only the ritual process, but also the authority and authenticity of the ritual experts, internal hierarchies of the participants (or of the groups which are represented by them) as well as relations beyond the ritual frame are evaluated, negotiated and reorganized. Ritual mistake and failure in this sense therefore originate inside as well as outside the ritual.

Brigitta Hauser-Schäublin in her contribution "Rivalling Rituals, Challenged Identities: Accusations of Ritual Mistakes as an Expression of Power Struggles in Bali (Indonesia)" exemplifies in one case study that critique may even be integrated into performances, and at the same time can influence action outside the ritual setting. The Intaran's deities manifest themselves in humans during the performances. These superhuman agents have the right to point out mistakes and to ask for their correction—which also implies the competence and power to continuously modify the 'script' of the temple festival, to induce change or to insist on conservatism. Since these local deities are 'lower' deities (as opposed to the 'higher' deities of the immigrants), their voicing of ritual mistakes represents a 'ritual of rebellion' which, however, does not only keep alive the recollection of the local deities as powerful leading figures, but also has a lasting practical impact on the social structures beyond the ritual context. In another case study Hauser-Schäublin discusses questions of ritual mistakes by drawing on one example from pre-colonial Bali. The village community consisted in the 17th century of autochthon villagers and a group of immigrants who were, in everyday life, bound together through economic and political ties. However, during temple festivals the cultural gap between these two groups became manifest in that each of them claimed that the animals appropriate for ritual sacrifice were those they had being using before. Here the mutual accusations mirror competitive power struggles within the village community (immigrants/locals). "The evaluation of mistakes and the mutual accusation of committing mistakes is the result of cross-references. Mistakes [...] were not the result of the wrong application of generally approved rules but stemmed from applying one's own rules to rituals of the others", Hauser-Schäublin concludes (p. 261). The allegation of 'getting it wrong' can serve to emphasise identity for all who are involved in the process: defining what others do 'wrong' implies the affirmation of one's own 'correct' values and norms. Challenging the validity of a ritual also touches upon the crucial issue of individual or group identity. "One's own ritual rules, seen as the exclusively correct way to perform rituals, are at the core of a group's identity construction" (Hauser-Schäublin, p. 263).

Similarly the constant struggle over 'ritual shares' between two Viṣṇuite groups in Ute Hüsken's case study ("Contested Ritual Property. Conflicts over Correct Ritual Procedures in a South Indian Viṣṇu Temple") points to a ritual's importance for identity formation. Moreover, in the context of 'ritual mistakes' Hüsken raises questions regarding the 'ownership' of rituals and of the right to perform them. She refers to Simon Harrison (1992) who characterises rituals as 'luxury goods' which are 'owned' and function to signify social, especially political, relationships. The right to perform certain rituals is owned by both individuals and groups, and as soon as ownership is challenged by one party, this feature of 'ritual shares' (the privilege to participate in one way or another in certain rituals) becomes evident. In that case certain ritual action is conceived of as a 'mistake' or even as an voluntary infringement of established norms from certain perspectives. Although these ritual shares are only nominally connected with economic privileges, they are hard-fought for, since they are 'property' and constitute identity. The outcome of the negotiations within the ritual will influence the wider context just as much as the outcome of negotiations in the socio-political field will influence the ritual performances. Ritual performance evidently also serves also as a medium to communicate changes and reorganisation in social structure.

The case study analysed in the article "The Unwanted Offering. Ubiquity and Success of Failure in a Ritual of the Hindu Right" by Christiane Brosius takes even more perspectives into account, namely that of the ritual's organisers and participants as well as external forces such as critics or state organisations. On the one hand, the threat of failure serves as a means of unifying the participants, on the other the actual events might lead to a decrease of the use of such rituals as a strategy of confrontation in the context of the Hindutva movement, Brosius suggests. Her enlightening contribution which draws upon different levels of relatedness and perspectivity reveals that complex ritual events rarely allow for a final conclusion with regard to the 'success' of the performance.

Michael Rudolph, with "Failure of Ritual Reinvention? Efficacious New Rituals among Taiwan's Aborigines under the Impact of Religious Conversion and Competition between Elites", gives an impressive example of a case where competing value systems and competition between elites in a globalizing and highly hybrid cultural context leads to the rejection of a reinvented ritual despite its evident efficacy. He clearly shows that it can be very difficult to create (or re-invent) a ritual with the 'appropriate atmosphere' which meets the expectations of all participants—even socially and religiously effective rituals can die when they are sabotaged by competing groups. Rudolph argues that "the described failure of ritual invention actually seems to be the result of the unfavourable collision of individual and collective agendas in a highly hybrid cultural context [...] individual definitions of ritual practices also have their limits and can bear unfavourable results, as there exists a historically rooted, collective dimension that is imminent to ritual and that transcends any individual intentionality" (p. 334).

References

Harrison, Simon 1992. "Ritual as Intellectual Property." *Man* (New Series) 27.2: 225–244.

Schieffelin, Edward L. 1996. "On Failure and Performance. Throwing the Medium out of the Séance". In: *The Performance of Healing*, Laderman, Carol & Marina Roseman (ed.). New York & London: Routledge, 59–89.

RIVALLING RITUALS, CHALLENGED IDENTITIES: ACCUSATIONS OF RITUAL MISTAKES AS AN EXPRESSION OF POWER STRUGGLES IN BALI (INDONESIA)

Brigitta Hauser-Schäublin

1. *Introduction*

The tiny island of Bali (Indonesia) is well-known for its 'thousand temples' and their prolific Hindu rituals—as advertised in tourist promotions all over the world. Though depicted as a backdrop to Balinese culture that has unchangeably existed for hundreds of years, temple rituals are a dynamic and contested arena. Most of the temple rituals are carried out according to a 'script' focussing on the day the ritual has to be carried out, the number, contents, and composition of the offerings to be dedicated to individual deities and their shrines, as well as on its plot and the main actors. To some extent rituals may indeed give the impression of being firmly standardised and simply reproduced at regular intervals. However, a ritual needs to be successful in order to reach its goal: to please the gods and the ancestors, and to ensure the well-being of the humans, their livestock and also their fields. This goal can be reached only if the rituals are carried out according to explicit rules on the one hand, and standards set by the gods, sometimes without conveying them in advance to the human actors, on the other. Such demands, therefore, are beyond human control. It is failure that people fear most, since this will result in catastrophes like illness and the unexpected death of humans and animals (even epidemics), or droughts destroying the fields. Failure implies a disrupted relationship between humans and gods/ancestors that can be restored, if at all, only with great difficulty and sometimes after much loss.

Each temple ritual inherently carries the risk of failure. Most risks of failure evolve around two crucial issues: 1) infringing the rules of purity, and, closely associated with this, 2) disrespecting taboos, breaking rules of conduct, such as sexual relations that fall under the incest taboo, and sexual intercourse with animals, constituting a violation of the boundaries between humans (*manusa*) and animals (*buron*). Impurity (*sebel*) is attributed to those who have been in intimate contact with death, illness, wounds, and menstruation. In one sense or another, these events are all associated with crisis. Death, the spilling of blood and the threat of disease attract beings of the world below, *buta kala/buta kali*, to invade pure space restricted to deities. *Buta kala/buta kali* are kept from the temples by blood sacrifices, and, among other offerings, rice wine and liquor poured onto the ground. Both, incest and bestiality result in cataclysms, the dissolution of categories that social order carefully separates. This sort of cataclysm inflicts *sebel* on the whole body of a village community and puts it into a state of emergency. No temples may be entered and no rituals held until whole cycles of purifications have been held. Impurity in this encompassing sense implies a collapse of distinct spaces, deities—and values; it invokes a world of chaos, destruction, and failure.

Apart from failure, it is possible for the actors to commit mistakes either unintentionally (Hüsken 2004: 2), these being only later acknowledged by the gods or, often in combination with the above, as part of a contentious issue among the rivalling actors. In contrast to failure, mistakes are subject to negotiation; they can often, at least partly, be corrected by repeating a sequence or juxtaposing an additional one. The boundary between the notions of failure and mistake becomes blurred as soon as actions perceived to be potentially failure-inducing—ineffectiveness or counter-productivity of the ritual—become subject to negotiation among the actors.

In this paper I shall put Balinese temple rituals in the context of power relations between different groups of people. The politically and socially sometimes tense relationship between such groups are reflected in the performance of rituals and the debates about the 'right' and 'wrong' ways of performing these. I shall describe and discuss contested temple rituals by using two different examples: a recent one from a village in South Bali, Intaran, and a historical one as reflected in oral histories and religious practices from Sembiran in North Bali.[1] The two villages today display remarkable differences concerning their social

[1] Fieldwork in Intaran was carried out between 1988 and 1993; for a detailed description of temples and temple rituals see Hauser-Schäublin 1997. Fieldwork in Sembiran and adjacent villages started in 1995 with several stays of different length, each ranging from two to eight months and totalling about two years. Fieldwork took place under the auspices of the Indonesian Institute of Science (Lembaga Ilmu Pengetahuan Indonesia), Jakarta, and Universitas Udayana in Denpasar with Prof. Dr. I Wayan Ardika as my sponsor. I am indebted to the German Research Council and the University of Göttingen for supporting my research between 1997 and 2004.

organisation. The former was ruled (in pre- and early colonial time) by a local lord who was part of a segmentary kingdom with hierarchically ranked title-bearing status groups. Apart from nobles, there were (and still are) several *brahmana* compounds located in the village. These were the ritual leaders with which the noble ruler cooperated not only to perform all the rituals necessary for a successful and prosperous life for himself and his people, but also in order to achieve his political goals (Hauser-Schäublin 2004a).

By contrast, at the time of the advent of the Dutch (mid-19th century), Sembiran was apparently more or less egalitarian in organization:[2] there was no local ruler attached to an overarching kingdom and there existed no clear-cut, hierarchically ordered status groups. Instead, to this day there are two associations, the assembly of delegates, one from each clan (*sekehe gede*), and the ritual village association (*kerama desa*) consisting of all married couples of the core village. This latter organisation is based on the sex and age (or rather the duration of their marriage) of its members. This village association and its mainly ritual tasks was formerly complemented by some temple priest and, additionally, by a Great Priest who held an outstanding position; nowadays he is only one among others. The priests, even the Great Priest, however, never had the status of a *pedanda*, a high priest of high descent such as *brahmana siwa, brahmana budha*, or other ritual specialists bearing respectable titles such as *sri empu, sri resì*. While such office-holders generally intermarried only with members of the same status group, the Great Priest did not.

The above, only briefly outlined differences in social, political and ritual organisation between Intaran and Sembiran do not represent unbridgeable oppositions. Rather, they have perhaps to be understood as poles within a wide range of variations that through time often underwent transformations from one form into the other (Ottino 2003a). Nevertheless, I suggest that disagreements about the way temple rituals should be properly carried out, the deities to be worshipped, and the contents of the offerings to be presented to these gods, can be related to the different social and political contexts of these two villages and, consequently, to the differing means the villagers have at their disposal to deal with such conflicts.

---

[2] As Ottino recently showed (2003b), those villages with no title-bearing status groups were far from being egalitarian; they nevertheless were less hierarchically ordered than others.

I shall start with Intaran (see Hauser-Schäublin 1997) and the particular way in which social difference here is translated into disagreements concerning rituals and the uttering of threats by the gods.

2. Brahmana's *ritual control and the complaints of deities from the nether world*

According to Intaran's stratified society, there exist deified ancestors and deities of different standing, too. Except for gods of the Hindu pantheon that recently gained supreme status due to their official recognition as a core part of Hindu religion (*agama Hindu*) within Indonesia and transnational Hindu movements, there are many other beings from the other world (*niskala*) worshipped in Intaran. These beings are either linked to a mostly autochthonous commoner clan and/or a status group, or they are bound to specific sites within Intaran and its surroundings. The most powerful deities are associated with the nether world and the sea rather than the upper world: these deities are much feared for their magical powers. The upper world is populated by those of 'real' Hinduism propagated by *brahmana* priests.

Like in many other villages in South Bali, each deity has a shrine at a particular site within the temple courtyard according to his or her standing within the hierarchy among the deities represented there. Since a clan or rather lineage is also responsible for the maintenance of 'its' deity's shrine, the arrangement of the shrines in a temple also reflects the relationship among the different social groups within a village. As historical analysis has revealed, several of the local temples already existed when gentry clans immigrated. Over time, these local temples became gradually appropriated by the immigrants. Through processes of temple renovation and expansion the local deities became spatially displaced and, thus, socially subjugated. As a result, many of the powerful deities associated with commoner clans are nowadays mostly located in the forecourt of a temple, while the ancestors and deities acknowledged by *brahmana* or nobles reside in the innermost court. As a rule, a worshipper usually proceeds from the outmost court to the innermost by praying at different shrines; however, people of high standing often do not stop in the first court but proceed directly to the innermost courtyard where the highest standing deities are located (Hauser-Schäublin 1997: 160f., 264–267).

Balinese temples are not visited except on fixed calendar dates. A temple comes to life on its anniversary, that is once a year, the length of which differs according to the calendar applied. During the temple festival, rituals are carried out in which the deities are invited to descend and to accept the offerings dedicated to them. In most temples where deities of different standing (nether-worldly as well as upper-worldly) are located, the ceremony reaches two completely different climaxes represented by contrasting, even rivalling, rituals. One of them is carried out under the guidance of a *brahmana* priest (*pedanda*). Accompanied by his assistants, the *pedanda* enters the temple almost unnoticed while hundreds of worshippers (with women carrying on their head an array of offerings consisting of towers of fruits, cookies and sometimes a chicken) continuously move in and out of the temple. In a small open hall opposite the shrines he physically establishes himself above the head of the worshippers. He carefully puts on his ritual attire while gradually preparing his paraphernalia and the holy ingredients for the ritual, of which the most important are the fire, the incense, flower petals and the holy water. The crown-like head covering is the last article of the *pedanda*'s dress that he puts on; he continues to perform *mudra* and utter *mantra* while he sprinkles holy water over the whole arrangement and over himself. Once he has completed these preliminaries, people gather in front of him, sitting or kneeling on the floor facing the lavishly decorated shrines. Under the guidance of the *pedanda* (sometimes invited from somewhere else) the congregation communally prays together, the climax being reached when he rings his bell (*bajra*) as a sign that communication has been successfully established between the humans and the gods; the gods are then perceived as ready to accept the offerings and the devotion of the congregation. Shortly afterwards, the temple priests and their assistants distribute holy water (*tirtha*) and some previously blessed rice grains that everyone applies to their forehead and temples. While the community remains seated on the floor, waiting until the holy water and the rice grains have been distributed, the *brahmana* priest packs up his paraphernalia again and quietly leaves the temple, again without attracting the attention of the worshippers. The *brahmana* ritual is highly formalised and standardised.[3] Today, these rituals have almost reached the status of a *sine qua non* for every temple festival. At

[3] By contrast to 'ordinary' temple priests, the *brahmana* novice has his own master (*nabé*) who teaches him over the years and makes him read the *lontar* scriptures. His initiation into full priesthood is acknowledged by a large board of *brahmana* and other learned men; this board has developed a canonising function with respect to *brahmana* knowledge and the performance of rituals.

the same time the *brahmana* priest's performance is considered more or less to guarantee a successful ritual.[4]

In many temples of Intaran that I investigated, there is a second climax; during my fieldwork many people called it the climax of the temple festival, consisting of a ritual, too, that is completely different in character. Instead of a meticulously performed and almost rationalised ritual led and controlled by a single specialist who establishes himself above the congregation, a trance séance with many people actively participating, with outbursts of yells and abrupt motions, with people fainting and dancing about wildly is at the core of this second ritual (Hauser-Schäublin 1997: 158–168). Such rituals mostly take place late at night with the temple crowded with people. The ritual starts with the gong orchestra playing intensely; the temple priests kindle incense and incense sticks until a thick intoxicating smoke fills the temple. Together with the beats of the gong orchestra this creates an intense atmosphere. Then dozens of men and women clad in white or black and white chequered (*poleng*) attire sit down in the centre of the courtyard while the audience gathers around them. These men and women in white and *poleng* are *sadeg* or *kulit*, people chosen by the local deities as their human vessels. During this ritual, the deities are expected to descend into them in order to let those responsible for the organization of the temple festival and its rituals know how successful it was. At the moment when a god descends the person falls into trance.[5]

At the beginning of such a séance, the temple priests are busy kindling the sandalwood fires and the incense. Then, suddenly one of the *sadeg* starts to tremble and to whisper while another throws his/her arms up, accompanied by a sharp yell, and then slowly sinks back into the lap of somebody behind. Immediately, the gong orchestra reduces its pace and its volume. One after the other, the *sadeg* fall into trance; some

[4] I have never seen any disputes or disagreements between the worshippers, the representatives of the most important clans, and the *brahmana* priest arising over the *brahman's* ritual, whether it was successful or not. According to the official religious authorities, the Parisada Hindu Dharma, major temple festivals should ideally be complemented by the *brahmana* ritual even in villages which formerly had their own priests and denied access to *pedanda* (see Pidada 1999).

[5] Only if somebody is regularly visited by the same deity is he/she acknowledged by the assembly of the major *sadeg* as one of them. If somebody is visited by different deities that person is interpreted as not yet having reached the firmness and stability required for a *sadeg*; for the person concerned this carries the danger of becoming *gila*, haunted by ghosts and losing control over him/herself.

remain quiet with eyes closed and gently shaking, sometimes smiling, while others start to cry, to shout or to talk. Some stand up and begin to dance, either slowly or violently, the audience trying to escape from the bold steps of the *sadeg* who sometimes grabs a weapon and fiercely waggles it in the midst of the crowd, or a piece of glowing coal which he or she puts into his or her mouth. The temple priests immediately try to calm down those gods who behave violently by sprinkling holy water over them and fanning the smoke of incense sticks onto them in order to bring the *sadeg* back to consciousness. The descent of the gods is a testimony that the efforts invested in the temple festival to attract the deities in order to promote well-being and prosperity have not been in vain. However, this does not automatically confer the accolade of a successful temple festival since the gods are expected to 'talk' and to 'evaluate' the performance. The priests and the audience anticipate that the gods will reveal mistakes, the breaking of taboos, incompleteness—thus a lack of ritual efficacy. In several such rituals, I was able to witness how the gods—through their human vessels—uttered not only severe criticism but also disappointment. Some even cried. The deities informed the human actors of the mistakes they had made, and interpreted these as signs of disrespect and maltreatment.

A subsequent interrogation conducted by the temple priests aims at appeasing and satisfying the deities. They attempt to bring the temple festival to a successful conclusion in spite of the flaws or mistakes they are accused of having committed earlier. The audience—participants not only of commoner descent—was in all cases that I followed up ready to comply with the wishes and demands of the gods since nobody wanted to be responsible for the consequences in the event of the deities' wishes being denied.

On some occasions I witnessed, the gods uttered some wishes for food or ingredients they had not received but which they had expected. Sometimes they even called the name of a particular brand of cigarettes or biscuits. Some wished some cloths fetched from an offering tray to be spread over them. These were wishes that could be easily fulfilled. If the deities are satisfied, they will withdraw, thus signalling that the ritual and the whole temple festival has been successful. In this case the ritual is immediately concluded and the aim of the temple festival has been accomplished. Some of the deities leave only after they have given orders regarding their expectations for the next temple festival; sometimes they ask for the promise that the temple will be renovated or that they will be given a new site within the temple courtyard.

Sometimes the deities cannot be easily satisfied, as I once witnessed in a trance séance in the innermost court of a temple now owned by a *brahmana* family. There, one of the deities who descended revealed herself as a goddess from the nether world. In other rituals (ritual dance dramas) this female deity usually appears in a (demon-like) *rangda*-mask. Her shrine is located in a forecourt of the *brahmana* temple. When the deity descended into her *sadeg* she asked for her mask (displayed on a shrine) to be brought into the innermost court. This was immediately done. She (it was, as far as I can remember, a male *sadeg* who represented the goddess) put it on and started to dance. Usually, it would be unthinkable to have such a mask performance in this most sacred part of the temple. While she slowly danced, she lamented that she had been separated from 'her brother' who had a shrine in the innermost court whereas she had only been given a shrine outside. Those responsible for the temple and its festival had allocated her the wrong site; how did they dare to commit such a mistake that implied disrespect and humiliation, apparently even without fearing retaliation? She asked to be reunited with her brother by being given a shrine in the same courtyard. The priests tried to appease her by telling her that she now (during her performance) was reunited with her 'brother'. However, she did not give in easily and asked to be given a blood sacrifice. One of the priests therefore fetched a small chicken which he killed on the spot—though under 'normal' circumstances, a blood sacrifice there would be regarded as inappropriate or even as pollution. The deity immediately grabbed and devoured it, thereby displaying her bloodthirsty nether-worldly character. She also asked for liquor and rice wine, both liquids offered to deities of the world below. It took quite a long time until she agreed to the promises that the priests gave to upgrade her status in the near future, formulated however in words that left open a variety of interpretations. The deity was finally satisfied and withdrew.

Another such ritual took place in a temple owned by commoner clans. These clans were attached to a *brahmana* compound. This *brahmana* family therefore sent two of their (adult) sons to the temple festival in order to acknowledge the bonds between the two families of unequal status. When they entered the temple, the preparations for the final ritual had already started and everybody was sitting on the floor as usual to ensure they were seated lower than the gods. When the two *brahmana* men entered the temple, they went to an open hall and took a seat on an elevated platform.[6]

Very shortly after the gong orchestra started its thrilling rhythms; from the incense containers rose thick smoke. The *sadeg* had already seated themselves and it was only a little later when they gradually fell into trance and the deities took possession of them. It was a violent performance. One *sadeg* sprang up and began to run back and forth speaking in a foreign language (said to be Chinese) while wildly gesticulating. Some deities pointed out mistakes committed during the temple festival; the priest tried to appease them by presenting them with everything they asked for and by begging pardon.

The trance lasted for quite a long time and while all other *sadeg* regained consciousness once the gods had retired, one deity still was not satisfied and threatened to disrupt the concluding ritual. All attempts by the temple priests to bring the *sadeg* back to his normal state of mind failed. The (male) deity refused to withdraw and criticised those responsible for the temple and its annual festival for various mistakes. Finally, he requested black and white chequered cloth offerings—such patterns are preferred by nether-worldly deities—to be brought to him by one of the two *brahmana* men; those men already had moved down to floor level. Their facial expression and physical gestures had drastically changed. Instead of displaying pride and self-confidence, they looked intimidated. Under the eyes of a staring audience the two men fell into a trance, acting as the deity's servants and moving on their knees to the offerings and fetching what the deity had ordered them to bring. Slowly one of them approached him in an attitude of total deference. The deity first seemed unwilling to accept the offerings, but when the man implored him to accept he finally did, though more or less reluctantly. With a sigh the *sadeg* regained consciousness when the deity finally withdrew, satisfied. The temple priests together with all the participants were relieved that the ritual, in spite of what they had anticipated, ended in harmony.

The two rituals, those of the *brahmana* priest and the trance session, are in sharp contrast to one another. First of all, a *pedanda* is not supposed

[6] Ruling nobles as well as *pedanda* rarely sit on the floor like ordinary people but demonstrate their higher standing by choosing a higher seat as well.

to fall into a trance. He is a learned man, a specialist in the scriptures and also the holder of an office restricted to privileged descent, that is, *brahmana* descent. Self-control or control over the clearly structured ritual (he 'guides' the ritual) characterise his performance. Except for assistants and temple priests acting on his behalf, the *brahmana* priest is the only—superior—actor; it is he who directly and exclusively communicates with the gods and invokes them for the benefit of the worshippers. There is almost no direct interaction between him and the congregation. As his elevated position shows—and this is underscored by the ritual investiture—, he is not an ordinary human being but transforms himself into a god (mostly Siwa) when he puts on his ritual attire, the necklaces, and finally his crown (*bauwe*). As a matter of fact, the well-known Hindu gods of Indian mythology (and their Balinese variations) never reveal themselves in trance séances, this being a privilege or characteristic (depending on the perspective and the social standing of the speaker) of the local deities. By contrast, the séance ritual is a public revelation. When the deities descend into the *sadeg*—who are ordinary members of the community—they do so in front of all the participants. Moreover, it is never settled in advance which of the worshippers (without being a *sadeg*) may be touched by one of the gods and therefore fall into a trance as well. In contrast to the *brahmana* ritual, the actual sequence of the trance séance as well as the identity of the gods that descend, the issues that are negotiated, and the outcome are all open.

The major mistakes criticised by the deities are, apart from requests for personal care and deference, social in origin and political in their implications: the nether-worldly deity in the *brahmana* temple did not like it that the humans had dedicated this courtyard to different, allegedly 'higher' standing deities, the deified *brahmana* ancestors, and their shrines. She played her power off against other 'purer' deities; she performed in a way that would have been unthinkable during the *brahmana* ritual that had taken place at the same site a few hours earlier: the request for a blood sacrifice and her wearing a *rangda*-mask with fangs protruding from mouth, bulging eyes and wild hair, are features typical of demon-like beings.

The deity was able to behave in such a way since, as Schieffelin has pointed out, every ritual—and in Bali a temple festival as a whole—bears the risk of failure (1996: 88). Thus, all the deities who descend into *sadeg* and inform the congregation of their opinion about the degree of success or failure exert power over the organisers of such temple festivals and over the whole congregation—regardless of the social standing of its individuals; all of them have contributed to the festival with money and labour. This deity's performance contained rebellion (Gluckman 1954): her objection to having been displaced and degraded by being allocated a shrine only in the forecourt aimed at a reversal of the order established by the temple 'owners'. This displacement within the temple area also implied a displacement in social space (see Hauser-Schäublin 2004b). Her rebellion also mirrored the 'commoner' clan's discontent with regard to its standing in relation to the superior *brahmana* that nowadays dominates both the temple and the 'commoner' clan.

In the second ritual described, the rebellion even ended in a reversal of the existing everyday hierarchy by turning a *brahmana* man into the servant of the deity from the nether world. Gluckman (1954) and Turner (1969) have suggested that ritual rebellion or even reversal of the social order ultimately serve to reinforce the established social order of everyday life. However, two dimensions seem to be commonly present: 1) Intaran's stratified society is the result of the immigration of title-bearing groups that probably started in the 17th century and continued even during the early colonial period.[7] Oral traditions tell of how immigrant nobles and *brahama* (thus, both gentry clans) established themselves above today's 'commoners'. The redesigning of temples and rituals constituted an important way of subduing local clans and their deities (Hauser-Schäublin 2004b). Therefore, these trance séances also serve as a means of preserving the memory that the social order of men and deities once differed from today's. Through the ritual, resistance is kept alive, probably even containing a grain of revolution. 2) The 'mistakes' the deities convey to the temple community, followed by the request for compensation, also have a bearing on the future. The redesigning of temples and shrines, and the alterations carried out during the rituals are initiated by gods, and humans are eager to comply with their wishes. In one case, the main deity insisted that he did not want any renovations to be carried out. Thus, the deities exert

[7] Intaran lies next to the famous tourist resort of Sanur. Most of the adult inhabitants work in one way or the other for its hotels, restaurants, and shops. Some are even wealthy owners; others have reached high positions in government administration and in business life. Mobility in space—immigration as well as emigration—and in social life are part of these processes that intensified since the 1970s. These aspects are beyond the scope of the present article, although they have consequences on temples and rituals as well.

much power with regard to sustaining traditions, promoting cultural conservatism as well as change.

The relationship between all these rituals in which the deities reveal themselves to humans and those with *pedanda* reflects in many ways the relationship between 'commoner' clans and those of noble or *brahmana* origin. It is indeed a kind of relationship between 'dominant' and 'demotic' discourse (Foucault 1994), though each of these rituals is raised to dominant discourse during its performance and the other is subdued; it is therefore a dynamic, changing relationship. The example of the *rangda* mask that danced in front of the *brahmana* ancestor shrines illustrates this well. Many of the temples housing local deities are interrelated (Hauser-Schäublin 1997), as are the clans and wards responsible for them. The members of these clans and wards, or at least their *sadeg* and temple priests, often participate in the annual festival of several such temples. Through the same *sadegs*, who are often formally invited, the deities of other temples are present, too; they all interact with each other. Therefore, during these trance séances a community with a shared identity becomes manifest, an identity that is regularly reconfirmed through the rituals. It is an identity that ties its members to a specific locality, the place where people live and amidst whom the gods have their shrines and temples (see also Platvoet & Toorn 1995: 351–353). This identity was framed until recently in the term *adat*, the village-specific 'traditional way of life' and its 'customs'. Over the past few years, however, the term *adat* has been replaced by the term *agama* (religion) (Picard 2002, 2004, Hauser-Schäublin 2004a). In an effort to define an independent pan-Balinese Hindu identity, *adat* increasingly implies 'belief' only and also locally limited idiosyncrasies rather than membership in a world-wide recognized religion, Hinduism. *Adat* runs the risk of entailing 'inappropriate' or even 'wrong' if applied to rituals with a pan-Hindu claim. It is *brahmana* rituals, the reference to canonised religious literature (emphasizing its Indian roots) promoted by religious and intellectual elites that is considered to be true *agama* and thus able to serve as a basis for a pan-Balinese identity. This pan-Balinese identity stresses what the Balinese—though dispersed in many different regions with separate histories—see as a unifying force, especially with regard to the non-Hindu Balinese, constituting a boundary and exclusion line in a state that is dominated by a large Muslim majority. The political side to this identity—constructed through ritual—is self-evident. The *brahmana* ritual in Intaran, therefore, has to be seen in this context. It conveys an identity based on belonging to a community encompassing individual villages. The two rituals described above for Intaran, therefore, also supplement each other from the perspective of identities, but on unequal levels.

3. *Rivalling rituals, challenged identities*

The negotiation of identity between different groups by designating some ritual practices as more appropriate than others seems however, to have already existed in pre-colonial times, as the example of Sembiran proves (Hauser-Schäublin 2004a). There exist no written sources on how such a process of negotiating rituals associated with once separate identities took place in pre-colonial times. The memory of how two groups, immigrants and the autochthonous villagers with contrasting rituals, finally achieved a common ritual practice and, as a consequence, a shared identity has been kept alive by the telling of oral histories, the performing of ritual practices, and calling the names of particular deities. Although historical memory in Sembiran is in many respects weak, the recalling of the mediation of difference and mutual exclusion is still a lively topic. The stories have to do much with Sembiran's identity as a village, with a particular *adat* that differs significantly from that of others. At the same time these oral traditions have a normative function in so far that they constitute a kind of script for correctly performing the rituals; they contain instructions as to what kind of offerings should be presented to which deity.

As I have described elsewhere (Hauser-Schäublin 2004a), Sembiran had been exposed to contact with the outside world due to its location near the coastline, where foreign traders stopped on their way to the spice islands and back for thousands of years (Ardika & Bellwood 1991). An international harbour and a community of foreign merchants, probably of Indian origin, are mentioned in 10th century copper plate inscriptions for the area. This important nodal point of transmaritime trade relations seems to have existed until the beginning of the 18th century. Sometime in the 17th century Muslim migrants arrived in Sembiran and decided to stay there.[8] There are indications that the Moslem immigrants were traders with connections across the island. One of the major deity's names, Ratu Pasisi or Ratu Subander,

[8] This date is the outcome of my attempt to reconstruct the context and the process of these interactions between the immigrants and the locals.

indicates that this deified ancestor once had the function of harbour master in charge of levying taxes on imports; he was also responsible for the security of foreign merchants, most likely on behalf of a king who resided in the interior of the island. Most of the tasks under the harbour master's responsibility were presumably carried out in cooperation with the local population. The immigrants seemed to have gained a leading position within the village. Furthermore, two major figures among these immigrants, Ratu Pasisis/Ratu Subander and Ratu Kamasan, are described as cultural heroes who attempted to reorder the social organisation and the religious practices of the village.

As explained above, economic bonds and everyday necessities tied the Muslim immigrants and the autochthonous group together. They seem therefore to have formed in some respects a well-defined local community. Beyond everyday economic cooperation, however, there apparently existed fundamental disagreements with regard to rituals, each group accusing the other of using the wrong animals for sacrifice. The disputes on these questions threw the village into one of its most serious crises and led it to the verge of disintegration. While the autochthonous population insisted that pork was the major food to be offered to the deities, the Muslim community strictly refused to accept this view and declared that the practice of the autochthonous villagers was impure and represented an insult to their ancestors. Instead, the Muslim claimed that their deified ancestors required from time to time a cow to be slaughtered. For the autochthonous villagers this was an abhorrent idea since cows, which were raised for different purposes, were not considered food, neither for humans nor for gods. The killing of cows for food therefore represented a violation of a taboo that would cause pollution. The Muslim called their sacrifice *suci*, pure, an attribute not used in relation to the sacrifice of pigs; the offerings of the locals were called *kala*, those representing the local traditions. These contrasting views seemed irreconcilable because they involved fundamentally diverging notions of edibility/inedibility of animals, purity/impurity and taboos.

As Connerton (1989) has pointed out, the crucial point in the constitution of a community's identity are not stories or even myths but rituals. An oral tradition can be reproduced without agreeing with its contents; in addition there always exists more than one version of a myth, thus leaving space for individual variations. In contrast, performing a ritual implies compliance with its rules and acceptance of its basic meaning. Though different participants may attribute various meanings or goals to a ritual, one has to consent to its general outline and the nature of sacrifice in particular, especially if tabooed animals are at stake. Therefore, it is obvious that within Sembiran the conflict over the appropriate animals to be sacrificed—each being categorically banned by the opposite group—touched the heart of each group's identity in spite of the bonds that otherwise tied them together.

The oral histories mention that the Muslim immigrants had succeeded in establishing themselves above the locals. The leaders of the traditional village association seem, however, to have retained an important say in the rituals and sacred sites, all clearly embedded in Sembiran's geocosmology. The Muslim reformers faced severe resistance from the locals, who did not want to give up what perhaps over centuries had constituted the core of the villagers' identity, namely their rituals.

One of the oral histories tells that at a certain stage in the process of integrating the immigrants into Sembiran village, the boundaries between people practicing different food habits (either eating pork or not) gradually dissolved. Before, intermarriage had given rise to conflicts even within families, separating brothers from each other. According to one of the stories, the Muslim younger brother decided to leave for Java (considered the homeland of Islam) after he had lived in disagreement with his elder brother who followed the *kala* rituals. Before he left he instructed this brother how he should pay respect to the deified Islamic ancestors/deities by presenting them with *slem* offerings. Conversely, he continued, humans would hence be free to choose pork as well as palm wine/liquor since it was no longer a strict form of Islam that was practiced in the village but a kind of syncretism. Everybody should personally decide on his/her food habits depending on individual taste and situation.

We do not know any details of the negotiations carried out between the two groups or how mediation was achieved, especially whether or not violence was involved. However, the result is clear: the locals and the immigrants managed to find an agreement that apparently satisfied both parties. It also resulted in a single community that today displays a common identity through shared rituals. However, some of the deities—those associated with the immigrants and their deified ancestors—are still never allowed to be offered pork; they are by origin what is known as *agama slem* (of Islamic religion). Instead, such offerings contain only flowers and leaves, sometimes with some additional chicken. For deities associated with the locals, pigs need to be sacrificed. Still, both types of deities reside side by side in the same temples.

Nowadays, the offerings presented during temple festivals consist, as a rule, of twenty-one offerings with pork and twenty-two without; the former being called *baktian bauwi* (pig offering), the latter *baktian slem* (Islamic offerings). People argue that they stick to the rule of different offerings in order to maintain purity and avoid impurity for particular deities. These distinct offerings dedicated to different categories of deified ancestors/deities are, as people nowadays say, a characteristic trait of Sembiran, and constitute their *kalapatra*, ritual practices as a means of performed identity.

It is interesting to note that cows—in contrast to pigs and chicken—are never killed in the temple today; their meat is never deposited on a shrine. Cows and cow meat apparently are never brought into temples. The sacrifice of cows—all of them associated with the sea, the dark side of the year, and death—therefore takes place outside the temples of even those with deities adhering to *agama slem*; the same applies to the sacrifice of goats. Although the deities are still distinguished by their preferred offerings (either *slem* or *kala*) there exist no binding rules of conduct for humans. I have never met a living person in Sembiran who categorically refused to eat pork in Sembiran (though I have never carried out a systematic investigation in this respect). Conversely, there were several people who said they would not eat cow meat even if these animals were slaughtered during a ritual.

Apart from the instructions and the legitimisation that the history of the conflict over rivalling rituals provide for the performance of rituals today, their main goal is to emphasize people's capacity for integration by means of which something new is produced. This is the true importance of these stories. It is perhaps this message that enables the people of Sembiran nowadays to abandon without resistance some of their traditions in favour of innovations such as the new forms of prayer and ritual propagated by intellectuals and a religious elite. These new forms correspond with the new pan-Balinese Hindu identity that people are able to acquire through following this ritual form of modernity already mentioned above.

4. *Contested animals: dogs, cows, pigs*

As has been demonstrated, the conflict between the immigrants and the locals arose over the appropriate animals to be sacrificed in rituals. Therefore, these animals are apparently at the core of identity constructions and the question is, why. In this paragraph I shall attempt to outline the facts about animals in Sembiran as known today.[9]

In the stories told, a prominent immigrant Muslim man is described as a 'black dog' who stealthily married a girl, the 'daughter of a pig'. The couple was expelled from the village since this union was considered a mismatch. This is an important aspect to be considered below. The dog, though impure to Muslims, is portrayed as the ancestor of today's population of Sembiran. Conversely, the daughter of a pig symbolises the indigenous inhabitants, exemplified by a woman[10] who married an immigrant. Even today, the pig remains the most important animal that the people of Sembiran sacrifice and consume. The stories emphasise the fact that a human child was born to the dog and his wife, the daughter of a pig. The human being born to the couple, therefore, displays unequal descent, the father being a fully-fledged animal, the mother a semi-animal. Through procreation the couple achieved a transformation from animality to humanity.[11]

Dogs are, by contrast to pigs, not seen as food even though dogs are also sacrificed in certain contexts. Both pigs and dogs are linguistically classified as animals and therefore characterized by a marker that distinguishes them clearly from humans. The dog is considered man's closest companion, though there exist different categories of dog, some being closer to humans than others. The one closest to humans is called *asu*: this type of dog has a long muzzle and possesses, in contrast to other dogs, a thumb-like finger on each of his paws. *Asu* dogs are mainly used as watchdogs, for the hunt (at least in earlier times, since there are now no longer any deer or wild pigs), and also as companions. Another task dogs had (formerly, before toilets were established) was to clean up the faeces of humans.

Asu are said to be quick to learn whatever humans expect from them. The relationship between a man and his dog is a personal relationship. The dog is assumed to understand what his master tells him; the dog is also able to communicate with him. An *asu* dog definitely wants to be fed by his master and tries to follow him wherever he goes. *Asu* females

---

[9] Many impulses in the following paragraph originate from Ellen (1999) and Valeri (2000).

[10] In fact, Sembiran's character, given by the gods, is that of a woman who shrinks back rather than attacks, the latter behaviour said to be typical of the neighbouring Julah village.

[11] In similar stories from other islands, the dog is explicitly interpreted as the ancestor of the (immigrant) Muslim (Van Eerde 1902, Kleiweg de Zwaan 1915).

give birth to their puppies in the immediate vicinity of the house or even inside it. The intimate relationship that exists between a man and his dog is also expressed in calling the dog by a name. These names may be identical with those of humans or may be taken from some particularities of the dog, due either to its behaviour or the patterns of its coat. No other animals are called by names, not even cats or fighting cocks that are so carefully and intensively nurtured. Nevertheless, a clear distinction is kept between dogs and humans, reflected also in the names given them. Humans not only bear personal names but also birth order names (first-born, second-born etc.) while dogs do not. To call a person by his/her name is considered impolite, even rude; instead, either the birth order name is used or teknonomy (such as 'father of x', x implying the name of his child) is practised. This is an important distinction that separates man from his closest animal companion. They are not equal partners, nor are both 'persons' as Ellen suggests for the Nuaulu (1999: 63). What they have in common is personality, certain individual traits allowing mutual communication, and the acknowledgment of similarities; however, they do not display shared identities.[12] The relationship between both is shaped by various elements of superiority and inferiority as well as dependency, these being continuously reconfigured depending on the context (see also Ellen 1999: 62). The dog used as a metaphor for the Muslim man was of the *asu* type. From the perspective of the man/dog relationship this metaphor, although it attributes full animality to the foreigner, expresses closeness also in terms of master/subject.

Other types of dogs, like *kuluk* and *kizing*, are said to have no 'thumb' and only a shorter muzzle; these dogs are said to be "naughty" because they steal food. Dogs are ambiguous beings: they belong to some extent to the world of the humans and are, therefore, not generally considered as edible food. Nevertheless they are (or rather were) used as sacrificial animals, that is, food for specific categories of deities. A food offering implies, at least theoretically, its ultimate consumption by humans. Dogs are killed during rituals addressed to the ground/sea in order to avert ill fate and danger. If destined for sacrifice, a dog is not selected according

[12] A 'person' is constituted through relations to other living members of the community on the one hand, and to the invisible birth sibling (*kanda mpat*), their foreparents, and the ancestors on the other. A person undergoes various transformations in the course of his/her life, accomplished through life cycle rituals (see Ottino 2000 and Riemenschneider & Hauser-Schäublin 2006).

to its behaviour and its skill but according to the patterns of its coat.[13] This means that a different type of classification is applied, one that is not concerned with 'intelligence' but with colours and patterns, a typical practice in selecting animals destined for sacrifice.

Dog meat is considered 'hot' (*panes*), as are cow and goat meat. The classification 'hot' is applied to the flesh of ambiguously classified animals. 'Hot' alludes to its inherent power that may have negative consequences on its human consumers. Moreover, it is meat that not all deities may consider to be appropriate; some may relish it, while others may perceive it as impure and, therefore, strictly refuse it. All animals or rather their meat, if classified as hot, share the fact that they may not be killed within a temple and their meat may not be deposited on an (elevated) shrine. Such meat offerings are deposited on the ground; they are destined to appease deities of the nether world, in other words deities feared for their power which may easily turn against humans.

It is important to note that the dog metaphor for a human actor is not restricted to the story of the Muslim immigrant. Perhaps even more importantly, creation myths have it that Bhatara Guru, the highest god, often identified with Siwa, created dogs as primeval beings who made the world inhabitable for humans. It was dogs that, by depositing excrement in the semi-flooded world and by treading the still swampy ground in order to prepare a place for sleeping, produced the first solid ground. The dogs expanded the ground in all directions until there was enough space for humans to live in. It was these primeval dogs, too, that implored Bhatara Guru to create humans. And, again, it was dogs that taught humans how to behave as human beings, to work the land, to prepare food etc. The first dogs, created by Bhatara Guru, were intermediaries between the most respectable gods and humans. Without these dogs, mankind would never have come into existence.

From this perspective the dog metaphor for the Muslim immigrant gains a further new facet, one that turns animality into a kind of semi-divinity. The dog as a sacrificial animal illustrates well the ambiguity of this animal, an ambiguity that oscillates between the extremes of man/dog relationships, namely the dog as 1) humankind's divine promoter and protector, 2) man's closest companion and assistant in

---

[13] During my fieldwork I never came across a case in which a dog was indeed sacrificed. People explained it in terms of the difficulty of finding a dog with the required patterns. Instead, the dog was replaced by a sack of Chinese *kepeng* coins.

the hunt, 3) the scavenger devouring man's faeces, and 4) a sacrificial animal whose meat is to be consumed by deities of the nether world (and only rarely by humans).

The cow, one of the animals that plays a part in the conflict about the appropriateness of animals to be sacrificed, is also classified as ambiguous. People cannot say why it is taboo to sacrifice a cow in the temple nor why cow meat should not be deposited on a shrine. As is well-known, the cow is intrinsically linked to Hinduism in general and to Siwa in particular. There are, from an outsider's perspective, many Siwaitic elements in Sembiran culture though the people themselves do not see it this way. As regards cattle, it is never adult individuals that are sacrificed but always calves (*godel*) of either sex, the only exception being in a death ritual for high-ranking members of the ritual village association. In this case a castrated bull (ox) accompanies the deceased from his home to one of the temples where cattle are usually sacrificed. The ox is killed in front of this temple. From there the corpse is carried to the burial ground.

Cows are kept in stables in the gardens, their dung being used for fertilizing the gardens. In earlier times they were also used for ploughing but nowadays, due to climatic change, only horticulture is possible, the hoe being the major tool. To some extent, cattle represent wealth; it takes years until they are mature and start to reproduce. In this dry region, a peasant or his wife sometimes spend several hours a day gathering enough fodder for these animals. Cattle are well cared for and regularly taken to the sea-shore or to a well to be washed. Calves are continuously needed for sacrifices (mainly in the context of life cycle rituals) and can therefore easily be sold.

The ambiguity arising over cows also has another dimension. One of the most severe taboos in Sembiran is bestiality. Bestiality, of course, needs to be brought to the attention of the village community in order to be recognized as such. Here, a further divide between humans and animals becomes visible. Animals are associated with unregulated sex. Among animals, sexual intercourse takes place even between siblings, parents and their children, as people say with abhorrence. What characterises humans are rules of conduct, especially regulations regarding incest. Committing bestiality, therefore, not only demolishes the boundaries between animals and humans in general but is also a threat towards what is considered the basis of human order: the regulation of sexual relations, in particular the incest taboo. The violation of these taboos puts the whole village in a state of impurity (*sebel*) that needs elaborate and costly rituals to bring the resulting crisis to an end and to restore the village to normality. During a period of *sebel*, no rituals and temple festivals may be held; the contact with the gods is disrupted.

The cases of bestiality I heard of always involved a man and a cow. The idea of sacrificing a calf that contained a man's sperm, and then offering its meat to deities only to be eaten later by humans, is one of the most horrifying ideas, and is dangerously close to cannibalism. The socially established and carefully maintained separation of sexual partners (= humans) from animals, divine offerings, and food thereby collapses.

In this context it needs to be pointed out that the story of the *asu* dog (the Muslim man) also employs the violation of the taboo of bestiality: the dog impregnated the girl, the daughter of a pig. The story thereby emphasises the social cataclysm that the clash between the immigrants and the locals brought upon the village.

In contrast to the classification of dog and cow meat as 'hot',[14] pork is regarded as *nyem*, 'cold', and therefore not as a dangerous food for humans.[15] Pigs are nowadays kept in pigsties at some distance from the dwelling houses (sometimes in the gardens); however, in earlier times they were kept in the immediate vicinity of the living quarters. Pigs are given all sorts of food though people emphasise that they regularly need to be fed with cooked food especially prepared for them. Male pigs are castrated after one month and seven days. This time schedule corresponds with that of a ritual performed on babies,[16] though this analogy receives no further explanation. The pig is the major sacrificial animal. All meat is first and foremost presented to the deities, the essence of the offerings (or rather its fragrance) being consumed by them; their materiality, in this case the actual meat, remains to be consumed later by humans. Some rituals require piglets (of either sex), *kucit*, to be sacrificed. But mostly the decision whether a piglet or a grown-up pig is killed depends on the amount of money to be spent. The term *celeng*, usually translated as pig, applies only to castrated males; these are the

---

[14] As briefly mentioned, goat meat is considered 'hot', too, as is that of snakes and monkeys. The latter two animals, however, are never sacrificed.

[15] The same applies to the meat of the water buffalo. The sacrifice of such animals rarely takes place in Sembiran.

[16] After a month and seven days a purification ritual is held for the baby and its mother. Before this ritual is held, a baby is supposed not to be brought into contact with the ground nor to leave the house because it is liable to attacks from demons. After the ceremony these restrictions are lifted.

only pigs to be sacrificed. Sows (*bangkung*) which have already littered are not fit for sacrifice, nor are boars.

Sembiran's major indigenous female deity, Bhatara Licin, who according to one set of creation myths raised the first humans, is also called Ni Bangkung, Lady Sow; thus this primordial deity is associated with the nurturing qualities of a sow and her 'litter', the humans. Again, this throws an additional light on the story of the immigrant Muslim (dog) who married the daughter of a pig; the pig metaphor, therefore, indeed symbolises a woman of indigenous descent.

The sacrifice of a *celeng* goes far beyond the mere presentation of its meat to the deities. A pig is butchered and cut up into pieces attributed with hierarchically ranked values and meanings. The most highly valued piece of pork is the right ear, followed by the left ear, then the right hind thigh, the left hind thigh, the lower right hind leg, the lower left hind leg, the right jaw, the left jaw, etc. The most highly valued piece, the right ear, is always presented to the deity whose annual festival is being celebrated. As a rule, each deity residing in a temple has his/her individual annual festival celebrated at his/her shrine while some others only 'witness' this ceremony and are served with a minor part of the pig only. After the deities have consumed the essence of the pig, the individual pieces of the pig are reassembled and then divided up according to the hierarchically organized individual positions (according to principles of seniority) within the ritual village association: the right ear is put on the *kawos* (a portion of food containing all elements of the earlier food offerings displayed in the long assembly hall) for the highest ranking member of the ritual village association; the left ear is put on the *kawos* of his junior. Each member of the ritual village association thereby receives a portion of the pork (sometimes in the form of a little bit of sausage or minced meat etc.). The reassembling of the pig (*wangun urip*) and its display in the long hall symbolizes the unity of the ritual village association. The consumption of these 'leftovers' from the deities' meal represents a communion of the whole village body and, at the same time, also a communion with the deities. The pig, therefore, is one of the strongest social as well as religious unifying symbols of Sembiran.[17] Without pigs, Sembiran's village community would, at least on a symbolic level, not exist.

[17] The individual parts of a calf are divided up also according to the status of deities and humans though in a very limited way and never displayed in the long hall of the village temple.

Looking back at the story of the conflict between the immigrants and the autochthonous villagers, one begins to understand why the animals so hotly debated did indeed constitute a crucial issue in the construction of formerly separate identities.

5. *Conclusion*

The two examples given of how accusations of ritual mistakes are dealt with in two villages in Bali allow, in spite of their apparent difference, some general conclusions: I should like to put forward my conclusion in four theses:

First, the question of committing mistakes in the performance of rituals has to be put into the context of power relations. In the case of Sembiran the mutual accusation of sacrificing the wrong animal in rituals as reported in oral traditions was made between immigrants and locals. The immigrants apparently were in such a powerful situation that they were not forced simply to follow the ritual norms of the autochthonous population but were able to set up claims concerning the appropriateness of the ritual sacrifice.[18] Here, in contrast to the case of Intaran, the evaluation of mistakes and the mutual accusation of committing mistakes is the result of cross-references. Mistakes in this sense were not the result of the wrong application of generally approved rules but stemmed from applying one's own rules to rituals of the others. We can assume that the conflict did not arise over the form, the structure or the sequences of the rituals. Rather, the two groups disagreed upon the interpretation of ritualistic norms with regard to the core sacrifice of animals, and, consequently, their implications for ritual purity/impurity. Nevertheless, these mutual interactions and accusations mirror competition—power struggles expressed in the mutual claim to possess the authority to decide on the correct ritual norm for sacrifices for the village community as a whole.

In the case of Intaran, the right to point out mistakes and to ask for their correction is held by a transcendental authority, the deities who speak through their human vessels. Their ritual criticism cannot be anticipated in detail by the organisers of the temple festivals and

[18] One has to take into account the fact that the immigrants probably also had missionising goals. By contrast, other oral histories emphasise the fact that a local lord ruling over Sembiran requested that every immigrant give up the rituals and beliefs he brought with him and follow those of Sembiran if he wanted to stay there.

the participants though everybody knows that the descending deities always have a censorious voice. To them is attributed the right and the power to continuously modify the script of the temple festival, and so inducing change or insisting on conservatism. Characteristically, this transcendental authority is held by the subdued local deities who also revolt against their (human) suppressors. These deities have managed to appropriate the power to finally evaluate whole temple festivals even if these are organised by high standing title-bearing groups. They are acknowledged by all parties involved to have the ultimate performative authority (Schieffelin 1996: 80). The power context here, as in the case of Sembiran, is that of immigrants and locals. However, the interactions apparently differed from those reconstructed for Sembiran. Among the socially and politically high-standing status groups that migrated to Intaran were ritual specialists, the *brahmana*. Through their contact with their place of origin, the *brahmana* ritual specialists were able to continuously draw on external sources of prestige and power, such as prestigious holy water from outside the village, the assistance of personnel and additional ritual paraphernalia. Moreover, they were backed by the noble lord (of *wesia* or *satria* noble descent) in whose service and on whose behalf they acted. The immigrants therefore managed to establish themselves above the local clans—and their deities: the asymmetrical relations between them were turned into a social hierarchy with the immigrants at the top.

The local deities and their voicing of ritual mistakes represent a ritual rebellion but not one, as Gluckman and Turner have it, that has its final effect in re-enforcing the social structure that dominates everyday life. Their appearance and their voices serve as a kind of memory that keeps alive the recollection of the local deities as powerful leading figures associated with mainly commoner lineages and clans; such rituals contain a germ of subversion. It is an earlier and still latent social reality that emerges during the performance (Schieffelin 1996: 81).

Sembiran's immigrants apparently lacked the continuous translocal contacts that were enjoyed by the *brahmana* and their noble lords of Intaran. There appears to have existed no external sources from whence these Muslims could draw ideological support. If ever they cooperated with a superior lord, this cooperation definitely was not in matters of rituals but economics. This lack of external support may be one of the reasons why the immigrants were unable to permanently establish themselves above the locals.

Second, the negotiation of the correct manner in which to perform rituals reflects a socially and politically tense relationship between two groups. Such mutual accusations may be experienced as a threat to the individual group. As a reaction to such threats, rituals that lie at the heart of their identities, and ritual rules as their normative setting, are doubtlessly bound to become standardised and even canonised. Under such conditions inequality between these groups persists as long as they perceive each other as entirely different—even though they are dependent on one another in other respects. If one group is no longer able to display legitimising proofs and means of superiority over the other, but at the same time both groups decide (or are forced) to stay together in the same place, a process of levelling of social inequality sets in. According to oral tradition, such a process was initiated by intermarriage with the result that a dissolution of boundaries between formerly separate ritual communities took place. It is likely that the immigrants were for whatever reason unable to establish or maintain endogamy. Only when intermarriage becomes 'normal' do rituals begin to change and 'syncretism' is produced, as in the case of Sembiran.

In the case of Intaran, inequality has remained, but not the existence of two separate ritual communities. Endogamy among gentry clans is favoured, though both groups form an integrated but stratified society with a specific social division of labour.

Third, as both examples have shown, one's own ritual rules, seen as the exclusively correct way to perform rituals, are at the core of a group's identity construction. For this reason, the practice of mutual accusation reflects separate identities, as the case of Sembiran demonstrated. The case of Intaran reveals not mutually exclusive identities but those on different levels: a local identity supplemented by a translocal identity that gradually has become more and more important in today's pan-Hindu Balinese context within a state dominated by Islam. The present-day processes taking place in Sembiran—with its reformation of the temple rituals carried out at great pace and following pan-Balinese standards—strongly supports this thesis. Therefore, a new form of identity arises that is also expressed in its reformed rituals. There, too, I suggest, power plays an important role: the reformist movement is led by a new elite, the intellectuals and publicly acknowledged ritual specialists from urban and semi-urban centres, and not by the traditional leaders of the ritual village association.

Fourth, the definition of mistakes as described in the two Balinese examples moves along the parameter either of 'incompleteness', or the threat of loss of purity and the violation of taboos, with the ultimate threat of the imminent chaos implicit in ritual failure—the collapse of the ordered world. In both ethnographic examples, retaliation from deities is feared. Accusations of ritual mistakes made by outsiders and the threat of failure therefore are strategies employed in a power context—strategies, I suggest, whose target is well beyond the merely ritual. In Intaran, the uncovering of mistakes only comes from one party, the subdued local deities, while in Sembiran the accusations were mutual. Such strategies of accusing one another of serious mistakes also serve as self-defence, and to maintain and reinforce one's own group identity by attempting at the same time to undermine the other's. Mutual accusations of ritual mistakes with the potential to end in failure are socially explosive; they do not, however, seem necessarily to lead to social disintegration or chaos.

References

Ardika, I. Wayan & Peter Bellwood 1991. "Sembiran: the beginnings of Indian contact with Bali". *Antiquity* 65: 221–232.

Connerton, Paul 1989. *How societies remember*. Cambridge: Cambridge University Press.

Ellen, Roy 1999. "Categories of animality and canine abuse. Exploring contradictions in Nuaulu social relationships with dogs". *Anthropos* 94: 57–68.

Foucault, Michel 1971. *L'ordre du discours: leçon inaugurale au Collège de France prononcée le 2 décembre 1970*. Paris: Gallimard (German translation used: *Die Ordnung des Diskurses*. Frankfurt: Fischer Wissenschaft, 1994).

Gluckman, Max 1954. *Rituals of rebellion in South-East Africa. Frazer Lecture 1952*. Manchester: Manchester University Press.

Hauser-Schäublin, Brigitta 1997. *Traces of gods and men. Temples and rituals as landmarks of social events and processes in a South Bali village*. Berlin: Reimer.

—— 2004a. "'Bali Aga' and Islam: Ethnicity, ritual practice, and 'Old'-Balinese as an anthropological construct". *Indonesia* 77 (April): 27–55.

—— 2004b. "The politics of sacred space. Using conceptual models of space for socio-political transformations in Bali". *Bijdragen tot de Taal-, Land- en Volkenkund* 161.2–3: 283–314.

Hüsken, Ute 2004. *Proposal for the Publication titled 'Ritual Failure, Mistakes in Ritual and Ritual Dynamics'*. Internal paper of the workgroup 'Ritual Failure' Collaborative Research Group 619, 'Dynamics of Ritual'. University of Heidelberg. URL: http://www.ritualdynamik.uni-hd.de/pdf/Proposal_Fehler_im_Ritual.pdf (date of last access: 17/08/2006).

Kleiweg de Zwaan, J.P. 1915: "De hond in het volksgeloof der inlanders van den indischen archipel". *De Indische Gids* Februari-Aflevering: 173–201.

Ottino, Arlette 2000. *The universe within. A Balinese village through its ritual practices*. Paris: Karthala.

—— 2003a. "Ritual subordination to the core-line and Bali Aga cultural Identity: some preliminary research notes on the *kabayan* of Gunung Batukau". *Antropologi Indonesia* 70: 1–19.

—— 2003b. "Revisiting kinship in Bali. Core lines and the emergence of elites in commoner groups". *The Asia Pacific Journal of Anthropology* 4.1–2: 52–70.
Picard, Michel 1999. "The discourse of kebalian: transcultural constructions of Balinese identity". In: *Staying local in the global village*, Rubinstein, Raechelle & Linda H. Connor (ed.). Honolulu: University of Hawai'i Press, 15–49.
—— 2002. "Religion, tradition et culture. La construction dialogique d'une identité balinaise". *L'Homme* 163: 107–136.
—— 2004. "What's in a name? Agama Hindu in the making". In: *Hinduism in Modern Indonesia*, Ramstedt, Martin (ed.). London & New York: Curzon, 56–75.
Pidada, I Gede 1999. "Status struggle and the priesthood in contemporary Bali". In: *Staying local in the global village. Bali in the twentieth century*, Rubinstein, Raechelle & Linda H. Connors (ed.). Honolulu: Hawai'i University Press, 181–201.
Platvoet, Jan & Karel van der Toorn 1995. "Pluralism and identity". In: *Pluralism and Identity. Studies in ritual behaviour*, Platvoet, Jan & Karel van der Toorn (ed.). Leiden & New York & Cologne: Brill, 349–360.
Riemenschneider, Christian & Brigitta Hauser-Schäublin 2006. "...yang hidup disini, yang mati disana." *Upacara hingkaran hidup di desa Sembiran, Bali (Indonesia)*. Berlin: LIT (Göttinger Studien zur Ethnologie, 15).
Schieffelin, Edward L. 1996. "On Failure and Performance. Throwing the medium out of the séance". In: *The performance of healing*, Laderman, Carol & Marina Roseman (ed.). New York & London: Routledge, 59–89.
Turner, Victor 1969. *The ritual process. Structure and anti-structure*. New York: Aldine Publishing Company.
Valeri, Valerio 2000. *The forest of taboos. Morality, hunting, and identity among the Huaulu of the Moluccas*. Madison: The University of Wisconsin Press.
Van Eerde, J.C. 1902. "De kalanglegende op Lombok". *Tijdschrift voor Indische Taal, Land- en Volkenkunde* 45: 30–58.

CONTESTED RITUAL PROPERTY. CONFLICTS OVER CORRECT RITUAL PROCEDURES IN A SOUTH INDIAN VIṢṆU TEMPLE

Ute Hüsken

In the present approach to the field of 'ritual mistakes', my focus is on the 'internal'[1] mechanisms involved in the processes of evaluating deviations from a 'ritual norm'. Labelling certain ritual behaviour as a 'mistake' is a negative judgement of the action in question. If this judgement is shared by the majority of the participants (or if it is voiced by more influential participants), it tends to remain undisputed and is thus seemingly beyond doubt. However, in the present case study this evaluative process involves negotiations between groups or individuals who are not unanimous as to what behaviour is perceived as 'normal' or as a 'deviation': the ritual actions are only evaluated as a 'mistake' by some of the participants, whereas the members of the 'mistaken' group insist on the rightfulness of their actions. It is clearly perceptible here that the evaluation of the rituals in questions always depend on the point of view of the interpreter. A 'mistake', I would argue, is inseparably connected with the perspective from which a particular behaviour is evaluated, because it is based on a certain set of norms and values which might be not be shared by all participants.

The present paper will examine a case of conflicting agenda among the participants in ritual events, namely the conflicts between two rivalling groups over ritual performances within a particular South Indian Hindu temple. For the last 150 years there have been fierce fights between the proponents of two sects[2] over their ritual rights and duties within the temple, and over the distribution of ritual honours. These contestations are constantly expressed by accusing the other of 'doing it wrong', or of 'performing the wrong action'. However, these 'mistaken' deviations from 'normal' ritual procedure are not interpreted as such

[1] That is, internal to the ritual/religious tradition analysed here.

[2] I use the term 'sect' here not in a pejorative sense but instead to distinguish this subdivision among the Śrīvaiṣṇavas from subdivisions in separate ritualistic 'schools' (see also Colas 1995: 111).

by all ritual participants, but only by one of the two groups vying for precedence within the multilayered ritual landscape of the temple.[3]

In the theoretical literature on rituals, it is frequently demonstrated that rituals not only depict a certain status quo of power relations but also actively influence their context.[4] In such processes, rituals tend to implement a hierarchical order and to (re)arrange the contextual, socio-cultural setting. Thus in many cases, deviations from a prescribed ritual procedure do not occur incidentally or just by chance, but are employed intentionally. The performers and participants use these deviations in the ritual procedures as an important means to challenge prevailing power relations. One important point at stake is the question of who can implement his/her set of values and thus has the power to successfully define certain behaviour as 'wrong'. This process is therefore inseparably interconnected with the power relations in the realm beyond the ritual performance.

1. *The case study*

The Varadarāja Perumāḷ temple[5] in the South Indian town of Kāñcipuram is a very large complex with more than 80 employees. The temple is a famous and important Viṣṇuite pilgrimage site visited throughout the year by tens of thousands of Hindu pilgrims from all over India. Most of the temple employees as well as many other Viṣṇuites who are involved in the daily temple rituals reside in the vicinity of the temple. Some of them hold for many generations a specific relation to the temple and the deities worshipped therein. These specific relations are generally expressed through participation in the ritual procedures pertaining to the deities.

The conflicts dealt with in this paper relate to this individual or group participation in the temple rituals, mainly because—as has frequently been argued—in South Indian Hinduism the temples have a crucial role for assigning social status, for validating social leadership and authority

[3] During these conflicts, no single element of the performances is put in question, but rather the appropriateness of the inclusion of certain ritual elements in the given context. Therefore, this paper deals with a particular class of 'ritual mistakes', namely, the 'proper ritual in the wrong setting'.

[4] For references see Wulf & Zirfas 2004: 8.

[5] Varadarāja Perumāḷ is the name of the specific form of Viṣṇu worshipped in this temple.

(Mukund 2005: xii; references there). "The temple is clearly synonymous with community, both as a domain of discourse and a field of action, [...] the temple is (inter alia) about social identities, worship is (inter alia) about social relations" (Dirks 1987: 212). This holds true not only for pre-colonial and colonial South India, but—to a somewhat lesser extent, but similar in structure—also for present day India.

Arjun Appadurai's 'transactional model' explains the crucial role of the South Indian temple for society at large.[6] As he and Carol Breckenridge (1976) convincingly argue, South Indian temples constitute the frame in which individuals and groups participate in an important and dynamic redistributive process. The amount and degree of participation in these processes is expressed by the distribution and redistribution of material resources as well as by 'shares' (*paṅku*) and honours (*mariyātai*) in the temple rituals. These ritual shares and honours are neither definite in regard to their content nor in regard to their recipients (Appadurai & Breckenridge 1976: 197). The participants in the diverse rituals, from the 'ordinary' devotee to the temple priests, each claim a unique and individual relationship to the deity. This relationship is expressed through separate and autonomous shares in the ritual and economic advantages received. Since the distribution of honours and shares is in most cases before the eye of the general public, not only the content is of prime importance for their recipients, but so is the sequence of such distributions. Appadurai & Breckenridge (1976: 198) argue that "[...] these honours are not simply denotative emblems of culturally privileged roles in relationship to the deity... [T]he receipt of specific honours, [...] renders authoritative the individual's share (*paṅku*) in the temple..." Depending on the context, "[...] one's share in the ritual process would have a different concrete content. But the sum of one's rights, over time, would constitute one's share in the ritual and redistributive process of the temple. This share is given public expression and authoritative constitution by some combination of a finite set of substances transvalued by association with the deity, which are referred to as 'honours'." Material expressions of ritual shares are, for example, the leavings of the deity's food (*naivēttiyam*) and the water which was used

[6] I disagree with Mukund (2005: 50), who argues that "this model bears little relevance for understanding the role of the temple in South India under colonial rule". Rather, I follow Dirks (1987: 383) who highlights the fact that we rather have to perceive this change as "a shift in forms and structures of meaningful activity".

as the deity's drinking or washing water (*tīrttam*).[7] These materials are collectively called *piracātam*, 'blessings' of the god. After consumption by the deity, they are distributed among the participants according to a certain multi-layered scheme which varies according to the ritual occasion. Another important honour is, for example, the placing of a 'metal crown' (*caṭāri*) on one's head.[8] In addition, "the right to offer service (*kaiṅkariyam*) to the deity, [. . .] the right to move the resources allocated for the specific ritual event, the right to command the relevant persons involved in the actualization of the given ritual, the right to perform a single part of a complex ritual event, and [. . .] the right to worship the deity, by simply witnessing the ritual" (Appadurai & Breckenridge 1976: 198), are all perceived of as a ritual share.

In the case of the comparatively large Varadarāja Perumāḷ temple in Kāñcipuram, these shares are distributed among many groups and individuals. These include temple priests (*arcaka*), their assistants (*paricāraka*), other temple servants, such as the cooks, those who provide certain materials, substances or services for and during the rituals, the donors who sponsor certain rituals, representatives of the temple administration, the devotees who visit the temple on a regular basis or occasionally, and many others, among them the congregations of the two rivalling Viṣṇuite sects Teṉkalai and Vaṭakalai.

2. *The two sects involved in the conflicts*

Those of the Viṣṇuite employees and devotees who are Brahmin by caste belong to either the Vaṭakalai ('Northern') or Teṉkalai ('Southern') Viṣṇuite sect.[9] However, while for many of the employees of the

[7] Holders of this right are called 'Tīrttakarar'. In the Varadarāja temple, the first ten portions of holy water (*tīrttam*) are assigned to certain personalities. They can depute the right to receive this water to others, should they be unable to attend the rituals in person.

[8] Viṣṇu's feet are represented on the top of this *caṭāri* 'crown'. After worship it is placed by the priest (*arcaka*) on the devotee's head. This act symbolises the complete submission under the feet of Viṣṇu. In 2004, some of the 'ordinary' devotees complained in court that they received *caṭāri* and *tīrttam* only long after the local Vaṭakalai- and Teṉkalai share-holders. Since then, the performers of the ritual have been forced to distribute *caṭāri* and *tīrttam* to all devotees present, immediately after having finished the worship.

[9] The Teṉkalai' traditional 'intellectual centre' is situated in the South Indian town Śrīraṅgam, the Vaṭakalais' centre is considered to be Kāñcipuram, which is slightly further to the North. Moreover, the Vaṭakalai tradition is generally viewed as

Varadarāja Perumāḷ temple their affiliation to one sect or the other is mainly derived from the temple's alleged affiliation to this sect,[10] there are also groups among these two sects which consciously and proudly refer to their communities' specific history. Their main identity marker in the context of the temple and its surroundings is the sect affiliation inherited or adopted by them.

These two sects are found not only in the Varadarāja Perumāḷ temple, but in almost every important Viṣṇuite temple in Tamiḻ Nāṭu. The subdivision of Viṣṇuites into a 'Northern sect' and a 'Southern sect' has a long standing history in South India. It dates back to a doctrinal split within the philosophical school Viśiṣṭādvaita. This philosophical school is traced back to the Viṣṇuite reformer and philosopher, Rāmānuja (trad. dates 1017–1137 CE), and his spiritual teachers. However, in the past seven centuries this school has gradually split into the two above-mentioned, sectarian groups. Although both sects recognise Rāmānuja as their religious teacher, the lists of his successors as spiritual and religious leaders of the sects differ. While the 'Southern sect' considers Maṇavāḷamāmuṉi (1370–1443 CE) as the spiritual successor to Rāmānuja, and also its founder, this position is attributed to Vedānta Deśika (trad. dates 1269–1369 CE) by the 'Northern sect'.[11]

Today, the differences between the two sects relate to doctrine and ritual.[12] However, although most of the ritual differences are traditionally

emphasising the 'Northern' language Sanskrit as the language of transmission of their sacred texts, whereas the Teṉkalais are mainly linked with the 'Southern' language Tamiḻ. Although not only Brahmins belong to either of the two sects, the members of the rivalling groups happen all to be Brahmins, and in the present paper I refer only to them. For the relation of sect and caste affiliation in the South Indian Viṣṇuite context, see Mumme 1993; on the necessary distinction between the general category 'Śrīvaiṣṇava' and the Brahmin groups among them see Pratap 1993: 5f.

[10] Although most of the South Indian Viṣṇu temples are under the control of the Teṉkalais (see Appadurai 1987: 74–101), the Varadarāja Perumāḷ temple is affiliated with the Vaṭakalai sect, as is evident from the Vaṭakalai sect-marks on the shrines, temple walls, most of the paraphernalia and also on other prominent portions of the temple. However, the authenticity of the temple's affiliation to this sect is disputed (see e.g. Subramanian 1996: 249, who quotes Annangāracharīyār, P.B. 1954. *History of Rāmānuja Deyapātram. Granta Office*, Little Kanchipuram, 23f.; see also Raman 1975 and Varada Tatacharya 1978).

[11] Since the two teacher-pupil lines of succession were established only when concrete differences between the two sects emerged in the 16th and 17th centuries, these two teachers are retrospectively regarded as the 'founders' of the two sects (see Siauve 1978: 23f.).

[12] The doctrinal differences refer to the nature of the god, to soteriology, to the role and importance of the spiritual teacher on the way to salvation, etc. (see Colas 1995: 121f.). The traditional number of 18 differences refers to doctrinal points. For

explained by doctrinal differences, the actual conflicts between the two sects pertain to ritual differences alone (see Subramanian 1996: 250).

3. *The local context and content of the disputes*

In spite of the supra-regional character of the ritual differences between the two sects, the practices and symbols actually disputed within the context of the Varadarāja temple do not refer to general ritual expressions of doctrinal differences, but rather to their local manifestations. The objects of the concrete disputes are invariably the details of several ritual procedures and symbols within the specific local context of the Varadarāja Perumāḷ temple.

The most palpable ritual differences between the two sects are the forms of their sect marks.[13] Accordingly, some of the conflicts in the Varadarāja temple circle round the question of which sect-mark should be engraved on several places of the temple and which should be painted, e.g. on the forehead of the temple elephant during processions.[14]

Another smouldering conflict again relates to the local manifestation of a general ritual difference between the two sects. The collections of Tamil̲ hymns in praise of Viṣṇu (*tivviyappirapantam*), which were composed by Tamil̲ saints (Āl̲vārs), are revered, learnt and recited by members of both sects. However, the introductory eulogistic verse (*tan̲iyan̲*) differs; while the 'Northern' version is in praise of Vedānta Deśika (*rāmānuja dayāpātram*), the 'Southern' version praises Maṇavāḷamāmun̲i (*śrīśaileṣa dayāpātram*) (Doraiswamy 1983: xlii). The local conflicts, based on this general difference, concern the question of which introductory verse (*tan̲iyan̲*) is to be recited during temple worship. It is obvious that the praise of the spiritual teacher and 'founder' of one sect or the other as commencement of the recitation of the Tamil̲ hymns is tantamount

---

a detailed description and analysis of the doctrinal differences, see Doraiswamy 1983 and Siauve 1978.

[13] These sect marks, *ūrdhvapuṇḍra*, is applied by male Vaiṣṇavas on twelve parts of their body. It has the form of a white U or Y, with a vertical red or yellow or orange line in the middle. The U/Y symbolizes Viṣṇu's feet and therefore his spiritual presence. The 'Southern' sect wears the Y, the 'Northern' sect wears the U.

[14] Some of these conflicts in the Varadarāja Perumāḷ temple in Kāñcipuram are described by Ramaswamy 2003.

to public approval of the superiority of that spiritual teacher and 'his' sect over the other, and therefore clearly refers to the context external to the actual ritual performance.[15]

Taking into account the above-mentioned fact that the supremacy in the temple amounts to supremacy in society at large, it might not be surprising that there were and still are fierce fights between the proponents of the two sects over whose *taṉiyaṉ* is legitimately recited.

With the breakdown of the 'old regime' and the gradual establishment of colonial rule, these conflicts were taken to legal courts. The colonial state was drawn into these conflicts as "an unwilling arbitrator and mediator" (Mukund 2005: 62). The disputes between the two sects over ritual details within the temple reached their climax in the last decades of the 19th, and in the beginning of the 20th century. Since then most details of the relevant ritual procedures have been sanctioned and regulated by court orders. Many employees of the Varadarāja temple therefore told me that the rituals in the temple are nowadays regulated by court orders rather than by the relevant prescriptions of the Sanskrit ritual texts (*āgama*). Also the conflicts pertaining to the recitation of the eulogistic verse in the Varadarāja temple have been dealt with in the courts since the beginning of the 19th century. Both parties took their cases to court where they were decided on the basis of what was convincingly presented to the judges as 'custom and usage'. Thus, for example, in the middle of the 19th century the 'Northern sect' tried to introduce its *taṉiyaṉ*. The case was taken to court by the Teṉkalais. In 1888 it was confirmed by court order that only the Teṉkalai *taṉiyaṉ* may be recited in the temple and during processions. Moreover, it was confirmed that the Teṉkalai congregation alone holds the hereditary right (*mirās*) to lead the recitation of the Tamiḻ hymns. This issue was taken to court again in the beginning of the 20th century (judgement from 1915). At that time the Teṉkalais wanted to secure that only their eulogistic verse may be recited in the Varadarāja Perumāḷ temple, and that the Vaṭakalais could only join the Teṉkalai congregation, but could not form a separate congregation (*ghoṣṭi*). The Vaṭakalais, however, argued that as ordinary worshippers they should be allowed to recite

[15] Similar conflicts are common to all the South Indian Viṣṇuite temples in which the two sects vie for precedence. Since disputes about these Dayapātra verses were very common in South Indian Viṣṇu temples, the British judges collectively called them 'pātram cases' (see Subramanian 1996).

whatever they liked, and that they in fact had the right to invoke their religious teacher (and thus recite their *taṉiyaṉ*) as long as they did not disturb the Teṉkalai congregation. They wanted to form a separate congregation behind the deity during processions. It was decided that the Vaṭakalais could join the Teṉkalai recitation as individual worshippers, but they were refused the right to form an independent congregation (Ramaswamy 2003: part 3). Nowadays—notwithstanding the general 'Northern' sect's affiliation to the temple—only the 'Southern' eulogistic verse may be recited as the commencement of the recitation of the Tamiḻ hymns there.

However, although the relevant judicial decisions are now legally binding and generally adhered to, the conflict has never ceased to exist. The fact that no member of the most influential Vaṭakalai families ever joins the recitation of the Tamiḻ hymns, although most of them are also very well versed in these texts, attests to the smouldering conflict. Although the Vaṭakalais may join the group reciting the Tamiḻ hymns from the second row, members of the Tātācārya families, the most fervent defenders of Vaṭakalai othodoxy, are "not interested" in doing so, as some of them put it.

In these conflicts the temple festivals are of crucial importance. Especially during the temple festivals the importance of the temple becomes evident—not only for the few who have a claim to precedence and a share of the temple honours, but to all the local inhabitants as a symbol of their collective religious and social identity (see Mukund 2005: 65). Temple festivals are public events: their performance comprises of the deity's processions through the streets of the town which are of great significance to the general public. Mukund (2005: 72f.) argues that processing the deities essentially signifies that the god (as paradigmatic sovereign) comes from his privileged seclusion of the temple to the people, to mingle with them and be accessible in public space. In people's general perception these processions signify a properly functioning government, public order, and stability. Consequently, all internal disputes regarding temple matters were and still are strategically enacted and negotiated at the time of these festivals. The 'ordinary' devotees are then spectators and participants on the one hand, but on the other they become judges of a conflict which has to be won by one of the two parties through performance.

In Kāñcipuram the god Varadarāja is accompanied by both groups during his processions. The Vaṭakalais recite the Veda and walk behind the deity;[16] the Teṉkalais recite the Tamiḻ hymns and walk in front of the deity. This spatial separation is the result of the conflict between the two groups and visibly attests to it. On these occasions there is a high risk that members of the two sects will try to sneak into the 'ritual domain' of the other party and take over at least part of it. Sometimes conflict erupts and disturbs the ritual, or even leads to its cancellation. Therefore, many policemen have to be present during these festivals in order to 'maintain law and order'. During several temple festivals I witnessed such occurrences: the members of one sect suddenly infiltrated the rows reserved for the other sect. The situation nearly ended in an abrupt termination of the ritual because of the scuffle that ensued from this transgression.

Also for example during the daily 'invocation' (*ārādhana*) of the deity during the temple festival Pavitrotsava (see Hüsken 2006), members of the two congregations recite their respective texts simultaneously. This looks very much like a reciters' contest: each party tries to drown the other out. The atmosphere during ritual occasions like this is highly competitive.

The conflicts thus have become an integral part of the ritual procedures, but nevertheless are by no means purely 'symbolic' in character.

There are two perspectives on what is 'correct' ritual performance, or what it should be, and neither of the two parties involved in these conflicts tolerates even the smallest deviation from 'the rule'.[17] Deviations are clearly marked as a 'mistake' by those who see their ritual share endangered. On the surface, these rituals, therefore, seem to be rather inflexible. Yet I argue that the rituals under consideration are in fact very flexible because the 'rules' that govern their performance undergo constant change. The frequent appeals of both sides to legal courts and the outcome of these appeals attest to this supposition. The decisions made by the legal bureaucrats were and are consistently based on the one or other representation of past enactments of the rituals under consideration. "Historians have observed that the English administrators

---

[16] As per court order, only the Vaṭakalais hold the right in the Varadarāja Perumāḷ temple to chant the Vedas.

[17] Within the temple, the holder of the so-called Maṇi(ya)kkāraṉ ('superintendent') office specifically has to have an eye on the performers of the rituals and has to ensure that they follow the rules (see Hüsken 2006).

in India had a deep-rooted belief that following old usage and precedent was the only way to preserve societal stability and tranquillity, with the added rider that Indian society was timeless and unchanging", says Mukund (2005: 68).[18] However, this attitude was also fostered by the local petitioners themselves. "Custom—more often the term used was mamūl—was claimed to have overriding legitimacy and authority and any innovation was inherently neither legitimate nor acceptable" (*ibid.*). In this process 'custom' is in fact reinvented to suit the interest of any concerned party.[19] What is presented as 'age-old custom' to the judges is itself a reconstruction of the past and becomes 'factual past' only through its acceptance by the judges in their court orders. Thus, in many cases 'mistakes' or transgressions in the context of temple ritual result in the creation of new texts which are supposed to fix norms and rules for the 'correct' ritual procedure, namely the court orders. These texts are invariably based on one out of two perceptions of the past, of 'custom and usage'. "The reinvented history created by the petitioners now became official history validated by the state" (Mukund 2005: 68).

4. *The South Indian temple as place of worship, of power negotiation and of redistribution*

As in other South Indian temples, the ritual shares in the context of the Varadarāja Perumāḷ temple are of great value to the diverse share holders. It is mainly for this reason that contradicting notions of 'mistaken' and 'correct performance' of ritual are constantly renewed and redefined by the participants and performers. Therefore, we need to look more closely at the value system which forms the basis for interpreting deviations-as-mistakes in the context at hand. While in the pre-colonial and colonial periods ritual honours and shares and the social ranking expressed through them were often linked to substantial material advantages, nowadays this aspect is rather insignificant. Nevertheless, the privileges of doing service to the deity, of receiving *mariyātai* in front of

[18] This perception is based on the Orientalist construction of India as a timeless society whose norms do not change, such that 'custom' was allowed to become the main governing principle in the legal system (see Mukund 2005: 4).

[19] Dirks (1987: 290) even says that temples were 'reinvented' as a means to secure social and economical supremacy, not only from the colonisers' side, but as a dialogic process furthered by both, local groups and colonials (see also Irschick 1994: 4–7).

the deity, of reciting one's own eulogistic verse, and so forth evidently have great value for the participants. Here, Simon Harrison's (1992) interpretation of 'ritual shares' as 'property' helps to understand the mechanisms involved. He shows that even when ritual shares do not have any material expression they can be perceived of as a form of property, namely 'intellectual property'. According to Harrison, ritual actions are 'luxury goods' which serve to signify social, especially political, relationships.[20] Their characteristic as property, Harrison (1992: 236f.) argues, becomes evident as soon as ownership is disputed, that is, as soon as a certain ritual action is conceived of as a 'mistake' from one perspective. However, the notion of ritual as property presupposes a common value system: "[...] intellectual property presupposes a shared system of information and meaning, [...] not only for its value, but also for its mere existence" (Harrison 1992: 235). Harrison argues that ownership in entitlement to ritual is based on a distinctive conception of property, similar to that of the gift exchange as analysed by Marcel Mauss (1923–24). Property is a symbolic representation of individuals or groups and a gift, such as the right in ritual, is a piece of one's identity. "[T]he performer of ritual [...] is simultaneously projecting his identity into, and drawing identity from, a universe of social relations transcending his own time and place. Participation in this larger world is an important privilege, and the measure of a man's rank or status", Harrison argues (1992: 239). Only on the basis of this conception of 'ritual as intellectual property' and at the same time as an essential part of the participants' identity, are some features of the conflicts within the Varadarāja Perumāḷ temple intelligible, which seem to be trivial if one presupposes a solely material notion of property (see also Appadurai & Breckenridge 1976: 205). In the present case study rituals do in fact contribute enormously to individual and (sub-)group identity[21] within the temple context: the integration of the rivalling self-representations of the participating groups into the ritual performances described above,

[20] "Tournaments of value are complex periodic events that are removed in some culturally well-defined way from the routines of economic life. Participation in them is likely to be both a privilege of those in power and an instrument of status contests between them", says Appadurai (1986: 21). The conflicts about ritual shares could therefore be well interpreted as a specific expression of these tournaments of value. This fact and the identification of ritual shares as 'luxury goods' by Harrison indicate that the conflicts under investigation are mainly contests between elites.

[21] Pratap (1997) convincingly argues in favour of the presence of sub-group identities as opposed to either monistic collective identities or individual identities.

especially when conflict erupts during the performances and leads to scuffles, attests to this. Ritual shares comprise both an expression and constituent of identity, and serve—especially when highlighted in the negative through the accusation of 'ritual mistake'—to demarcate separation and distinction. "[R]ituals present a social network of relationships which are not self-contained but rather mutually organized along variously defined sub-group identities. And it is along these sub-identities that bargaining for power and privileges in our modern world takes place" (Pratap 1997: 13).

5. *Grave consequences of small deviations*

An independent value is therefore attributed to ritual shares. At the same time they are perceived of as easily perishable and difficult to maintain. This second characteristic is in clear contradistinction to the widespread notion that rituals are somewhat static and unchanging, that they are enduring rather than short-lived. Yet, here it is argued that changes in the performance of the rituals investigated have more often than not a direct impact on future performances as well as on the perception of the past.

Raman (2003: 47ff.) describes an incident which took place in the year 1969. At that time a member of the Tātācārya family wanted to recite the eulogistic verse praising his ('Northern') sect's founder Vedānta Deśika on the occasion of this religious leader's annual birthday celebration in the Varadarāja temple, where also an image of this sectarian leader is kept. Although recitation of a verse praising the religious teacher's birthday could be perceived of as appropriate to the occasion, this request was denied because of massive objections from the 'Southern' sect. Evidently there was great concern that making a single exception to the rule, namely that in the Varadarāja temple the 'Southern' eulogistic verse alone be recited, would set a precedent and soon become a general challenge to the rule itself.

Similarly, certain offices and individual rights to offer certain services to the deity are ardently defended. One of the office-holders, for example, is in charge of fetching the water for the daily worship of the main image of the deity in the temple. He inherited this right from his father. Now, however, he has massive health problems and thus the strenuous task of carrying many buckets of water is difficult for him to perform. Nevertheless, although his own son is still too young to fulfil this task, he refuses to allow others to assume this duty. He openly fears that his family would lose this right permanently if he temporarily handed it over to some unrelated person.

In fact, there are several cases which attest to the view that it is actually the performance of rituals rather than their (normative) texts which decides on whether to change or maintain a ritual practice. Recently there was a dispute between several ritual share holders in the Varadarāja temple about the question of whether the processions through the streets of the town during temple festivals can be performed when major portions of the temple are under renovation. The general question of which rituals are to be performed during temple renovation is dealt with in detail in the Āgamas, the ritual texts in Sanskrit which are considered to be the highest authority for all ritual procedures within the temple. However, even though many participants who wanted all temple festivals to be performed during the renovation explicitly referred to the relevant passages in these texts, the actual decision was based on ritual practice alone. Because in 1992, during the last renovation of the temple, only those festivals took place that are performed within the temple walls, this was finally considered the proper procedure. This clearly shows how a singular exception to the rule (the 1992 case) has the power to 'rewrite' the rules and thus to establish a new 'tradition'.

6. *Repetitions and references to the past as a means to maintain and defend ritual shares*

As we have seen, ritual shares are highly contested at the Varadarāja Perumāḷ temple. What is more, even the slightest deviation from the 'regular procedure' has the power to initiate a fundamental and lasting change in the performance of rituals and therefore in the distribution of ritual shares. These changes are then canonised by the subsequent creation of new texts (namely court orders) which are supposed to fix norms and rules for the 'correct' ritual procedure. This process at first glance indicates a high degree of inflexibility in the rituals. The accusation of making ritual mistakes leads to the petrifaction of a system with an ever increasing number of rules. Yet it is based on the existing flexibility of the rituals: only when changes are possible is the creation of measures which prevent change necessary. Paradoxically this entire procedure reflects the actual flexibility of the rituals.

Yet this actual flexibility is covered up by the 'repetitions'—or rather by the potential repeatability—of the ritual procedures. In ritual, as is evident from the court orders which are based on subjective versions of the past, it is the reconstruction of former performances, of 'custom and usage', of pasts, that decides on the norms, irrespective of what might actually have happened.[22] Wulf & Zirfas (2004: 5, 21) point to the importance of ritual performance in this process. They argue that rituals—through repetition—inscribe themselves 'into' the performers, and that these repetitions then refer to the future as well as to the past. Repetition creates the impression that it has always been like that and must always be like that. Ritual practice is thus an effective means to change rituals and can be perceived of as a frame that knits together tradition and innovation.

It shall be emphasised here that the aspect of repeatability, in particular, refers to a past which is mainly constituted by the actual performance of a ritual. This new version of the past serves then to legitimise all present and future performances: through new and changed performances new facts are created which are at the same time perceived of as 'tradition' or (if recognized as innovation) as 'return to the original tradition'. Rivalling versions of the past, however, are rejected and excluded by marking them as 'mistaken'.

Ritual performance thus has an immediate effect on the perception of the 'past' and is in the position to legitimise or challenge claims to ritual shares. The texts subsequently created are based on these performances, but consistently refer to 'custom and usage' as having been established by preceding texts, such as temple inscriptions or other documents, in order to serve as an authoritative interpretation of the past and as a point of reference for the future. These texts, therefore, legitimise reconstructed pasts in order to evaluate present day practice and to establish the 'correctness' of future performances. Nevertheless, they cannot rule out the normative power of ritual performance, which

[22] The strategy of using ritual to establish identities is based on the fact that ritual practice suggests continuity with the past and thus serves to establish 'fixed' traditions. Ritual can be interpreted here as a "[...] good form for conveying a message, as if it were unquestionable, and it is often used to communicate those very things which are most in doubt.... [T]he connection between ritual and the unquestionable is often at the core of its doctrinal efficacy as much in social and political settings as in religious ones" (Moore & Myerhoff 1977: 24). See also Hobsbawm (1983), who argues that rituals are an important means of reconstructing pasts, which in their turn serve to provide an unquestionable basis for claims in the present and future.

in the present example is so decisive that even the smallest deviations are marked as 'mistakes' in order to devalue their normality. The emphasis on the importance of performance within this process is especially helpful for understanding the present case study.[23] Since it is the 'mistakes' in these performances through which future norms are defined, the norms that are supposed to guide ritual performances are paradoxically confirmed through the categorisation of certain performances as 'mistaken'.

7. *Conclusion*

To term a certain ritual action or behaviour a 'mistake' is a negative evaluation and always depends on the respective point of view. In the conflict under consideration in this paper it is not claimed that a certain ritual procedure is 'wrong' but that the ritual in the given context is 'wrong': all parties involved invariably argue that the invocatory verse of the other sect is not appropriate in the present temple. It has become clear that dealing with 'mistakes' therefore necessitates the researcher to be explicit about the question of whose perspective he or she represents.[24] The present case study points moreover to the fact that the negative assessment 'mistake' or 'doing it wrong' can even from an 'insider' perspective exist side by side with a positive assessment of the same practices. Then conflict is likely to emerge, especially in contexts where ritual procedures reflect and shape social hierarchies to a considerable degree, as is the case in South Indian Hindu temples.

It is the subjectivity of the evaluation which prompts the participants to try to make their point of view the general norm, to shift it beyond doubt and discussion: courts are resorted to by both parties as a means to create a normative script for the ritual (in the form of court orders) which is invested with authority and which can be referred to in future. These then fixed scripts obscure the subjectivity of their own basis. This process of objectifying subjective points of view is

[23] Thus, Wulf & Zirfas (2004: 19) argue that the techniques and practices not only enable repetitions of performances, but also help to single out flaws.

[24] What Dirks says about his ethnohistorical approach holds true for the investigation of 'ritual failure' as well: "...since I believe that ethnohistory must concern itself with power [...] the constituted object must never be permitted to speak (or to appear to speak) only for itself; it speaks with 'interests' and in situations that must be identified and decoded" (Dirks 1987: 405).

time-consuming, expensive, and intricate. Since the whole conflict centres around one single verse in the present case study, the question has to be posed why so much time, money and effort is invested. The answer to this question is that the 'ritual shares' are perceived of as 'property' and as such as inalienable constituents of individual or group identity: contesting ritual procedures by marking them as mistakes, therefore, is tantamount to contesting identities. Moreover, although rituals are frequently perceived of as expressions of doctrinal differences, it seems that it is the ritual procedure rather than the doctrine which in fact marks identity. Ritual as an extension of identity is as flexible as identity itself. It acts upon the context in which it is performed, but at the same time it mirrors the 'external' conditions in which it is negotiated during performance. Thus, it is not surprising that the ritual history of the Varadarāja temple is and was mainly constituted by (performative) deviations from the norm and their consequences. However, the critique is only superficially directed at the proper performance of the rituals in the temple. The right to perform certain rituals in South Indian temples is not only part of a complex process of the redistribution of resources and ritual shares, but at the same time is a public expression of hierarchies and power structures in the locality.

The fights over 'ritual shares' express the desire of the parties involved to implement their version of the truth and thus to achieve permanent acceptance for their norms against the norms of the other party. A closer look at the method of how this perspectivity is ostensibly eliminated reveals that repetition and repeatability play a key role here. Repeatability and repetition are features generally ascribed to ritual. These features anchor rituals in the past and refer them to the future. At the same time, the potential repeatability constitutes the ritual's potential for innovation: ritual is newly constructed in each performance but is perceived of as a repetition of former enactments. In the present case study, the Orientalist perception of India as an unchanging society and the tendency of the colonial judges to try to preserve 'custom and usage' which has been followed 'since time immemorial' contribute very much to this effect.

The frame of reference for the notion of 'ritual as property' therefore is a notion of the past. Since in this case rivalling notions of the past exist or shall be established, the allegation of making ritual mistakes is resorted to. Different concepts of the past compete with each other in the process of establishing and legitimising identity. In our case, "[t]here is tension between groups that have an enduring corporate interest in temple control. In the expression and resolution of these conflicts, the 'pasts' of these groups play a direct and important role." Therefore, to understand the example given in this paper, "[...] it is especially vital to understand the politics of the past in the present" (Appadurai 1987: 201) and the role attributed to rituals therein.

Applying (re)constructed pasts in this way is a common means of establishing and defending new ritual practices. Ritual innovation is based on the critique of present practices and on successfully declaring certain practices as 'mistaken'. And more often than not, innovation appears disguised as a 'return to an original practice'.[25] The interpretation 'ritual mistake' thus not only points to the system(s) of rules and to the value system which form(s) the basis of the ritual performances, but it also indicates the irresistible normative power of these performances.[26] It is their repeatability, in particular, which makes rituals open to the dynamics of change.

References

Appadurai, Arjun 1978. "Kings, Sects, and Temples in South India, 1350–1700 AD" In: *South Indian Temples. An Analytical Reconsideration*, Stein, Burton (ed.). New Delhi: Vikas Publ., 47–73.

—— 1986. "Introduction: commodities and the politics of value". In: *The social life of things. Commodities in cultural perspective*, Appadurai, Arjun (ed.). Cambridge: Cambridge University Press, 3–63.

—— 1987. "The Past as a Scarce Resource". In: *Temples, Kings and Peasants: Perceptions of South Indian's Past*, Spencer, George W. (ed.). Madras: New Era Publ., 196–221.

—— & Carol Appadurai Breckenridge 1976. "The South Indian Temple: Authority, Honor and Redistribution". *Contributions to Indian Sociology* (NS) 10.2: 187–211.

Colas, Gérard 1995. "Cultes et courants du vishnouisme en Inde du Sud. Quelques observations á partir des texts". In: *Les ruses du salut: Religion et politiques dans le monde indien*, Reiniche, M.-L. (ed.). Paris (*Puruṣārtha* 17), 111–138.

Dirks, Nicholas B. 1987. *The Hollow Crown. Ethnohistory of an Indian Kingdom*. Cambridge: Cambridge University Press (Cambridge South Asian Studies).

Doraiswamy Iyengar, M.A. 1983. "Appendix II: Tenkalai Vatakalai Divisions in Srivaisnavism". In: *Two Great Acharyas. Vedanta Desika and Manavala Mamuni*, Varadachari, V. (ed.). Madras: Prof. M. Rangacharya memorial Trust, vii–lxiii.

---

[25] See Humphrey & Laidlaw 1994: 12; see also Harrison 1992: 232.

[26] Dirks's observation regarding the Aiyanar festival in the Pudukkottai region attests to this finding: "Many of the meanings of the Aiyanar festival, as is true of all rituals, only emerge when we find that such festivals were the foci of tremendous dispute and conflict within villages (or natus, castes, lineages, etc.). Ritual, as we see here, denoted and sustained not only unity, but also disunity. What was significant was not that ritual always resulted in order and integration, but that even disorder and conflict manifested themselves first, and most conspicuously, in ritual arenas" (Dirks 1987: 304f.).

Grimes, Ronald L. 1988a. "Infelicitous Performances and Ritual Criticism". *Semeia* 43: 103–122.
—— 1988b. "Ritual Criticism and Reflexivity in Fieldwork". *Journal of Ritual Studies* 2: 217–239.
Harrison, Simon 1992. "Ritual as Intellectual Property". *Man* (New Series) 27.2: 225–244.
Hobsbawm, Eric 1983. "Introduction: Inventing Traditions". In: *The Invention of Tradition*, Hobsbawm, Eric & Terence Ranger (ed.). Cambridge: Cambridge University Press, 1–14.
Humphrey, Caroline & James Laidlaw 1994. *The Archetypal Actions of Ritual. A Theory of Ritual illustrated by the Jain Rite of Worship*. Oxford: Clarendon Press.
Hüsken, Ute 2006. "Pavitrotsava: Rectifying Ritual Lapses". In: *Jaina-Itihāsa-Ratna. Festschrift für Gustav Roth zum 90. Geburtstag.* Hüsken, Ute & Petra Kieffer-Pülz & Anne Peters (ed.). Marburg: Indica et Tibetica Verlag (Indica et Tibetica 47), 265–281.
Irschick, Eugene F. 1994. *Dialogue and History: Constructing South India 1795–1895*. Berkeley: University of California Press.
Mauss, Marcel 1923–24. *Essai sur le don*. Presses Universitaires de France: Paris (German translation used: *Die Gabe: Form und Funktion des Austauschs in archaischen Gesellschaften*. Mit einem Vorwort von E.E. Evans-Pritchard. Übers. von Eva Moldenhauer. Frankfurt: Suhrkamp [Suhrkamp-Taschenbuch Wissenschaft 743], 1996).
Moore, Sally Falk & Barbara G. Myerhoff 1977. "Introduction. Secular Ritual: Forms and Meanings". In: *Secular Ritual*, Moore, Sally Falk & Barbara G. Myerhoff (ed.). Assen & Amsterdam: Van Gorcum, 3–24.
Mudaliar, Chandra 1976. *State and religious endowments in Madras*. Madras: University of Madras.
Mukund, Kanakalatha 2005. *The View From Below. Indigeneous Society, Temples and the Early Colonial State in Tamil Nadu, 1700–1835*. New Delhi: Orient Longman.
Mumme, Patricia Y. 1993. "Rules and Rhetoric: Caste Observance in Śrīvaiṣṇava Doctrine and Practice". *Journal of Vaiṣṇava Studies* 2.1: 113–138.
Pratap, Kumar P. 1993. "Religious Institutions: Ritual and Power Dynamics in India". *Journal for the Study of Religion* 6/2: 69–89.
—— 1997. "Ritual and Hierarchy: A Case of Shrivaishnavas". *Journal for the Study of Religion* 10.1: 3–18.
Raman, K.V. 1975. *Srī Varadarājaswāmi Temple—Kāñchi*. Abhinav Publications: New Delhi.
Ramaswamy, T.S. 2003. *Judicial Solutions for Temple Disputes—A Critical Analysis*. Madras: RNR Printers.
Siauve, Suzanne 1978 (ed., transl.). *Aṣṭadaśabhedanirṇaya. Explication des dix-huit differences (entre les deux branches de l'École de Rāmānuja) de Śrī Vātsya Raṅganātha*. Pondichery (PICI 58).
Subramanian, P. 1996. *Social History of the Tamils (1707–1947)*. New Delhi: DK Printworld (Reconstructing Indian History and Culture 7).
Varada Tatacharya, R. 1978. *The temple lord Varadaraja, Kanchi: a critical survey of Dr. K.K. Raman's Sri Varadarajaswami Temple, Kanchi*. Kanchi.
Wulf, Christoph & Jörg Zirfas 2004. "Performative Welten. Einführung in die historischen, systematischen und methodischen Dimensionen des Rituals". In: *Die Kultur des Rituals. Inszenierungen. Praktiken, Symbole*, Wulf, C. & J. Zirfas (ed.). München: Zink-Verlag, 7–45.

THE UNWANTED OFFERING. UBIQUITY AND SUCCESS OF FAILURE IN A RITUAL OF THE HINDU RIGHT

Christiane Brosius

> *If the saints agree, I would not hesitate to even dump these shilas (pillars) into the gutter.*
> Mahant Devendra Prasad Acharya, religious leader, Ayodhya, March 2002[1]

> *The successful completion of the 'shila daan' ceremony on schedule constituted a victory for the forces of Hinduism... Today, the VHP overcame all obstacles sought to be placed in its path, and successfully completed the 'shila daan' on deadline.*
> Praveen Togadia, International Secretary, VHP, at a press conference in March 2002[2]

> *...ironically, the Vishwa Hindu Parishad's 'shila puja' and 'shila daan' campaign ended with its working president, Ashok Singhal, being shouted down by the couple of hundred supporters who had collected around the 'karsevakpuram' compound this morning. The gathering of 'sadhus', indigent 'pujaris' and 'mahants' and a handful of young men said it was incensed at having been 'tricked into accepting a deal which fell far short of expectations... Mr. Singhal maintained silence on the day's events. It was Vinay Katiyar, BJP MP from Ayodhya and Bajrang Dal leader, who admitted that the VHP's campaign had not gone 'according to its plan'. And that some things had gone wrong.* (Mody 2002a).

These three quotes have been chosen as introductory landmarks designating parts of the territory through which this paper will move in its discussion of failure in Hindu nationalist ritual performances. All three represent different perspectives on the so-called *shila puja* ('pillar ceremony') or *shila daan* ('pillar offering'), a ritual that was performed by orthodox Hindu nationalist leaders in the north Indian pilgrimage city of Ayodhya in March 2002. The first one is from the head of a

---

[1] "No takers for shilas in Ayodhya". In: *Rediff.com news*, 22/Mar/2002 (http://www.rediff.com/news/2002/mar/22ayo3.htm; date of last access: 17/08/2006).

[2] "VHP wins, anti-Hindu forces lose: Togadia". In: *Rediff.com news*, 15/Mar/2002 (http://www.rediff.com/news/2002/mar/15ayo15.htm; date of last access: 17/08/2006).

temple in Ayodhya, who angrily refused to allow the allegedly sanctified pillars to remain in his compound after the procession's conclusion. The alliance of sanctity and "gutter" do not need much explanation and clearly refer to the provocative denial of the ritual authority and credibility of this particular event, as well of its performers. The rejection of an offering in a ritual context points to the fact that something had really gone wrong!

The second quote stems from Praveen Togadia, International Secretary of the World Hindu Congress (*Vishwa Hindu Parishad*, hereafter VHP), one of the fiercest and best-known speakers of the extreme Hindu Right, the last one from an analyst of an Indian weekly. These quotes show that the question of risk occurs on various levels of ritual performance, and for various agents involved in its conduct. The fact that risk emerges in different ways points us towards the dynamics of ritual in terms of its imagined (expected) and its actual efficacy. Even if a ritual may have no further consequences for the appearance of a religio-political movement in public (on the long run, for example, that it becomes a 'landmark', a recurring point of reference for the movement), its discussion enables us to ponder relationships between various social agents in a field of conflict, and the issues that are at stake here, as well as *how* they are negotiated. While both the ritual as well as its potential failure may be perceived as a real threat to organisers and critics, it 'works' equally powerfully as a virtual emblem and challenge to others. I want to show here that the risk of ritual failure is an important factor for ritual performers, participants and those opposed to, or trying to stop it for various reasons. Before, during and after the ritual, the 'right balance' and tension between success and failure has to be kept, and a whole ecology of rhetoric is developed in order to do so. Hardly ever would ritual performers acknowledge that things could be 'done the wrong way', that something or somebody went 'out of control'. At the same time, there are moments when this risk is consciously worked in, either to adjust the ritual dynamics to external factors (for example, a ban on the ritual), or internal factors (lack of support among the 'members' of the movement). Thus, ritual failure constantly works within, or moves along the lines of shifting and contesting frames of credibility and authority.

In order to tackle this multi-layered notion of 'doing things wrong', the question of perspectivity onto a particular ritual must be a central focus of attention for us. While Togadia interpreted the overall performance of the particular ritual that is at centre-stage in this article, the *shila daan* ('pillar offering') as a great "victory" against all odds, the author of the third quote gives us an idea of the failure and loss of credibility in the eyes of the audience of the leading performers of the ritual during its enactment, hinting at a lack of conviction, direction and message. The participants felt cheated and articulated their protest against the 'authorised' leaders. In the end, many of the participants no longer wished to deal with the ritual objects, that is, the 'sanctified' pillars. What is otherwise received and perceived as a great honour had turned into an unwanted offering.

Above, we read that Vinay Katiyar, a Hindu nationalist hardliner, famous for his leadership of the VHP's militant youth wing (*Bajrang Dal*), acknowledged that "some things had gone wrong". But what might have gone wrong, where, when and how? To analyse this, the article looks at the offering ritual from various perspectives. Involved in this are the agents who look at, participate in and read meaning into the ritual performance: organisers and leaders, participants, and external agents.

1. *About the context*

In order to map the question of perspectivity in ritual failure in the case of the ritual procession that is the focus of this article, a few remarks about the political context are necessary. The ritual around which the discussion evolves was referred to as *shila puja* (sacred pillar ceremony) and *shila daan* (pillar offering).[3] It was organized and performed in the north Indian pilgrimage city of Ayodhya, on March 15, 2002, by speakers and sympathisers of the VHP. In the debate surrounding nationality in contemporary India, the VHP is no blank sheet and has gained itself the reputation of being a 'toughie' in terms of its role in national/ist politics, reserving the right of high morale and conduct, and not shying away from sanctifying violence of different kinds.[4] We are dealing with an organisation that claims to represent 'the Hindu people' as a nation, in particular their religious sentiment, and to preserve or revitalise their heritage and 'Hindu way of life' (Hindutva) both in India and

[3] Since the objects of this devotional act were two pillars, the term 'pillar' will be used instead of stone. However, at the famous *shila puja* of 1989, the ritual objects collected from all over India, and even the world, to be offered for the reconstruction of Ram's birth temple at Ayodhya, were bricks.

[4] For further information on the VHP, see Katju 2003.

worldwide. Founded in 1966 to challenge the alleged dilution of this way of life through secularism and inadequate governance, the VHP distances itself from parliamentary concerns and activities and calls itself a religious organization that cares for national welfare. It is made up of a variety of religious leaders from different Hindu sects, many of which are members of the 'religious parliament' (*Dharma Sansad*), as well as strategic experts that have been delegated from its 'mother organisation', the Rashtriya Swayamsevak Sangh (National Volunteer's Association, hereafter RSS) to serve the interests of Hindutva. The VHP is involved in social and educational grassroots work, runs schools for economically and socially marginalized groups like the Dalit ('untouchables') or Adivasi (tribal aboriginals), in economically backward rural areas or urban slums. Despite its proclamation that its ethics are based on tolerance and doors are open to every 'Indian', the VHP's rhetoric is strongly anti-Muslim, anti-Christian, and also anti-Communist. It is part of the so-called 'Sangh', a family of organizations aligned to the RSS that dedicate their activities towards Hindutva, the interests of the 'majority' of Indians—the Hindu people and their cultural heritage. In the 1980s and 1990s, the organization started to show a great concern for territorial issues. A topography of threatened and/or destroyed Hindu sites was superimposed on the map of India. In the course of this, more than 3000 Hindu sites have been located by 'historians', archaeologists and other 'scientific experts'. These sites are mostly Hindu temples that were allegedly destroyed, occupied and desecrated over the centuries by the construction of buildings of different religious origin, particularly Islam. In order to 'liberate' these 'dominated sites' and convert them into 'dominant' sites (Kritzman 1996), the VHP created a set of religious rituals that would purportedly help the Hindu people to awaken, unite and claim back their holy sites, thus revitalizing their lost pride. Thus the ritual discussed here can be understood as a territorial ritual, contesting, conquering and establishing imagined and physical sites of religious meaning and mythological and historical relevance in the attempt to transform the 'dominated' site into a 'dominant' site.

To some extent, these territorial rituals have enjoyed the support of political representatives such as the Bharatiya Janata Party (Party of the Indian People, hereafter BJP). This is not without reason: there is an intimate relationship between the framing and conduct of 'religious' rituals and parliamentary elections. Thus, the Hindu Right rituals always surface in politically sensitive times, when public opinion-making is sought to be shaped by 'waves', that is, highly emotional issues. In this context, these rituals have often been accompanied by and triggered off ethno-political violence, especially between Hindus and Muslims. The rhetoric of the rituals and other propaganda means are clearly anti-Muslim, some of them calling openly for violence against those Muslims who do not succumb to Hindutva and its various *avatars*, for example, Mother India or Lord Ram and his birth temple.

The VHP's attempt to map 'vulnerable', sacred and 'humiliated' Hindu sites as the stage of its ritualised rhetoric has been mentioned: the site on which the pillar offering was to take place in March 2002 is such a highly contested and powerful location. For more than 20 years now, the VHP has performed a range of rituals there, requesting the 'liberation' of Lord Ram (also defined as a 'national hero') from his 'Muslim' prison, the Babri Mosque. The mosque, built in 1528, was allegedly erected on and through the demolition of Ram's birth temple. It is defined as a symbol marking the beginning of Muslim invasion and Hindu colonisation. Only the reconstruction of the Ram temple, so the argument goes, can reinstall Hindu pride. After almost ten years of agitation, on December 6, 1992, thousands of so-called *kar sevaks*, voluntary workers in the service of God, associated with the Sangh, stormed the fenced ground on which the mosque stood and demolished it in less than five hours. The demolition was accompanied and followed by pan-Indian riots, claiming thousands of dead, both among Hindu and Muslim communities. Since then, a makeshift temple for the child-form of Ram, Ramlalla, has been erected. The area is heavily protected by barbed wire and security forces; *puja* is only allowed in a very restricted way. Public access to the site is not permitted, except for small groups of Hindu devotees wishing to perform *puja*.[5] The land is now partly in government hands. Since 1992, VHP spokespeople demand that the land is handed over to its 'legitimate' owners, the VHP-near Ramjanmabhoomi Nyas (a Trust set up for the reconstruction), and, in the final consequence, the 'Hindu people'. But there are further agents involved in the negotiation of territoriality: disputes between representatives of Muslim groups, the Hindu Right, and the Indian government are ongoing and to this day no decision has been reached about the future of the site; the case is pending in the Supreme Court. Even though the Archaeological Survey of India presented a report in 2003 in which it 'proved' the existence of a Hindu temple

[5] See "Supreme Court's intervention". In: *Frontline* 19 (7).

at the site of the demolished mosque, this evidence has been strongly questioned. Internally too, the agents have to be differentiated when we look at the question of ritual failure. Today, the so-called Ram temple movement, made up of various quasi-religious organizations and until 1992 relatively united in its appearance and agenda is fragmented. Furthermore, in the course of the BJP's 'domestication' following its electoral access to governmental power in a big coalition in 1998, the VHP had been increasingly marginalised.

Through rituals such as the pillar offering, so it was hoped by the VHP, its old position could be reaffirmed and the fragmented movement's unity reinstalled. But the ritual was also meant to speed up the decision-making processes and apply pressure on the government to hand over the land so that the VHP could begin with the temple construction and could once again push itself to the forefront of public discussion on nationality. Albeit, even ten years after the mosque demolition nothing had happened in this context, much to the contrary and disappointment of large segments of the Sangh Parivar, the issue had instead been put on the backburner. The VHP also did not know whether the Ram temple issue could catch the imagination and sympathies of the majority of Hindus-as-a-nation. We have to understand the ritual as a test, or 'reality-check': to investigate whether support for the Ram temple construction could still be mobilised along the broadest possible lines.

Ten years after the demolition of the Babri Mosque, arguments and actions had barely changed but were now imbued with different meaning and had different consequences. Stating that the Hindus could not wait any longer to revitalise their lost (and destroyed) past and glorious identity, two *dramatis personae*—Ashok Singhal, general secretary of the VHP, and Mahant Ramachandra Paramhans, the head of the Ramjanmabhoomi Nyas, announced plans for the successful and even victorious construction of a Ram temple. On March 15, 2002, so the proclamation, the VHP would start moving two foundation pillars that had been carved especially for the proposed temple. Construction of the temple would begin shortly afterwards, at an auspicious moment, to be determined through astrological consultations (Muralidharan 2002b). The ritual could not fail because divine will was with the performers, sanctifying their actions. Thus the framing of another ritual had begun, and the agenda set—on the basis of religious 'ingredients' that are required for any temple construction.

Everything was set, it seemed. Until the Supreme Court, two days before the auspicious moment, on March 13, ruled that *no* kind of religious activity may be performed on government acquired land covering an area of almost 70,000 acres on and around the demolished site (Muralidharan 2002b, Noorani 2002a and b). Suddenly the risk of failure was in the air.

2. *Successful failure and multi-perspectivity*

Platvoet is certainly correct when he designates the politico-religious Ayodhya rituals of the Hindu Right as 'rituals of confrontation', for a dramatic polarisation of forces is central to these ritual performances. And not without reason: the majority of studies analysing the ritual rhetoric of the Hindu Right argues that they were, overall, a successful strategy in positioning Hindutva interests at centre-stage of the public domain and challenge those forces who purportedly undermine them, and in particular the Hindu sentiment (see Brosius 2005, Jaffrelot 1993, Platvoet 2004, van der Veer 1994). Yet beyond the helio of success, many such performances that were staged with vociferous confidence and mediagenic spectacle were highly unstable, risky and contested—always close to failure. One reason why these nationalist chauvinist rituals were not questioned as to the efficacy of their dynamics might be because the ritual performances are generally linked to the rapid rise and success of the Hindu Right since the beginning of the Ram temple movement in 1989[6] and the BJP's speedy growth in parliamentary representation. Until then, no other political player had dared to exploit religious rhetoric as openly as the BJP (this does not mean that, for example, other parties such as Congress did not piggyback on religious themes and practices). Religious issues were still closely intertwined with political and economic interests, or could be instrumentalised for such reasons. Various Hindutva representatives trusted that success was granted whenever a quasi-religious ritual was involved (even at the risk of inviting violence against minority groups), and several previously

[6] The first mass agitation was organised by the VHP in 1983. However, only when the movement gained political momentum when the BJP officially joined the 'struggle for Ram's liberation' and turned many of the rituals into parallel election campaigns, did the agenda become a 'wave'.

successfully organized rituals were used as a reference point in order to affirm this trust (see also Schieffelin 1996: 66).

I propose that the VHP depended on those rituals to make itself and its ideas 'real' and 'graspable', and to participate in the public opinion-making process. This supports Schieffelin's argument that agents "are reproduced through these practices and activities" (1996: 61), whether their power is affirmed or challenged. In this context, it could even be argued that the Hindu Right rituals could never completely fail. However, I also wish to argue that underlying this 'inbuilt' success is the constant presence of risk of failure. And the risk of failure concerns more than the organisers and participants, it also pulls into its complex web external forces such as critics or state organisations. Looking closely at the performance of the rituals and the different agents involved in organising and staging them, it becomes evident that there are many instances in which the rituals (almost) 'slipped' into failure, were interrupted, broke apart, did not manage to create "presence" (Schieffelin 1996: 59f, 82), that is, tactile credibility, or find accreditation and support by all kinds of agents.

Schieffelin has proposed that risk is inscribed in every ceremonial performance, and that "the ritual performances are necessarily subject to the variable competencies of the major performers, the competing agendas and ongoing evaluations of all the participants, as well as unforeseen contingency and blind luck" (1996: 80). On the following pages, some of the agents involved in conducting, disturbing, and participating in the performance are discussed in order to argue that we must understand Hindu nationalist rituals as a field of discourse made up of a variety of positions, all enforcing each other. In this paper, I hope to show that the performance of a ritual, like Schieffelin (*ibid.*) has argued, is a risky undertaking on many levels and in various ways, vulnerable to various internal and external structural factors and contingencies. Failure is caused by and impacts on a range of social and religious agents who are directly or indirectly involved in the ritual's organisation and proceedings. And it is by no means obvious for those involved in its organisation that the ritual will have a 'successful' ending. Close vicinity to ritual failure would be never admitted, and face-saving strategies developed instead to prevent the ritual from being stamped as a 'flop', both by participants and critics. I want to show that 'failure's presence' is ubiquitous, lingering on various levels of those religio-political rituals of the Hindu Right, and argue this on four levels of enquiry: 1) the level of internal critique, 2) the level of confrontation with external forces, 3) the level of organisers and speakers of the Hindu Right, and 4) at the level of support/mobilisation.

This way, the issues of perspectivity and intentionality, through which authenticity, authority and validity are attributed to the ritual's potential 'efficacy', can be analysed with respect to the fact that the notion and attribution of 'success' and 'failure' depends on the agents' status and interests as they seek to position themselves competitively in the field of discourse. What might be failure for some, is successful performance for another; whereas the whole ritual flopped for some, for others a few 'mistakes' occurred that could, however, be sidelined for the sake of a larger agenda. The notion of ritual failure is employed here not to come up with an ultimate judgement on a ritual's efficacy. Rather, it enables us to look at the individual agents involved in the struggle for authority, positioning themselves in and through the ritual—around the issue of territorial identity/nationality—as they attempt to hold it in a state of stability or enforce imbalance, and thus engage in crisis management.

3. *Building up drama and announcing the ritual*

At the outset, it all looked like a successful beginning.

On January 27, 2002, Atal Behari Vajpayee, the Indian Prime Minister, received a VHP delegation. This was after the VHP had staged a seven day *sant chetavani yatra* ('holy men's warning mach') that had culminated at Delhi's vast Ramlila grounds. The delegation announced that it was following the suggestions of the Marg Darshak Mandal,[7] a committee close to the Sangh, claiming the authority to direct and guide religious ceremonies, ethics and morals of Hindu society. It set an ultimatum on the government "to hand over the land at Ayodhya or face a situation in which the *sants* (holy men) would forcibly take it over and build a Ram temple" (Muralidharan 2002a). Earlier in the

[7] Members of the Mandal represent different Hindu sects. It has c. 200 members, and meets twice a year to advise VHP in 'socio-religious' questions. The Mandal had decided on the construction date of the Ram temple and is assisted by the *Sadhu Sansad* (Parliament of Sadhus), another Hindu Right organisation that was converted into the *Dharma Sansad* in 1984, with thousands of participants. The Dharma Sansad decides the course of action for the VHP, mainly through processions, and supports the VHP through public participation, while the Mandal is responsible for decisions only, not for executing them (Kaur 2002).

morning, a meeting of the VHP had adopted a resolution demanding that the 67 acres of land acquired by the government of Uttar Pradesh in 1993, after the demolition of the Babri Mosque, must be handed over to the Ram Janmabhoomi Nyas (a VHP controlled trust). This, so it was argued, would finally enable the VHP to start with the construction of the proposed temple at the disputed site on any auspicious day after Shivratri of the same year (which fell on March 12). The delegation addressing the PM announced that from February 24 onwards, another mass agitation would begin. Fiery VHP speakers such as Praveen Togadia announced that more than a million people would follow the call 'Ayodhya chalo' (go to Ayodhya), and thousands of 'devotees' with their families would start gathering there, to be part of the temple reconstruction (Noorani 2002). Coincidence or not: on February 27, a compartment of an express train to Bombay, filled with Ram devotees returning from Ayodhya, burnt and claimed around 60 lives in Godhra, a town in the western state of Gujarat. Hindutva representatives accused a Muslim mob of setting the train on fire. This led to some of the worst pogroms against Muslims since India's Partition. Even though these events will remain largely unexplored in this article, the connection between ritual and violence in the context of the Ayodhya debate is an important backdrop to understand the extent to which territorial rituals of the kind discussed here impact on public life and discourse.

4. *Critique and refusal from within: religious experts*

> *At the simplest level, this [failure] is a matter of basic performance competence: the ability to create and maintain a credible persona and activity and carry it off acceptably within the limits of the genre* (Schieffelin 1996: 66–67).

In order to tackle ritual failure's ubiquity, I want to discuss the *shila puja* by starting with critics from within the movement. Since the credibility of such rituals depends on the public appearance and acknowledgement of leading representatives (in terms of their creation of 'charisma'), and is a 'test' of strength in terms of mass support and competence to manage or create conflict, critical voices from insiders are an essential threat to authority.

One of the levels on which the pillar offering of 2002 'failed' is in the lack of organisers to create a ritual atmosphere and ritual commitment among the participants, be they religious leaders or grass-roots cadres from the Sangh. Various claims have been made by individual religious experts that the ritual was neither conceived, nor organised, nor performed properly. And thus, for various reasons, the ritual and its 'owners' failed to convince previous supporters from within the so-called 'Ayodhya movement' to participate. Reasons for not convincing are varied and concern framing, execution, form, and means: there was openly announced protest by staying away, silent protest by backing out without excuse, there was the critique that the ritual was hijacked by political interests, and that the performance of *shila puja* was redundant and thus invalid. Furthermore, the fear that further politicisation will enhance ongoing tensions within the Ayodhya dispute led to the fact that the 'gift', the pillars donated by religious leader Paramhans, turned into an unwanted offering. The interruption of the flow of reciprocity that echoes the rejection or denial of divinity (and with it, religious expertise and authority communicating this sanctity) in this context is, I argue, a major sign of ritual failure. Overall, the authority of the VHP and the religious leaders associated with it in the context of the ritual performance was seriously questioned and challenged.

In the case of the VHP, many of the leaders take their charismatic leadership and authority for granted, and assume that their supporters do likewise. There is a competition for charismatic authority, and each leader has his—or her—particular rhetorical strategy to appeal to the crowds, and the playground for doing so is generally a ritual performance. The different audiences catered to by leaders such as Ashok Singhal, Praveen Togadia or Paramhans can be an advantage in terms of the broadest possible mobilisation, and there is a lot of team-working when it comes to present the 'movement' as one based on the solidarity of the 'brotherhood'. But the charismatic appeal, the ritual competence, of the leaders is not always taken for granted by the participants of a performance. Rather, it has to be affirmed anew in and through each and every public appearance. It is here where challenges by individual or collective agents may lead to conflicts that introduce imbalance, lack of consensus and finally, threat of failure of the performance.

In the case of the *shila puja*, several affiliates of the Ram temple movement did not want to align themselves to the agenda and/or the leaders performing the ritual. Various reasons caused this dissociation. During fieldwork, I frequently heard of situations in which tensions arose among 'small leaders' and grassroots cadres whose members felt that there was a lack of communication and concern for their own interests from the side of the 'big men'. This ignorance became particularly manifest in ritual performances, leading to feelings of frustration when participants of all ranks felt sidelined and treated as 'props'. What can be particularly harmful to a spokesperson's authority, and thus to a ritual's credibility, is the open or covert critique from spokespeople within his or her own ranks—be it by means of verbal articulation or demonstrative absence.[8] However, the critique has to be placed in such a way that it must be heard. A few examples will underline the management of critique and the issues at stake therewith.

The *shila puja* of 2002 indicated that the taken-for-granted fraternity of leaders faced serious instability—in particular tensions surfaced shortly before the day of the ritual performance, partly because of the confusion that arose following the Supreme Court's ruling, partly because the 'movement' did not pull the same support as it had done in the period before 1992. Disbelief was above all expressed by local religious leaders with gard to the competence, authenticity and authority of the pan-national VHP leaders and their motivations. The credibility of the ritual performance was questioned by local leaders, formerly associated as firm supporters of the movement, who now stated that they no longer wanted to be identified with the ritual, or silently protested by staying away from the ritual altogether. One news magazine even reported a "complete boycott of the event by the local religious institutions" (Muralidharan 2002a).

In one case, the ritual itself then turned into a field of conflict and discourse over power—the competition over authority and ownership of the right to know how, when, and by whom a ritual could be effectively performed. One figure of resistance and competition for power was Ayodhya's Mahant Jaganath Das, head of the Nirmohi Akhara.[9] Once closely associated with the VHP, he distanced himself from that position, questioning the VHP leaders' legitimacy: "This [*shila puja* as

---

[8] The story of the failure of the pillar offering ritual in 2002 does not end here: other religious heads from Ayodhya formerly closely related to VHP activities chose to express their dissent by staying away from the ritual, purportedly having to attend other religious functions elsewhere. This, of course, clearly indicates both protest and disapproval by evolving a hierarchy of rituals allegedly 'more important' than the *shila puja*. Other specialists did not even bother to give an excuse and simply refrained from showing up.

[9] Ayodhya is made up of different *akharas*, seats of religious scholarship and training, representing various Hindu sects/schools, see van der Veer 1987.

representative of the Ram temple campaign, the author] is for them just a way to generate money. [...] The VHP is packed with *dalals* [brokers, the author] who trade religion for power" (Muralidharan 2002a). This statement introduces a critique of the ritual as an instrument of selfish and commercial enterprise instead of being a selfless vehicle of ideological values and convictions. Such arguments have been raised before by voices within and outside the Sangh, accusing VHP leaders and *sants* of misusing monetary donations for their own purposes when they were intended to finance the construction of the Ram temple. This is partly in tune with the orthodox claim that religious leaders should not interfere in political matters, but follow their tradition of 'detachment and silence' that befits them (see Muralidharan 2003). Jaganath Das's accusations could also have been fed by other sources of discontent: jealousy, internal political issues, to mention only a few aspects. The critique of the ritual performance and the performers' authority was certainly not just based on selflessness.[10] For example, in 1992, before the demolition of the Babri Mosque, the then BJP-dominated state government of Uttar Pradesh, under Chief Minister Kalyan Singh, had ordered the demolition of more than sixteen temples that were under administration of Jaganath Das's Akhara. The temples had been standing close to the Babri Mosque, so people alleged that they (together with several Muslim graveyards) had fallen victim to religious tourism development, or, as is also possible, preparations for the removal of the mosque. However, this competition for land and sites might well have triggered off personal tensions and feelings of marginalisation in the Mahant. Mahant Jaganath Dasnow felt that it was the right time to position himself once again, in a vengeful manner, and provoke dissent from the ritual legitimacy.

Another example shows critique of a different kind that indicates that the *shila* offering failed because it was ritually illegitimate: it was a mere replica, a rhetorical copycat, of an identical ritual performed previously. Jaganath Das and Mahant Gyan Das (head of the Nirvani Akhara),

[10] It was his order, a religious institution going back several centuries (van der Veer 1987) that filed a case in January 1885 with the sub-judge of Faizabad, "seeking consent to construct a temple over the Ram Chabutra, adjacent to the [then still standing, the author] Babri Masjid [...] Permission was declined" on the basis of domination of Hindu structures over Muslim structures, but the *akhara* went on fighting and still claims today that it has a privileged right over the disputed site.

"were dismissive, asking what earthly meaning the donation of a stone could have when the foundation stone has been ostensibly laid in 1989" (Muralidharan 2002a). This example is interesting because it points to the fact that in 1989, the VHP, supported by the BJP and other Sangh organisations, had already offered and laid a foundation stone for the proposed Ram temple in a massive public ritual entitled *shila puja.* Ten thousands of sanctified bricks had been assembled by means of processions and small *pujas* from all over India and the world, to symbolise and enable the construction of the Ram temple. At that time, the ritual had taken place outside the boundaries of the still existing Babri Mosque. The *shila puja* is today seen as the prototype of success for the Ram temple movement, and for the ability of the VHP to mobilise millions of people, and rupees, for this purpose (see Brosius 2005, Jaffrelot 1993). Clearly, the Mahants's critique is focused on the authenticity of a ritual, the fact that the *shila puja* of 2002 was nothing but a dramatic 'make-up' of something that can only be performed once.

Another point of critique was directed to the authorisation of ritual performances through sacred scriptures. Mahant Ramdas, the chief priest of Ayodhya's oldest temple, the Hanuman Garhi, argued that, "the way the so-called shila pujan or shila daan was carried out was meaningless as it did not conform to the procedures laid down under the Hindu scriptures" (Muralidharan 2002a). Even though he did not specify what kind of Hindu scriptures he actually referred to, his pointing to a canon of existing sacred rules that regulate the 'authenticity' of (temple) rituals, and thus their efficacy, shows that he was out to define the ritual as a failure, with no right to claim sanctity. Allegedly on this basis, and despite being one of the key trustees of the Ramjanmabhoomi Nyas, Mahant Ramdas refused to have anything to do with the ritual performance. Another former ally, Mahant Jugal Kishore Shastri, Chief Trustee of the Ramalaya Trust, one of the other organisations involved in the Ram Temple movement, claimed that "the whole exercise of March 15 was a farce".[11] It seemed that the delegation that had approached the Prime Minister in January had somewhat miscalculated the fact that the claimed support had been successively withdrawn, that the movement had run out of steam.

[11] "No takers for shilas in Ayodhya". In: *Rediff.com news*, 22/Mar/2002 (http://www.rediff.com/news/2002/mar/22ayo3.htm; date of last access: 17/08/2006).

These examples are clear indications that rituals do not always create communitas, and consensus, and that Platvoet's term 'rituals of confrontation' for the Hindutva movement can also be applied to internal negotiations and conflict over the 'right way' to do a ritual. Another point of internal critique, and thus failure of the ritual to convince and constitute the 'right communitas', was the inclusion of laymen at the centre of the *puja*, that is, the pillar offering. According to Jaganath Das, a further 'mistake' was made by the Mahant of Ayodhya's Digambar Akhara, Paramhans, by ritually donating the foundation stone to Shatrughan Singh, an official representative of the Ayodhya cell at the Prime Minister's office. The point of conflict here was that Singh attended the ceremony as a representative of the secular government, and that he was not an authorised religious specialist. Furthermore, he was not a Brahmin, and Jaganath Das underlined the inauspiciousness implied for a Brahmin like Paramhans to "bestow his material favour upon a Kshatriya". Many things can be read into these lines, for example, the claim to and affirmation of Brahmin superiority within the Ram temple movement. In the religious ritual context, this transfer of power could also be read as a secularisation and de-auratisation of a sacred object. Having transformed the pillar into a mundane object, so Das, the recipient could now "grind masala with it in his kitchen" (Muralidharan 2002a). The offering had begun to be 'unwanted'.

Interestingly, though, the same kind of 'pollution' of an object sanctified through ritual by a Brahmin priest did *not* seem to occur in 1989, when the foundation stone laying ceremony at the *shila puja* was carried out by a Dalit—a person from the lowest end of the caste and ritual hierarchy, and defined per se as possessing polluting *guna* (quality). In other contexts, hardly any incident could have been more scandalous than designating a Dalit to partake in a Brahmin ritual, and at such a central point within the choreography (Brosius 2005: 203). However, in 1989, when the movement was at its height, it was part of the ritual's open strategy that the Ram temple movement, generally attributed with the reputation of being elitist, treated each and everyone as an equal. This point once again emphasises the importance of perspectivity in ritual dynamics when it comes to the conscious inclusion or exclusion of elements within the framing and conduct of a performance and its negotiation.

In the final example of this section, the question of the unwanted offering is addressed. Ritual authority was challenged on other grounds too, pinpointing the field of conflict between politics, business and 'pure' religion. Because of the Supreme Court's decision on 13. March 2002 that no public religious ceremony may be carried out in the vicinity of the demolished site where the Babri Masjid had stood, the original plans for holding the final pillar offering at the site where the temple was to be built had to be changed. Since this implies that no governmental permit had been granted to commence with the construction work, the laying of the foundation stone was merely virtual. After being offered, a suitable storage place for the pillars had thus to be found. Once more the credibility of the ritual was at stake: Devendra Prasad Acharya, who was head of the Badasthan temple where the pillars were first kept after the ceremony, and who had refrained from participating in the ritual, asked for them to be instantly removed. He feared that by being the host to such controversial symbols, his temple could turn into a playground for VHP representatives' interests. Mahant Devendra Prasad Acharya further expressed anger over the fact that his temple had been (ab)used as a storage place despite his absence and rejection of the idea. And provocatively, he told media persons that he had called for a meeting of Ayodhya *sants* on that particular issue: "If the saints agree, I would not hesitate to even dump these shilas into the gutter". In his view, "other prominent temples of Ayodhya [were] also wary of accepting the controversial pillars".[12]

The refusal to accept the pillars as a 'donation' until they could be used for their original purpose is crucial. It demarcates the interruption of the flow of symbolic and real goods between people who appreciate reciprocity as a sign of an ecology of solidarity. The rupture, the breaking of this invisible 'bond' of imagined fraternity points towards a major shift and the fragility within the internal alliances that constitute a movement. The example also indicates that the pillars' meaning and value had, in and through the ritual performance itself, been shifted from that of 'authentic' religious objects to that of symbols of political rhetoric and economic interest. The disruption of the flow on one level of ritual economy must be understood as a major catalyst that changed the flow and emergence of commitment to the ritual.

On March 28, the pillars were put in steel boxes and deposited at the Faizabad district treasury. This act resulted from an order by the

[12] "No takers for shilas in Ayodhya". In: *Rediff.com news*, 22/Mar/2002 (http://www.rediff.com/news/2002/mar/22ayo3.htm; date of last access: 17/08/2006).

district magistrate and the Union home ministry, who argued that the safety of the unwanted pillars had become a matter of concern for national security (Pradhan 2002b).

5. *Organising ritual failure from outside: the secular government's fear of violence*

According to the quotation at the beginning from the VHP's international secretary, Praveen Togadia, the *shila puja* did *not* fail. Quite to the contrary, he proposed that it marked the triumph of the Hindutva forces over secularism because the fact that the ritual was performed proved that the government had in principle accepted the VHP's demand, and right, to start temple construction.

The government, however, did not share this view. In this passage, I explore the means used by the state apparatus to let the ritual fail *as much as possible* [sic.] but not *completely*. The underlining intention of 'portioned' or controlled failure was to restrict ritual performance to such an extent that a major public conflict with the Hindutva forces as well as a feared outbreak of communal violence could be avoided. Unlike the 1989 rituals, when the BJP supported the Ram temple movement from the opposition, the BJP was now in the government, bent by loyalties towards its coalition allies and bound by its promise to put the Ram issue on the backburner.

We shall see that several strategies were employed to minimise the *shila puja* to quasi-invisibility, and put pressure on its conduct from various sides. But its complete failure was to be prevented for various reasons. First, the Prime Minister's office did not want to alienate the VHP since it was an ally of the Sangh Parivar and an important partner in terms of election campaigning. Secondly, because it was feared that in the light of the pogroms simultaneously taking place in the aftermath of the Godhra carnage in Gujarat, violence could further spread throughout the country if the VHP leaders wanted to make the failed ritual an issue to blackmail the government.[13] The intention was to reduce all participation in the ritual to such an extent that the ritual would fail

[13] The pogroms in Gujarat 2002 claimed the lives of 2,000–3,000 people, mostly Muslims, leaving 250,000 people homeless, many of whom still do not dare to return to their home villages due to threats by Hindu Right organisations. The VHP, arguing that the train was set afire by a Muslim mob, interpreted (and to some extent physically and financially supported) the violence as just 'revenge' by the Hindu people.

to create a 'wave' of support. This way it was hoped that the ritual would fail on its own.

We now move from the inner circle of ritual specialists and critics to the external forces that challenged the VHP, the central government of India, legislature and police forces. The individual and collective agents that played an important role in orchestrating the 'right' balance for a successful ritual failure were: the Prime Minister's Office, the Supreme Court, police and military forces, and a crisis management committee set up to negotiate between VHP spokespeople and the government.

6. *The Prime Minister's office*

In 2002 the Indian government was led by the BJP, sharing however, power with partners of the large coalition of the National Democratic Alliance since 1998. The more orthodox and radical affiliates of the Hindu Right had become disappointed and felt betrayed: the BJP had deleted its promise to build a Ram temple from its election manifesto, and despite a few public announcements by senior BJP leaders that the Hindu sentiment will be appeased and the Ram temple built if consensus is created, nothing much had happened that promised to bring fresh wind into the VHP's sails en route to Ayodhya. Despite his close proximity to the Sangh, particularly the RSS, since his teenage days, then Prime Minister A.B. Vajpayee was in favour of shifting all decision-making responsibilities with respect to the temple construction to the Supreme Court. He declared his full support of the court's most recent decision that no religious ceremony may be performed on the disputed and the undisputed site. Praveen Togadia argued that by ordering that the foundation stone was to be received by a government employee, the government had already given in and "endorsed the plan for the construction of a temple". Vajpayee announced that he rejected any such statement that the government's permit to perform the *shila daan* was a symbolic climbdown and a 'recognition in principle' of the construction of the temple at the disputed site: "He clarified that he had given no assurance to the VHP on any date of commencement of temple construction.... followed the rule of law strictly and at the same time, respected the sentiments of people" (Ansari 2002). Vajpayee and his ministerial office at South Block emphasised that the "Ayodhya issue could be resolved either through a mutual agreement between the parties to the dispute or a judicial verdict".[14] Ritual, however, was not acknowledged as an adequate means for creating mutual consent.

7. *Legal means of making ritual failure: court, bans and legal codes*

Legislature also contributed to the creation of ritual imbalance and failure. The Supreme Court's decision to impose territorial and thus performative restrictions on the *shila* offering just two days before the ritual was to take place invited its failure because firstly, the final ceremony was to take place on the ground where the Ram temple was proposed to stand, and secondly the verdict eliminated any space for public participation and thus recognition. But Hindutva rituals are explicitly public events. In that they differ, for example, from such temple rituals which require no witnesses but simply the presence of priests and deity in order to be tentatively successful.

The Supreme Court had declared the whole plot on which the Babri Mosque once stood as disputed and banned the performance of *puja* exceeding a specific number of people. The interim order passed on March 13, 2002, declared that, "no religious activity of any kind by anyone either symbolic or actual including 'bhumi puja' or 'shila puja', shall be permitted or allowed to take place" on the almost 70,000 acres of land acquired by the central government in 1993 (Venkatesan 2002a).[15] Furthermore, Section 144 of the Indian Penal Code came into force, which states that not more than four people can assemble in public without causing offence. By means of the court verdict, even the undisputed site had now been turned into a disputed site.[16]

---

[14] "We will implement court order: PM". In: *The Hindu*, 15/Mar/2002.

[15] Land described in the Schedule to the Acquisition of Certain Areas at Ayodhya Act, 1993. The modified text as of 13/Mar/2002 reads: "no religious activity of any kind by anyone, either symbolic or actual, including bhoomi puja or shila puja shall be permitted or allowed to take order". See "SC clarifies Ayodhya order". In: *The Tribune*, 15/Mar/2002, Venkatesan 2002a and b. One argument by Attorney General Sorabjee was that "there were 14 temples in the acquired land where 'puja' was going on...for years which should not be stopped under the court orders" (Venkatesan 2002b).

[16] "We will implement court order: PM". In: *The Hindu*, 15/Mar/2002. Even the Supreme Court's stand was accompanied by internal differences. Following the court verdict on the denial of access to the site, Attorney General Soli Sorabjee from the Supreme Court ordered that at least a temporary and 'symbolic' *puja* could be performed on the undisputed site (*The Tribune*, 14/Mar/2002) and asked for a permit to perform a

On the other hand, the VHP had identified plots of land belonging to the Ramjanmabhoomi Nyas (c. 43 acres) that had been acquired by them before being taken over by the government, and now demanded this land to be returned so that temple construction could begin (Noorani 2002b). It rejected the fact that government land must be used for a 'public purpose' only, and not in a way that favours just one party, such as the VHP. After 1993, it was decided that the land should be made available to two trusts, one acting for a temple, one for a mosque as well as for the planned development of the area (Noorani 2002a). However, since the Supreme Court could not come to a decision, the status quo had to be maintained.

Even a ban on a religious procession or ritual performance does not necessarily mean that the event as such runs the risk of failing completely. In some cases, a legal ban imposed on a ritual could in fact become handy for the reinterpretation of the ritual as a passion-play of Hindu martyrdom. Furthermore, Hindutva leaders defined the legal restriction as a sign of 'success' because the government, so the allegation, therewith acknowledged and, undemocratically, censored its power.[17] Imposition of a ban can also cause an event's success in that it therewith becomes a focus of media attention, and where new modes of agency, and face-saving, can be staged, such as the threat of suicide by leaders or the breaking of the ban by performing a ritual, followed by the leaders courting arrest. A journalist of the weekly *Frontline* reports that the ban on the *shila puja* produced a successful failure, for at times, "mediapersons outnumbered VHP members... The drama was a well-orchestrated one... The different faces of the Sangh Parivar acted out their roles. Despite the arrests, their mission was accomplished. They were able to grab centrestage. The level of Hindutva hysteria was raised" (Bunsha 2002). In this context, the risk of possible failure of the ritual by not taking place due to the legal ban imposed on it provoked a shift initiated by the performers. They threatened to reject the ban, and to embrace arrest and imprisonment, which, in one step, would

three hour symbolic *puja* with adequate conditions and restrictions (Venkatesan 2002b). The suggestion was debated but finally laid aside.

[17] Yatras, particularly with respect to their role as supporters of election campaigns, have frequently been banned before. The latest ban imposed by the Election Commission of India was on the VHP's Vijay Yatra in Gujarat, where a week before the Assembly Elections, and just a few months after the Gujarat riots, the VHP wanted to stage a procession commemorating the 10th anniversary of the demolition of the Babri Mosque (see Bunsha 2002).

invite—at least among sympathizing audiences—a heroic reputation, and, in another step, strategically pull the ritual out of the dilemma of having failed before it even started by catching the attention of the media through dramatic performance and public attention.

The ritual of confrontation has a two-folded kind of failure implanted in its structure: either the performers and their ritual could fail, in this case because of the Supreme Court's decision. Or the performers manage to redirect the potential failure of the ritual by questioning the Supreme Court's legitimacy as a secular institution and blaming it for being biased by preventing 'true Hindus' to perform 'simple' religious rituals. This tendency to shape narratives of martyrdom in such a case becomes evident in the following example.

8. *Security forces and arrests*

The potential of imposing but also of breaking a ban and courting arrest as a means of creating dramatic plots of martyrdom has been mentioned above. Another strategy of paving the ground for ritual failure by means of external agents was developed on the level of security through state organs, such as the police and special army forces:[18] the Rapid Action Force as well as the Central Reserve Police Force. The aim was to diminish the VHP ritual's influence in the public domain by physically controlling and preventing *kar sevaks* (voluntary workers) from reaching the ritual performance site and making it a 'successful mass event' by the sheer presence of supporters.

The government suspended long-distance bus services as well as trains travelling through the nearby city of Faizabad. As early as March 12, 8,500 security personnel were positioned in Ayodhya. And access to the holy city by both individuals as well as groups was restricted, so that at the eve of the scheduled ritual hardly more than 500 people had reached it (as opposed to the thousands that were announced by the VHP). An estimated number of 35,000 people was arrested across the country to prevent them from participating in the ritual, and, most of all, stir up new violence between Hindus and Muslims *en route* to Ayodhya or on their way back home.[19] Previously, particularly in 1990, in the context

---

[18] By March 14, for instance, 10,000 Central Reserve Police Force, and 2,000 policemen were stationed in Ayodhya (Mody 2002b).

[19] BBC World "Ayodhya Hindus march peacefully", 15/Mar/2002. The BBC reported that the largest number of arrests (19,000) were made in Madhya Pradesh,

of the Ram Rath Yatra (Chariot Procession of Lord Ram) under the auspices of the BJP party president LK Advani, the government of Uttar Pradesh had enforced similar strategies of restriction of participation in politico-religious processions in and to Ayodhya, and thus caused the failure of the ritual becoming a symbol for a mass movement. Related to this is a range of narratives on the heroic martyrdom of those *kar sevaks* who gave their lives for the successful completion of the ritual (see Brosius 2005: chapter 6).

The presence of security forces put the town into a curfew-like situation. Day by day more security companies arrived, criss-crossing the city, demonstrating their presence even in small lanes. Interestingly, VHP leaders re-interpreted the presence of security forces, the control and arrests of *kar sevaks*: they were there *not* because the Bajrang Dal was dangerous but because it was feared that, especially after the September 11 events, Muslim terrorists could enter the town "in the guise of *kar sevaks*".[20] Again, ritual failure surfaces as a complex notion filled with manifold meaning, where interpretations go as far as involving ethno-political conspiracy theories and the strategy of rumour in order to trip up sensation and tension in the participants.

We can see that the question of ritual failure has to be approached from various sides, all of them negotiating and contesting their positions in and through the ritual performance. What requires highlighting here, however, is the seemingly paradoxical fact that even in the light of its failure, the ritual can nevertheless be 'successful'. Thus, to modify Platvoet here, rituals of confrontation are carefully negotiated and often results of compromises *because* of the in-built creativity and agency of ritual failure.

9. *(Mis)managing ritual shifts and face-saving: organisers and speakers*

The Supreme Court's decision became a key factor in the risk that the pillar offering ritual could fail as such due to external conditions. I have already referred to aspects of internal critique that threatened

c. 10,000 were picked up in Mumbai, and 'failure' of staging the ritual successfully was also aided by authorities banning "phone text messaging to prevent rumour-mongering", one of the most dangerous and effective means of creating violence. Praveen Togadia's response to the arrests and restrictions was that the government terrorised pilgrims and people (Singh & Sahay 2002).

[20] "Curfew-like situation in Ayodhya". In: *The Tribune*. Chandigarh, 15/Mar/2002.

the ritual with a loss of credibility even before it was conducted, and then, ultimately, with the refusal to accept the offered centre-piece of the ritual. In this section, the course of the ritual performance shall be explored insofar as its form and means came to be constantly negotiated and improvised anew in order to save it from failing.

To introduce yet another perspective on ritual failure and the agency and agents related to it, the key focus of this section is the organisers and speakers of the VHP ritual. Attention shall be on the notion of 'impression management' (a term developed by Erwin Goffman in his concept of social drama, arguing that individual agents seek to consciously shape their appearance, as if on stage), or rather 'mis-management'. At centre-stage is one particular politico-religious agent and the ways in and through which he attempted to use and shape ritual performance in order to install himself as a major player in the Ram temple movement. At stake here is a different kind of risky failure, that of the emergence or decrease of personal competence and intentionality (see Schieffelin 1996: 62). But the agency surfacing here also has to be seen as an attempt to re-establish the disturbed order that was imposed on the larger frame of ritual conduct as it was re-shaped by the external forces and decisions mentioned above.

In this context I want to introduce the term 'structured improvisation' because even though they are shaped on the formula of previous religio-political rituals or fragments, Hindutva rituals generally lack firm rules that are based on religious texts or formulae.[21] These rituals are more theatrical and performative in that they change gear, direction and develop their momentum *in statu procedenti*, reacting to sudden events from both within and without (see Köpping 2004).

The original plan of the VHP leaders and associated religious agents was to perform a procession through Ayodhya and finally conduct *shila puja* by offering the pillars at the disputed site itself. This was to mark the (second) foundation stone laying ceremony and the much-awaited and talked about beginning of temple construction. After the court

[21] With respect to the form and choreography of the pillar offering ritual, standard elements of Hindu rituals were used: there was a procession of religious leaders and supporters led by the pillars that had been loaded onto a wagon; participants sung vedic hymns, and fire ritual was offered at the *puja*. In the introductory quote of this article, reference is even made to Paramhans moving to the makeshift temple at the disputed site in order to take *darshan* (*darshan lena*), that is, to be seen and blessed by Ram's eyes.

decision, this was ruled out, not because the VHP follows orders given by a secular court, but because its leaders felt that breaking the law this time would not increase its power (despite frequent announcements by VHP speakers that they were ready to break the law). This was already seen as a major climb-down by orthodox Hindutva supporters. But pragmatics felt that only compromise could save their face, and the ritual from failing and vanishing into invisibility.

At times, all differences between *shila puja* and *shila daan* are erased while in other instances, a vital difference between the two is underlined in debates about the event. What seems to be a rhetorical gimmick, and in fact might not even be more than that for the VHP leaders, is to me an interesting facet of ritual dynamics. Since the terms *puja* and *daan* are used, value is negotiated, quite like in the above-mentioned case of the *shilanyas* (sanctified bricks) that were rejected by the Mahants of Ayodhya Akharas because an inappropriate attitude or a lack of ritual commitment 'de-sanctified' and transformed them into kitchen utensils or objects to be dumped in the gutter. One day after the Supreme Court decision, the General secretary of the VHP, Ashok Singhal, announced that the much-hyped plan of conducting a 'symbolic *shila puja*' at the disputed site in Ayodhya had been changed. Ramchandra Das Paramhans, religious leader, chairman of the Ramjanmabhoomi Nyas and well-known Hindutva supporter who was to conduct the *puja* at the site, proposed a *shila daan* performance (offering of the pillar) instead. This has been widely perceived as a 'climbdown'. Why? Paramhans insisted that there was no difference between a *shila puja* and *shila daan*, "because a lot of things were offered to Lord Ram". However, his announcement indicates that the authority and authenticity of the ritual were about to run the danger of being transposed from the status of a 'purely religious' to that of a secular and almost bureaucratic performance, because the recipient of the offering was not Lord Ram but the Kshatriya Singh, representative of the Prime Minister's office. While *puja* often implies the affirmation of the divine recipient as well as the devotee's desire to be blessed by the deity, those points of reference changed their meaning and significance in the case of a government employee. The de-auratisation of the ritual through the transfer of significant and significance was further increased by the fact that a formal receipt was handed over to Paramhans for the offering by recipient Singh. Through this bureaucratic act, the VHP was pulled off its own symbolic territory and onto that of the secular government, which, in some supporters' eyes, signified the movement's climbdown instead of the beginning of a new phase in Hindu history.

Both Köpping (2004) and Schieffelin (1996) elucidate the theatrical aspects of ritual performances as well as the importance of agents to position themselves as competent players on the field. However, as Schieffelin further argues: the "structure of the enactment is inherently subject to the contingencies of the enactment itself" (1996: 61). This shall be further elucidated by analysis of the performance dynamics as they rapidly changed in the course of action, criss-crossing, or rather balancing, between failure and success. Paramhans's performance was seen as a 'second climbdown'; he was blamed for making concession after concession, and some supporters were forced to accuse Paramhans of performing a theatre play instead of a ritual performance. What caused Paramhans to make 'mistakes' that must not be made and invite participants' protest?

The confrontation between the VHP and the government administration and legislature had almost brought the ritual to an end before it could even start. Without an actual site at which to perform the ritual, and with diminished support due to critique both from religious experts as well as laymen, in the last minute the VHP leaders came up with an alternative strategy in order to prevent complete failure of the already doomed ritual. They threw in one of the most respected religious speakers and hardliners of the Ram temple movement, Ramchandra Das Paramhans, head of the Digambar Akhara, president of the Ramjanmabhoomi Trust and a strong VHP ally. A day before the announced ritual was to take place, the old man, who had been involved in the temple movement for almost 20 years, appeared at a press conference. He announced that he would end his tenure on planet earth (*jeewan leela*, lit. game of life), that is, he would commit suicide, if he was denied the possibility to perform the ritual at the site of his choice and reach his final aim, the reconstruction of the Ram temple (Muralidharan 2002a). He told media persons that it was the birth right of every Hindu to perform rituals, and threatened that if he failed to perform it, for instance because he was stopped by the police, "then I will consume chemical [sic.] and sacrifice my life for the sake of Lord Ram and construction of Ram temple" (Satyanaranayan 2002).

This was a strategically clever move to heighten drama and shift responsibilities into the government's court, and it is almost certain that the threat of a religious authority to commit suicide would have created a wave of sympathy for the VHP. No one could say whether Paramhans was serious about taking his life or whether he was blackmailing the government by staging this martyrdom drama. The threat was furthermore a good move because it pointed the media's attention to the ritual's agenda. The attempt to slow down the ritual's downfall succeeded: a whole range of political and religious agents rushed to visit or call upon the Mahant to change his mind, the titular Raja (king) of Ayodhya—who tried to persuade the suicide candidate to withdraw from his decision—recalls desperate phone calls from senior BJP leaders such as Home Minister L.K. Advani (one of the procession heroes of the early years of campaigning for the Ram temple, and a Hindutva hardliner) or Uma Bharati, another leading and fiery speaker of the Ayodhya campaign. The Prime Minister, however, kept silent, for he tried to present himself as neutral (see Muralidharan 2002a).

Finally, a crisis management team was installed, made up of state government speakers, and an agreement was found: Paramhans offered to perform the ritual in Ram Kot Mohalla, a site close to the acquired land, instead of the disputed territory. In his view, this move was justified because the location was sacred; according to the legend, it was the village in which Ram was born. The government was in favour of this suggestion and tensions seemed to be reduced. It was hoped that from this point onwards, the ritual performance would move peacefully and be concluded with little attention and attraction. Nevertheless, surprises from VHP hardliners like Ashok Singhal and Vinay Katiyar were still expected until the last moment. And in fact, underlying the ritual dynamics of many public Hindutva performances was the subtle or open threat of leaders that violence would take over in case their claims were not respected. Government forces were thus constantly worried that the situation could get out of hand if Singhal and Katiyar called upon the *kar sevaks* to save the movement's and the Hindu nation's honour.

The chain of changes in the ritual programme did not end. The second climbdown, or—depending on the perspective—step towards the failure of Paramhans's credibility occurred when Paramhans communicated his 'vision'. By then, the procession had already begun its march to Ram Kot. It was fronted by a decorated cart carrying the carved pillars and followed by *sants* and participants chanting vedic hymns and "Jai Shri Ram" (Victory to Lord Ram).[22] Only a group

---

[22] "Paramhans switches venues, *shila daan* complete". In: *Rediff.com news*, 15/Mar/

of about 300 supporters followed the religious and VHP leaders (as opposed to the thousands previously announced). On the way, and passing Paramhans's *akhara*, the crowd learnt that the Mahant all of a sudden "had the vision that he should perform his ritual obeisance to the stones at his own institution" (Muralidharan 2002a). Up to that moment, the plan for the ritual performance had been that he would perform a *puja* with fire ritual (*homa*) at his *akhara* before continuing, with the pillars, to Ram Kot, where the *shila daan* was planned to be executed, a site defined as 'under ban' by the Supreme Court (Pradhan 2002a). Questioning the 'authenticity' of the vision, other sources refer to speculations that his move was intended to stage the ritual under the eyes of media persons and *kar sevaks* at the grounds of the *akhara*. In public, and thus also in Ram Kot, Section 144 of the Indian Penal Code would have applied: not more than a handful of people could have attended this ritual.[23] Frightened of the crowds getting out of control and perhaps deciding to storm the fortified disputed site if the march continued to Ram Kot and the exclusive manner of the final performance became public, the crisis management team gave in to this seemingly moody announcement of the religious leader and allowed the performance of the ritual on the premises of his *akhara*. And considering the VHP's and Paramhans's perspective, the latter's 'vision' could have just been an excuse to prevent the ritual from failing (without giving in to government restrictions): had the procession continued its march to Ram Kot, it could have been stopped altogether by security forces due to the Supreme Court's verdict.

Besides the rhetoric of vision, blackmailing, so it seems, was alleged to have saved the ritual, and thus the movement, from failing. For example: Katiyar, one of the founders of the VHP's militant youth foresaw the possibility of losing control over his own people who, angry and worried that the ritual might fail, would try to enter and take over the disputed site with the makeshift temple. Indeed, the VHP's youth wing, the Bajrang Dal[24] is well-known for its aggressive dedication to

2002 (http://www.rediff.com/news/2002/mar/15ayo12.htm); date of last access: 17/08/2006.

[23] "Paramhans switches venues, *shila daan* complete". In: *Rediff.com news*, 15/Mar/2002 (http://www.rediff.com/news/2002/mar/15ayo12.htm); date of last access: 17/08/2006.

[24] 'Hanuman's organisation'; Hanuman, divine leader of the monkeys, is commonly referred to as Lord Ram's most dedicated devotee.

'solving problems' by main force and symbolical threat, be it in the context of the Ram temple movement or the Gujarat pogroms of 2002. Disappointed *kar sevaks*, possibly already disillusioned by the low-key atmosphere of the event (some of whom may have travelled from as far as Karnataka or Tamil Nadu, fired by indoctrination etc.) and then prevented from participating, were feared to stage their own protests—a result of failure of negotiations, and 'proper', that is, charismatic and competent conduct of the ritual.

Why did Katiyar propose unlimited anger of 'his' people in this case? Negotiations with the government had reached a point where the VHP was allowed to perform the ritual at Ram Kot, but only with a small number of participants (Section 144). This, however, was not in the VHP leaders' interest. For them, the ritual would fail if no larger audience could attend and give evidence to the legitimacy of their claim. And the *shila* ritual was also a 'test' of its popularity and support among various groups within Indian (Hindu) society.

A whole net of activities dedicated to prevent the *shila puja* from failing was spun in VHP leader's rhetoric, covering the national territory and involving a whole range of other rituals and strategies (including civil war) through which the 'imagined nation' of Hindus could be visualised. As stated above, the VHP is an organisation of threats and blackmail, and a speaker such as Praveen Togadia repeatedly called for a 'civil war' if the Muslims would not begin to behave like 'proper Indians', that is for instance, to pay devotion to Mother India and Lord Ram. Underlining the call, he furthermore stated that the VHP had the facilities to lead such a war, and that it was high time that the Hindu people came out openly on the streets and defend their honour. Thus, do we need to see the prospect of ritual failure, at least in some cases, as a force uniting those who are fragmented? It was in this light that he made the following announcement, carrying a similar pathos as Paramhans's statements: "If one *sant* was arrested or a shot was fired in Ayodhya tomorrow, it would be treated as the announcement of the beginning of a mass agitation throughout the country".[25] Support for the *shila puja* was also claimed by announcing that "the Parishad would stage protest *dharnas* [sit-ins, the author] all over the country on March 16 in case the saints were stopped from performing puja and

[25] Satyanarayanan 2002; see also *The Tribune News Service*, 14/Mar/2002.

arrested."[26] Togadia also announced that *sants* would select an auspicious time for the VHP leaders who wanted to 'fast-unto-death' if the ritual failed due to external hindrances. Ram devotees all over India would chant 'Ram Ram' at exactly 2.15 p.m., when the procession in Ayodhya started, to well-wish the whole performance.[27] Whether or not those nation-wide symbols of ritual support really took place has to be doubted. Their announcement rather has to be understood as a rhetorical safety-net, created to erase possible doubts about ritual failure. It is important to point out that at this stage such messages were also addressed to potential supporters who it was feared had ceased to believe in the ritual's success due to its announced ban. The last section of the paper shows that such fears were not too far-fetched, and support was indeed decreasing. But the reasons for this lie elsewhere.

10. *Ritual failure as incompetence: angry crowds and face-saving leaders*

Despite all the leaders' attempts to sell the *shila puja* as a great success, they failed to convince and create ritual commitment among the participants at the site. Instead, the performance was predominantly perceived as a 'theatre', 'fooling' the participants. In this context, it is important to consider Köpping's claim that the distinctions between 'acting' and ritual performance are often defined by the audience or participants:

> The effectiveness of the performance of a ritual is thus closely connected with the 'acting' skills of performers who determine the recipient's judgement of quality. [...] All must perceive that what is going on in a particular domain of social action is 'ritual', and thus has the iconic quality of a collectively shared imagery about the frame, nonwithstanding the

[26] "Don't stop shila puja, warns VHP". *Rediff.com news*, 14/Mar/2002 (http://www.rediff.com/news/2002/mar/14ayo15.htm); date of last access: 17/08/2006.

[27] "Hand over disputed land: VHP". *The Hindu*, 15/Mar/2002. Media reports narrate the following incidents: "Hundreds of Vishwa Hindu Parishad activists on Friday performed an *aarti* at the organisation's state headquarters at Paldi in Ahmedabad praying for the success of the *shila daan* programme in Ayodhya" (*Rediff.com*, 15/Mar/2002 [http://www.rediff.com/news/2002/mar/15ayo11.htm]; date of last access: 17/08/2006), and "The Vishwa Hindu Parishad and its militant arm, the Bajrang Dal, on Friday launched multiple programmes in Gujarat to coincide with the *shila dan* in Ayodhya. The programmes would include chanting of mantras and religious assemblies all over the state. [...] In Godhra, where over 50 kar sevaks returning from the disputed site in Ayodhya were set ablaze in a railway bogie by a mob, Hindus would congregate at the Ram Lalla temple for a prayer session" (*ibid.*).

> fact that the ritual action is performative in terms of being meticulously staged, prepared, rehearsed, with rules which are followed (and negotiated). But the performativity lies in the very fact that the staging has to be competent in order [for the ritual, the author] to be effective [...] (Köpping 2004: 101–2).

To use Schieffelin's words: the ritual failed to "create and make present realities" (Schieffelin 1996: 59). The agency of leaders such as Paramhans was perceived to be based on "bad impression management, strategic manoeuvre and improvisation" (*ibid.*: 61).

The supporters of the march, both *sadhus* and *kar sevaks*, saw the change of ritual venue as a sign of weakness from the VHP leaders. Many had apparently expected that the *shila puja* was another means of finally appropriating the disputed site, even by physical force. Thus, to them the 'ending' of the ritual at the grounds of Paramhans's *akhara* almost looked like betrayal and capitulation. It was now to the leaders to implement face-saving manoeuvres. As the crowds started shouting at Singhal and Paramhans, the two leaders, embarrassed by the loud protests, asked the police present at the site to evacuate witnessing media persons and shouting *sadhus*, at the same time appealing to the angry participants to calm down. One of the removed *sadhus* complained to the press that, once cherished as a supporter, he was now being humiliated by being pushed out off the *akhara's* premises. The *sadhu* termed Singhal as a 'contractor of religion',[28] whereas another Mahant from Faizabad called Singhal and Paramhans traitors of the *sant samaj*, abusing both holy men and *kar sevaks* for their meagre game: "If this was the drama that he [Paramhans] was going to stage, then what was the need to put the entire population of Ayodhya under so much misery and what was the need to have so many sadhus here?" (Pradhan 2002a).

Singhal and Paramhans were thus accused for lacking a sincere interest in the performance of a proper ritual and being more focused on power politics, at the cost of participants and the risk of losing their authority. While both returned the ball into the audience's court by arguing that it had been a conscious choice to reduce crowds and change the performative language and itinerary in order to 'tame' the angry crowds. Tentatively, the failure of the 'full-fledged' ritual was legitimised by emphasising the 'mob's' anarchic structure. Further

[28] The *sadhu* is named as Mahant Ram Das of Hanuman Garhi. See Pradhan 2002a.

face-saving was dramatised, for example, when Togadia, at a press conference, told media persons that the shift of venue had been decided instantly to prevent the crowds becoming 'unmanageable', "because of the sudden turnout of so many *karsevaks* and other local people". In the light of the low turnout of participants both from outside Ayodhya as well as the vicinity, and the fact that the VHP is otherwise not too concerned about such issues, this statement is a cheap excuse. And Bajrang Dal leader Vinay Katiyar added that the VHP feared the presence of 'zealous activists' whose violent behaviour might cause disgrace and embarrassment fort he entire movement, clearly referring to the defence strategies played out by BJP and VHP speakers after the demolition of the Babri Mosque. Then, the Sangh had also tried to shift responsibilities to a few scapegoats instead of taking responsibility for the fact that the demolition had been carefully organised (see Pradhan 2002a). Paramhans too tried to re-interpret the lack of mass support as 'intended', as he told media persons at a press conference in Ayodhya a day after the ritual had come to an end: "I abided by the Supreme Court's decision. I saved the Government's *lajja* [honour, the author]. [...] There could have been bloodshed, had I gone ahead with my plan of donating the 'shila' near the acquired land. That is why I dispersed the kar sevaks who had come along with me."[29]

What is interesting though is that apparently even the face-lifting strategies of the VHP leaders in order to regain their standing with the disappointed cadres failed to appeal to the constituencies they claimed to represent. This, one would assume, must have been a disillusioning experience for the ritual organisers, because it showed that the issues on which mobilization was sought did not work anymore, and that only a few full-fledged supporters from within the disciplined cadre structure of the Sangh Parivar had remained faithful.

Despite all the efforts of face-saving, senior VHP functionaries assembled at a two-day-meeting at Karsevakpuram in Ayodhya just four days after the *shila puja*. Their aim was to "review the Ram temple agitation and chalk out the future course of action".[30] This, of course, does not mean that possible failure was publicly acknowledged. Instead of acknowledging failure, the VHP announced another, even bigger,

---

29 "Ayodhya security curbs to be eased". In: *The Hindu*, 17/Mar/2002: front page.
30 "VHP to review Ram temple movement at two-day meet". In: *Rediff.com news*, 19/Mar/2002 (http://www.rediff.com/news/2002/mar/19ayo4.htm; date of last access: 17/08/2006).

mass movement to occur in June 2002: by then, so the message to the government, the courts will have to have reached a decision.[31]

11. *Concluding notes*

Our exploration of the success and failure of ritual drew upon different levels of relatedness and perspectivity. On one level, the territorial rituals performed by the VHP are clearly a means of confrontation, putting pressure on and negotiating particular 'hot issues' with the government. In that sense, they can fail when the aim is not reached, and the government or another secular institution remains the key player setting the rules for the performance. However, we have also seen that the rules are constantly shifted and played out anew before and during the process of the ritual's performance, and that both sides play with the notion and the risk of failure. This is also due to the government's fear that things might get out of control once the ritual is doomed to failure, and would lead to ethno-politically motivated violence. Furthermore, crisis management agents can intervene in limited ways, and often they have to be prepared to step back from former agreements and succumb to a new situation that emerges in *statu procedenti*, as was the case in the act of shifting the ritual from Ram Kot to Paramhans's *akhara*.

On yet another level, it became evident that individual players also contributed to the diminished success of performing a ritual like the foundation stone laying ceremony: by refraining from attending the ritual ceremony, and demonstratively attending other festivities, religious specialists withdrew charismatic power from the organizers and indicated the heterogeneity and lack of consensus within the purportedly solidary 'mass movement'. In such an incident, new players, previously not very involved in the conducting of a ritual, like Paramhans, could move in and define their own rules in order to save the ritual as well as their reputation as competent religious leaders. Other agents can articulate their critique of the sincerity of a ritual, as the case of Jaganath's

---

[31] This follows a proclamation issued by the Lucknow Bench of the Allahabad High Court that 'evidence' will be collected and recorded with respect to the question of whether a temple once stood at the site of the demolished Babri Mosque, and a commission has been assigned to do so. The VHP stated that if the findings would be against the 'Hindu claim' that there was a temple, thus continuing to 'hurt the Hindu sentiment'; the religious leaders of the VHP would come up with another row of ritual events in protest.

accusation of the VHP's irreligious, business-oriented motivations has demonstrated. Further harm to the credibility of the foundation laying ceremony was done by the reference to the ritual as a copy of an original, was something that must not be repeated for then both events lose their power: the foundation stone cannot be laid twice. In that case, ritual becomes a sheer rhetorical strategy.

On a third level, we could see that the prevention of supporters participating in the ritual by security measures to a decrease 'public presence' and efficacy, as much as the lack of support by local communities or the failure to mobilise other audiences contributed to a lack of credibility in VHP leaders' claims to representation. In that case, the only solution for the ritual organisers and speakers seems to be 'saving face': coming up with arguments that despite the alleged 'failure' the ritual has had its intended effects and positive results. Ritual thus is a complex ecology of agents trying to push their interests and expectations onto centre stage. Failure can be unintended and intended, consciously brought into play as a means of putting pressure on another agent, who might have completely different reasons for wanting to prevent the ritual from failing such as maintaining public security.

On the level of in-group formation, for example, I argued that the ritual failed to create solidarity and identification, ritual commitment, and a notion of there being a 'real issue' or agenda. This became especially clear in the case of the pillars turning into an unwanted offering. On the external level, too, there were several climbdowns or 'mistakes' by VHP representatives and religious experts. However, to conclude that this equals a climbdown of the movement as such, would be dangerous. As much as ritual will remain an important strategy of confrontation in the context of the Hindutva movement, ritual failure will have to be considered in its complexity and multi-perspectivity.

References

Ansari, Javed M. 2002. "Court is the final authority, says PM". In: *The Hindu*, 17/Mar/2002: front page.

Brosius, Christiane 2005. *Empowering Visions. The Politics of Representation in Hindu Nationalism.* London: Anthem Press.

Bunsha, Dionne 2002. "Yatra Drama". In: *Frontline*, 23/Nov/2002–06/Dec/2002: 10–11.

Jaffrelot, Christophe 1993. *The Hindu Nationalist Movement in India.* London & New Delhi: Viking.

Katju, Manjari 2003. *Vishva Hindu Parishad and Indian Politics.* Hyderabad: Orient Longman.

Kaur, Naunidhi 2002. "Ambiguity as Strategy". In: *Frontline* 19(7), 30/Mar/2002–12/Apr/2002: 17–18.

Köpping, Klaus-Peter 2004. "Failure of Performance or Passage to the Acting Self? Mishima's Suicide between Ritual and Theatre". In: *The Dynamics of Changing Rituals. The Transformation of Religious Rituals within their Social and Cultural Context*, Kreinath, Jens & Constance Hartung & Annette Deschner (ed.). New York et al.: Peter Lang, 97–114.

Kritzman, Lawrence D. 1996. "In Remembrance of Things French". In: *Realms of Memory. Rethinking the French Past.* Vol. 1, Nora, Pierre (ed.). New York: Columbia University Press, ix–xiv.

Mody, Anjali 2002a. "Government keeps its fingers crossed as VHP plans 'shila daan'". In: *The Hindu*, 13/Mar/2002.

—— 2002b. "Security blanket over Ayodhya as VHP is firm on shila daan". In: *The Hindu*, 15/Mar/2002.

Muralidharan, Sukumar 2002a. "Temple Interrupted". In: *Frontline* 19(7), 30/Mar/2002–12/Apr/2002: 4–8.

—— 2002b. "Ayodhya Offensive". In: *Frontline* 19(4), 16/Feb/2002–01/Mar/2002.

—— 2003. "A new Phase of Adventurism". In: *Frontline* 20(15), 19/Jul/2002–01/Aug/2002.

Noorani, A.G. 2002a. "Land and legality". In: *Frontline* 19(4), 16/Feb/2002–01/Mar/2002: 14–16.

—— 2002b. "The Supreme Court's Intervention". In: *Frontline* 19(7), 30/Mar/2002–12/Apr/2002: 9–12.

Platvoet, Jan G. 2004. "Ritual as War. On the Need to De-Westernize the Concept". In: *The Dynamics of Changing Rituals. The Transformation of Religious Rituals within Their Social and Cultural Context*, Kreinath, Jens & Constance Hartung & Annette Deschner (ed.) New York: Peter Lang Publishing (Toronto Studies in Religion 29), 243–266.

Pradhan, Sharat 2002a. "Singhal, Paramhans booed by karsevaks". In: *Rediff.com news*, 15/Mar/2002. URL: http://www.rediff.com/news/2002/mar/15ayo19.htm; date of last access: 17/08/2006.

—— 2002b. "Shilas deposited with government treasury". In: *Rediff.com news*, 27/Mar/2002. URL: http://www.rediff.com/news/2002/mar/27ayo.htm; date of last access: 17/08/2006.

Satyanarayanan, S. 2002. "Paramhans threatens to end life". In: *The Tribune*, 15/Mar/2002.

Schieffelin, Edward L. 1996. "On Failure and Performance. Throwing the Medium Out of the Séance". In: *The Performance of Healing*, Laderman, Carol & Marina Roseman (ed.). New York & London: Routledge, 59–89.

Singh, Onkar & Tara Shankar Sahay 2002. "Lift ban on pilgrims travelling to Ayodhya: VHP". *Rediff.com news*, 16/Mar/2002. URL: http://www.rediff.com/news/2002/mar/16ayo1.htm; date of last access: 17/08/2006.

Van der Veer, Peter 1987. "God must be liberated. A Hindu Liberation Movement in Ayodhya". *Modern Asian Studies* 21.2: 283–303.

—— 1994. *Religious Nationalism. Hindus and Muslims in India.* Berkeley & Los Angeles & London: University of California Press.

Venkatesan, J. 2002a. "Order encompasses entire acquired land, clarifies SC". In: *The Hindu*, 15/Mar/2002.

—— 2002b. "Supreme Court says 'no' to puja, orders status quo". In: *The Hindu*, 14/Mar/2002.

FAILURE OF RITUAL REINVENTION? EFFICACIOUS NEW RITUALS AMONG TAIWAN'S ABORIGINES UNDER THE IMPACT OF RELIGIOUS CONVERSION AND COMPETITION BETWEEN ELITES

Michael Rudolph

1. *Introduction*

Theoretical reflections on the reasons for ritual failure suggest that the rejection of a certain ritual or ritual element as false or mistaken is often due to the perception that ritual efficacy is endangered—a perception that may be evoked by the violation of ritual rules or by incompetent performance.[1] My contribution on the failure of a reinvented efficacious ritual among Taiwan's Aborigines shows however that such criteria cannot always serve as a satisfactory explanation of why certain ritual traditions are rejected while others are not: competing value systems and competition between elites in globalizing and highly hybrid cultural contexts also seem to be decisive factors in the process of selection. Ritual architects who deliberately use aesthetical patterns inscribed into the cultural memory of a people to activate collective agencies should be aware that such icons—if loaded with certain historical experiences—can also assume the function of (warning) signals.

The context of my research is Taiwanese nativism since the beginning of the 1990s. As a part of its multicultural policy, Taiwan's government today officially welcomes and financially supports any kind of cultural revitalisation if it is only connected to the island's multifarious cultural heritage. The main aim of this policy is to cure and to readjust the negative results and shortcomings of the former homogenisation policy of the Chinese National Party (KMT) that tried to make Taiwan appear a part of China. Western-trained scholars and politicians hope that an increasing engagement of the people in their own traditional cultures may enhance the development of a feeling of 'unity in diversity', as well as a sense of responsibility for their country. Simultaneously, such a demonstration of diversity can of course also serve as a falsification

[1] Grimes 1988: 113; Schieffelin 1996; Schieffelin in the introduction to this volume.

of the claim that Taiwan is Chinese, not only in cultural terms, but in political terms as well.[2]

Encouraged by this general trend in cultural politics, which is closely connected to Taiwan's need for self-authentication, intellectuals and artists of Taiwan's so-far twelve recognized Aboriginal groups today compete with each other in their endeavours to revitalise their Malayo-Polynesian cultures in a modern cultural context. As Aborigines have been severely discriminated against for their 'backwardness' in past decades by Han people, this is sometimes not an easy task. In addition, most Aborigines have become Christians today. On the other hand, elements of the former religious beliefs and cultural traditions are still alive in the form of 'old superstitions' and habitualisations. In the age of culturalism and tourism, Aborigines today become increasingly aware that the 'excavation' and exhibition of these rudiments cannot only help one to regain one's own ethnic pride and confidence, but also has its usefulness in economic terms. Aboriginal languages may be named as a concrete example here: in order to be eligible for certain subsidies and privileges, Aborigines today must testify to their language ability in special examinations.[3] It is this interrelation of religious, cultural, political and economic aspects that has a deep impact on all kinds of cultural practice in Aboriginal society today. This can also been seen from the following account of ritual reinvention in Taroko society, an Aboriginal group that lives in the mountainous regions of Taiwan's East Coast and that had not been officially recognized as an independent ethnic group before the presidential elections in 2004.[4]

2. *The Taroko's reinvented rituals*

Since all rituals in Taroko society were once closely connected to the Taroko's ancestor gods-belief and certain traditions linked to this belief

[2] For a discussion of the origins, the functions, and the problems of Taiwan's new multiculturalism see Rudolph 2003b.

[3] This policy was been implemented in 2001. Since that year, Taiwanese school children in general have to choose one of Taiwan's native languages as an obligatory supplement. This includes Taiwan's 12 Austronesian languages as well as the two Chinese dialects mainly spoken on the island, i.e., Hoklo and Hakka. All children are free to choose whatever language they like.

[4] Anthropologically categorized as a dialect group of the Sedeq—one of the two subgroups of the Atayal—the Taroko number approx. 25,000 individuals. The two other dialect groups of the Sedeq are the Dooda and the Dekedaya who are not recognized yet and who live in close neighbourhood with the Taroko (Rudolph 2003a: 305f.).

such as tattooing and head hunting,[5] the practice of collective rituals had been strongly discouraged during Japanese colonial rule in Taiwan. After Japan's surrender in 1945, a collective return to the ancestor gods-belief seemed impossible because the original ritual groups who once worshipped common ancestor gods had been torn apart by the resettlements instituted by the Japanese. Furthermore, the rapid spread of Christianity hindered any open practice of rituals connected to the old religious beliefs: by the end of the sixties, most Taroko had become Christians. As a result the Taroko—similar to the Atayal—did not practice any collective rituals at all for a long time.

A sudden change occurred in 1999. With the financial support of local government bodies, a group of politicians and educational elites arranged a first collective and ritual transcending village level in a Taroko village near to Hualian on Taiwan's East Coast. As the organisers of the association emphasized, their so-called 'ancestor gods rituals' were supposed to serve as a model for all further activities of this kind. In their view, an overarching Taroko-identity could only be forged and consolidated with the help of a common ritual collectively celebrated at least once a year, a habit that could actually be observed in all other Aboriginal groups except from the Atayal and the Taroko. If the Taroko wanted to be recognised as an ethnic group independent from the Atayal with its own representatives and financial resources, they had to engage in a common culture.[6] The revitalised ritual itself was reconstructed with the help of oral accounts of the old people and with Japanese sources from the colonial period. As nobody could remember its original name anymore, even the Taroko term for the ritual had to be taken from Japanese sources.[7] The ritual's most salient characteristic was that sequences that originally would have lasted several days were now put together like in a 'speed up', melting it down to a one-hour event.[8] One of its central elements was the blood sacrifice before hunting: the throat of a chicken was carefully cut, and the blood of the still living animal was collected in a bowl. Meanwhile, the ritual leader whose role was played by a Christian minister sang hymn-like verses,

---

[5] Personal notes from 1994–96. See also the documentary of Qiu Ruolong of 1999 "GaYa".

[6] Manual of the ancestor gods' rituals 1999 in Wanrong, p. 1. Kaji-Cihung 2003: 11–12.

[7] I.e., from a book by the Japanese ethnologist Sayama Yukichi (1917).

[8] For instance, the sequence of the ritual hunting was left out and only commented by the moderator, while the scenes before and after it were performed.

addressing the *rutux*—a very general term for god in Taroko-language which could signify the ancient ancestor gods as well as the Christian god—in a multitude of ambiguous and confusing terms, like '*rutux* of all *rutux*', '*rutux* of all our ancestors' etc.[9] The same actor subsequently spread parts of this blood on the hunter's weapons and on the soil. According to the traditional belief, such blood contained supernatural power and ensured victory and success. Other sequences put on stage in the collective ancestor gods rituals were the killing of the prey as well as the thanksgiving sacrifice after hunting, which was conducted with parts of the prey. As the organizers of the ritual emphasized, one main idea was central to all of these sequences, i.e., the idea of the forefathers' close observation of the *gaya*—the organisational rules and norms of the Taroko that had once guaranteed discipline and solidarity in the Taroko tribes and whose ethical and spiritual value should—for the sake of ethnic survival—not be forgotten (interview with Unang-Kasaw 22.11.2002). The ritual described here was framed in a way typical for most collective rituals of Aborigines in Taiwan today: speeches by politicians and church ministers preceded the performance, and after its completion it was followed by collective games, competitions and dancing.

3. *Failure of ritual canonization*

Until 2001, the ancestor gods rituals was performed four times at collective festivals,[10] hereafter it was gradually replaced by other forms of collective rituals organized by Christian elites, for instance a head hunting ritual in one case or a wedding ritual in another.[11] Both latter

---

[9] While *rutux rodan* literally means 'ancestor gods', *rutux baraw* (*baraw* = highest) stands for 'the Christian god'.

[10] The first occasion was in May 1999 in Wanrong, the second on the eve of the new millennium in Xiulin, the third 2000 in Wenlan, and the fourth 2001 in Tongmen. As the Xiulin township administration decided to support only village-festivals instead of village-overarching festivals from 2001 on, the subsequent festivals were organized by individual villages whose inhabitants mostly opposed further enactments of the ancestor gods rituals.

[11] This does not mean that public blood sacrifices totally disappeared: political and educational elites kept on performing blood sacrifices in those events that were organized by them. However, they were not labelled 'collective rituals'. In 2002, two such events took place in the Taroko village Fushi at the entrance of the Taroko National Park, one on the occasion of a car race organised by Han and the other on the occasion of an international Marathon. If the rituals' original designation was the beseeding

performances had in common that they no longer contained any real blood sacrifices: while the paraphernalia used in the head hunting ritual consisted of plastic head and red paint, the animal sacrifice in the wedding ritual were simply skipped. As the church people contended, the main function of their rituals should be to remember the achievements of the ancestors.

A number of reasons must be named as responsible for the difficulties in canonising the ancestor gods rituals as the Taroko's main ritual, the most important ones being its incompatibility with Christianity on the one hand and competition between elites on the other. Though not practiced openly and collectively anymore until the end of the 1990s, the worship of ancestor gods had actually been quite popular within Taroko families all the time. Whenever things were suspected to be outside of the range of the Christian god's competence, or when the ancient gods' competence was considered to be stronger (as after certain kinds of social transgressions or in times of passage within people's lifecycle), people still adhered to the 'old superstitions', as they called them pejoratively. This is why sacrifices like those mentioned above were still frequently done before hunting, at weddings, after childbirth, or even after the purchase of a new car. After the enactment of the collective ancestor gods rituals, however, the organizers were each time confronted with profound criticism, particularly from the side of the more fervent adherents of Christianity who denounced the sacrifices in the ritual not only as 'misleading', but also as 'blasphemous' and even 'dangerous' acts that 'negligently provoked supernatural powers'.[12] Most suspicion was aroused by the 'instrumentalisation' of the church minister as a 'ritual leader': shortly after the first enactment of the ritual, a letter was circulated in PCT-circles in which the ritual and the minister's participation were severely attacked.[13] Many of the opponents

---

of the ancestor gods to equip the sacrificer and his people with supernatural power (*bhring*) in order to lead them unharmed to success (Kaji-Cihung 2001), the rituals' observation in these particular situations could also be understood differently: now it also pointed to the powerlessness of the Han on the land that originally belonged to the Taroko. That blood sacrifices had already taken on the additional meaning of 'rites of rebellion' in some parts of Taroko society was also demonstrated by an activity by young Taroko intellectuals in 1999, who demonstrated against the occupation of their land by the cement industry with a blood sacrifice (see the documentary of Pan Chaocheng 2003).

[12] Interviews with Nanang 23.11.02; Jiro 15.04.03; Imy and Gu 10.04.03; also see Qiu Juanfang 2002: 9.

[13] Most people were convinced that Hayu Yudaw—a Taroko-minister and PCT-

were church ministers themselves or persons who were closely linked to the Presbyterian Church (PCT) that had once built the foundations for Taiwan's nativist movement.[14] At the high tide of nativism in the second half of the nineties, however, the fruits of this former commitment were increasingly monopolized by other ethnic elites, for instance local politicians who boasted that they were the savers and protectors of Aboriginal culture, as well as Taroko school teachers and directors who were now officially assigned the organization of Aboriginal mother languages curricula.[15] From the perspective of the Presbyterians, these traditionalist elites had to be treated with caution, because most of them had formerly been loyal to the authoritarian regime and still belonged to political circles in Taiwan today called 'conservative influences'. As their devotion for local culture had only begun after the spread of nativism, it was suspected that their interest in the rituals merely stemmed from their wish to dominate official cultural resources in favour of their own individual power, as the organisation of the festivals was prestigious.[16]

4. *Religious and social efficacy in the reinvented rituals*

From my description above it already became clear that the Taroko's reinvented ancestor gods rituals had in fact been quite 'efficacious'.

College teacher who had participated in the ancestor gods rituals several times as a ritual leader—had been 'misused' by the political elites. Hayu Yudaw himself dismissed these accusations, arguing that his only aim had been to 'intervene' and 'mediate' between Christian and non-Christian traditions. The motive of the traditionalists to let the minister participate, however, can only be explained as an attempt to 'borrow his authority'.

[14] Rudolph 2004: 243. Since the mid-seventies, the Presbyterian Church of Taiwan (PCT) was always the most active institution in terms of protecting of Aboriginal cultures in Taiwan. About half of the 84% Christians in Taroko society belong to the PCT. Although the Roman Catholic Church and the True Jesus Church also have large congregations in Taroko society, they very rarely engage in cultural activities.

[15] A policy that annoyed many church people was that they were now requested to pass special exams if they wanted to continue to pursue their education in mother languages, in spite of their previous role as sole protectors of native languages.

[16] A very outspoken commentary on the connection of ritual events and power politics can be found in Liu Huanyue 2001: 5. As for the conflict between political elites and PCT elites, it was also ideologically motivated: while the former usually only pleaded for a separation of the Sedeq from the Atayal, the majority of Taroko PCT-intellectuals participated in the 'Taroko-recognition-movement' that advocated the Taroko's independence even from the Sedeq (a claim that was finally achieved in the course of the Presidential election of 2004). The main reason for the PCT's claim for the Taroko's independence was the hope of an own autonomous zone in the future.

First of all, the worries put forward by the Christians indicated that the rituals were believed to be vested with a certain religious efficacy. Particularly the fact that real animals were killed and that the blood was treated in a way people still knew it from their private rituals at home seemed shocking and confusing at the time. This effect had actually been very much intended by the educational elites, who had not only tried to furnish the ritual with symbols familiar to all Taroko, but who also argued that people should 'face their common culture and their commonalities' in order to find their common identity, and who criticized the 'mental colonisation' exercised by the Church.[17] In postcolonial Taiwan, this kind of criticism was actually nothing revolutionary: facing a steady decrease of followers in recent years, even Aboriginal church people themselves often contended that Western Christianity had developed under special cultural conditions in ancient Israel and should be indigenized in order to become fully accepted as an indigenous religion. As a member of a PCT college, the Christian minister who had played the 'ritual leader' in all the ancestor gods rituals had in fact always been one of the most fervent advocates of such a request. This did not mean that he really wanted to revive traditional religion or that he really cooperated with the traditionalists: as he made clear in personal interviews, his participation in the ritual was just his own individual way to promote the kind of indigenisation[18] that was also welcomed by the intellectual superstructure of his church whose members did not have to work with the people and with the other churches in the villages.[19]

Apart from their religious efficacy, however, the reinvented ancestor gods rituals also had a manifest social efficacy inasmuch as they helped to re-negotiate certain social and psychological tensions in Taroko

---

[17] Personal interview with Lodi 2.12.02; interview with Kaji-Cihung 7.12.03.

[18] Personal interview with Hayu Yudaw 15.11.2002; see also the interview in Kaji-Cihung 2003: 25. In these accounts, Hayu not only emphasises that he had actually prayed to his Christian god during the rituals, but also admits that he had sometimes been afraid during the rituals, as he was not sure how the *rutux* would react.

[19] As the Aboriginal ministers who lived in the villages (most of them being opponents of the ancestor gods rituals) were in permanent contact with the people, not only did they have the deepest knowledge of the psychology of the people, they also had to cope with any negative results of 'cultural experiments' (interview with Jiro 15.04.03). In strong contrast, church intellectuals like Hayu Yudaw as well as most of the traditionalists were usually very assimilated in the corresponding social and intellectual strata in modern Han society.

society. In improvisations that were not mentioned in the ritual script prepared by the traditionalists, cultural attitudes, social hierarchies and ethnic relations were challenged and redefined. As an example of this kind of efficacy, the negotiations between traditionalist and Christian perspectives described in the section above may be named. Other examples of such improvisations were scenes of 'status inversion' in the Turnerian sense,[20] as well as scenes of 'reversed violence' and subversion of Han authority and culture.[21] Most striking was the way—or better the technique—for achieving these effects: in each case, cosmological specifications and ritual roles were synthesized or juxtaposed with certain aspects of the real life world of the Taroko (i.e., real social roles, experiences and memories of participants and audiences) in a way that certain interpretations were subtly—although not compellingly—evoked.[22] It was this technique of strategic exploitation of the ambivalence of ritual symbols that prevented the ritual from being interrupted during the performances in spite of the presence and the intervention of competing agendas.[23]

---

[20] In his notion of *communitas*, Victor Turner (1969) suggests that ritual is a medium that negotiates and mediates social relations. In this context, Turner also refers to 'rituals of status inversion' that mediate between the upper and the lower strata of a society. In the case of the ancestor gods rituals, rites of status inversion could for instance be observed between influential politicians and the ordinary people in the moment when the more prestigious traditional roles were played by the ordinary people and *vice versa*.

[21] A concrete example of this kind of subversion was the offering of raw liver not only to participating Taroko who ate it in the conventionalised way, but also to the invited Han school directors who observed the ritual from the guests tribune. They reacted rather embarrassed and finally pretended to act according to the convention. While the raw liver cosmologically symbolizes vigour and power that will be instilled in those who participate in the ritual, its use indexically aims at a revenge for the Han's centuries-long bullying and subjugation of Aborigines in Taiwan.

[22] For details see Rudolph (forthc.). The kind of indexical usage of ritual symbols described here has first been pointed out by Tambiah (1979: 153).

[23] A similar dynamic has been pointed out by Bell (1997: 231) in her reflections on the efficacy of invented rituals. Referring to the Olympics as a new international ritual that successfully forges a new common identity and negotiates between different political positions, she contends: "The ambiguity of the Olympics is one of its most striking features. Various scholars of ritual have examined [...] the way it simultaneously combines sports, games, warfare, and ritual. [...] Heavy on the rhetoric of common values while open to a great deal of variation in each participant's purposes, ritual makes few of the pragmatic or substantive statements so vulnerable to disagreement and contention".

5. *By way of conclusion: the interplay of individual and collective agendas*

I would like now to return to my initial question: the question why rituals may fail in spite of their evident efficacy. As we can see more clearly now, one decisive reason for the failure of the canonisation of the Taroko's ancestor gods rituals was its undue religious efficacy: in a society whose members harboured an ambivalent belief system, religious efficacy seemed not to fit into a collective ritual that was supposed to craft a common identity. This was the reason why the ancestor gods rituals were finally replaced by the commemorative rituals of the Christian elites: rituals that also had—though to a smaller degree—social efficacy, but that tried to avoid any allusions to the ambivalent belief system of the Taroko today.[24]

The problem is more complex, however. Although deliberately disregarding Christian sensibilities, it was not the main intention of the cosmopolitan makers of the ancestor gods rituals to vest their ritual with religious efficacy, but to find a common denominator for an authentic 'Taroko identity' in the context of Han-Taiwanese nativism and multiculturalism.[25] Religious efficacy was very much a by-product, created in the course of ritual criticism initiated by the opposing elites and reinforced by the intervention of the Christian minister—an authority who represented the 'sacred' in contemporary Taroko society—who tried to mould the ritual's efficacy according to his own individual ideas. Not only confronted with the highly contradictory phenomenon that the ritual leader was in fact a representative of Christianity, but also witnessing that this person used aesthetical patterns from the

---

[24] As I have showed elsewhere (Rudolph forthc.), these commemorative rituals are in so far socially efficacious as they enhance the participants' positive identification with their own Taroko past (for instance by proudly wearing artificially applied tattoos that were for a long time looked down upon because of the discrimination by the Han, or by presenting the former headhunting habits as almost altruistic acts in a highly sophisticated social system). By means of performance, cultural memory is regenerated in such a way that it can serve as a basis for an unstigmatised and uninhibited Taroko identity. Here 'efficacy' exists in a sense similar to that pointed out by Köpping & Rao (2000: 12) in their reflections on the function of the performance of folklorised elements of a culture by its members: in spite of the acknowledgement of the discontinuity of the past, it is recognised as an immanent part of one's identity.

[25] Taiwanese multiculturalism not only propagates the necessity of respecting Taiwan's cultures, but also of making cultural continuity possible. As I mentioned above, the ancestor gods rituals was supposed to demonstrate the ancestors' close observance of the *gaya*—the organizational rules and norms of the Taroko—as an incentive to revive the 'gist' of this traditional legal code.

Christian as well as from the traditional repertoire (fresh blood!) at the same time, common people were no longer able to rule out the possibility that religious efficacy was involved. From this perspective, the described failure of ritual invention actually seems to be the result of the unfavourable collision of individual and collective agendas in a highly hybrid cultural context.

The persistence and sudden emergence of the collective dimension observed here points to a (particular) risk that might be inherent in any kind of ritual reinvention or ritual appropriation in comparable contexts: in their endeavour to instrumentalise ritual performances for identity constructions on national or regional levels, individual agents (politicians, intellectuals, activists) try to adapt rituals to meanings that have little in common with the traditional context of these practices. However, as this context still latently exists (in form of habitualisations, aesthetical patterns, 'superstitions' etc.), any ritual manipulation must refer to these rudiments in order to be efficacious (for instance by using icons from the traditional repertoire). This in turn leads to the phenomenon that these individual definitions of ritual practices also have their limits and can bear unfavourable results, as there exists a historically rooted, collective dimension that is imminent to ritual and that transcends any individual intentionality.[26]

References

Bell, Catherine 1997. *Ritual: Perspectives and Dimensions*. Oxford & New York: Oxford University Press.

Grimes, Ronald L. 1988. "Infelicitous Performances and Ritual Criticism". *Semeia* 43: 103–122.

Kaji-Cihung (Gariyi Jihong) 2001. "Tayazu dongsaidekequn chuantong yiliao gainian" [The traditional medicine conceptions of the Atayal-Sedeq]. In: *Convolute of the 'Conference on the traditional medicine of Taiwan's aborigines vs Western medicine'*. Taiwan: Foundation of Taiwan Aborigines.

—— 2003. "Zuling, shengling yu jisi de chaoyuexing: Saidekequn cunluo jidian gainian fenxi" [The transcendence of ancestor gods, god and the ritual leader: An analysis of the ritual conception in villages of the East-Sedeq]. In: *Convolute of the 'Symposium on the encounter of the aborigine's traditional culture and rituals with Christianity'*. Hualian: Taiwan World Vision Association.

[26] For this last line of thought I am indebted to my colleague Bernhard Leistle with whom I had endless discussions on the topic presented here. A question which evolves from this analysis is whether it is wise for nation states to rely on rituals as authentication tools in their multiculturalist nation-building projects.

Köpping, Klaus-Peter & Ursula Rao 2000. "Die 'performative Wende': Leben—Ritual—Theater". In: *Im Rausch des Rituals. Gestaltung und Transformation der Wirklichkeit in körperlicher Performanz*, Köpping, Klaus-Peter & Ursula Rao (ed.). Münster & Hamburg & London: LIT, 1–31.

Liu Huanyue 2001. *Taiwan Yuanzhumin jidian wanquan daolan* [A Comprehensive Guide to the Rituals of Taiwan's Aborigines]. Taipei: Changmin wenhua.

Pan Chaocheng 2003. *Women wei tudi er zhan* [We fight for our land]. 56 min. Taiwan.

Qiu Juanfang 2002. "Chuantong de jiangou yu wenhua de zhuanshi: Shixi Hualian Truku ren de zulingji" [Construction of Tradition and Change of Cultural Interpretations: Analysis of the Taroko Ancestor-Gods-Ritual]. In: *Convolute of the 'Symposium on Identity Construction, Ethnic Identification and the Breaking Up of the Atayal Ethnic Groups'*, 16.–17.11.2002. Taipei, 1–18.

Qiu Ruolong 1999. *GaYa: 1930 nian de Wushe shijian ya Saidekezu* [GaYa: The Wushe incident of 1930 and the Sedeq]. Taiwan.

Rudolph, Michael 2003a. *Taiwans multi-ethnische Gesellschaft und die Bewegung der Ureinwohner—Assimilation oder kulturelle Revitalisierung*. Münster & Hamburg & London: LIT.

—— 2003b. "The Quest for Difference vs. the Wish to Assimilate: Taiwan's Aborigines and their Struggle for Cultural Survival in Times of Multiculturalism". In: *Religion and the Formation of Taiwanese Identities*, Katz, Paul R. & Murray A. Rubinstein (ed.). New York: Palgrave Macmillan, 123–156.

—— 2004. "The Pan-Ethnic Movement of Taiwanese Aborigines and the Role of Elites in the Process of Ethnicity Formation". In: *The Politics of Multiple Belonging: Ethnicity and Nationalism in Europe and East Asia*, Christiansen, Flemming & Ulf Hedetoft (ed.). Hampshire, United Kingdom: Ashgate, 239–254.

—— forthc. "Ritual Reinvention and the Reconstitution of Ethnic Identity: The Efficacy of Contemporary Ritual Performances of Taiwan's Aborigines". In: *Qualifying Ritual in an Unstable World: Contingency—Embodiment—Hybridity*, Henn, Alexander & Klaus-Peter Köpping (ed.). New York, Berlin: Peter Lang.

Sayama Yukichi 1917. *Banzoku chosa hokokusho* [Research Report on the Barbarian Peoples]. Tokyo.

Schieffelin, Edward L. 1996. "On Failure and Performance. Throwing the Medium Out of the Séance". In: *The Performance of Healing*, Laderman, Carol & Marina Roseman (ed.). New York & London: Routledge, 59–89.

Tambiah, Stanley J. 1979. "A Performative Approach to Ritual". *Proceedings of the British Academy* 65: 113–169.

Turner, Victor 1969. *The Ritual Process. Structure and Anti-Structure*. Chicago: Routledge.

RITUAL DYNAMICS AND RITUAL FAILURE[1]

Ute Hüsken

The contributions to this volume clearly show that in many cases participants and spectators alike learn more about the 'correct' performance of a ritual by deviating from, rather than by adhering to the rules. One might even say that solely the definitions and examples of 'ritual failure' and 'error'—and how they are coped with—prove the existence of decisive norms for ritual actions, even when the former are imagined deviations from imagined norms. It therefore turns out that this slightly unusual view opens up new perspectives on ritual rules, expectations, procedures, and on the interactions which constitute these procedures and their context. 'Failed ritual' directs our attention to 'what really matters' to the performers and participants and others in one way or another involved in a ritual.

However, when talking about ritual failure and mistakes in ritual there is a need to be explicit about one's notion of 'ritual'. In scholarly literature, there is no lack of definitions of 'ritual', and not two definitions are alike.[2] Recently, there is an increasing tendency among ritual studies scholars to avoid the term 'ritual' altogether and to use other terms (such as ritualisation or public events) instead. Moreover, some of the traditions dealt with here do not even have an "indigenous" term equating 'ritual'.[3] Neither does this group of scholars from the diverse academic disciplines contributing to this volume agree on one uniform definition of 'ritual.' Nevertheless, the diverse notions and usages of 'ritual' in this volume are conceptually connected: our working definition of ritual is that of a *polythetic class*, that is: "(A) each member of the class has a large but unspecified number of a set of characteristics occurring in the class as a whole, (B) each of those characteristics is possessed by a large number of those members" (Snoek 2006).[4] The

[1] The final version of this essay was decisively influenced by Edward L. Schieffelin's introduction to this volume.

[2] See e.g. Snoek 2006.

[3] See Stausberg (ed.) 2006.

[4] To meet the requirements of a 'fully' polythetic class, no one of those characteristics would be possessed by every member of the class (Snoek 2006). The 'rituals'

plurality of potential characteristics of the members of this polythetic class[5] allows us to look at a very wide range of events, rather than at actions that are 'traditionally' recognised as rituals alone. We use this 'open' definition of ritual as a heuristic tool, not as an end in itself.[6] One very good example of the usefulness of such a loose analytical category even for studying actions which are not generally perceived as ritual is given by Hoffmeister in this volume. Rituals that go awry or deviations in ritual can be used as a tool to understanding what ritual can be or do.

1. *Deviation and evaluation*

Contrary to the widespread assumption that rituals are rather static and unchanging, most rituals do in fact undergo slight or even significant changes—be it in the course of time, as a result of their transfer to another cultural context, or simply because they are 'updated' to meet the requirements of changed circumstances. The notions of change, adaptation, invention and reinvention imply deviation from an original or earlier version of a ritual. Only if such deviation from explicit or implicit rules, values, expectations, norms or models is judged negatively do we find ourselves in the field of 'distortion', 'mistake', 'flaw', 'error', 'slip', 'failure' etc.[7] That means that not each and every deviation is necessarily marked as a mistake. Even an obvious difference between ritual prescription and performance can continue to exist for quite a long time without being judged negatively (see Hüsken 2006: 269f.).

dealt with in the present volume possess the characteristics of a 'polythetic class', but nor those of a 'fully polythetic class' because the characteristic of 'repetition' can be found in any of the rituals dealt with in this volume.

[5] Some of these characteristics are: religious, action, repetition, (cognitive) framing, formally stylized, based on scripts or models, perceived as different from everyday behaviour, invested with meaning, transcendence, symbolic communication, consisting of building-blocks, culturally constructed, traditionally sanctioned, taking place at specific places and/or times, multi-medial, rehearsed, structured, patterned, ordered, sequenced, and rule-governed (cf. Snoek 2006).

[6] A polythetic definition of 'ritual' comes close to a "field of possible forms of 'ritual'", as proposed by Handelman (2006) in order to avoid the banality of universal definitions. At the same time this is also a step towards the "de-Westernisation" of one of the concepts of the study of religion (Religionswissenschaft), as called for by Platvoet (2004: 243ff.).

[7] See also Stausberg 2004: 234. Moos (2001b: 5, note 27) gives a list of 40 English synonyms for 'mistake'. He argues that the vocabulary of a language betrays the interest (or lack of interest) in the concept of 'mistake' (Moos 2001b: 2).

It is obvious that ritual criticism precedes negative interpretations of deviations. The exploration of underlying values and the process of evaluation are therefore central issues when studying rituals that have gone wrong. Evaluation is an intersubjective process, executed by groups or individuals. It is based on certain sets of values which might stem from canons which the participants themselves have not created, but it might equally be based on the expectations, intentions and agenda of individual participants. However, Whitehouse (2006) reminds us that "much of human behaviour is normally inaccessible to conscious inspection—it operates on an implicit level". In many cases these implicit values or beliefs become conscious only in the process of discussing and explicitly evaluating a ritual. Grimes argues (2004): "Ritual change, ritual creativity, ritual conflict and ritual criticism are inextricably linked in practice; therefore they should be inextricably linked in theory [...] Rites, no matter how sacred, are assessed, judged wanting or judged adequate [...] Ritual criticism goes on informally all the time, and its contexts are various—both popular and scholarly. Criticism is not restricted to scholars. Ritual criticism is implicit in the normal course of conserving, transmitting, enculturating, and adapting rites. There is nothing abnormal about it, for the simple reason that humans evaluate and criticise everything, ritual included". He cautions not to "ignore change and critique by constructing theories that, by definition, exclude it" (Grimes 2004).

While dealing with and representing interpretations of 'mistakes' and 'failure' it is important to be explicit regarding the perspectives one depicts. In this volume mainly four perspectives on ritual deviations are represented: that of the individual or group acting against norms, that of the individual or group responding to this, that of those who wrote or edited texts reporting flawed ritual events, and the perspective of the researcher.

The form each of these interpretations and evaluations takes is influenced by several aspects which might or might not be directly linked to the ritual event. While the researcher tries to give an 'impartial' account and analysis of the ritual under investigation, his or her theoretical assumptions nevertheless are children of their times and place of birth, and are guided by taken-for-granted assumptions and worldviews (Grimes 2006: 12). "[I]t is wise to theorize as if the place where you do it matters", says Grimes (2006: 14). More specifically, Platvoet (2004: 246) questions the usefulness of the scholarly distinction between 'etic' and 'emic' views because "[our etic concepts] are the historically contingent and culturally particular concepts of modern Western society shaped by its peculiar Christian history." He therefore pleas for a sharp critical self-reflexivity, including a constant awareness of the inherent limitations our scholarly categories impose (2004: 247).[8] This holds particularly true for value-laden contexts such as 'failure' and 'mistake'.[9]

However, *within* the tradition(s), explicit critique and accusing others of having made mistakes is a common practice. Therefore we have to take the context into account and, above all, ask questions about modes and motives of representation.[10] The widespread perception that rituals never fail is reinforced by the fact that neither mistakes during a performance nor a ritual's failure are described frequently: they are not enjoyable and therefore one tends to draw the curtain over it. Moreover, if rituals or ritual systems fail in that they become irrelevant there is again no reason to report this failure. The other side of this coin is that we have in each and every case of a report of ritual failure to try to disclose the motivation(s) behind the report: rituals are always represented by somebody to somebody. Those papers in this volume dealing with conflicting assessments within certain traditions show that in many cases it is common practice to accuse other members of the same tradition of making mistakes or even of messing up the entire ritual—one party's failure can be the other party's success. This insight prompts Howe in his article "Risk, Ritual and Performance" to suggest a new metaphor for ritual, namely 'test', 'trial', 'examination' and 'contest' (Howe 2000: 76). In many rituals there are in fact winners and losers, whose assessment of the ritual event will be directly opposed to each other. The researcher then has to detect and represent the plurality of voices. The call for a high degree of reflexivity during field work, especially in such value-laden contexts, is certainly more than

---

[8] Grimes (1988a: 105) suspects: "Criteria for considering a ritual as successful or failed may be inescapably religio- or ethnocentric". Or, as Howe puts it: "While anthropologists may stress the purported meaning, participants care whether their doing is effective" (Howe 2000: 65).

[9] This issue is explicitly discussed by Emmrich and Snoek in this volume.

[10] 'Representation' in this essay is used to denote every mode of transmitting an account of a ritual, be it in written form, through oral narrative, or through visual and audio-visual media. Representation in this sense already *is* the outcome of interpretation.

appropriate.[11] All contributors therefore problematise the terms they use and the means and mode(s) of representing the respective traditions.

2. *Ritual, risk and criticism*

Ritual and the fact that something can go wrong have so far mainly been dealt with under the pretext of 'ritual serves to minimize risks'.[12] Social coherence and crisis mastery were the focus of attention. Only few scholars have systematically concentrated on the 'dangerous' sides of ritual. Schieffelin, in his "Introduction" to this volume, refers to the first scholars explicitly interested in rituals that go wrong: Clifford Geertz (e.g. 1973: 96–132), one of the first scholars to use a ritual that did not work properly as an analytical tool to point out non-explicit facets of the event, Ronald L. Grimes, who comes up with a preliminary classification of 'failed ritual' (1988a),[13] and Edward L. Schieffelin, who in his 1996 article shows that the failure of a ritual event can be used as a means of looking at "the inner construction of a particular 'ritual' or 'theatrical' experience involved" (1996: 62). Especially Grimes's and Schieffelin's contributions were extremely useful for the analysis of the instances of ritual mistakes and failure in this volume. Moreover, Schieffelin's notion of performance as the crucial connecting link between ritual texts and the context in which the rituals are enacted proved to be a good starting point for those contributions to this volume in which the relation of (normative) ritual texts and their concrete enactment are dealt with.

[11] In many cases, the competition underlying these conflicts is itself influenced by scholarly representations of the incidents. Many traditions since long reflect on their rituals, making use of the literature on ritual theories, too (see, for example, Stausberg 2004: 234). However, since the researcher is a human being interacting in the field of his or her research, he or she will always have an impact on the situation investigated. The only remedy is to be explicit about one's own positioning in the field.

[12] For references, see Howe 2000: 63 and 67, see also Platvoet 2004: 257.

[13] In this volume, Grimes preliminary categories prove to be central issues in analysing 'ritual failure' and 'ritual mistakes' in an intercultural and historical approach. However, while Grimes distinguishes in his 1988a article between 'failure *in* ritual' and 'failure *of* ritual', in this essay I prefer to use 'mistake' rather than 'failure *in* ritual'.

After 1996, more scholars gave examples of failed or distorted rituals.[14] These case studies are referred to frequently in this essay.[15]

3. *Sources and approaches*

On the basis of the material analysed the diverse contributions can be divided into three categories: those dealing with texts alone, those dealing with texts and performances, and those solely based on performances.

Many contributions to this volume deal with to notions of 'mistake' or 'failure' in the context of performances witnessed personally.[16] These case studies show that ritual atmosphere, the interplay and conflict of individual and collective agenda, charisma and authenticity, and ritual competence, but also the social and cultural context beyond the ritual frame are major issues when it comes to assessing a ritual performance. Doing field research has the undeniable advantage that the researcher can immediately experience, assess and interpret the relevant situation without having to rely on other media of transmission. The scholar witnesses how the incident is dealt with and how it is interpreted at the time it happens, he or she is in the position to notice whether there are diverse—maybe even conflicting—assessments, and how retrospective evaluations emerge (see also Colas 2005: 28). These issues might be the main reasons why thus far flawed rituals and their effects have almost exclusively been dealt with in the context of performance and participation. Undoubtedly these are central aspects of 'ritual failure', especially since many instances of 'mistake' and 'failure' require bodily presence (Moos 2001a: xv). Bodily presence moreover implies immediate interaction at the time the ritual is performed. This interactional aspect is—apart from historical circumstances and the question whether a ritual 'works'—, the major source of contingencies and risks, as Schieffelin (1998: 197f.) points out. Since it is extremely difficult in purely performance based rituals to single out the 'rules' that guide them, the

[14] See e.g. Chao 1999; Brückner 2001; Fuller 1993 and 2004; Gengnagel 2005; Gladigow 2004; Hüsken 2006; Kendall 1996; Köpping 2004; Schlehe & Weber 2001.

[15] In contrast to these essays, I refer to the case studies presented within this volume by simply mentioning the author's name.

[16] Brosius, Dücker, Emmrich, Hauser-Schäublin, Hüsken, Merz, Polit, Rudolph, Snoek, and Weinhold.

analysis of 'mistakes' and errors is especially helpful in detecting what deviation matters.

However, taking instances of exceptions to the rule as a key for understanding implicit structures is equally employed by those contributions that exclusively deal with texts (and other scripts) related to rituals.[17] These articles contribute substantially to an understanding of the many facets of 'ritual failure' in exploring the concepts internal to the respective traditions within their (remote) historical context as well as the use of narratives which represent 'ritual failure' in the sources. Partly in contrast to the first mentioned contributors to this volume, the scholars who have to rely solely on texts are in the difficult position of judging what the texts tell us about actual performances, whether they are idealisations, or even cover-ups. Phillippe Buc, who analyses the relationship between mediaeval documents and 20th century ritual theory, explicitly cautions that instead of immediately applying anthropology to textual sources one should first try to understand why and how authors wrote about 'bad rituals',[18] since the authors sought to influence the world around them through their narratives. Therefore, one has to detect the role of ritual in the economy of the respective narratives (Buc 2001: 3f.). Texts are not fixed entities with definite meanings, but are struggles about who can get what inscribed, says Howe (2000: 65). "By excluding alternatives, what is inscribed becomes authoritative, legitimate and even obligatory". All ritual texts are likely to express above all the agenda of those who composed the texts and of those in charge of transmitting them. Like a researcher who witnesses him/herself the incidents s/he analyses, the textual scholar is sometimes confronted with two or more conflicting assessments of one and the same ritual event. Thus in Ambos's essay the royal inscriptions tell a totally different story than the letters concerning the same incident which ritual specialists sent to the king. Moreover, the protocols of interrogations of serial killers which are dealt with by Hoffmeister reveal a different 'ritual script' than that ascribed to them by the court files pertaining to the same criminal cases. It is therefore of prime importance to detect what message is intended to be conveyed why and how to whom. The complexity of a ritual's textual representation

[17] Ambos, Buss, Hoffmeister, Michaels, and Stavrianopoulou.

[18] Buc (2001: 8) terms "rituals that social agents manipulate or rituals that break down" as 'bad rituals'.

is even more evident if the (historical) context changes: as soon as the content of ritual texts is no longer beyond ambiguity, commentaries are written in order to reconnect them with practice or a (changed) interpretation. Hence, it is not only important what is written down, but also what is not included in the texts. The analysis of the inherent fractures within the texts may reveal fractures in the actual ritual practice or in the way a ritual is perceived.

Those contributions which use (sometimes ancient) textual traditions as well as actual performances of the rituals as sources[19] reveal the complex relation of the representation of a ritual's risks as described in a ritual text with the risks lying in the actual performance. Even when there is a seemingly fixed structure or script, the creative acting of the participants and their inventive response to contingencies and to the concrete context of the performance is as crucial to the enactment of the ritual and to the perception of what is right or wrong as the (normative) ritual text (see Gengnagel 2005). Those scholars who deal with these heterogeneous materials have to constantly keep in mind that each source is the child of its time and circumstances.

4. *Ritual competence and the detection of mistakes*

The question as to who is competent and eligible to perform a ritual 'correctly', on the one hand, and who possesses the authority and competence to disclose mistakes and to correct them, on the other, is of utmost importance.[20] In many cases it seems that the ritual specialists, as competent ritual agents, do indeed have the power to react creatively to contingencies and to deviate from the normative. It is often only the performer himself or herself who decides whether a ritual—or a part of it—is 'correct' or 'distorted' (see Hüsken forthc.). Here, instances of unsanctioned 'deviations from the normative' on the part of the performer can also be viewed as pointing to the core of the ritual specialists' ritual competence: only they are in the position to 'make the right mistakes'.[21] It is largely through their legitimate

[19] Buss, Dücker, Emmrich, Hüsken, and Snoek.

[20] Brosius characterises this competence as "the ownership of the right to know how, when and by whom a ritual could be performed effectively" (p. 302).

[21] This expression was coined by Michael Houseman during the conference on 'theorizing rituals' organised in the context of the Collaborative Research Centre in 2003.

deviation from the normative that their superior ritual authority is made apparent. However, such a 'right to deviate from the norm' can also be challenged, as Snoek's example of Annie Besant's extravagant treatment of the 'wedding ring case' shows. It might well be that the degree of the right to deviate from 'rules' generally indicates the respective agent's degree of power, which transcends the ritual context. Since Annie Besant's power within the community was declining, her creative handling of the wedding ring case met with strong opposition. In a similar manner, in Weinhold's case study the community's acceptance of deliberate transgressions of ritual rules known to all participants is a clear indication of the transgressor's standing. However, it would be a misjudgement to reduce a performer's ability do deviate from the norms to being a simple reflection of social hierarchies. As in Howe's example (2000), rituals can also entail the enacting and consolidating of specific social relationships: the king tried to consolidate his superior position by the extraordinary sacrifice of a rhinozeros. This act was considered very risky because the king's authority was at stake (Howe 2000: 72ff.). Rituals, like other 'valuables', are both reflective and constitutive of social partnership and struggles for preeminence (see Appadurai 1986: 19 and 34).

Breaches of rules may in some cases be unavoidable. It might also be that the attempt to avoid an irregularity causes greater damage than the irregularity itself. The breach of rules may be preferred to a disruption of the flow of ritual performance. Here the performance's context is a decisive element for the negotiation and evaluation of deviations. Snoek shows that the 'mastery of the risk' involves the skills of obscuring and masking mistakes, since the disruption of the flow of a ritual would disturb the flow of emergence and commitment to the ritual in the participants, which is considered of utmost importance in the rituals of the freemasons. This 'flow' of the rituals has to be created and maintained during each and every performance. In Weinhold's case study a formalised dance serves to 'enhance the flow of energy between participants' in Santo Daime rituals. 'Holding the energy' during a performance is mainly the task of the ritual leader who decides whether a participant's deviation from the rules requires an interruption of the 'flow' or whether it is better to ignore it and to continue. Especially in contexts lacking explicit or strict norms it is often mainly the performer's ability which makes a ritual work.

The importance of 'ritual competence' for a ritual's assessment is explicitly dealt with in Stavrianopoulou's study of the role of the priest in Ancient Greek rituals. 'Ritual competence' here is explicitly attributed to certain individuals: a ritual is enacted 'correctly' only when performed by them. In this case 'competence' is completely detached from actual practise.

These examples clearly show that 'ritual competence' is not only established through knowledge of and adherence to rules.

5. *The creative power of deviations*

Although in most cases not explicit in theory, breaches of rules can—and frequently do—instantiate the creation of new ritual rules in practice. It is frequently under the pretext of 'returning to old (severer) rules' that in fact new regulative systems are formulated (see Humphrey & Laidlaw 1994: 12). Breaking rules therefore can also be valued as a creative process, even within a rather conservative tradition. Two strands seem to exist side by side, the fixed rules and the possibility to deviate from them in case of necessity. This is explicitly expressed in numerous Indian ritual texts which provide for both: rules and sequences are explicitly prescribed in minute detail, but at the same time the texts allow for exceptions to the rules in case the regulations cannot be followed. Since deviations in ritual performances bear in themselves the possibility of a modification or transformation of the ritual (Kreinath 2004: 267f.), they often serve to renovate ritual systems and thus contribute substantially to ritual dynamics.

There are also many instances of breaches of rules which are applied deliberately in order to effect sustained changes in rituals (such as performing an ecumenical Last Supper or an ordination of women as Catholic priests etc.), or even in order to disturb the ritual procedure and thus to invalidate it: rites are employed as critique of other rites and are subversive elements of rituals.

In some cases breaches of rules are even desired elements of a ritual: transgressions and rule-breaking can also be part of the ritual code. The most popularly known rituals of this kind are 'rituals of rebellion' (see Gluckman 1954 and Turner 1969) and 'rituals of confrontation' (Platvoet 2004), as analysed by Howe (2000) and by Brosius in this volume. Dücker also gives an example: on the occasion of the Nobel Prize banquet in 1999 Günter Grass welcomed the Swedish Monarch with "Sehr geehrter Herr König" ("Dear Mr. King"). This (deliberate) breach of rules was then perceived as a positive confirmation of the writer's unconventional and emancipated attitude and thus contributed to the value of the ritual, not to its devaluation. One of the case studies presented by Hauser-Schäublin is another example of the creative power of deviations. In the rituals of the Intaran the superhuman agency (of the 'lower' local gods) has the right to enumerate and even denounce mistakes. In doing so these agents have the power either to modify the 'scripts' of the ritual performances or to insist on conservative norms. Here again, 'ritual mistakes' are subversive elements of the rituals and are at the same time part and parcel of the 'correct' performance. This kind of 'ritual of rebellion' does not necessarily confirm order but contains the possibility of change.

6. *Failure of performance: charisma, authenticity and agency*

Notions of 'mistake' and 'failure' often depend on the character of the ritual, that is, whether the rituals are strictly rule governed or only loosely structured, following a commonly accepted 'traditional' form or set of (heterogeneous) expectations (see Howe 2000: 66). Here some factors governing the negative evaluation of a deviation or variation in a improvisational performance are dealt with.

A distorted 'relational aspect' is a factor frequently found in cases of negative evaluation: a ritual may be performed 'by the wrong person', 'aimed toward the wrong person', or be performed by an appropriate person, but 'at the wrong time', 'in the wrong place', etc. (see Chao 1999; see also Hauser-Schäublin). In these cases the relation between ritual action, performers, participants, symbols etc. is dissonant. The ritual symbol and action must be concordant with its bearer or performer, in particular when the performer represents a certain group. If this 'relational aspect' is malfunctioning the ritual is perceived as 'wrong' or inadequate.

This 'relational aspect' can also be related to the more diffuse field of 'ritual atmosphere'. Rudolph shows that a lack of uniformity of the cultural context can prevent the creation of a 'ritual atmosphere', perceived as 'appropriate' by all participants. Such rituals are bound to fail. In Hoffmeister's case study it is mainly the participants' (and not the main performers') 'inappropriate' acting which creates the 'wrong' atmosphere and therefore leads to the ritualised act's failure: the 'success' of many ritualised killings performed by serial killers depended on the 'appropriate atmosphere'. When this atmosphere was disturbed the serial killers interrupted their activity and some of the prospective victims were spared.

As indicated above, 'ritual competence' is not only established through knowledge of and adherence to rules. In primarily performative contexts it is frequently the main actor's responsibility to make the performance work through his/her competent acting. S/He must convince the audience and maintain this conviction. This dimension of rituals is connected with aspects of technique (Grimes 1988a). The use of language, for example, is one aspect of technique. As Madhav Deshpande (1996) illustrates, Sanskrit—which is considered the 'sacred language' in the context of Indian Brahmanical rituals—is highly valued mainly because it is the 'eternal language of sacred tradition'. However, in practice this language is not at all fixed and unchanging, but is updated and adapted to the regional and historical ritual contexts. Deshpande shows that the assumption that 'everything is done in holy Sanskrit' is much more important than the grammatical and linguistic correctness of the language actually used. Part of the success—or failure—of the priest's performance is therefore his technique, his ability to convey to the participants that they are actively involved in a holy ritual. Here, performance technique and perceived authenticity are more important than (grammatical) rules.[22] A performance, thus Schieffelin, is always inherently interactive and improvisational and therefore a fundamentally contingent process (1998: 198). Schieffelin sees in the interactive abilities of the performer the main force which makes a performance work or fail (1996: 62f. and 80). This assumption is confirmed by Merz's case study: the junior medium in a ritual that was conducted within a healing ritual 'overdid' her performance in an attempt to renegotiate hierarchical structures, and in the eyes of her audience lost her perceived authenticity.[23] It is a skill to keep the fine balance between one's personal agenda and other participants' expectations (see also Howe 2000: 70).

---

[22] This observation contradicts Frits Staal's thesis based on his impressive work *Agni* (1983) and proposed in his *Rules without meaning* (1989) that in these rituals the rules are more important than understanding what one is doing. However, since I do not agree with Staal that there exists one single meaning attributed to a ritual but rather that a multiplicity of meanings can be attributed to any ritual, I argue here that it is not the 'understanding of the meaning' but rather the competent acting of the ritual specialist which makes the ritual 'work'.

[23] This specific failure, as described by Merz, might also be the outcome of "an inadmissible border crossing from one socially defined level to a higher one" (Dücker, p. 80). In the long run, however, the medium's attempt to secure a better position was successful.

Here the close relation between ritual performance and theatrical performance comes to the fore: the 'value' of a ritual in many cases is measured on account of the main performer's ability to convince other participants. This kind of improvisational but competent acting often is a precondition for success. It seems that in some cases ritual performance fails because it is too obviously 'not real' but is instead rather perceived as theatrical performance. In many Indian traditions—where the god is perceived as the sole ritual agent—failure of performance is attributed to human performers, who are accused of acting 'as if' they were the god's 'mechanical vehicle'. This negative evaluation is based on the view that 'acting' means 'make-believe', 'illusion', 'lying', and 'falsehood'. Likewise in Schieffelin's case study the performance of the spirit séance failed since it turned out that the performer 'only pretended' to be the vessel of the god's presence. In both cases, seen from within the tradition, the agency involved is that of the gods. But since the main actor fails to come up with a convincing performance, s/he is held responsible (see also Chao 1999: 506).

However, Schieffelin (1998: 200f.) cautions that the Western notion of theatre could obstruct our view on performance because one aspect of this notion of 'theatre' is strategic manipulation. This, however, is not necessarily the case in other cultural contexts. As Kendall (1996: 19ff.) shows, a strict separation of ritual ('real', 'authentic') and theatrical ('false', 'only acting') performances can also be a misconception: a successful Korean shaman must be able to present emotionally compelling performances and a successful initiation of a shaman implies that the initiate, in appropriate costume, invokes the spirits in their proper sequence and manifests them through song, dance, mime, comic banter, and oracles. Therefore, Kendall points to the "delicate balance between theatricality and inspiration as shamans work with the initiate" rather than to a strict separation of ritual and theatrical performances (1996: 18f., 31, 34; see also Howe 2000: 68). Similarly Brückner refers to the distinction between 'spontaneous possession' and 'controlled possession' in a South Indian ritual tradition as artificial. From the participants' perspective the phenomenon is considered basically the same (2001: 318). Thus it must seriously be questioned whether a distinction between 'theatre' and 'ritual' is appropriate in such contexts. "The exact nature of the performative relationship between the central performers and the other participants (including spectators) in a cultural event cannot be assumed analytically, it must be investigated ethnographically" (Schieffelin 1998: 202).

The interplay between and the distinction of ritual and theatre is the main topic of Köpping's article "Mishima's Suicide between Ritual and Theatre" (2004). There he deals with a case in which the performer (Mishima) made a theatrical play a ritual. In the eyes of the audience he played the ritual and, therefore, did not produce 'ritual commitment' and failed to rouse the 'ritual stance' in the audience. Here Köpping refers to Humphrey & Laidlaw (1994: 5, 88ff.): the participants adopt a 'ritual stance', which conveys the message 'this is ritual'. Köpping argues that Mishima failed to convince his audience and therefore the act was not effective (as a ritual). Mishima failed because he broke the frames of both, ritual (he did not produce a ritual stance in the audience since he too obviously 'acted out') and theatre (real death instead of 'acted' death) (Köpping 2004: 113).[24]

Nevertheless, 'failure of performance' cannot be equated with 'failure of ritual': even if ritual performances do not convince the audience this does not inevitably invalidate the ritual as a whole (see Snoek).

7. *Emergence and efficacy*[25]

Rituals always bear some kind of risk (Schieffelin 1996: 80) and it is the degree of the obviousness of this risk, combined with personal involvement, intentions and agenda, which determines the attentiveness of the participants and audience to the procedures.[26] Within that complex

[24] Here, one can pose the more general question of whether the commitment 'to do it right' is inevitably part of the 'ritual stance'. One could think of many more examples of confused or broken frames of ritual and theatre. How for example does the performance of rituals as part of tourism programme, or as a cultural asset that is ordered to be preserved, affect the perception of successful performance? See Köpping 2000: 172, note 1; see also Schlehe & Weber 2001.

[25] 'Efficacy' is used here to denote the ability to produce an effect, but not only a specifically desired effect, whereas 'effectiveness' is used in the rather positive sense of the degree to which planned, intended or desired outcomes are achieved. These two issues, however, are closely interrelated. Since the agenda can be multiple and since diverse agendas may even conflict with one another, what is 'effectiveness' for one party can be 'efficacy' for the other (Schieffelin 1996: 80; see also Hauser-Schäublin, Hüsken). Here it becomes moreover evident that in many cases a strict separation of 'performer' and 'audience' is not necessarily fruitful, since the perception of 'the audience' as homogeneous and having one single common agenda is misleading (Schieffelin 1996: 67).

[26] "The enactment of all ceremonial (or theatrical) performances is inherently risky [since] the ritual performances are necessarily subject to the variable competencies of the major performers, the competing agendas and ongoing evaluations of all the participants, as well as unforeseen contingency and blind luck" (Schieffelin 1996: 80).

interplay of factors it is often a ritual's efficacy which earmarks the action as a 'success' or a 'failure'. "Most rituals are staged to achieve an end, so there is always something at stake in performances", says Howe (2000: 67).

However, the term 'efficacy' in ritual studies is used in a variety of ways.[27] While some scholars mainly concentrate on the 'postulated' or 'believed' efficacy of rituals (Hubert & Mauss 1902/03, Malinowksi 1954), some privilege the social effects (Radcliffe-Brown 1969, Bourdieu's 'social magic' [1982]), and others are concerned with questions regarding the relation of postulated efficacy and a ritual's empirically detectable effects (Lévi-Strauss 1949, Samuel 2001).

It is certainly necessary to distinguish diverse kinds or 'modes' of efficacy. Moore & Myerhoff (1977: 10ff.), for example, differentiate between 'doctrinal' and 'operational' efficacy. According to them, operational efficacy relates to the empirically detectable physical, psychological or social effects of a ritual, whereas doctrinal efficacy cannot be detected empirically[28]—it is postulated efficacy.[29] However, it seems that the mere distinction drawn between doctrinal and operational efficacy does not suffice to describe the diverse modes of efficacy dealt with in the contributions to this volume. Köpping (2004) introduces the useful notion of the 'emergent'. Taking the example of Mishima's 'failed' ritual suicide, Köpping proposes that 'ritual failure' *can* be interpreted as an outcome of the fact that the performer's intention is not achieved. Yet, Köpping argues, this kind of failure does not necessarily invalidate the act as ritual since "the emergent is what performance brings about in social reality", even if this is the opposite of the performer's intentions (2004: 101). These effects on social reality can be interpreted as 'operational efficacy'. However, since the contingent aspects of rituals can—as in Köpping's case study—render the outcome rather unpredictable, 'emergence' is understood here as the effects of a ritual which are generally

Moreover, he continues: "It is likely, however, that the nature of the risks involved for a performer vary according to the cultural genre and situation in which s/he is acting [...] Thus, where the risks lie in a given performative event or genre must be ethnographically determined—but they will be there and contribute to the quality of what happens."

[27] For a detailed account of the diverse uses of 'efficacy' in ritual studies, see Podeman Sørensen 2006.

[28] Moore & Myerhoff (1977: 12) are well aware of the technological difficulties of answering empirical questions, especially while doing ethnographic field research.

[29] Similarly Tambiah (1985) introduces the categories of subjectively and pragmatically effective rituals.

rather hard to predict and which stem from intricate causal relations across different scales and levels.[30]

A fourth mode of efficacy is 'performative efficacy': "all it needs in order to work is the local agreement that this is the way to do it", says Podeman Sørenson (2006) with reference to illocutionary speech acts, but this mode of efficacy can be detected not only in speech but in other ritual action as well. Many life-cycle rituals are mainly characterised by their performative efficacy: a marriage makes a married couple through its mere performance, and a naming-ritual gives a name to a newborn child.

Diverse modes of efficacy refer to diverse ways a ritual can fail. In many cases the postulated efficacy of a ritual is 'proven' by declaring certain phenomena the outcome of a ritual performance. More often than not this happens in the negative: the lack of doctrinal efficacy is postulated in that catastrophe, bad fate, disease, sudden deaths etc. are attributed to preceding failed ritual (see e.g. Ambos, Hauser-Schäublin, Stavrianopoulou). Retrospective failure of a performance (= the claim that a ritual has failed) here often functions as confirmation of the value of the same ritual, if performed successfully (see Howe 2000: 68). Doctrinal efficacy presupposes a shared set of beliefs, and this itself is another potential source of failure. Especially in instances where the expected effects cannot immediately be experienced, the question of who has the power to define ritual action as 'efficacious' and whether that person can implement his or her interpretation arises. Gengnagel (2005) for example shows in his article on text and performance of a pilgrimage in Benares (India) that even the costly and extensive efforts of textual scholars could not change the actual route of the procession which was considered 'wrong' (and therefore ineffective!) by the textual exegetes. This finding confirms Appadurai's thesis that authentication is often a matter in which popular understanding about ritual efficacy and folk criteria of authenticity play a major role (1986: 46).

Although 'performative efficacy' implies that the performance itself renders the ritual effective, this is no general infallible mechanism but depends on certain preconditions. The most important aspect, namely the local agreement that 'this is the way it works', in many cases encompasses several other restrictions with regard to the appropriate

---

[30] In a similar way, Schieffelin defines 'emergence' as the irreducible change arising from a performance (1996: 64f.).

conditions, performers and mode of performance. Moreover, the story of the failed initiation of a Korean shaman analysed by Kendall clearly shows that even *rites de passage* can and do in fact sometimes fail. Since the failure of this ritual is no exception but a frequent occurrence, it seems that it is even an integral part of the respective tradition, all the more so since its failure adds to the value of successful performances (see Kendall 1996: 19, 30).

Few scholars of ritual studies have considered the possibility and implications of a parallel existence of diverse modes of efficacy. As is shown here, a ritual can fail and be successful at the same time, depending on which kind of efficacy is focused on (see also Grimes 1988b). The diverse modes of efficacy are not mutually exclusive and can be at work at the same time.

The simultaneous existence of diverse modes of efficacy is most obvious in rituals which are supposed to immediately transform reality. If they fail to do so their emergent effects come to the fore: although there was a 'final' doctrinal failure of a ritual aimed at enabling a woman to conceive children, an emergent success of the same ritual was that it ended a long situation of suffering for two families. At the same time, the operational efficacy for the patient was rather negative, since the ritual's outcome (the confirmation of her infertility) had severe social consequences for her. Rudolph gives another example of the close interrelation of 'doctrinal' and 'operational' efficacy. In his case study the postulated doctrinal efficacy made the ritual reinvention fail on the operational level. The failure in canonising the Taroko's ancestor gods ritual was due to its religious efficacy: in a society with ambivalent belief systems, "religious efficacy seemed not to fit into a collective ritual that was supposed to craft a common identity", especially when there is a collision of individual and collective agendas, Rudolph (p. 333) argues (see also Chao 1999).

It therefore seems that ritual is not so much a method to create a single outcome by one single performance, but a field where postulated effects, participant's intentions, and the social reality which emerges from a ritual process are negotiated.

8. *Counteracting a ritual's risks*

Most ritual traditions are aware of the risks inherent in ritual performances and therefore have internal measures at their disposal to prevent mistakes and failure, or at least to avoid the negative consequences which might arise from them. Both strategies are closely related to each other.

Some of these measures refer to deviations which remain unnoticed by the participants, including the main performers. Michaels reports that in Vedic ritual three holy syllables are often uttered preventively to cure unnoticed mishaps. In cuneiform sources, too, the so-called 'disregard-formula' lists all kinds of possible mistakes which *might* have occurred without being noticed by the performer (see Ambos).

Such remedial rituals are often performed as preventive measures, not only in case of actual flaws (see Hüsken 2006). Many textual traditions attempt to exclude the possibility of flawed performances through atonement rituals, which are incorporated into the rituals proper.[31] Thus the yearly cycle of temple rituals in a South Indian temple begins with a festival called *pavitrotsava*. By performing this seven-day-long festival the priests ensure that the 'fruit' emerging from one year's ritual course accrues to them in spite of eventual mistakes or irregularities. Moreover, by performing *pavitrotsava* the ritual purity of the temple and the ritual actors is ensured and re-established. Ritual purity is a precondition for the effectiveness of future rituals performed in the temple. These rituals can be viewed humorously as a "kind of ritual spell-checker that scans the liturgical year fixing all your mistakes" (Grimes 2004). It is noteworthy that the 'corrective rituals' (for example in the case of corrective repetitions or in rituals of atonement) follow those rules which also apply to the ritual performance: the modes of speech and action used to rectify or prevent mistakes are basically the same as in the rituals proper. At times, the remedial actions can also simply consist of additional ritual activities which do not at all take another from than the 'normal' ritual course. Thus Howe reports from Bali that families that are exposed to misfortune often are burdened with extra ritual activity to 'compensate' for past ritual deficiencies (Howe 2000: 69).

Another way of dealing with a ritual's inherent riskiness is the 'internalisation' of the entire ritual process, as Michaels argues. He uses 'internalisation' in the sense of a shift of the ritual's performance from the outer, physical world to a mere inner, mental performance of it. In his study of mishaps in Vedic rituals, he argues that the idea of internalisation and a certain 'autonomy' of the ritual part and parcel of

[31] See Michaels, Buss, and Ambos.

any kind of ritual thinking: rituals, he says, are dynamic events in their own right that cannot really fail on the doctrinal level. Michaels sees in internalisation "the rituals' intrinsic capacity of self-healing". It must be mentioned, however, that this kind of 'internalisation' is not resorted to in each and every tradition dealt with in the present volume. Ambos, for example, demonstrates that in spite of the many expressions of criticism and desperation prompted by the unpredictability of a ritual's outcome, the cuneiform sources show only little sign of fundamental scepticism about the efficacy of divination and ritual.

If mistakes have been detected in a ritual's course they are sometimes considered so grave that they lead to the necessity of repeating the entire ritual,[32] while others can be rectified by repeating only a sequence of the whole. Nevertheless, sequences or elements of a ritual performance judged deficient are not repeated in all traditions and contexts. In many complex, long, and elaborate rituals one tends to avoid corrective repetitions. This might be due to economical reasons but holds also true for many rituals which take effect through their process in the first place. Here, corrective repetitions are also frequently avoided in order not to disturb the flow of action and the 'ritual atmosphere'.[33] During rituals which can be performed only at a certain point of time the participants will do everything to secure successful completion since there is no possibility for repetition of the ritual as a whole, but only for the repetition of some parts of it.[34]

Some ritual systems evidently cope with the riskiness of rituals in that they 'incorporate' deviations in rituals by attributing them to superhuman agency and thus considering them as part of the ritual process. Thus in many Indian traditions "nothing can go wrong, since the god is the ritual agent". The priest is not held responsible but is considered "the mechanical vehicle of god's will".[35] Ambos even shows that this attribution of ritual failure to superhuman agency is in cuneiform sources expressed in a complete literary genre, the so-called 'wisdom literature'. The topic of these texts are the words and actions of the

---

[32] Gladigow, referring to the Roman *instauration*, assumes that ritual failure definitely implies that the ritual is considered ineffective and thus has to be repeated in its entirety. This, he argues, might be one central difference between ritual and 'every day action' (Gladigow 2004: 72f.).

[33] See Snoek, Weinhold, Merz, and Brosius.

[34] See Michaels, Buss, and Polit.

[35] Śrī Srivats Goswamy during the 'Workshop on South Asian Rituals' held in Heidelberg (11/2003); see also Fuller 1993.

gods, which are beyond human understanding: "The plans of the gods were unfathomable to man, confusing even the ritual experts and diviners" (p. 28). Similarly, Hauser-Schäublin states that the rituals of the Intaran are performed according to a certain fixed 'script', but at the same time there are other standards, established by the gods, which are virtually unknown to humans. This realm of the ritual is therefore beyond human control. Or, as Emmrich concludes with respect to his study of the fall of god Matsyendranātha's chariot during a procession: "It is the god who gets angry and throws himself to the ground and he does this because the people act in a way that gives him reason to fall. [...] The god cannot do otherwise than interrupt the circle of his journey" (p. 160). In Weinhold's case study the god is also perceived as the main ritual agent. Interestingly, however, graver and more violent deviations from the rule are more likely to be attributed to 'superhuman agency' than minor transgressions, which are frequently attributed to the participants' 'ego'.

However, despite these 'systematic measures', mistakes are not totally excluded and the efficacy of the ritual is by no means secured—it is mainly the culpability of the performer(s) which is annulled (see also Howe 2000: 69). Mistakes are still possible and do in fact endanger the effectiveness of the ritual to a considerable degree. Thus, some traditions developed additional institutions, which are specifically designed to cope with ritual mistakes connected with the concrete context of the performance, such as the office of a 'temple superintendent' in South Indian temples, who supervises all ritual performances and takes care of unexpected situations (see Hüsken 2006), the *fiscal* in European Santo Daime rituals (Weinhold), or the 'Master of Ceremonies' in European freemasons' rituals (Snoek). These institutions clearly indicate that factors external to the ritual frame can render the ritual ineffective.

The reactions to failure of ritual and mistakes are closely related to the preventive measures described above. Many 'mistakes in ritual' that have actually happened are simply brushed aside, ignored, or even covered up. In Schieffelin's example of the failed performance of a medium during a spirit séance, the participants avoided openly declaring the medium's performance as a 'failure' during the ritual itself, mainly because of their heterogeneous agenda. In this way, the (failing) performer was not directly confronted with his failure but "the failure was allowed to become obvious" (Schieffelin 1996: 79). Again, the skills of obscuring and masking mistakes in favour of the atmosphere and flow of a ritual are considered an important aspect of 'ritual competence' in predominantly performative traditions.

The examples of variations and failures given by Brückner with respect to the annual festivals of a South Indian ritual tradition show that a high degree of variation in a ritual is even possible in situations with fixed scripts—as long as these are accepted by both audience and performers (Brückner 2001: 314f.). During the performance of South Indian temple rituals deviations from normative texts are ignored or silently corrected, but afterwards they might be criticised as ignorance and incompetence on the side of the performer. Outside the ritual frame, criticisms or discussions of the 'quality' of a ritual will frequently be heard.

Another mode of coping with flawed rituals is the imposition of drastic sanctions (Moos 2001a: xviii). In practice, mistakes that have happened are not only met with 'ritual' sanctions, but also non-ritual punitive measures are employed (beating, fines, court procedures, suspension, etc.; see Michaels, Stavrianopoulou, and Hüsken). Apart from these sanctions imposed by the ritual system, the fear of social sanctions which emerge during or after a ritual has failed, often makes people do their very best. The performance dealt with by Köpping is a vivid example of what social sanctions may look like in cases of 'ritual failure': the performer was directly and immediately confronted with the fact of his failing performance in that the audience laughed at him at the time he committed ritual suicide (Köpping 2004: 97; see also Polit and Merz).

9. *Rituals and their contexts*

Referring to Bateson's 1955 theory of cognitive, meta-communicative framing, Handelman (2004: 9) cautions that "...the frames vary...and even an imperative meta-message like that of *This is ritual* is not seamlessly self-referential, but may be negotiated." He therefore offers an alternative to Bateson's lineal framing, namely the theoretical concept of a ritual's 'moebius framing': "this framing is inherently dynamic, continuously relating exterior to interior, interior to exterior" (2004: 15). This concept implies a strong potential interaction of the 'inner' and the 'outer' sphere of a ritual, which is in perfect agreement with the mutual influence of ritual and its context in many contributions to this volume.

Critical judgements about various aspects of ritual performances are expressed verbally, through gestures, or through other bodily expressions. Such ritual critique evidently can 'correct' and revise not only ritual practice but also social interaction outside the ritual frame. In one of Brückner's case studies (2001: 321–324) the god—inhabiting a priest's body—shows great dissatisfaction with a patron's everyday behaviour. Likewise, in Hauser-Schäublin's case study critique is integrated into ritual performances, and influences action beyond this specific ritual: the Intaran's deities manifest themselves in humans during the performances. These superhuman agents are eligible to point out mistakes and to ask for their correction. They thus have the power to continuously modify the 'script' of the temple festival, to induce change or to insist on conservatism. Since these local deities are 'lower local' deities (as opposed to the 'higher' deities of the immigrants), their voicing of critique represents a 'ritual of rebellion' which, however, does not only keep alive the recollection of the local deities as powerful leading figures, but also has a lasting practical impact on the social structures. Social, political and other relations of individuals and groups beyond the ritual context may be negotiated through the accusation of making ritual mistakes.

The connection of politics and ritual is crucial in yet another example: the frequent falls of the god Matsyendranātha during processions are reported by chronicles which generally tend to try to explain certain events at the royal court, be it political decisions or changes in power (see Emmrich).

Ritual mistakes are a common topic in contexts of rivalry among individuals or groups. Fuller describes how younger but more educated priests 'show off' in public during a major temple ritual and from time to time accuse other (less educated) priests of 'getting it wrong', correct them and thereby demonstrate their own superior ritual knowledge (Fuller 2003: 15). Likewise the medium in Merz's case study tried to demonstrate her ritual competence in that she accused participants of not adhering to the rules of (ritual) purity. She thereby signalled that she is 'stricter' than other—hierarchically superior—mediums. In Hauser-Schäublin's case study of the Sembiran, mutual accusations mirror competitive power struggles within the village community (immigrants/locals). Obviously, the evaluation of the gravity of mistakes depends very much on the role of the ritual as a field for negotiating hierarchies outside the ritual. In South Indian Viṣṇu temples, where 'ritual shares' constitute values in their own right, ritual is an important means to position oneself in the wider social context (see Hüsken). Here, as in Merz's case study, ritual performance serves also as a medium to communicate changes and reorganisation in social structures. Consequently, failure (or looming failure) can also be a signal for shifted power structures. In Brosius's case study some of the participants contributed to the devaluation of the ritual performance by not attending the ritual ceremony: religious specialists withdrew charismatic power from the event and indicated lack of consensus with the political aims of the performers. During such public processes of competition, ritual mistakes are frequently employed as a strategic instrument to position oneself in the socio-cultural or political field of society.

Ritual thus can even be used to *destroy* unity when employed in power struggles as means to rearrange hierarchies (Platvoet 1995: 213; Howe 2000: 69f.; Wulf & Zirfas 2004: 8).[36] In these contexts, rituals as well as the accusation of making mistakes function as political instruments.

In none of the case studies is the influence of context on ritual and vice versa unidirectional. In many instances, a changed socio-cultural context initiates—sometimes drastic—changes of ritual norms. Such a shift in context may refer to time and/or space. Schieffelin explicitly points to the link of historicity and contingency in the concrete time and circumstances of a ritual's performance. Since a performance always articulates cultural symbols and ritual genres of that particular time, it is subject to its particular circumstances: "It is only if the performance succeeds in encompassing this particular occasion that the ritual actually 'works'" (1996: 66).

Likewise, the specific local context of a ritual is one of the factors that decides whether a deviation is considered relevant or not. Thus, the transfer of rituals in space can lead to shifts in perception. Writing on rituals performed by Hindu immigrants in the U.S.A., Venkatachari (1992) clearly shows that here a rapidly changing context heavily influenced the concept(s) of 'ritual mistake'. In his study of freemasons' rituals, Snoek gives another example: one of the criteria for accepting somebody as a member of the first freemason's Grand Lodge (formulated in 1723 CE) was that the candidate had to be "of mature and discreet Age" (i.e. at least 21 years old). Despite this rule, in the 18th century, hardly any of the members of a lodge in Leyden

[36] Buc (2001: 8), with reference to textual representations of mediaeval political rituals even states: "If read as evidence for the real, the abundance of depictions of manipulated or failed rituals suggests that far from creating consensus or order, rituals could be positively dangerous [...] To perform a ritual, then, must in many cases have been a gamble, because one's enemies might manipulate or disrupt it. [...] and far from automatically legitimizing the this-worldly hierarchy, ritual references to the exemplary heavenly order never stood beyond the challenge of the disaffected."

was 21 when initiated, since most of them were students from abroad. Moreover, although in the beginning membership to the lodges was restricted to men, nowadays there exist a number of 'mixed' and even female orders.

Ritual critique and the evaluation of deviations as 'mistake' are means to create distinction. The allegation of 'getting it wrong' can serve to emphasise identity for all who are involved in the process: on the one hand, critique is directed towards important matters only,[37] on the other, defining what others do 'wrong' implies the affirmation of one's own 'correct' values and norms. Since rituals in many cases function as markers of identity (Platvoet & van der Toorn 1995), challenging the validity of a ritual also touches upon the crucial issue of individual or group identity. "One's own ritual rules, seen as the exclusively correct way to perform rituals, are at the core of a group's identity construction" (Hauser-Schäublin, p. 269).[38] Evaluating certain ritual practices as a mistake can be an effective strategy for establishing group identities by means of exclusion. These kinds of confirmation or (re)construction of identities play an important role in situations of cultural (ex)change, of assimilation of certain groups into a context different from their original context and can be detected in ancient[39] as well as in contemporary cultures.[40]

10. *Conclusion*

The instances dealt with in the diverse contributions to this volume clearly show that rituals can in fact go wrong, they can fail: rituals, as modes of human interaction in the social world, always bear some kind of risk. The risks are situated on diverse levels of the ritual.[41] The

---

[37] See Dücker's example of the sabotage of the ritual presentation of the Büchnerpreis: "The revolutionary students confirm the importance of the conventional consecration ritual by trying to convert it into a platform on the basis of which they can announce their interpretation of the given situation and the demands ensuing from it" (p. 91).

[38] See Wulf & Zirfas 2004: 23f.

[39] In Stavrianopoulou's case the 'authentic Egyptian' ritual specialist is called for; and in Ambos's study it is important not to perform 'foreign' or 'new' rituals.

[40] See Hauser-Schäublin, Rudolph, and Hüsken. As Brosius shows, even the imposition of a ban on performing a certain ritual does not necessarily imply that it is going to fail: a ban can instigate the creation of dramatic plots of martyrdom on the side of the performers.

[41] These factors can be the process, the result, the sequence of ritual elements, the

degree and the variety of risk in a ritual performance determine the efforts to prevent mistakes and failure. However, it seems that some rituals are more liable to failure than others. It is therefore on the one hand a matter of determining where the risks lie in ritual, and on the other, a matter of determining which risk matters.

Failure is an integral part of order. A 'ritual mistake' thus connects a specific performance to past and future enactments of the same ritual. At the same time, it refers to its contemporary socio-cultural context where the deviation initiates a discourse about rules. "Deviation is the most latent element of the existing order, offering a new interpretation of the existing normality as and when it is activated," says Dücker (p. 79). The analysis of ritual failure therefore contextualises the ritual. 'Failure' or 'mistake' does not exist independently from the individual or group who or which interprets an action as such. Deviations are always to be found, but only their negative evaluation makes them 'mistakes'. The criteria for appraisal, i.e. the values on which this interpretation is based, emanate from a very broad spectrum of factors, which include normative written ritual prescriptions on the one end of the scale, and factors such as 'ritual atmosphere' or a sense of 'ritual appropriateness' on the other. Therefore, rituals can simultaneously fail *and* succeed and the notion of 'mistake' and 'failure' does not necessarily presuppose a set of explicit or commonsensical rules which have been broken. Yet examples of 'ritual failure' and of 'mistakes' in the ritual context do give an indication of decisive norms—albeit norms which might be relevant only for an individual in a very specific context.[42] Defects thus contextualise rituals not only with respect to other performances, but also with respect to the performers and participants. Frequently, if not always, the social and political standing of individuals and groups beyond the ritual context are negotiated through the evaluation of ritual. Not only the ritual process, but also the authority and authenticity of the ritual experts, and hierarchies among the participants (or of the groups which are represented by them) are evaluated and, eventually, reorganised. Moreover, whose definition of 'right' and 'wrong' has a lasting impact on a ritual tradition reveals how the power relations in the

participants, the reaction or resonance of the participants, the context, the preconditions, the rules, the underlying ritual system, its retrospective (discursive) evaluation, or other issues.

[42] Thus Weinhold describes a case where one and the same person committed and detected the 'mistake', a deviation which only this person considered a 'mistake'.

wider socio-cultural field are structured. This close connection of ritual and its context accounts for the fact that deviations from a prescribed ritual procedure are often purposely employed in order to challenge the form of the rituals and through it the prevalent power relations as well. Reports of deviations and failure clearly refer to the realm external to the ritual. The analysis of 'ritual mistakes' thus highlights the fact that ritual and its interpretation cannot be separated from its context.

Failure directs attention, it makes us remember: "The effectivity [of rites] depends on the effect on memories" (Grimes 2000: 5). Successful (i.e. durable/long-lasting) representation of ritual performance in many cases shapes our notion of rituals more than 'ritual-in-performance'. If different representations of the same ritual event are given, the success of the one or other account depends on whose interpretation achieves acceptance in the long run, but not on the question of 'what really happened'. Even—or rather especially—negative assessments of ritual events create and maintain distinct identities for the performers: similar to a ritual that went beyond all expectations, a failed or sabotaged ritual is more likely to be inscribed in collective memory than unspectacular, dull performances.

Failure and mistakes initiate change: they are invariably part of ritual dynamics. Criticism or discussions of the 'quality' of a ritual influences future performances. Corrections of a ritual's script or its rules indicate that a former practice is not considered appropriate (any more). Breaking rules can instigate the creation of new rules deemed more pertinent to the ritual event.

Last but not least, analysing 'ritual failure' can help to understand actions which are not culturally defined as 'ritual'.[43] Hoffmeister in this volume metaphorically categorises 'serial killings' as 'ritual'. Rather than 'murder *is* ritual' Hoffmeister analyses 'murder *as* ritual'. Her paper shows how analysing a failed ritualised activity as 'failed ritual' helps to understand underlying patterns and structures, and reveals collectively shared ideas and the way in which they are 'superimposed' on the performers. Through her analysis of the factors leading to the 'failure' of some of the killings Hoffmeister can clearly distinguish the killers' 'personal scripts' as opposed to the society's 'social script'. Moreover, her paper once again discloses that it is the durable (long-lasting) representation which shapes our notion of rituals (and other actions and events) rather than its performance.

---

[43] See Grimes 2000: 26, 28, *et passim*.

The possibility of making mistakes and of failure is a constitutive feature of rituals. The contributions to this volume reveal several factors which strongly influence a ritual's assessment, two of which shall be highlighted here: first, the type of ritual and the character of the ritual tradition is an important factor when it comes to the appraisal of errors and deviations. For example, a ritual's assessment is immediately linked to the frequency of its performance and hence to the arousal it evokes (Whitehouse 2006). Another important issue in the process of detecting (or hiding) flaws are the media of transmission and the media employed during performance: the chosen method for communicating rituals strongly influences their perception, the retrospective control of the rituals and, consequently, their future performances.

Ritual mistake and failure originate inside as well as outside the ritual. A central difference between 'ritual failure' and 'mistake' is that failure rather refers to the efficacy of a ritual, whereas a mistake refers to its performance and is closely related to competence and agency. The scale of entitlement to deviate from rules indicates the respective agent's power, which transcends the ritual context. Moreover, the effectiveness of a ritual is consolidated only through its possibility of failure. Here, the distinction between postulated efficacy, the participants' intentionality, and a ritual's emergence points to the fact that not only rituals but also their outcome is dynamic.

References

Appadurai, Arjun 1986. "Introduction: commodities and the politics of value". In: *The social life of things. Commodities in cultural perspective*, Appadurai, Arjun (ed.). Cambridge: Cambridge University Press, 3–63.

Austin, John L. 1955. *How to do things with words: The William James Lectures Delivered at Harvard University*. Oxford: Oxford University Press.

Bateson, Gregory 1955 (1972). "A Theory of Play and Fantasy". In: *Steps to an Ecology of Mind: Essays in Anthropology, Psychiatry, Evolution, and Epistemology*. New York: Ballantine, 177–193.

Bourdieu, Pierre 1982. *Outline of a theory of practice*. Cambridge: Cambridge University Press (Cambridge Studies in Social Anthropology 16).

Brückner, Heidrun 2001. "Fluid Canons and Shared Charisma: On Success and Failure of Ritual Performance in a South Indian Oral Tradition". In: *Charisma and Canon: Essays on the Religious History of the Indian Subcontinent*, Dalmia, Vasudha & Angelika Malinar & Martin Christof (ed.). New Delhi: Oxford University Press, 313–327.

Buc, Philippe 2001. *The Dangers of Ritual. Between Early Medieval Texts and Social Scientific Theory.* Princeton: Princeton University Press.

Chao, Emily 1999. "The Maoist Shaman and the Madman: Ritual Bricolage, Failed Ritual, and Failed Ritual Theory". *Cultural Anthropology* 14.4: 505–534.

Colas, Gérard 2005. "Rites Among Vaikhānasas and Related Matters: Some Methodological Issues". In: *Words and Deeds. Hindu and Buddhist Rituals in South Asia*, Gengnagel,

Jörg & Ute Hüsken & Srilata Raman (ed.). Wiesbaden: Harrassowitz (Ethno-Indology. Heidelberg Studies in South Asian Rituals 1), 23–44.
Deshpande, Madhav 1996. "Contextualizing the eternal language. Features of priestly Sanskrit". In: *Ideology and Status of Sanskrit. Contributions to the History of the Sanskrit Language*, Houben, Jan (ed.). New York: Brill, 401–436.
Fuller, Christopher J. 1993. "Only Śiva can worship Śiva: ritual mistakes and their correction in a south Indian temple". *Contributions to Indian Sociology (n.s.)* 27.2: 169–189.
—— 2003. *The Renewal of the Priesthood: Modernity and Traditionalism in a South Indian Temple.* Princeton: Princeton University Press.
Geertz, Clifford 1973. *The interpretation of cultures: selected essays.* New York: Basic Books (German translation used: *Dichte Beschreibung. Beiträge zum Verstehen kultureller Systeme*, Luchesi, Brigitte & Rolf Bindemann [transl.]. Frankfurt, 1983).
Gengnagel, Jörg 2005. "Wenn Pilger vom rechten Weg abkommen: Ein Fallbeispiel aus Benares (Nordindien)". In: *Die Welt der Rituale. Von der Antike bis heute*, Ambos, Claus & Stephan Hotz & Gerald Schwedler & Stephan Weinfurter (ed.). Darmstadt: Wissenschaftliche Buchgesellschaft, 121–128.
Gladigow, Burkhard 2004. "Sequenzierung von Riten und die Ordnung der Rituale". In: *Zoroastrian Rituals in Context*, Stausberg, Michael (ed.). Leiden & Boston: Brill (Studies in the History of Religions 102), 57–76.
Gluckman, Max 1954. *Rituals of rebellion in South-East Africa. Frazer Lecture 1952.* Manchester: Manchester University Press.
Grimes, Ronald L. 1988a. "Infelicitous Performances and Ritual Criticism". *Semeia* 43: 103–122.
—— 1988b. "Ritual Criticism and Reflexivity in Fieldwork". *Journal of Ritual Studies* 2: 217–239.
—— 2000. *Deeply into the Bone. Re-inventing Rites of Passage.* Berkeley & Los Angeles & London: University of California Press.
—— 2002. "Ritual and the Media". In: *Practicing Religion in the Age of the Media. Explorations in Media, Religion, and Culture*, Hoover, S. & L. Schofield Clark (ed.). New York: Columbia University Press, 219–234.
—— 2004. Response to the contributions presented on the occasion of the panel 'Ritual Mistakes and Failure of Ritual' during the AAR conference, held in 11/2004 in San Antonio, Texas (unpublished).
—— 2006. *Reimagining ritual theory: John Bourke among the Hopis.* Nijmegen: Thieme MediaCenter Nijmegen.
Handelman, Don 2004. "Re-Framing Ritual". In: *The Dynamics of Changing Rituals. The Transformation of Religious Rituals within Their Social and Cultural Context*, Kreinath, Jens & Constance Hartung & Annette Deschner (ed.). New York: Peter Lang (Toronto Studies in Religion 29), 9–20.
—— 2006. "Conceptual Alternatives to 'Ritual'". In: *Theorizing Rituals: Classical Topics, Theoretical Approaches, Analytical Concepts, Annotated Bibliography*, Kreinath, Jens & Jan Snoek & Michael Stausberg (ed.). Leiden: Brill.
Harrison, Simon 1992. "Ritual as Intellectual Property". *Man* (New Series) 27.2: 225–244.
Harth, Dietrich & Gerrit Schenk (ed.) 2004. *Ritualdynamik. Kulturübergreifende Studien zur Theorie und Geschichte rituellen Handelns.* Heidelberg: Synchron Publishers.
Howe, Leo 2000. "Risk, Ritual and Performance". *The Journal of the Royal Anthropological Institute* 6.1 (March 2000): 63–79.
Hubert, H. & Mauss, M. 1902/03. "Esquisse d'une théorie générale de la magie". *Année sociologique* 7 (1902–1903): 1–146.
Hüsken, Ute 2006. "Pavitrotsava: Rectifying Ritual Lapses". In: *Jaina-Itihāsa-Ratna. Festschrift für Gustav Roth zum 90. Geburtstag*, Hüsken, Ute & Petra Kieffer-Pülz & Anne Peters (ed.). Marburg: Indica et Tibetica Verlag (Indica et Tibetica 47), 265–281.

—— forthc. *Viṣṇu's Children*. Habilitation thesis; to be published in: Ethno-Indology. Heidelberg Studies in South Asian Rituals. Wiesbaden: Harrassowitz.
Humphrey, Caroline & James Laidlaw 1994. *The Archetypal Actions of Ritual. A Theory of Ritual illustrated by the Jain Rite of Worship*. Oxford: Oxford University Press.
Kendall, Laurel 1996. "Initiating Performance: The Story of Chini, A Korean Shaman". In: *The Performance of Healing*, Laderman, Carol & Marina Roseman (ed.). London: Routledge, 153–176.
Köpping, Klaus-Peter 2004. "Failure of Performance or Passage to the Acting Self? Mishima's Suicide between Ritual and Theatre". In: *The Dynamics of Changing Rituals: The Transformation of Religious Rituals within Their Social and Cultural Context*, Kreinath, Jens & Constance Hartung, & Annette Deschner (ed.). New York: Peter Lang Publishing (Toronto Studies in Religion 29), 97–114.
—— 2000. "Transformationen durch performative Verkörperung in japanischen Ritualen". In: *Im Rausch des Rituals*, Köpping, Klaus-Peter & Ursula Rao (ed.). Hamburg: LIT, 172–190.
Kreinath, Jens 2004. "Theoretical Afterthoughts". In: *The Dynamics of Changing Rituals. The Transformation of Religious Rituals within Their Social and Cultural Context*, Kreinath, Jens & Constance Hartung & Annette Deschner (ed.). New York: Peter Lang Publishing (Toronto Studies in Religion 29), 267–282.
Lévi-Strauss, C. 1949. "L'efficacité symbolique". *Revue de l'histoire des religions* 135: 5–27.
Malinowski, Bronislaw 1954. *Magic, Science and Religion and Other Essays*. New York: Doubleday.
Moos, Peter von 2001a. "Einleitung. Fehltritt, Fauxpas und andere Transgressionen im Mittelalter". In: *Der Fehltritt. Vergehen und Versehen in der Vormoderne*, Moos, Peter von (ed.). Köln & Weimar & Wien (Norm und Struktur. Studien zum sozialen Wandel in Mittelalter und Früher Neuzeit 15), 1–96.
—— 2001b. "Vorwort". In: *Der Fehltritt. Vergehen und Versehen in der Vormoderne*, Moos, Peter von (ed.). Köln & Weimar & Wien (Norm und Struktur. Studien zum sozialen Wandel in Mittelalter und Früher Neuzeit 15), xi–xxiv.
Platvoet, Jan G. 1995. "Ritual as Confrontation". In: *Pluralism and Identity*, Platvoet, Jan & Karel van der Toorn (ed.). Leiden: Brill (Studies in the History of Religions 67), 187–226.
—— 2004. "Ritual as War. On the Need to De-Westernize the Concept". In: *The Dynamics of Changing Rituals. The Transformation of Religious Rituals within Their Social and Cultural Context*, Kreinath, Jens & Constance Hartung & Annette Deschner (ed.). New York: Peter Lang Publishing (Toronto Studies in Religion 29), 243–266.
—— & Karel van der Toorn 1995. "Pluralism and Identity". In: *Pluralism and Identity*, Platvoet, Jan & Karel van der Toorn (ed.). Leiden: Brill (Studies in the History of Religions 67), 349–360.
Podeman Sørensen, Jørgen 2006. "Efficacy". In: *Theorizing Rituals: Classical Topics, Theoretical Approaches, Analytical Concepts, Annotated Bibliography*, Kreinath, Jens & Jan Snoek & Michael Stausberg (ed.). Leiden: Brill.
Radcliffe-Brown, A.R. 1969. *Structure and Function in Primitive Society*. London: Cohen and West.
Samuel, Geoffrey H. 2001. *Law of obligations and legal remedies*. London: Cavendish.
Schieffelin, Edward L. 1982. "The bau a Ceremonial Hunting Lodge: An Alternative to Initiation". In: *Rituals of Manhood. Male Initiation in Papua New Guinea*, Herdt, Gilbert H. (ed.). Brunswick & London: Transaction Publishers, 155–200.
—— 1996. "On Failure and Performance. Throwing the Medium out of the Séance". In: *The Performance of Healing*, Laderman, Carol & Marina Roseman (ed.). New York & London: Routledge, 59–89.
—— 1998. "Problematizing Performance". In: *Ritual. Performance, Media*, Hughes-Freeland, Felicia (ed.). London & New York: Routledge, 194–207.

—— 2006. "Participation". In: *Theorizing Rituals: Classical Topics, Theoretical Approaches, Analytical Concepts, Annotated Bibliography*, Kreinath, Jens & Jan Snoek & Michael Stausberg (ed.). Leiden: Brill.
Schlehe, Judith & Helmut Weber 2001. "Schamanismus und Tourismus in der Mongolei". *Zeitschrift für Ethnologie* 126.1: 93–116.
Snoek, Jan A.M. 2006. "Defining 'Rituals'". In: *Theorizing Rituals: Classical Topics, Theoretical Approaches, Analytical Concepts, Annotated Bibliography*, Kreinath, Jens & Jan Snoek & Michael Stausberg (ed.). Leiden: Brill.
Staal, Frits 1989. *Rules Without Meaning. Ritual, Mantras, and the Human Sciences*. New York etc.: Peter Lang.
Staal, Frits & C.V. Somayajipad, et al. 1983. *Agni, the Vedic ritual of the fire altar.* Berkeley: Asian Humanities Press.
Stausberg, Michael 2004. "Patterns of Ritual Change among Parsi-Zoroastrians in Recent Times". In: *The Dynamics of Changing Rituals. The Transformation of Religious Rituals within Their Social and Cultural Context*, Kreinath, Jens & Constance Hartung & Annette Deschner (ed.). New York: Peter Lang Publishing (Toronto Studies in Religion 29), 233–242.
—— (ed.) 2006: "'Ritual': A lexicographic survey of some related terms from an emic perspective". In: *Theorizing Rituals: Classical Topics, Theoretical Approaches, Analytical Concepts, Annotated Bibliography*, Kreinath, Jens & Jan Snoek & Michael Stausberg (ed.). Leiden: Brill.
Tambiah, Stanley J. 1979. *A Performative Approach to Ritual. Radcliffe-Brown Lecture*. London: British Academy.
—— 1985. *Culture, Thought, and Social Action. An Anthropological Perspective.* Cambridge, Mass.: Harvard University Press.
Turner, Victor 1969. *The ritual process. Structure and anti-structure.* New York: Aldine Publishing Company.
Venkatachari, K.K.A. 1992. "Transmission and Transformation of Rituals". In: *A Sacred Thread. Modern Transmission of Hindu Traditions in India and Abroad*, Williams, Raymond Brady (ed.). Chambersburg: Anima Publications, 177–190.
Whitehouse, Harvey 2006. "Transmission". In: *Theorizing Rituals: Classical Topics, Theoretical Approaches, Analytical Concepts, Annotated Bibliography*, Kreinath, Jens & Jan Snoek & Michael Stausberg (ed.). Leiden: Brill.
Wulf, Christoph & Jörg Zirfas 2004. "Performative Welten. Einführung in die historischen, systematischen und methodischen Dimensionen des Rituals". In: *Die Kultur des Rituals. Inszenierungen. Praktiken, Symbole*, Wulf, Christoph & Jörg Zirfas (ed.). München: Zink-Verlag, 7–45.

INDEX

249, 253, 257–260, 262, 263, 265, 266, 293, 305, 314
corrective 6
rejection of 292
unwanted 291, 293, 301, 305, 323
oracle(s) 202, 204, 350
oracle of Apollo 193
oracle interpreters 183
oracular session 202, 204, 206
oracular pronouncement 8
oracular queries 21, 31
oracular utterance 32, 33
outcome (of a ritual) x, 3–5, 7, 13, 15, 16, 178, 197, 351–353, 355, 363
failure of 5
uncertainty of the 197
unexpected 197
unpredictable 351
worldly 5

Paramhans, Ramchandra Das 296, 301, 305, 314–318, 320–322
participants
attentiveness of the 350
creative acting of the 344
evaluations of all the 241, 298
experience of the 49, 56
expectations of the x, 197, 243
heterogeneity of the 71
hierarchy of 70, 241, 361
intentions of the 241
misbehaviour of the 22
perspectives of the 21, 56
subjective theories of the 21, 49, 63
participation
degree of 60, 275
limitations of 192
mode of 218
public 309
restriction of 312
unlimited 73
past
perception of the 284
rivalling notions of the 288
Pasternak, Boris 82
penance(s) 78, 127
perfection 121, 122, 130, 131
performance(s)
archetypical 130
core of the 150
cultural 219
deviation(s) in 109, 110, 114
error-free 5
evaluation of the 198
failed ix, 11, 209, 219
failure of 2, 9, 225, 235, 347, 349, 350
flawed 17, 166, 199, 354
frequency of 363
improper ix, 3, 6
incorrect x, 5, 21, 35, 177, 197
infelicitous 2, 232
messy 5, 131
mode of 353
normative power of 289
patterns in the 228
proper 3, 18, 192
social 9
symbolic 81
variant 10
performance technique 348, 349
performative dynamics 2, 17
performative surplus 225, 230
performer(s)
'acting' skills of 319
culpability of the 356
expectations of the 159, 197
interactive abilities of the 348
motivations of the ix
political aims of the 359
shortcomings of the 6
skills of 319
Pergamon in Asia Minor 189
'perseverance' 229
perspectivity 243, 288, 292, 293, 297, 299, 305, 322
pillar ceremony 291, 293
pillar offering 291, 293, 295, 296, 300, 302, 305, 306, 312, 313
Platvoet, Jan G. 297, 305, 312, 339, 346, 359,
& Karel van der Toorn 256, 360
point of view 2, 16, 65, 84, 85, 87, 89, 96, 126, 167, 179, 198, 224, 236, 273, 287
pollution 145, 215, 216, 252, 258, 305
of the material 22
polythetic class 337, 338
portents, evil 36
possession 49, 55, 178, 210, 212, 217, 253, 349
controlled 349
spontaneous 349
power(s)
balance of 234
creative 346, 347
cultural 236
curative 55